1982

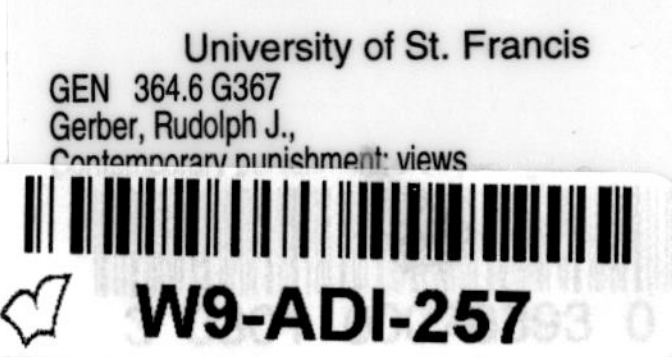

Contemporary Punishment

Contemporary Punishment

VIEWS, EXPLANATIONS, AND JUSTIFICATIONS

With a foreword by
NORVAL MORRIS

RUDOLPH J. GERBER
AND
PATRICK D. McANANY
Editors

UNIVERSITY OF NOTRE DAME PRESS
NOTRE DAME LONDON

The editors wish to acknowledge a debt of gratitude to the many people who encouraged them to undertake and continue the work of putting this book together. Special thanks should be paid to the Center for Studies in Criminal Justice and its two Co-Directors, Norval Morris and Hans Mattick, for their continual support, both financial and moral, during the long birth process. Also, we would like to single out John P. Conrad, a scholar and a friend who pointed out to us the need for such a book. Henry Balikoff, of the University of Chicago Law School, assisted greatly with the work of editing the texts.

Library of Congress Catalog Card Number: 72-185410
Manufactured in the United States of America by NAPCO Graphic Arts, Inc., Milwaukee, Wisconsin

Contents

Foreword

Express or implied, most exercises of discretion by police, prosecutors, judges, and parole board members are determined by their views of the purposes of punishment in general, as well as in the particular case. Police discretion to arrest will turn not only on the policeman's decision on the existence of a "probable cause," but also on his opinion concerning the utility of taking the first step toward punishment. As one looks further into the whole system of criminal justice, this process becomes even more obvious. Every sentence imposed on a convicted offender, for example, is clearly a product in part of legislative and judicial views of the purposes to be served in this type of case, and in this particular case, by criminal sanctions. The topic to which this book is addressed is thus of central importance to criminal law practice and to the jurisprudence of crime control.

To refuse to articulate our punitive purposes is to take Pilate's choice, and this is frequently done. Decisions gain immunity from criticism in inverse relation to the extent to with which they are sought to be explained. The advice to the newly appointed judge to act with confidence and never give reasons is sound, at least if he seeks to avoid criticism. But an effective, consistent, and reasoned criminal justice system requires the emergence of a common law of prosecuting, sentencing, and paroling–of effective controls of our almost random exercises of discretion.

The criminal justice system is, of course, multi-purposive; and different purposes may well properly be pursued for different crimes and at different levels of the system. Our reasons for invoking the criminal law differ when the offense is murder from when it is vagrancy, and likewise, there is no reason to expect the policeman and the probation officer to agree on the mix of purposes to be served by their quite different roles in the criminal justice system.

Analysis of this multi-purposive system of punishment requires acquaintance with research and scholarship in law, philosophy, and a range of social sciences. Gerber's and McAnany's *Contemporary Punishment: Views, Explanations, and Justifications* provides just such a comprehensive and thoughtful overview. Its comprehension is greatly assisted by concise and effective commentaries. It will be of use to student, scholar, and all practitioners in the criminal justice system who care to lift their eyes from the routine path to the direction they wish to travel.

NORVAL MORRIS
Julius Kreeger Professor of Law and Criminology,
University of Chicago

Introduction

The study of criminal law has a fascination which betrays some of man's more primitive traits. It deals with human actions which bring injury to others and, in turn, bring injury to an often stupid and irresponsible individual, the criminal. But despite its unsavory subject matter, the social elements at work in the attempt to curb men's passions are some of the most fundamentally human and humane.

The irony of all the newsprint devoted to describing crime's bloodshed and anguish is that it often ignores the problems which underlie efforts to construct an effective yet just way of ordering social life. When the question is asked why society punishes criminals, the answer must touch the foundations of our political, social, and moral life together. The law and order debates, today so compelling but always in fashion, ultimately concern how society's coercive power shall be applied to those who break the rules. The fact that we have spent centuries discussing the same problem and devising means of controlling the excesses of rage and retaliation is no guarantee that a solution has been found. As Max Weber said, "It is a fact that most 'fundamental' questions are often left unregulated by law even in legal orders which are otherwise thoroughly rationalized." This implies that each generation must grapple anew with the problem and fashion an answer which satisfies its sense of justice.

The following selections speak of the fact that our present generation has recognized the grave need to come to terms with the perennial problem of crime and punishment. This is a task not only for lawyers, though they share a special burden, but for all disciplines dealing with man in his social setting. This includes social scientists, philosophers, politicians, religious experts, doctors, and policemen. While the question is fundamentally one of the justification one offers for the social process called "punishment," almost any discussion of the system will betray how one stands on the basic moral issue. This is why we have chosen widely from authors and articles on punishment and have not confined ourselves to the technical philosophic discussion.

The arrangement of the material conforms to the classical distinctions among purposes for punishment developed over the last two centuries: retribution, deterrence, rehabilitation, and incapacitation. We have given an introductory chapter in basic elements of criminal law to provide our readers with a context in which to view the problem. A final chapter is devoted to the theme of creating a working unity among conflicting values attached to punishment and gives the best thinking of contemporary scholars on the subject. The essays have been selected for their focus on the problem of justification of punishment, but they also treat many other critical issues in punishment.

JUSTIFICATION OF PUNISHMENT

We might then ask why in any discussion of punishment the topic sooner or later reverts to the question of *justification*. Participants all assent to the relevance of justification as *the* point of departure. Even where there is a difference of opinion as to how one defines what we do to criminals, a justification for the process is in order. What is it about punishment that requires us to harbor a defensive approach to it, attempting to justify what is, in fact, such a common practice?

The clearest motivation for justifying punishment lies in its negative and deprivative character. When society punishes it is imposing on the individual a series of socially painful deprivations. It does so, not only knowingly, but out of a sense of duty. There is present a will to inflict certain specified pain with no explicit goal to be achieved except that the law calls for it. Not unwittingly the law speaks of the convicted person as "paying back" or "satisfying his debt to society," when it refers to the pain that he undergoes through imprisonment, fine, or other penalties. But who gets paid? Even a fine, more clearly a tangible exchange for the crime, does not properly pay back anyone. Further, because the punishment process begins with condemnation of the convicted person, it may seem paradoxical if not contradictory to follow it up by inflicting a pain not easily distinguishable from that of the crime. It is this seeming reciprocity of evils that needs justification. Whereas an individual may have been beset by overwhelming passion which mitigates, if not excuses, his crime, the state inflicts its pain within the impersonal framework of law, through trained officials, and with every opportunity to hear the complete details of the accused's defense. It is this impersonal and self-righteous use of pain as *the* means of social control that must be justified.

But apart from its pain-inflicting and moralizing features, punishment requires justification as an interference by society into the privacy of the individual. Suppose punishment were not steeped in the tradition of the gibbet iron and lash but had been therapy-oriented throughout its history. Suppose, too, that there were no condemnation of the offender, only a factual finding that he did the prohibited act. Even in this case, if the treatment were applied to the individual through the coercive power of the state, it would have to be justified as a public intervention into the private sphere at a level of intimacy not easily acceptable. This is especially true where the purpose is to reshape fundamental values of the offender so as to conform them to those shared by the "majority" of society. Even if the individual consented to this process of change, one would feel uneasy that the state, with its concentrated power, was entering the life of the individual with a patently political purpose. Added to this, of course, would be the question of how long the state could keep trying to change the convicted person. If he had not changed in the *first* ten years, would the state be justified in trying for *another* ten?

It should be clear by now that this preoccupation with the issue of justification is prompted by the nature of punishment, even when we call it by more euphemistic names such as "treatment" or "rehabilitation." While all can agree that punishment needs to be justified, the nature of such justification is much in dispute. Nearly all writers will speak of justification of punishment as an attempt to give a moral account of the use by the state of coercive and pain-inflicting power. But they fail to agree on what morality means. Here we touch on another primary issue in jurisprudence raised by punishment: the relationship between law and morality. If one adheres to a utilitarian profession of a faith, morality in this context means the achieving of a measurable social goal at a cost which is not incommensurate with its value for society. Punishment is moral if it achieves the prevention of crimes at a price which is not too dear in terms of the pain it inflicts on the offender and society at large. If one is more inclined toward a natural rights philosophy, the morality will be cast in terms of personal freedom and responsibility. Punishment is moral if it is inflicted only against an individual who has acted freely in committing a crime. A third species of morality is proposed, although confusedly, by the humanitarians who insist that personal welfare of the individual is the guiding norm, so that coercive treatment is moral only when it relates to the welfare of the individual. In all of these attempts at justification of punishment one fact is in evidence: the real moral crux is the conflict of rights between the individual and society.

APPROACHES TO A UNIFIED THEORY OF JUSTIFICATION

Searching for a justification to punishment is a quest that unites an otherwise fragmented field of endeavor. The several traditional arguments for punishment agree on the need to rationalize for society its role of judge and jailer. But here unity ends and diversity begins.

Retribution as a school of punishment argues that society punishes a man because he has broken the law. The justification for inflicting the pain and suffering of a criminal sanction is totally explained in the assumption that the individual is responsible for his action and that justice demands that the suffering which he gave be returned upon him in like amount. The focus is the individual wrongdoer and his free *choice* in breaking the law.

Deterrence shifts the focus to society. There is need to punish a wrongdoer whenever the drama of his deed solicits others to act likewise. Punishment is justified by its preventive quality whether this be a low-grade fear of suffering or a sophisticated reinforcement of belief in law abidance. The utilitarians would argue that the justification of using punishment to prevent other crimes depends upon the amount of pain and suffering caused the individuals over against that caused society by threatened crimes. Since the effect of punishment on others is highly conjectural, that judgment is difficult to make if empirical proof is demanded.

Rehabilitation argues several ways. It can insist that punishment is justified only insofar as it can be shown to reform the individual. This approach may consist in inflicting suffering on the individual as a condition for self-reform. Or it can be the use of the coercive power of the state to impose a regime of social and psychological therapy. In the latter case punishment as such is ruled out and the use of confinement or control is subordinated to the rehabilitative goal. Again it is evident that the focus has shifted back to the individual, away from society.

Finally, social defense theory argues that society needs protection against crime and the only sanction allowable is that of *restraining* those dangerous to society. Thus punishment is not justified at all, since it presupposes an ability both of the individual to freely choose crime and of society to judge moral guilt. What is justified is the identification and control of dangerous individuals. The key factor is *danger;* any control imposed must relate to that. Again the shift is back to society and its right to protect itself against an aggressor, even though he is not judged as responsible.

TOWARD A SOLUTION

None of the schools denies the right of society to protect its survival by declaring certain acts as prohibited. This is the underlying principle for all criminal law: our right to unite for survival and to adopt means to that end. Punishment is a way of backing up the prohibitions set out in criminal law. It has succeeded in varying degree over the centuries and has moved from crude forms of retaliatory victim-revenge, gradually controlled by the state, to a contemporary emphasis on the diagnosis and rehabilitation of offenders.

It seems to us that what punishment implies is the right of society to make moral choices, to set up a line between right and wrong, and to condemn individuals who fall on the wrong side of the line. Punishment takes its characteristics from this moral process of asserting values and denigrating their opposites. The emphasis lies not in the fact that a man can be physically restrained from doing acts that harm others, but rather that he can be morally restrained. The prevention of crime as a goal of society is not ultimately achieved by either crass fear or huge detention centers but by a successful communication of disapproval. It is a moral process which depends for its success on a widely accepted system of laws which reflect a consensus of values and embody a fairness in procedure that guarantees equality of enforcement. One of the serious flaws in today's system is its selectivity, whereby the vast majority of offenders escape and a symbolic few are punished. This selectivity may seem in accord with certain utilitarian principles of punishing the few to instruct the many but it is not that at all. It is the product of an inefficient system that selects the easy cases based on irrelevant qualities of poverty, race, and psychological imbalance. The purpose of punishment or its justification, from this perspective, is to create a system of self-restraint and self-reform. If the system has failed to achieve an accurate reflection of the values held most deeply by society at large, or has not been fair about equally imposing the prohibitions of criminal law, then the self-restraint which derives from this moral basis of the system is impaired. People begin to fall back upon the weak restraints of merely coercive threats of penalty. Where the erosion of the moral base has progressed far enough, the commission of a crime might even itself become a moral imperative, as expressed in the draft record destruction cases.

More to the point of punishment itself, any notion of self-reform depends on the ability of the offender to identify with the norm violated. If unfairness has clouded the picture, he will have the distraction and even the justification which he will naturally be seeking. He can concentrate on the unfairness of the system to the exclusion of his own responsibility. Punishment unfortunately has a greater possibility of becoming unfair or immoral because of its nature as communication. While the substantive criminal law may communicate quite clearly its moral basis in community values, once a penalty is assigned to it and applied to an individual, through the medium of other individuals, many other factors may begin to join the communication effort. Justice needs to be ultra-pure if it is to have its basic impact as moral message. Thus self-reform through the process of punishment depends on a system of men and laws which must be constantly purged of unfairnesses.

Naturally, the success of such a system is its best justification. Here we find the current criminal punishment system much in arrears. If it is impossible to communicate the basic moral message to offenders by the existing system of penalties, then it must be replaced by a system that works. That is perhaps the subrosa debate contained in the following pages. But as will be evident, communication may be successful even if the message gets through more to those speaking than to those spoken to. We may find that the moral process of crime and punishment is really a reforming technique for those who have never offended. But it would be basically wrong, we feel, to ever exclude the welfare of the individual offender in this process. It is the balance of values between the good of the individual and that of the community which should characterize the means of securing an ordered society.

PART I

The Context for Punishment

CHAPTER ONE

CRIMINAL LAW AND CRIMINAL PUNISHMENT

As will become evident in the readings which comprise this book, punishment can have a broad meaning which includes anything from a father's reprimand to execution. But for the most part the theme of justifying punishment as raised in this book is concentrated in the field of criminal law. It is here that the problems of social control by coercive means take on crucial significance. Not only are the means frequently harsh, such as loss of liberty, but they always involve that latent quality of moral condemnation noted by Professor Henry Hart in the first selection included in this chapter.

There are two concepts of criminal law that every first-year law student learns quickly and retains easily—if not with great comprehension: *actus reus* and *mens rea* (to give their familiar Latin titles). These two ideas formulate the nature of every crime, which must embody an external, voluntary act done with criminal intent. Without act and intent there is no crime. This explains why accidents which take more innocent lives by far than murder are not punished as crimes. This also explains why we do not punish a man for his evil intentions, even where these are as totally antisocial as treason. When there is no crime (act plus intent), then there can be no punishment. Looked at in this way, responsibility and conduct are the basis or justification for imposing punishment. We cannot punish a man as a criminal until we have proven beyond reasonable doubt that he did the prohibited act with criminal intent.

Taking a closer look at the issue of responsibility, we can say that the prohibited action, the crime, must be the voluntary and intended act of a person capable of choice. Lawyers are not psychologists and have not attempted, for the most part, any sustained analysis of the meaning of *intended*. Rather they argue from common sense when they assert such things as "every conscious act is intended," "if a man acts on knowledge he also has willed his act," etc. The basic assumption is that a man does have choice and if he commits a prohibited act consciously he has intended to do it; he has responsibility. It is on the basis of such assumptions that the characteristic quality of criminal punishment—blame—is built.

Blame is what the magistrate does when he passes his judgment. The jury finds the defendant "guilty," which is a *factual* statement—he did it. Judgment is an *ethical* statement—"he is blameworthy." Sentence is a consequence of blameworthiness—"he must serve five years in prison." We often consider punishment in the narrow sense of the actual sentence, the five years dragged out day by day. But in truth punishment is more essentially the denunciatory action by the judge, who illustrates, as it were, society's rejection of the crime by imposing a term of imprisonment. In fact, the moral condemnation of judgment is itself the essence of punishment.

Since we speak of criminal *justice*, can we call the sentence, whether it be payment of money or of days in jail, a restoration of something belonging to another? Hardly. But as absurd as this notion may sound under present conditions, criminal law was not always as removed from the notion of "giving every man his due." In earlier days the victim, rather than the state, was the one who exacted the debt from the culprit. When a crime involves property we can imagine how the return of stolen goods, plus an extra portion as reminder of the wrong, could well fit this pattern of just desert. But once we get into personal injury, the repayment notion gets blurred. It is interesting to note, however, that some retributivists will insist on this strict model of "just debt" and substitute vengeance for property as the thing to be returned.

Finally, we must cope with the problem of defining what we mean by punishment. We began this introduction with the idea that criminal punishment would be our prime analogate. We end the chapter, however, with a definition that goes beyond law. This does not mean that the heart of Professor Flew's definition is not rooted in the law tradition. We think that it is. But he has generalized the concept to include other important punishing situations, all of which look back to the standard set by criminal law.

Professor Henry Hart makes his argument for a moral interpretation of the criminal sanction from the condemnatory process of judgment. It is a theme clearly sounded throughout the history of common law and appears again in all of the essays of the first chapter. Herbert Packer is more cautious in his attempt to explain what criminal law means by morality. The concept of morality is further explicated in Richard Wasserstrom's analysis of H. L. A. Hart's utilitarian explanation of moral blameworthiness.

Bittner and Platt are also concerned about the moral quality of punishment. They show how that quality has been changed by historical development from personal moral confrontation of victim and criminal to the "neutral" atmosphere of society vs. the individual who commits an antisocial act.

Professor Flew's definition is widely accepted and serves as a proper bridge between a more technical discussion of criminal law and the basic theories of punishment.

CRIMINAL PUNISHMENT AS PUBLIC CONDEMNATION*

Henry M. Hart, Jr.

Henry M. Hart, Jr., was professor of law at Harvard University for many years until his death in 1969. In the selection given below he shows that criminal law is unique in that it includes moral denunciation of the criminal. As a consequence, the punishment shares the moral quality of this condemnatory process, and it is this which sets it apart from other sanctions the law employs to gain conformity.

What do we mean by "crime" and "criminal"? Or, put more accurately, what should we understand to be "the method of the criminal law," the use of which is in question? This latter way of formulating the preliminary inquiry is more accurate, because it pictures the criminal law as a process, a way of doing something, which is what it is. A great deal of intellectual energy has been misspent in an effort to develop a concept of crime as "a natural and social phenomenon"[1] abstracted from the functioning system of institutions which make use of the concept and give it impact and meaning.[2] But the criminal law, like all law, is concerned with the pursuit of human purposes through the forms and modes of social organization, and it needs always to be thought about in that context as a method or process of doing something.

What then are the characteristics of this method?

1. The method operates by means of a series of directions, or commands, formulated in general terms, telling people what they must or must not do. Mostly, the commands of the criminal law are "must-nots," or prohibitions, which can be satisfied by inaction. "Do not murder, rape, or rob." But some of them are "musts," or affirmative requirements, which can be satisfied only by taking a specifically, or relatively specifically, described kind of action. "Support your

* Excerpted from Hart, *The Aims of the Criminal Law* and reprinted with permission from a symposium on Sentencing appearing in LAW AND CONTEMPORARY PROBLEMS (Vol. 23, No. 3, Summer 1958), published by Duke University School of Law, Durham, North Carolina. Copyright 1958, by Duke University.

[1] See the discussion of the Italian positivists and their influence in American criminology in JEROME HALL, GENERAL PRINCIPLES OF CRIMINAL LAW 539–51 1947), especially at p. 549.

[2] *Cf.* Llewellyn, *Law and the Social Sciences—Especially Sociology*, 62 HARV. L. REV. 1286, 1287 (1949): "When I was younger I used to hear smuggish assertions among my sociological friends, such as: 'I take the sociological, *not* the legal, approach to crime'; and I suspect an inquiring reporter could still hear much of the same (perhaps with 'psychiatric' often substituted for 'sociological')—though it is surely somewhat obvious that when you take 'the legal' out, you also take out 'crime.'"

wife and children," and "File your income tax return."[3]

2. The commands are taken as valid and binding upon all those who fall within their terms when the time comes for complying with them, whether or not they have been formulated in advance in a single authoritative set of words.[4] They speak to members of the community, in other words, in the community's behalf, with all the power and prestige of the community behind them.

3. The commands are subject to one or more sanctions for disobedience which the community is prepared to enforce.

Thus far, it will be noticed, nothing has been said about the criminal law which is not true also of a large part of the noncriminal, or civil, law. The law of torts, the law of contracts, and almost every other branch of private law that can be mentioned operate, too, with general directions prohibiting or requiring described types of conduct, and the community's tribunals enforce these commands.[5] What, then, is distinctive about the method of the criminal law?

Can crimes be distinguished from civil wrongs on the ground that they constitute injuries to society generally which society is interested in preventing? The difficulty is that society is interested also in the due fulfillment of contracts and the avoidance of traffic accidents and most of the other stuff of civil litigation. The civil law is framed and interpreted and enforced with a constant eye to these social interests. Does the distinction lie in the fact that proceedings to enforce the criminal law are instituted by public officials rather than private complainants? The difficulty is that public officers may also bring many kinds of "civil" enforcement actions—for an injunction, for the recovery of a "civil" penalty, or even for the detention of the defendant by public authority.[6] Is the distinction, then, in the peculiar character of what is done to people who are adjudged to be criminals? The difficulty is that, with the possible exception of death, exactly the same kinds of unpleasant consequences, objectively considered, can be and are visited upon unsuccessful defendants in civil proceedings.[7]

If one were to judge from the notions apparently underlying many judicial

[3] For a discussion of types of legal duties generally, see HENRY M. HART, JR. AND ALBERT M. SACKS, THE LEGAL PROCESS: BASIC PROBLEMS IN THE MAKING AND APPLICATION OF LAW I (mim. ed. 1957), at 121–23. Account should also be taken of a peculiar type of criminal prohibition, baffling analysis, which purports to forbid not conduct, but certain kinds of personal condition. See Lacey, *Vagrancy and Crimes of Personal Condition,* 66 HARV. L. REV. 1203 (1953); FOOTE, *Vagrancy-Type Law and Its Administration,* 104 U. PA. L. REV. 603 (1956). To the extent that these crimes are valid and enforceable, however, it seems that they reduce themselves to prohibitions of the conduct bringing about the condition.

[4] See HART AND SACKS, *op. cit. supra,* note 3, at 114–17.

[5] Many of the duties of the civil law, of course, are open-ended, the specific nature of what is to be done being privately determined, as in contracts, and wills. In the criminal law, in contrast, officials bear the whole burden of prescribing the details of private conduct. But the same thing is true, for the most part, in the law of torts and other areas of civil law. See *id.* at 108–10, 129–31.

[6] In many legal systems, moreover, private persons may institute criminal proceedings, as, of course, they could in the English common law and still can in contemporary England.

[7] Thus, debtors were once imprisoned. Insane persons, aliens held for deportation, and recalcitrant witnesses still are. Juvenile delinquents are put on probation. A judgment for the payment of money, which objectively considered is all that a fine is, is, of course, the characteristic civil judgment. And the amount of the civil judgment may be "punitive," and not merely compensatory or restorative.

opinions, and the overt language even of some of them, the solution of the puzzle is simply that a crime is anything which is *called* a crime,[8] and a criminal penalty is simply the penalty provided for doing anything which has been given that name. So vacant a concept is a betrayal of intellectual bankruptcy. . . . Moreover, it is false to popular understanding, and false also to the understanding embodied in existing constitutions. By implicit assumptions that are more impressive than any explicit assertions, these constitutions proclaim that a conviction for crime is a distinctive and serious matter—a something, and not a nothing.[9] What is that something?

4. What distinguishes a criminal from a civil sanction and all that distinguishes it, it is ventured, is the judgment of community condemnation which accompanies and justifies its imposition. As Professor Gardner wrote not long ago, in a distinct but cognate connection:[10]

> The essence of punishment for moral delinquency lies in the criminal conviction itself. One may lose more money on the stock market than in a court-room; a prisoner of war camp may well provide a harsher environment than a state prison; death on the field of battle has the same physical characteristics as death by sentence of law. It is the expression of the community's hatred, fear, or contempt for the convict which alone characterizes physical hardship as punishment.

If this is what a "criminal" penalty is, then we can say readily enough what a "crime" is. It is not simply anything which a legislature chooses to call a "crime." It is not simply antisocial conduct which public officers are given a responsibility to suppress. It is not simply any conduct to which a legislature chooses to attach a "criminal" penalty. It is conduct which, if duly shown to have taken place, will incur a formal and solemn pronouncement of the moral condemnation of the community.

5. The method of the criminal law, of

[8] See, *e.g.*, State v. Dobry, 217 Iowa 858, 861–62, 250 N.W. 702, 704 (1933): "In finding what shall constitute a crime, the legislature has unlimited power. In other words, they can make it include certain elements or omit certain elements therefrom as in their judgment seems best."

[9] See, *e.g.*, in the Constitution of the United States, art: I, § 3, para. 7 (preserving safeguards of criminal trial in matters of impeachment); art. I, § 9, para. 2 (habeas corpus); art. I, § 9, para. 3 (forbidding passage of bills of attainder and ex post facto laws by Congress); art. I, § 10, para. 1, cl. 6 and 7 (forbidding passage of bills of attainder and ex post facto laws by any state); art. III, § 2, para. 3 (jury trial and venue in federal criminal cases); art. III, § 3 (definition and regulation of conviction and punishment for treason); art. IV, § 2, para. 2 (extradition); amendment IV (unreasonable searches and seizures and search warrants); amendment V (indictment by grand jury, double jeopardy, self-incrimination, and due process clauses); amendment VI (rights in criminal cases of speedy and public trial, jury trial, local venue, knowledge of accusation, confrontation of witnesses, compulsory process for obtaining witnesses, and assistance of counsel); amendment VIII (prohibition of excessive bail, excessive fines, and cruel and unusual punishments); amendment XIII (recognition of involuntary servitude as punishment for crime); and amendment XIV (due process and equal protection of the laws in state action).

[10] Gardner, *Bailey v. Richardson and the Constitution of the United States*, 33 B.U.L. REV. 176, 193 (1953). It is, of course, to be understood that Professor Gardner's statement and the statements in the text do not accurately describe the significance of a criminal conviction under many modern regulatory and other statutes which penalize people who have had no awareness nor reason for awareness of wrong-doing. The central thesis of this paper . . . is that a sanction which ineradicably imports blame, both traditionally and in most of its current applications, is misused when it is thus applied to conduct which is not blameworthy.

course, involves something more than the threat (and, on due occasion, the expression) of community condemnation of antisocial conduct. It involves, in addition, the threat (and, on due occasion, the imposition) of unpleasant physical consequences, commonly called punishment. But if Professor Gardner is right, these added consequences take their character as punishment from the condemnation which precedes them and serves as the warrant for their infliction. Indeed, the condemnation plus the added consequences may well be considered, compendiously, as constituting the punishment. Otherwise, it would be necessary to think of a convicted criminal as going unpunished if the imposition or execution of his sentence is suspended.

In traditional thought and speech, the ideas of crime and punishment have been inseparable; the consequences of conviction for crime have been described as a matter of course as "punishment." The Constitution of the United States and its amendments, for example, use this word or its verb form in relation to criminal offenses no less than six times.[11] Today, "treatment" has become a fashionable euphemism for the older, ugly word. This bowdlerizing of the Constitution and of conventional speech may serve a useful purpose in discouraging unduly harsh sentences and emphasizing that punishment is not an end in itself. But to the extent that it dissociates the treatment of criminals from the social condemnation of their conduct which is implicit in their conviction, there is danger that it will confuse thought and do a disservice.

At least under existing law, there is a vital difference between the situation of a patient who has been committed to a mental hospital and the situation of an inmate of a state penitentiary. The core of the difference is precisely that the patient has not incurred the moral condemnation of his community, whereas the convict has.[12]

[11] Art. I, § 3, para. 7; art. I, § 8, cl. 6; art. I, § 8, cl. 10; art. III, § 3, para. 2; amendment VIII; and amendment XIII.

[12] For a convincing statement that the difference does not lie in the necessarily greater gentleness of the treatment administered in the hospital, see de Grazia, *The Distinction of Being Mad*, 22 U. Chi. L. Rev. 339, 348–55 (1955). Of course, there are also differences in the legal provisions governing the possibility of release, but these are mostly corollaries of the basic difference in the nature of the judgment directing detention.

CONDUCT AND PUNISHMENT*

Herbert L. Packer

Professor Herbert Packer is a member of the law faculty of Stanford University and author of many articles and books on criminal law. The present piece sets out his notion of conduct as a limitation on punishment. Criminal law does not deal in thoughts or emotions short of external action. It can only justify the imposition of punishment where conduct has been voluntary and thus culpable.

It may hardly seem a startling notion that the criminal law, or law in general for that matter, is concerned with conduct—people's actions (including their verbal and other expressive actions) and their failures to act. Yet there is nothing in the nature of things that compels this focus. The criminal law could be concerned with people's thoughts and emotions, with their personality patterns and character structures. It is true that if this rather than conduct was the focus, it would still be expedient in most cases to ascertain these essentially internal characteristics through inquiry into conduct. But if these internal characteristics were the focus, conduct would simply be evidence of what we are interested in rather than the thing itself; and we would not hesitate to use other evidence to the extent that it became available. If, for example, we could determine through projective tests like the Rorschach or through other and more sophisticated forms of psychological testing that a given individual was likely to inflict serious physical injury on someone, someday, somewhere, and if we viewed conduct as a prerequisite rather than as merely evidentiary, we would presumably not hesitate to inflict punishment on that person for his propensities, or, as the old cliché has it, for thinking evil thoughts. We might rationalize this simply by saying that we were punishing him for the offense of having flunked his Rorschach test, but we would then be acting on a somewhat Pickwickian definition of "conduct."

Why do we not do so? The obvious historical answer is that, aside from a few antiquarian anomalies such as the offense of imagining the King's death, we have not been sufficiently stirred by the danger presented or sufficiently confident of our ability to discern propensities in the absence of conduct to use the instruments of the criminal law in this fashion. For some it may be enough to rejoice that historically this was so and to rest on that historical accident for the present and the future, but I think that a further answer is required. This answer turns, in

* Reprinted from The Limits of the Criminal Sanction by Herbert L. Packer with the permission of the publishers, Stanford: Stanford University Press; London: Oxford University Press.

my view, on the idea of culpability, that necessary but insufficient condition of criminal liability that is an important part of our integrated theory of criminal punishment.

Among the notions associated with the concept of "culpability" are those of free will and human autonomy. I do not mean this in any deep philosophical sense but in a contingent and practical social sense. It is important, especially in a society that likes to describe itself as "free" and "open," that a government should be empowered to coerce people only for what they do and not for what they are.

If this is important for law generally, it is *a fortiori* important for that most coercive of legal instruments, the criminal law. Now, this self-denying ordinance can be and often is attacked as being inconsistent with the facts of human nature. People may in fact have little if any greater capacity to control their conduct (some say in part, some say in whole) than their emotions or their thoughts. It is therefore either unrealistic or hypocritical, so the argument runs, to deal with conduct as willed or to treat it differently from personality and character.

This attack is, however, misconceived. Neither philosophic concepts nor psychological realities are actually at issue in the criminal law. The idea of free will in relation to conduct is not, in the legal system, a statement of fact, but rather a value preference having very little to do with the metaphysics of determinism and free will. The fallacy that legal values describe physical reality is a very common one. We shall encounter it in its most vulgar form in connection with the so-called insanity defense. But we need to dispose of it here, because it is such a major impediment to rational thought about the criminal law. Very simply, the law treats man's conduct as autonomous and willed, not because it is, but because it is desirable to proceed as if it were. It is desirable because the capacity of the individual human being to live his life in reasonable freedom from socially imposed external constraints (the only kind with which the law is concerned) would be fatally impaired unless the law provided a *locus poenitentiae*, a point of no return beyond which external constraints may be imposed but before which the individual is free—not free of whatever compulsions determinists tell us he labors under but free of the very specific social compulsions of the law. The law is full of such points of no return.

Conduct should not be confused, as it sometimes is, with the infliction of harm. We are simply forcing the criminal law onto a Procrustean bed when we attempt to assimilate the diverse kinds of conduct with which it may be concerned to the occurrence of harm. The infliction of harm may well be a useful classifying device, serving for some analytic purposes to distinguish certain kinds of crime from others; and it may afford an important prudential criterion of limitation for the scope of the criminal sanction; but the use of the term "harm" to embrace all of the kinds of conduct that have been or rationally might be comprised within a criminal code is at best illusory. What is the harm inflicted by an unsuccessful attempt to kill someone who does not even know that he is in danger? Or by driving in excess of the speed limit without becoming involved in an accident? Or by possessing tools that are adapted for committing burglaries? Yet attempted murder, reckless driving, and possession of burglar's tools are all well-established examples of criminal conduct. And even the most ardent proponents of the "harm" theory have never charged that calling these forms of conduct criminal is inconsistent with any important legal principle.

. . . The problems that offenses of this sort raise are essentially definitional problems, as we shall see in succeeding sections. That does not disqualify them from congruence with the first and most basic requirement of the criminal law: that the subject with which it deals is conduct.

It may seem anomalous, particularly to those with some training in the conventional doctrines of the criminal law, that we should fasten here on conduct as a limitation on culpability. The orthodox view is that culpability is primarily a matter of the actor's mental state, rather than of the conduct in which he engages. Indeed, it is those offenses whose commission is established by proof of conduct irrespective of the offender's mental state that are referred to as offenses of strict liability and that are denounced, and rightly so, as being incompatible with culpability limitations. And yet, the paradoxical fact is that the limitation of criminal punishment to conduct constitutes the first and most important line of defense against erosion of the idea of culpability, for it keeps the criminal law from becoming purely the servant of the utilitarian ideal of prevention.

A clue to why this is so is afforded by the universally recognized doctrine that conduct that occurs while the actor is in an unconscious state—sleepwalking, epileptic seizures, automatism—may not be dealt with criminally. Conduct must be, as the law's confusing term has it, "voluntary." The term is one that will immediately raise the hackles of the determinist, of whatever persuasion. But, once again, the law's language should not be read as plunging into the deep waters of free will vs. determinism, Cartesian duality, or any of a half-dozen other philosophic controversies that might appear to be invoked by the use of the term "voluntary" in relation to conduct. The law is not affirming that some conduct is the product of the free exercise of conscious volition; it is excluding, in a crude kind of way, conduct that in any view is not. And it does so primarily in response to the simple intuition that nothing would more surely undermine the individual's sense of autonomy and security than to hold him to account for conduct that *he* does not think he can control. He may be deluded, if the determinists are right, in his belief that such conduct differs significantly from any other conduct in which he engages. But that is beside the point. *He* thinks there is a difference, and that is what the law acts upon.

Thus we see that limiting criminal punishment to cases of conduct *pro tanto* detracts from the utilitarian goal of prevention and is, in fact, the first in a long series of trammels that the rationale of the criminal law places on a purely preventive orientation. The conduct limitation is the main distinction between criminal law and civil commitment, although the difference does not make the outcome of either process any the more or the less a form of punishment. Finally, the conduct limitation in the criminal law has been powerfully reinforced by the development of alternative legal processes for dealing with the prevention of future undesired behavior.

PUNISHMENT AND RESPONSIBILITY*

Richard A. Wasserstrom

Richard A. Wasserstrom is a professor of law and philosophy at the University of California, Los Angeles. In the present essay he examines and criticizes the attempt of Professor H. L. A. Hart to develop a purely utilitarian meaning for criminal intent and responsibility as the basis for punishment.

In both the English and the American legal systems, a person's liability to punishment is generally made dependent upon certain mental conditions (in addition, of course, to the commission of certain proscribed acts, etc.). In order for a person to be held criminally responsible for his acts, so the generally acknowledged doctrine goes, *mens rea* must have been present. In his writings on the criminal law, Professor H. L. A. Hart has been concerned in large measure with providing a reinterpretation of the doctrine of *mens rea* and a new rationale for and defense of the doctrine of criminal responsibility that depends upon it.[1] For Hart the challenge is to defend these doctrines against two positions which threaten them from opposite directions. The first is the claim that the requirement of *mens rea* only makes sense within the confines of a retributive theory of punishment—within the context of a view that makes the requirement of *mens rea* dependent upon the appropriateness of punishing people for the immorality of their conduct. The second is the claim that the doctrine of criminal responsibility (and hence *mens rea*) could profitably be "eliminated" from the criminal law, and the focus of the criminal law shifted thereby from a punitive to a preventive intention. . . .

Any retributive theory of punishment depends in some quite fundamental sense upon the presence of a morally wrong act. Thus, it is not surprising that in one of his most important and influential articles, "Legal Responsibility and Ex-

* Excerpted from Wasserstrom, *H.L.A. Hart and the Doctrines of* Mens Rea *and Criminal Responsibility,* 35 University of Chicago Law Review 92 (1967). Reprinted with permission.

[1] Among the writings by H. L. A. Hart that deal most directly with these topics are: The Concept of Law (1961); The Morality of the Criminal Law (1964); Punishment and the Elimination of Responsibility (1962); *The Ascription of Responsibility and Rights,* in 49 Proceedings of the Aristotelian Society 171 (new series 1949), and in Logic and Language 145 (1st series A. Flew ed. 1960); *Intention and Punishment,* 4 Oxford Rev. 5 (1967); *Legal Responsibility and Excuses,* in Determinism and Freedom in the Age of Modern Science 81 (2d ed. S. Hook (1965); *Negligence, Mens Rea and Criminal Responsibility,* in Oxford Essays in Jurisprudence 29 (A. Guest ed. 1961); *Prolegomenon to the Principles of Punishment,* in 60 Proceedings of the Aristotelian Society 1 (new ser. 1959), and in Philosophy, Politics and Society 158 (2d ser. P. Laslett & W. Runciman ed. (1962) [all citations hereinafter are to the latter volume].

cuses,"[2] Professor Hart seeks to criticize the thesis, which he attributes to Jerome Hall, that criminal responsibility depends on moral culpability. This, says Hart, is a mistake. *Mens rea* is not required in order to assure the existence of *moral* culpability. Instead the doctrine's desirability can be seen to depend both upon maximization of the choices that it allows to individual members of society and upon the prevention of the punishment of those who did not voluntarily violate the law.

Hart begins his exploration of these topics by proposing an interpretation of the requirement of *mens rea.* Those mental conditions that must be present before liability to punishment is allowed can, says Hart, be viewed most profitably in their negative form. As such, they are the conditions that exempt one from punishment on some ground or other. Thus, one way to view these mental conditions is as excusing conditions:

> [T]he individual is not liable to punishment if at the time of his doing what would otherwise be a punishable act he is, say, unconscious, mistaken about the physical consequences of his bodily movements or the nature or qualities of the thing or persons affected by them, or, in some cases, if he is subjected to threats or other gross forms of coercion or is the victim of certain types of mental disease. This is a list, not meant to be complete, giving broad descriptions of the principal excusing conditions; the exact definition of these and their precise character and scope must be sought in the detailed exposition of our criminal law. If an individual breaks the law when none of the excusing conditions are present, he is ordinarily said to have acted of "his own free will," "of his own accord," "voluntarily"; or it might be said, "He could have helped doing what he did."[3]

Given this interpretation of the *mens rea* requirement, the next question is, of course, why we either do or ought to recognize these excuses as properly exempting persons from criminal liability. The view that Hart wants to reject is that which regards the importance of excuses to any determination of criminal responsibility as being itself dependent upon "the more fundamental requirement that for criminal responsibility there must be 'moral culpability,' which would not exist where the excusing conditions are present."[4]. . .

. . . Hart is concerned to establish that Hall's view is mistaken. . . . It supposes that criminal liability must either be based on moral culpability or it must be "strict," *i.e.,* based "on nothing more than the outward conduct of the accused."[5] Given this dichotomy, it does seem to follow, says Hart, that the only plausible explanation as to why we inquire into the mental state of a defendant is that we are concerned to establish the presence or absence of moral culpability.

The difficulty here, Hart tells us, is

[2] Hart, *Legal Responsibility and Excuses, supra* note 1, at 81.

[3] *Id.* at 81. For an earlier statement by Hart of this same general view, see Hart, *The Ascription of Responsibility and Rights, supra* note 1, at 171.

Whatever other difficulties may inhere in viewing the concepts of *intentional* or *voluntary* action as defeasible ones, it is clear that not all cases of intentional actions can be regarded in this defeasible sense, *e.g.,* the *intention* required by a statute that makes it a crime to enter a dwelling with the intention of doing X. This is what Hart has in one place called "doing something with a further intention." Hart, *Intention and Punishment,* 4 OXFORD REV. 5, 8 (1967). I think Hart would agree that this concept of intention is not a defeasible one.

[4] Hart, *Legal Responsibility and Excuses, supra* note 1, at 88.

[5] Hart, *Legal Responsibility and Excuses, supra* note 1, at 90.

that the dilemma is an unreal one. There is, in short, a third alternative; namely, that the actor's mental state is relevant just in order to establish that the actor acted *voluntarily*. There is, Hart insists—and this seems to me to be the central point—a rationale for the system of excuses that is different from the one proposed by Hall. It is simply that there is a principle worthy of respect that holds that "it is unfair and unjust to punish those who have not 'voluntarily' broken the law."[6] This, Hart quite rightly insists, is a very different principle from that which holds that "it is wrong to punish those who have not 'voluntarily committed a moral wrong proscribed by law.' "[7] Thus, if Hall had not mistakenly supposed that all liability must be either strict or based on moral culpability, he would have seen the possibility of a rationale for the excuses based upon the fundamental principle that it is unjust to punish a person who did not voluntarily violate the law.

Hart's thesis raises at least three further questions. First, what is there that is unfair or unjust about punishing someone who did not voluntarily break the law? Second, even if it is unjust to punish someone unless he voluntarily broke the law, might it not only be just to punish those who have voluntarily broken the law? And third, is it just to punish those who have voluntarily broken the law? That is to say, even if Hart is right concerning the injustice of punishing in the presence of one of the excuses, this does not imply the justness of punishing in the absence of the excuse—and in particular in the absence of "moral fault." It is important to notice, I think, that one reason why Hart's contribution to legal philosophy has been so meaningful and so substantial is that he is prepared to give a response to each of these questions.

Thus Hart is not content to rest, as would many, on the "inherent" attractiveness of the principle that it is unjust to punish a person who did not voluntarily break the law. Instead, Hart proposes the following as an answer to the question of why it is unjust to punish in the absence of a voluntary action. Imagine, he says, what it would be like to live in a society in which accidents, insanity, duress, and all of the other excuses were not regarded as entitling an offender to exemption from criminal liability.[8] Imagine what it would be like to live under a system of criminal law that operated on the basis of total 'strict liability.' At least three things would happen. First, "our power of predicting what will happen to us will be immeasurably diminished." This is so because we cannot predict very accurately when we will, for example, do something by mistake or by accident. Secondly, what happens to us will be dependent very largely on things other than our own choices. And thirdly, "we should suffer sanctions without having obtained any satisfactions."[9]

Thus, *in support* of the principle that it is wrong to punish someone who did not voluntarily violate the law, Professor Hart points to three undesirable consequences that would attend the systematic neglect of that principle. Professor Hart's analysis is surely convincing and illuminating. It does appear wrong to *punish* persons in the face of one or more of the

[6] *Id.* at 91.

[7] *Id.*

[8] An analogous set of cases that Hart considers particularly instructive consists of the invalidating conditions in the civil law sphere, such as mistake or duress with respect to the validity of contracts.

[9] Hart, *Legal Responsibility and Excuses, supra* note 1, at 99. *See also* H. L. A. Hart, Punishment and the Elimination of Responsibility 28 (1962).

excuses, and, in part at least, for reasons similar to those given by Hart.[10] We can understand the need for excuses in any punishment system, and we can do so without recourse to appreciably more problematic theories such as retributivism.

. . . At present . . . I want to consider the additional but related claim advanced by Hart that there are *affirmative* virtues to a system which recognizes the excusing conditions. Hart identifies at least three advantages in such recognition:

> First, we maximize the individual's power at any time to predict the likelihood that the sanctions of the criminal law will be applied to him. Secondly, we introduce the individual's choice as one of the operative factors determining whether or not these sanctions shall be applied to him. He can weigh the cost to him of obeying the law—and of sacrificing some satisfaction in order to obey—against obtaining that satisfaction at the cost of paying "the penalty." Thirdly, by adopting this system of attaching excusing conditions we provide that, if the sanctions of the criminal law are applied, the pains of punishment will for each individual represent the price of some satisfaction obtained from breach of law.[11]

Here, too, Hart's analysis does provide us with a new and useful way of looking at the role of excusing conditions in the law. By emphasizing the significance that the presence of choice alone can make, Hart permits us to view the criminal law in a substantially more "positive" fashion than is typically the case. It permits us to see the sense in which the criminal law can be seen not so much as a system of prohibitions, the punishment for which is justified either as a means of securing compliance or as a fitting response to wrongdoing, but as a system of "prices" for alternative courses of conduct.

One real danger in this analysis is, of course, that it may lead us significantly to underestimate and understate the nonoptional character of criminal laws, that it may lead to an interpretation of criminal laws as mere hypothetical imperatives. Hart has himself acknowledged the force of this objection on a variety of occasions,[12] but in one place, at least, he

[10] However, I am far from certain that none of the traditional excuses is relevant even in the typical strict liability statute. *See* Wasserstrom, *Strict Liability in the Criminal Law*, 12 STAN. L. REV. 731 (1960). Three additional points merit mention:

(1) Nothing that Hart has said rules out the plausibility of regarding the excuses as essential because their presence would prevent an assessment of moral culpability. Hart has not, by this argument, refuted Hall's view. He has simply provided an alternative rationale.

(2) Under Hart's analysis, it is clear that mistake of law, just as much as mistake of fact, must be recognized as an excuse. Hart is quite consistent, therefore, in insisting that the present doctrine in respect to mistake of law ought to be changed. Hall, on the other hand, insists that mistake of law not be deemed an excuse—a position that, given his general view, seems extraordinarily difficult to defend. *See* J. HALL, GENERAL PRINCIPLES OF THE CRIMINAL LAW 376–414 (2d ed. 1960).

(3) It should be noted that Hart is also quite willing to accept numerous modifications of the principle concerning voluntary acts in the name of practical problems of the administration of justice, particularly of problems of proof. *See, e.g.*, H. L. A. HART, PUNISHMENT AND THE ELIMINATION OF RESPONSIBILITY 20–22 (1962).

[11] Hart, *Legal Responsibility and Excuses, supra* note 1, at 99. *See also* H. L. A. HART, PUNISHMENT AND THE ELIMINATION OF RESPONSIBILITY 28 (1962).

[12] *See* Hart, *Legal Responsibility and Excuses, supra* note 1, at 96-97, where he says: "I do not of course mean to suggest that it is a matter of indifference whether we obey the law or break it and pay the penalty. Punishment *is* different from a mere 'tax on a course of conduct.' What

does so in an atypical, most curious fashion. Immediately after the passage quoted above[13] Hart goes on to say that this view:

> can sound like a very cold, if not immoral, attitude toward the criminal law, general obedience to which we regard as an essential part of a decent social order. But this attitude seems repellent only if we assume that all criminal laws are ones whose operation we approve. To be realistic we must also think of bad and repressive criminal laws; in South Africa, Nazi Germany, Soviet Russia, and no doubt elsewhere, we might be thankful to have their badness mitigated by the fact that they fall only on those who have obtained a satisfaction from knowingly doing what they forbid.[14]

Now this is, I think, a most curious way to acknowledge the point. On one basic issue his position is surely sound and important: criminal laws can be bad, they can make illegal conduct that is not blameworthy and they can fail to prohibit conduct that ought surely be prevented and condemned. There are bad and repressive criminal laws in the United States, to say nothing of the countries mentioned by Hart. Yet, it is, nonetheless, odd to put the point in the fashion in which Hart has. For in the first place there is no guarantee whatsoever that bad and repressive systems of criminal law will necessarily recognize the excuses.[15] Thus, there is no reason to assume that their badness will be mitigated in the fashion described by Hart. And in the second place, it would appear that the distinction between laws we should obey and those we should not could be preserved merely by acknowledging that the obligation to obey the law is an obligation that can be overriden by more stringent moral obligations on a variety of occasions and in virtually every social order. Thus, the non-optional character of criminal laws could be maintained more easily through the recognition that their non-optionality is not absolute and that it is in fact susceptible of being replaced by more compelling moral demands.[16]

I do mean is that the conception of the law simply as goading individuals into desired courses of behavior is inadequate and misleading; what a legal system that makes liability generally depend on excusing conditions does is to guide individuals' choices as to behavior by presenting them with reasons for exercising choice in the direction of obedience, but leaving them to choose."

In another work, Hart develops the nonoptional character of the criminal laws more fully: "The idea that the substantive rules of the criminal law have as their function (and, in a broad sense, their meaning) the guidance not merely of officials operating a system of penalties, but of ordinary citizens in the activities of nonofficial life, cannot be eliminated without jettisoning cardinal distinctions and obscuring the specific character of law as a means of social control. A punishment for a crime, such as a fine, is not the same as a tax on a course of conduct, though both involve directions to officials to inflict the same money loss. What differentiates these ideas is that the first involves, as the second does not, an offence or breach of duty in the form of a violation of a rule set up to guide the conduct of ordinary citizens." H. L. A. Hart, The Concept of Law 38–39 (1961).

[13] *See* text accompanying note 11 *supra.*

[14] Hart, *Legal Responsibility and Excuses, supra* note 1, at 111-12.

[15] I suppose that one sort of defect, among others, that attached to the Nuremberg Decrees was that they did not permit the traditional excuses; that is, they made being a Jew a crime.

[16] *See* Wasserstrom, *The Obligation to Obey the Law,* 10 U.C.L.A. L. Rev. 780 (1963).

THE RIGHT OF THE STATE TO PUNISH*

Egon Bittner and Anthony Platt

Egon Bittner is professor of sociology at Brandeis University, and Anthony Platt is professor of criminology at the University of California, Berkeley. In this article the authors combine their interests in social science and law in tracing the historical development of punishment as it moved from a private right to a public duty. It is interesting to note that restitution was the original sense of "making the punishment fit the crime." This personal dimension of answering to the demands of the victim has been swallowed up in the impersonal—and neutral—demands of society.

THE HISTORICAL ROOTS OF PUNISHMENT[1]

Evidence from studies of life in preliterate societies and from studies of ancient law indicates that legal punishment, in the now current sense, is a relatively recent phenomenon.[2]

Leaving aside disciplinary chastisement by heads of families, which in the past encompassed a much wider scope than is the case today,[3] we find that early societies are devoid of mechanisms for the *ex officio* prosecution of delicts. This does not mean that they lack the concept of crime and punishment, or that they have no laws. Quite to the contrary, laws and litigations are encountered in the most primitive societies. Moreover, not only do we find laws everywhere but in primitive and archaic societies virtually

* Excerpted from Bittner and Platt, *The Meaning of Punishment*, 2 Issues in Criminology 82 (1966). Reprinted with permission.

[1] Sir Henry Maine, writing about the topic we are now addressing, stated, "What mankind did in the primitive state may not be a hopeless subject of inquiry, but of their motives for doing it, it is impossible to know anything," *Ancient Law*, 149, (1954). To the good fortune of posterity Sir Henry did not remain silent about the motives and intended meaning of the practices of ancient people. He offered surmise where he could not know, and we shall avail ourselves of this method, without, needless to say, claiming his powers of discernment.

[2] For the former consider Hoebel, E. Adamson, *The Law of Primitive Man*, (1954); for the latter, Weber, Max, *On Law in Economy and Society*, 54 ff., (1954), and the literature cited therein.

[3] The disciplinary rights of parents in ancient law have been exaggerated by some modern commentators. The apparent severity, for example, of Talmudic Law has been literally interpreted without reference to rabbinic commentaries. The doctrine of the "stubborn and rebellious son" in *Deuteronomy* has led some writers to conclude that fathers had the absolute right of death over their children. The true motivation of this law seems to have been to *limit* the paternal authority by compelling the parent to bring such a case before the elders for adjudication. Furthermore, the rabbinic attitude towards the capital punishment of children was generally humanitarian and so many ingenious legal restrictions were required that an execution was almost rendered impossible; cf. Goldin, Hyman E., *Hebrew Criminal Law and Procedure*, 166–175, (1952).

all litigation was concerned with delicts.[4] Under ordinary circumstances of archaic life the function of the polity was confined to the interpretation of the principles of justice. In a variety of ways, many of them involving augury and divination, the collectivity as a whole, or its deputized agents, would ascertain the fact of a delict and stipulate an appropriate remedy. The manner in which the process of judging was set into motion and the manner in which the judgments executed were devoid of procedural formalizations. To take the initiative was wholly the burden of the aggrieved person, who, upon obtaining a favorable judgment, was also left with the task of executing it. In this task his own resourcefulness was augmented only by such help from kin and friends as he was able to mobilize privately. The official judgment merely licensed the compensation and stipulated its terms. Within these general limitations the manner in which a case in law could be raised and executed varied considerably.

It is worth noting that in all but the most primitive circumstances there existed procedures which provided for compensations along the line of the Roman maxim *omnis condemnatio est pecuniaria.* This was the case not only in those parts of the world that were exposed to Roman influence, as for example, the earliest English laws, but also among such people as actually had no money and employed trade objects.[5] In this way, or in some other ways, archaic law always brought the punishment of offenders into some sort of relationship to the loss of the injured party. Such systems of administration of justice provided a general framework for the peaceful rectification of wrongs, at least to the extent of making final settlements possible.

It could be maintained, of course, that such remedies are not analogous to what we perceive to be punishment and that they resemble cases in tort. There are no objections to this formulation provided that it will be remembered that these actions encompassed virtually all that we now find under the scope of criminal procedure, and that it will be remembered that the stipulated compensation stressed punitive significance.[6]

The absence of a formal law enforcement apparatus in so-called primitive societies is, of course, not a remarkable fact in itself. As social evolution becomes identified with the increase of functional differentiation, the term "primitive soci-

[4] The seemingly exclusive concern of early jurisprudence with wrongs has led Durkheim to assert the logical and chronological priority of criminal law over civil law; cf. his *On the Division of Labor in Society,* (1933).

[5] Though such stipulations are not ubiquitous in archaic law they are quite common. Where they occur, they indicate a tendency toward objectivity in the determination of the substance of the punitive reparation and a tendency towards regulating the measure of punishment in detailed manner. Concerning the making of peace on a "financial" basis in the ancient civilizations of the Near East see Professor Woolley's remarks in Hawkes, Jacquetta and Sir Leonard Woolley, *Pre-History and the Beginning of Civilization,* 487, (1963). Another example, taken from an altogether different cultural context is furnished by the practices of remedial compensation employed by the Ifugao of Northern Luzon; cf. Hoebel, *op. cit.*

[6] In early Roman jurisprudence, for example, the finding against a party in this sort of litigation involved *infamy* in addition to the duty to make restitution; the same is true of Homeric Greeks, as is shown in Keller, Albert G., *Homeric Society: A Sociological Study of the Iliad and the Odyssey,* 282 ff, (1902) ; furthermore, recent interpretations of the Assyrian and Hittite Codes lead to the conclusion that they too were based on systems of justice relying on punitive-tort type procedures, cf. Woolley, *loc. cit.*

ety" implies the absence of specialized organs of all kind.[7] The official passivity of the society in the matter of executing its judgments, however, requires an additional explanation. Weber argued that the lack of concern for implementation was related to the belief that the judgments have been arrived at "by the interpretation of oracles or other magical devices, or the invocation of magical or divine powers, [which] carried with it sufficient magical authority to enforce itself, so that disobedience constituted a kind of serious blasphemy."[8] When this mechanism of *quid pro quo* justice broke down recourse was open to other kinds of retribution involving untempered and unmitigated violence. It is important to emphasize, however, that the procedures involving direct reciprocity made up the bulk of the routine administration of justice. The relatively sterner measures, though not infrequent, were certainly extraordinary. The feature of ordinary administration of archaic justice which we wish to emphasize is that it encompassed the principle of proportional punitive sanction and that it provided for the conveyance of the benefit of the sanction to the aggrieved party. This is true even in cases where the injured party obtained no material compensation but merely the satisfaction of inflicting commensurate pain on the assailant. The role of society remained morally unproblematic as it confined itself to "citing" the code to the contesting parties. The offender suffered at the hand and pleasure of the offended party whose right to compensation was patently given in the facts of his injury. Furthermore, the restitution was, in an important sense, voluntary. This is not to suggest that the offender volunteered to suffer the punishment but that he had the option of either paying the price of his transgression and retaining his membership in the society, or placing himself outside of the scope of the protection of the moral order, which he enjoyed even as an offender.[9] Whatever was done to him then was no longer accountable in terms of the prevailing calculus of right and wrong. Upon such persons early man descended with awesome harshness. The mortification of the *morally exterritorialized* person appeared to have inhumane aspects because he was perceived to be more an obnoxious object than a person. Thus, if we insist in our definition of punishment, that it be a morally significant act then we cannot define what happens to a person standing outside the horizon of morally regulated reciprocal relationships as punishment. To be sure, universalistic ethics, especially the ethic of Christianity, have made it difficult for us to even think of a human as other than morally significant, and of any action against man as entirely devoid of moral significance.[10] This was not always the case, for in archaic societies the boundaries of

[7] cf. Parsons, Talcott, Evolutionary Universals in Society, 29 *American Sociological Review* 339–357, (1964).

[8] Weber, *op. cit.*, 51.

[9] Durkheim's discussion of "altruistic suicide" could be considered as an instance of volunteered suffering of punishment; cf. his, *Suicide: A Study in Sociology,* (1951). Ethnographic documentation of such cases can be found in, Malinowski, Bronislaw, *Crime and Custom in Savage Society,* (1932).

[10] In this respect, it is interesting to note that the mentally ill in English law have often been characterized as "wild beasts" and metaphorically compared with dumb animals. Cf. Platt, Anthony M., and Bernard L. Diamond, The Origins and Development of the "Wild Beast" Concept of Mental Illness and Its Relation to Theories of Criminal Responsibility, 1 *Journal of the History of the Behavioral Sciences* 355–367, (1965).

morality were largely coextensive with the boundaries of membership in the collectivity. That is, it was possible for a ritually or ethnically alien person to be devoid of all rights, which is just a way of saying that it is possible for him to have no moral status.[11] About him it could not be said that he *deserved* any particular sanction, but if he was in some sense obnoxious, as he was generally perceived to be, then he had to be eliminated. Thus, persons who were so sullied by blasphemous conduct as to be beyond the redemption by punishment were not, strictly speaking, punished but merely objectively destroyed.[12]

These acts of destruction of morally exterritorialized persons can be found to accompany the normal and routine administration of justice. In the Near East, for example, licensed acts of mob violence against persons who offended some religious taboo run parallel with normal retributive justice administered in accordance with the *lex talionis.*[13] Similarly, the Eskimo recognize, in addition to the highly regularized contests between offenders and victims, a procedure whereby "the obnoxious person is first ostracized, then *liquidated.*"[14] From such evidence it may be inferred that, in its primordial forms, remedial action was either part of a private settlement of grievances, the terms of which were set by the society, but which was executed entirely by the aggrieved persons, or acts perpetrated either collectively or individually upon persons defined as standing outside the bounds of the moral order. In the first instance, it was punishment, a moral act located in the private sphere of the activities and interests of individuals. In the second instance it was merely an act in which the ritually impure person did not so much deserve to be destroyed, as the society was entitled to be rid of the jeopardy into which his presence placed it. In these latter actions no distinction was made between ethnic strangers, persons who were perceived as polluted as the result of some impieties, and persons who displayed some other signs of ritual impurity. Thus, for example, stigmata resulting from physical illness could produce the same results as adultery. In either case, the act of the society can no more be described as punishment than the acts of soldiers destroying their adversaries. In sum, it may be said that initially at least, society destroyed its adversaries but did not punish. Punishment, that is an act meted out in the interest of justice, and which conferred upon the punished the benefits of redemption, was a right of the aggrieved and his alone.

[11] Jacquetta Hawkes notes in *op. cit.* 127, "It need hardly be said that the social morality evolved by long custom for the protection and well being of members of a tribe or other group did not apply to 'foreigners.' " Consider also the following: "A social attitude toward a member of another group is . . . unthinkable. A snake, a leopard, a slaughtered sheep, or a crushed worm is not more abstractly treated. It is felt that an attitude of this sort cannot by any stretch of meaning be taken to include punishment." Farris, Ellsworth. The Origin of Punishment, 25 *International Journal of Ethics* 64, (1914). We can point to a vestigial survival of this belief in the *sub rosa* legitimacy of the rule that wrongs perpetrated upon ethnic outsiders do not carry the same stigma of moral turpitude as wrongs perpetrated upon co-ethnics; cf. Garfinkel, Harold, Research Note on Inter and Intra-Racial Homicides, 27 *Social Forces* 369–381, (1949).

[12] Concerning the redemptive functions of punishment see, Burke, Kenneth, *The Rhetoric of Religion: Studies in Logology,* 175–176, *et. passim,* (1961).

[13] The apothegm about Christ and the adultress might well be taken as an attack against ritual outlawing and destruction rather than an argument against punishment in general.

[14] Hoebel, *op. cit.,* 90, (emphasis supplied).

The establishment and development of an *official machinery* for the prosecution of delicts and the execution of punishment is extremely difficult to trace historically. Only in the most general sense is the migration of the competence to punish from private to public hands a concomitant of the growth of large territorial states encompassing ethnically heterogeneous populations. It appears that public law enforcement entered the field of delicts by way of aiding tribal folk justice. According to Professor Woolley, the great lawgivers of the ancient Near East were not legal innovators and in their codes the law of delicts remains essentially a private law. They merely attempted to insure a relatively homogeneous administration of justice, and they typically did not establish special offices for this purpose but used existing deputaries of the central government and garrisoned armed forces as aids to local judges. The reticence of the governments of the early territorial states to assume responsibility for the prosecution of delicts and the execution of punishment can be documented from many sources. Even where the idea of the public delict is fairly well established as, for example, in Republican Rome and in Anglo-Saxon law, the functions of the state remain narrowly circumscribed. States that have the most elaborate administrative and military organization have not even a remotely comparable system for the administration of justice.[15] Often the dealings with delicts became the proper business of the central government or the sovereign only when customary law ceased to function adequately.[16] The customary law operating at the local level did not, of course, retain the purity and formalism of the old tribal folk law. It is more likely that the local judiciary, such as it was, operated with a particular variant of the syncretized versions of folk law that are contained in virtually all archaic codes, from the Code of Hammurabi to the Dooms of the Anglo-Saxon Kings. But even in this attenuated situation, the authority and power of the monarch was initially available mainly to enforce the payment and acceptance of composition.[17]

The definition of the state as a competent litigant in matters involving delicts came as a result of a tortuously slow development. Initially some select offenses were treated as "botless," that is, cases in which the offender could not redeem himself by restitution to the aggrieved person but was at the king's mercy. In

[15] Concerning Rome, Kirchwey writes, "The assumption by the state of the right and duty to punish criminal offences . . . began as a legislative or as an executive rather than judicial procedure." That is, public offences were treated as political rather than criminal acts. The authority invested in the procedures to deal with them was remarkably limited. For example, customary Roman law of delicts contained provisions for the death penalty, but the state was not empowered to invoke it in dealing with public delicts, except under conditions of martial law. Cf. Kirchwey, George W., Criminal Law, 2 *Encyclopedia of the Social Sciences*, 569–579.

[16] Virtually all existing legal documents from ancient Egypt pertain to cases in which the royal court functioned as a court of appeal, and contain references to the corruption of local judiciaries, cf. Woolley, *loc. cit.* Concerning Anglo-Saxon justice Pollock and Maitland wrote: "The king had judicial functions, but they were far removed from our modern ways of regarding the king as a fountain of justice. His business is not to see justice done in his name *in the ordinary course,* but to exercise a special and reserved power which a man must not invoke unless he has failed to get his cause heard in the jurisdiction of his own hundred." 1 *History of English Law,* 40–41, (emphasis supplied).

[17] It bears mentioning that the monarch collected a fee for this, which the offender had to pay in addition to paying compensation.

medieval Europe the legal construct under which the king's right to impose punishment took precedence over the aggrieved's right was the "King's Peace." In this way, however, the early forms of public prosecution and punishment still retained the form of a private quarrel. In later development, the fact that the monarch was the ultimate source of the feudal benefice, added significance to this construct. Insofar as a person's property, livelihood and peace were grants from his liege, in return for the promise of service, all offences against persons could readily be perceived as offences against the person of some lord and his domain. To punish offenders became part of the *noblesse oblige.* The rights of feudal lords were, however, very early limited by the special jurisdictions of the Church, and later by the special jurisdictions of chartered municipalities.[18]

It is an understatement to say that criminal law, during the middle ages was in a state of confusion and neglect. Acts of political rebellion were not easily distinguishable from crimes and the virtually permanent state of warfare mitigated against public law enforcement. The institution of systematic public prosecution of delicts and execution of punishment belongs to the 16th century. It starts with legislation enacted in Italian and German cities and culminates in the *Constitutio Criminalis Carolina* of 1532, a uniform code of criminal jurisprudence governing the actions of courts in the entire Holy Roman Empire of the German Nation. At the same time, though without formal codification, Tudor England experienced a surge in the administration of criminal justice, the best-known aspect of which is the enormous increase of public executions which took place under Henry VIII. More important, however, is the fact that Henry eliminated the last vestige of locally authorized criminal jurisdiction in subjugating the Marcher Lords. The further development of criminal jurisprudence in England is of particular interest because it highlights the last step in the definition of the state's right to punish. The concept that the authorization of the state to punish derived from the fact that an offence was an affront against the monarch carried over from the middle ages to the absolute monarchy. Contrary, however, to the feudal lord, the absolute monarch claimed complete freedom of jurisdiction as the sole and unchecked source of all law. In absolute monarchy the will of the crown need not be based on, or reconciled with, some concept of public interest or morality; it defines it. Insofar as an action is authorized by the king it is *ipso facto* justified. As is well known, the doctrine that the judges are "lions under the throne" was attacked by the great hero of Common Law, Sir Edward Coke. Coke's argument asserted that the law has "an independent existence of its own, set above the king as well as his subjects, and bound to judge impartially between them."[19] Under this concept the state had the duty to initiate criminal proceedings and to execute judgments on behalf of some larger interest. To define the nature of the larger interest, and the way it legitimizes the use of punishment, has become the abiding interest of jurists, philosophers, and penologists since the eighteenth century.

It is important to emphasize that the defence of punishment is not a new moral

[18] Ganshof, F. L., *Feudalism,* (1952); Beard, Charles A., *The Office of the Justice of the Peace in England, Its Origin and Development,* (1904); Davis, John P., *Corporations,* Chapters 3, 4, and 5, (1961).

[19] Trevelyan, G. M., *History of England,* 391, (1926).

argument. One can find statements about this as far back as he cares to trace it in the literature. However, where older arguments and practices appear to put restraint on punitive practices while relating them to concepts of just dues to the aggrieved, the eighteenth century writers seek to establish the value of punishment without any regard for the aggrieved's interest.[20] With the elimination of the competence of the victim, and of the feudal concept of *noblesse oblige,* and the prerogative of the absolute monarch, the justification of punishment had to be placed on *disinterested considerations.* That is, there was no real or fictitious person who could lay claims that the injury he suffered at the hands of an assailant entitled him directly or indirectly to benefit from punishing the offender.

In point of fact punitive practices have always contained some aspects of a "disinterested tendency to inflict punishment."[21] In the latter part of the eighteenth century, however, these practices met with an unprecedented wave of expressions of moral scruples. To be sure, the attack was not directed against punishment as such but mainly against the existing forms of punishment. But this brought forth the question of what proper punishment should be, and what the definition of propriety should be based on. Whereas earlier apologists would have regarded it proper to define punishment in such terms as would appease the affronted person's desire for vengeance and intended only to restrict his right to conform with prevailing standards of humane decency, the modern penologists deny the relevance of this consideration entirely.

[20] We point here to a shift of emphasis rather than a radical contrast. Earlier literature does contain some statements indicating a categorical value of punishment that is independent of considerations of situational redress; cf. Plato, *Gorgias,* 145, (1960) ; Horowitz, George, *The Spirit of Jewish Law,* 195, (1953) ; and, the *Dooms of King Canute* (c. 1017), Chapter II, 69.

[21] The term "disinterested tendency to inflict punishment" is borrowed from the work of the Danish sociologist Svend Ranulf who has amassed a large body of evidence in favor of the hypothesis that the tendency is related to sentiments of moral indignation which characterizes the outlook of the lower middle classes. According to Ranulf, societies in which the lower middle classes are politically powerful will have zealous, cruel and "disinterested" systems of penology. Cf. his, *Moral Indignation and Middle Class Psychology,* (1938) .

DEFINITION OF PUNISHMENT*

Antony Flew

Antony Flew, professor of philosophy at Oxford University, specializes in linguistic analysis. In the following excerpt, published in 1954, he applies his skills to the difficult concept of "punishment." The definition which he arrives at has proven to be an accepted point of departure for subsequent discussion by many serious scholars. If quarrels must be picked with such a masterly performance, one might raise the question of punishment for the breach of rules outside the legal realm.

Punishment. (i) This term is both vague and 'open-textured' (Waismann).[1] Vague; because in several directions there is no sharp line drawn at which we must stop using it: when does punishment of the innocent or illegal punishment cease to be properly called punishment at all? (Here we must beware the scholasticism which F. P. Ramsey attacked in Wittgenstein, when the latter insisted that we *cannot* think illogically. For though there does come a point at which 'thinking' is so illogical, 'punishment' so wayward, that we should refuse to call them thinking or punishment at all, there is nevertheless a wide margin of toleration. And of course, as usual when we say there comes *a point at which,* what we really mean is that there comes *a twilight zone after which.*) Open-textured; because many questions of its applicability could arise over which even full knowledge of current correct usage might leave us at a loss. Not because this case fell within a more or less recognized No-Man's-Land of vagueness across which no sharp line had been drawn but because it was of a sort which had simply not been envisaged at all: would it be punishment if no effort was made or even pretended to allocate the 'punishments' to the actual offenders, but only to ensure that the total of hangings, say, balanced the total of murders; irrespective of who was hung? (See Ernest Bramah[2] on thus "preserving equipoise within the Sacred Empire.") A third feature, which partly overlaps both the other two, is that several logically independent criteria are involved. Ideally these are all simultaneously satisfied, but there is no strict unanimity rule here to paralyze action: so the word may be applied, and correctly, where one criterion is definitely not satisfied (and not merely where, through its vagueness, there is doubt as to whether it is or is not satisfied).

Once these features, which this concept shares with so many others, are recognized it becomes clear that it would be well as a prelude to possible discussions

* Excerpted from Flew, *The Justification of Punishment,* 29 PHILOSOPHY 291 (1954). Reprinted with permission.

[1] *Logic and Language.* (Edited Antony Flew), Vol. I, pp. 119–20.

[2] *The Wallet of Kai Lung, Kai Lung's Golden Hours,* and *Kai Lung Unrolls His Mat.*

of the ethics of punishment to list the criteria. This usually useful preliminary is in this case exceptionally important. Both because there is—since ideas here have certainly developed and are still changing and controversial—every reason to expect there are minority users of the word "punishment": that some people will insist that certain elements are essential which others will not so regard. And because in ethical controversy the temptation to produce from up one's sleeve at later stages in the argument apparently decisive definitional jokers is very strong: and can only be removed by making clear from the start what is and what is not to be involved in the central notions.

In listing the criteria satisfied by what, without honorific intentions,[3] we may call a standard case of punishment, in the primary sense of the word, we have to realize: both—as we have already mentioned—that there are some non-standard users with their private variations on this primary use; and that there are secondary uses of the word (with which those intending to discuss the ethics of punishment are not directly concerned); and that it is correctly applied even by standard users in its primary sense to non-standard cases of punishment, i.e. cases in which not all the criteria are satisfied, but which because of its vagueness the word can cover.

I am going to present my remarks here as *proposals*. Not because I regard them as arbitrary; for on the contrary they are based on what I take to be the general or at least the dominant tendencies in current usage; though I shall not give as many illustrations as would otherwise be necessary, because Mabbott has already done a large part of this work, in his "Punishment" (in *Mind* 1939: this is quite the most valuable article I know on this subject). But because it needs sometimes to be emphasized that no philosophical analysis of the meaning of any term worth so analysing can ever leave things exactly as they were—however conservative the intentions and protestations of its protagonists. For it must necessarily tend to change the meaning for us and our usage of the terms it analyses—ideally by precisifying it and making clear its implications.

(ii) I *propose*, therefore, that we take as parts of the meaning of "punishment," in the primary sense, at least five elements. *First*, it must be an evil, an unpleasantness, to the victim. By saying "evil"—following Hobbes—or "unpleasantness" not "pain," the suggestion of floggings and other forms of physical torture is avoided. Perhaps this was once an essential part of the meaning of the word, but for most people now its employment is less restricted. Note in this connection the development of an historically secondary use of the word; as applied first to a battering in boxing, then extended to similar situations in other sports where there is no element of physical pain (e.g. as an equivalent to "trouncing," of bowling in cricket).

Second, it must (at least be supposed to) be for an offence. A term in an old-fashioned public school, though doubtless far less agreeable than a spell in a modern prison, cannot be called a punishment, unless it was for an offence (unless perhaps the victim was despatched there for disobedience at home). Conversely, as Mabbott most usefully stresses, if a victim forgives an offender for an injury which was also an offence against some law or rule, this will not necessarily

[3] There is, for instance, nothing honorific in saying that this car is a standard model; not 'custom built' or bespoke.

be allowed as relevant to questions about his punishment by the institution whose law or rule it is. A mnemonic in the 'material mode of speech': "Injuries can be forgiven; crimes can only be pardoned."

Third, it must (at least be supposed to) be of the offender. The insistence on these first three elements can be supported by straightforward appeal to the *Concise Oxford Dictionary,* which defines "punish" as "cause (offender) to suffer for an offence."

Notice here that though it would be pedantic to insist *in single cases* that people (logically) cannot be punished for what they have not done; still a *system* of inflicting unpleasantness on scapegoats—even if they are pretended to be offenders—could scarcely be called a system of punishment at all. Or rather—to put it more practically and more tolerantly—if the word "punishment" is used in this way, as it constantly is, especially by anthropologists and psychoanalysts,[4] we and they should be alert to the fact that it is then used in a metaphorical, secondary, or non-standard sense: in which it necessarily has appropriately shifted logical syntax (that is: the word in this case carries different implications from those it carries in a standard case of its primary sense). A likely source of trouble and confusion.

Fourth, it must be the work of personal agencies. Evils occurring to people as the result of misbehaviour, but not by human agency, may be called penalties but not punishments: thus unwanted children and venereal disease may be the (frequently avoided) penalties of, but not the punishments for, sexual promiscuity. To the extent that anyone believes in a personal God with strong views against such sexual behaviour, to that extent he may speak of these as divinely instituted punishments (though, allowing the linguistic propriety of this, the fact that so often the punishments fall on the innocent and can be escaped by the guilty should give pause still).

(Note here. First the distinction often and usefully made—but rarely noticed even by those making it—between the 'natural' penalties *of* and the prescribed penalties *for* such and such conduct (gout *of* port-bibbing: free kicks *for* fouls). Second, that the expression "to the extent that" is peculiarly appropriate to beliefs about God and a quasi-personally sustained moral order in the universe: for with most people these meander somewhere between complete conviction and complete disbelief; and hence to offer the present distinctions between the uses of "punishment," "penalty of" and "penalty for" as if these were already completely given in present (correct) usage would be seriously to misdescribe the confused situation which actually confronts us.)

Fifth, in a standard case punishment has to (be at least supposed to) be imposed by virtue of some special authority, conferred through or by the institutions against the laws or rules of which the offence has been committed. Mabbott brought this out clearly. A parent, a Dean of a College, a Court of Law, even perhaps an umpire or a referee, acting as such, can be said to impose a punishment; but direct action by an aggrieved person with no pretensions to special authority is not properly called punish-

[4] Cf. e.g. J. C. Flugel, *Population, Psychology, and Peace,* pp. 70–I. "Another germane example is the stigma of 'illegitimacy', and this example illustrates the important fact that the punishment or suffering in question need not necessarily be endured by the culprit" and "There is such a thing as vicarious punishment".

ment, but revenge. (Vendetta is a form of institutionalized revenge between families regarded as individuals.) Direct action by an unauthorized busybody who takes it upon himself to punish, might be called punishment—as there is no unanimity rule about the simultaneous satisfaction of all the criteria—though if so it would be a non-standard case of punishment. Or it might equally well be called pretending (i.e. claiming falsely) to punish. The insistence on these fourth and fifth criteria can be supported by appeal to the *Oxford English Dictionary* which prefaces that same definition as that given in the C.O.D. with "As an act of superior or public authority."

Besides these five positive criteria I *propose* negatively that we should not insist: *either* that it is confined to either legal or moral offences, but instead allow the use of the word in connection with any system of rules or laws—State, school, moral, trades union, trade association, etc.; *or* that it cannot properly be applied to morally or legally questionable cases to which it would otherwise seem applicable, but instead allow that punishments, say, under retrospective or immoral laws may be called punishments, however improper or undesirable the proceedings may be in other respects. Laxity in both these directions conforms with normal usage; while in the second it has the merit of separating ethical from verbal issues.

I shall say nothing about "collective punishment" except that: while no doubt the original unit on which punishment was inflicted was not the individual but the family, tribe, village, clan, or some other group; nevertheless for most of us today "collective punishment" is somehow metaphorical or secondary: it is a matter of regarding a group as an individual, for certain purposes.[5]

Justification. This term is multiply relational. A justification has to be of A, rather than B, against C, and to or by reference to D; where A is the thing justified, B the possible alternative(s), C the charge(s) against A, and D the person(s) and or principle(s) to whom and/or by reference to which the justification is made. The variables may have more than one value even in one context: there may, for instance, be more than one charge. But they do not all have to be given *definite* values *explicitly*. Indeed the point of saying all this lies precisely in the fact that in most cases of justification the values of some of the variables are given only implicitly by the context, and perhaps rather indefinitely too: hence, just as in the notorious case of motion, it is possible to overlook (some of the implications of) the relational nature of the concept. The alternative(s), for instance, may be unstated and even very hazily conceived: but that there must be at least one alternative is brought out by considering that "There is no alternative" is always either a sufficient justification or a sufficient reason for saying that the question of justification does not arise. Finally, and most important—again compare the case of motion—the reference point, the fourth variable (the person(s) or principle(s) by reference to which justification is made) has the same rather indefinite value implicit in most actual

[5] Compare here (*a*) K. R. Popper's examination of the appropriateness and limitations of the metaphor involved in regarding rogue states as criminals: *Open Society,* Vol. I, pp. 242 ff. (*b*) the Nuremberg Trials: a colossal effort to discover what the guilt of the Nazi régime amounted to in terms of the particular guilt of particular Germans. This point I owe, like so much else, to Mabbott, privately, and later to his *The State and the Citizen.*

contexts: the value "(whom I consider) reasonable people, and what (*fundamentally*) they agree on."

Presumably this has contributed to the use of "justification" as a near synonym for "reason for." Which in turn has been a very minor determinant of the modern fashion—for which there is much to be said—of presenting moral philosophy as an enquiry into what are and are not *good reasons* in ethics. But note here. First, that the word "justification" may, even in contexts where all the variables have the same values, be used in two relevantly different ways: either implying that the proposed justification is or not implying that it is morally or otherwise acceptable to the user; in the latter case if it is *very* unacceptable the word may be put in protest quotes. (*Mutatis mutandis* the same is true of "reason.") Second, that this mode of presentation tends to conceal the existence of really radical ethical disagreements. This point has been pressed in a critical notice of S. E. Toulmin's *The Place of Reason in Ethics* by J. Mackie (*Australasian Journal of Philosophy* 1951). Presumably Toulmin would answer, on Kantian lines, that he was elucidating the *nature of ethics as such*: from which the fact that certain reasons were relevant and good, and others irrelevant and bad, followed necessarily. This would imply that those who seem to be doing ethics but admit different reasons to that extent cannot be doing ethics at all, or at least are very unreasonable people: by definition. Which is perhaps fair enough: providing that steps are taken to bring out just what must be involved in rejecting the definitions implicitly accepted by Toulmin, and that many would reject some of the implications of these definitions, and that their position in so doing is monstrous. To say this last is abandoning pure analysis to take sides, as all men must, in a struggle: making a normative, participant's utterance; and not a purely analytic, neutral's observation.

The. The assumption behind the use of the definite article is that there is one and only one (unless the whole expression is interpreted, as it rarely is, as strictly equivalent to "justifying punishment"). This is questionable twice over, at two levels: first, because the variables admit of various values—what would serve as justification against one charge and for a Roman Catholic could be simply irrelevant against another and for an atheist humanist; and, second, because in any one context (i.e. where the same values are given to all the variables) there may be two logically separate acceptable justifications both independently sufficient. And surely this is not merely possible but likely: for the fields of human causation, motivation, and justification are precisely those in which 'overdetermination' (Freud) is most common. (An action is said to be *over-determined* when at least two motives were at work to produce it, either of which alone would have been sufficiently strong to do so separately. The concept, *mutatis mutandis,* obviously can and should also be applied to matters of causation and justification.)

PART II

Four Basic Views of Punishment

CHAPTER TWO

RETRIBUTION

A vast amount has been written on the aims and justification of criminal punishment. Perhaps this is because, as a political institution devoted to the infliction of pain on human beings, punishment has never rested easily on the conscience of civilized man. Of the various attempted justifications of punishment, it is probably that of retribution which sits least comfortably on the human conscience, at least insofar as one finds therein the explicit argument that it is a good thing for an evildoer to suffer for his evil.

In the words of one of its critics (A. C. Ewing, *The Morality of Punishment* [London: Kegan Paul, 1929, p. 13]), the retributive theory holds that "the primary justification of punishment is always to be found in the fact that an offense has been committed which deserves punishment, not in any future advantage to be gained by its infliction." Such a description will fit most if not all the various formulations of retribution, since it emphasizes the following common features: that punishment should primarily view the offender rather than society at large; that the gravity of the offense should roughly dictate the extent of the sanction; and above all, that the offender must suffer because he is responsible for his evildoing, i.e., he could have done otherwise but chose not to.

From a historical point of view, one of the earliest formulations of one variety of retribution can be found in the ancient biblical dictum "an eye for an eye, a tooth for a tooth." The proportionality of crime and punishment finds therein one of its most lasting expressions. Similarly, one notes that the ancient Jewish law manifested an inseparable blending of philosophical, humanistic, moral, and religious justifications of punishment. Indeed, in later thinkers this blend becomes as recurrent as it is ambiguous. Aristotle never doubted the freedom of the will, and while distinguishing various degrees of voluntariness, he nonetheless maintains that it is at all times within man's power to be good and to do what is right. His justification of punishment thus reflects the belief that man is responsible for what he does, deserving punishment for his evil acts exactly as he deserves rewards for his good ones. With the philosophical seeds thus implanted, St. Thomas Aquinas adopts much of the Aristotelian defense of retributivism, but adds to this humanistic approach a reflection of religious and moral values suggesting a need to balance the metaphysical scales of justice as well as to give the offender his "due." The abstract metaphysical version of the retributive theory is given one of its classic statements by Immanuel Kant in his *Philosophy of Law*. According to Kant, punishment "can never be administered merely as a means for promoting another Good either with regard to the Criminal himself or to Civil Society, but must in all cases be imposed only because the individual on whom it is inflicted has committed a Crime." The great Russian novelist Fyodor Dostoyevsky points out the difficulties of making punishment fit the moral gravity of the offense; he cites inevitable inequalities of moral guilt in the commission of the same crime and inequalities of suffering from the same punishment. Yet Dostoyevsky adds to Kant the assertion that punishment is as much a matter of moral insight as it is of an objective of impersonal justice, since the offender becomes morally rehabilitated through his experience of retributive deprivation and pain.

From the foregoing brief sampling of opinions, it is obvious that retribution has a number of differing formulations, as is evidenced by the distinguished authors in this section. J. D. Mabbott boldly announces that he will defend a retributive theory of punishment. His retributivism, however, is of a legalistic kind, with little in common with Kant or Dostoyevsky and a great deal in common with rule-theory. Professor Jerome Hall clashes with Mabbott's positivist approach to punishment in arguing for a necessary connection between morality and law, so that punishment reflects not merely a legal but also a moral violation. The excerpts from Pius XII's speech illustrate his sympathy with Hall's attitude on the close alliance between morality and legality but also add a purely religious dimension to the sphere of retributivism. Sir Walter Moberly continues this moral and religious approach in arguing that punishment views not primarily society but the individual, who has "consented" to the punishment in choosing wrongdoing and for whom punishment is both a privilege and an honor reflecting his rational responsibility. Finally, in a critical overview of retributive theories, Nigel Walker discusses varieties of formulations of retributivism which express the legal, moral, and religious motivations of their authors without solving, to his mind, the new problems which this blend creates.

PUNISHMENT AS A COROLLARY OF RULE-BREAKING*

J. D. Mabbott

J. D. Mabbott, one of Oxford University's foremost analytical philosophers, illustrates the perennial interest in punishment among this century's English philosophers of logical and linguistic bent. In the 1939 selection below, still a touchstone for penal debate, Mabbott discusses the inadequacy of utilitarian justifications of punishment and suggests the primacy of a retributivist rationale based on a form of rule-theory. The critical issue for Mabbott is the relation between law and morality: Are they congruous or discrete spheres of authority?

I propose in this paper to defend a retributive theory of punishment and to reject absolutely all utilitarian considerations from its justification. I feel sure that this enterprise must arouse deep suspicion and hostility both among philosophers (who must have felt that the retributive view is the only moral theory except perhaps psychological hedonism which has been definitely destroyed by criticism) and among practical men (who have welcomed its steady decline in our penal practice).

The question I am asking is this. Under what circumstances is the punishment of some particular person justified and why? The theories of reform and deterrence which are usually considered to be the only alternatives to retribution involve well-known difficulties. These are considered fully and fairly in Dr. Ewing's book, *The Morality of Punishment*, and I need not spend long over them. The central difficulty is that both would on occasion justify the punishment of an innocent man, the deterrent theory if he were believed to have been guilty by those likely to commit the crime in future, and the reformatory theory if he were a bad man though not a criminal. To this may be added the point against the deterrent theory that it is the threat of punishment and not punishment itself which deters, and that when deterrence seems to depend on actual punishment, to implement the threat, it really depends on publication and may be achieved if men believe that punishment has occurred even if in fact it has not. As Bentham saw, for a Utilitarian apparent justice is everything, real justice is irrelevant.

Dr. Ewing and other moralists would be inclined to compromise with retribution in the face of the above difficulties. They would admit that one fact and one fact only can justify the punishment of this man, and that is a *past* fact, that he has committed a crime. To this extent

* Excerpted from Mabbott, *Punishment*, 48 Mind 152 (1939). Reprinted with permission.

reform and deterrence theories, which look only to the consequences, are wrong. But they would add that retribution can determine only *that* a man should be punished. It cannot determine how or how much, and here reform and deterrence may come in. Even Bradley, the fiercest retributionist of modern times, says "Having once the right to punish we may modify the punishment according to the useful and the pleasant, but these are external to the matter; they cannot give us a right to punish and nothing can do that but criminal desert." Dr. Ewing would maintain that the whole estimate of the amount and nature of a punishment may be effected by considerations of reform and deterrence. It seems to me that this is a surrender which the upholders of retribution dare not make. As I said above, it is publicity and not punishment which deters, and the publicity though often spoken of as "part of a man's punishment" is no more part of it than his arrest or his detention prior to trial, though both these may be also unpleasant and bring him into disrepute. A judge sentences a man to three years' imprisonment not to three years *plus* three columns in the press. Similarly with reform. The visit of the prison chaplain is not part of a man's punishment nor is the visit of Miss Fields or Mickey Mouse.

The truth is that while punishing a man and punishing him justly, it is possible to deter others, and also to attempt to reform him, and if these additional goods are achieved the total state of affairs is better than it would be with the just punishment alone. But reform and deterrence are not modifications of the punishment, still less reasons for it. A parallel may be found in the case of tact and truth. If you have to tell a friend an unpleasant truth you may do all you can to put him at his ease and spare his feelings as much as possible, while still making sure that he understands your meaning. In such a case no one would say that your offer of a cigarette beforehand or your apology afterwards are modifications of the truth still less reasons for telling it. You do not tell the truth in order to spare his feelings, but having to tell the truth you also spare his feelings. So Bradley was right when he said that reform and deterrence were "external to the matter," but therefore wrong when he said that they may "modify the punishment." Reporters are admitted to our trials so that punishments may become public and help to deter others. But the punishment would be no less just were reporters excluded and deterrence not achieved. Prison authorities may make it possible that a convict may become physically or morally better. They cannot ensure either result; and the punishment would still be just if the criminal took no advantage of their arrangements and their efforts failed. Some moralists see this and exclude these "extra" arrangements for deterrence and reform. They say that it must be the punishment *itself* which reforms and deters. But it is just my point that the punishment *itself* seldom reforms the criminal and never deters others. It is only "extra" arrangements which have any chance of achieving either result. As this is the central point of my paper, at the cost of laboured repetition I would ask the upholders of reform and deterrence two questions. Suppose it could be shown that a particular criminal had not been improved by a punishment and also that no other would-be criminal had been deterred by it, would that prove that the punishment was unjust? Suppose it were discovered that a particular criminal had lived a much better life after his release and that many would-be criminals believing him to have been guilty were influenced by his fate, but yet that the "criminal" was punished for something he had never done, would these excellent results prove the punishment just?

It will be observed that I have throughout treated punishment as a purely legal matter. A "criminal" means a man who has broken a law, not a bad man; an "innocent" man is a man who has not broken the law in connection with which he is being punished, though he may be a bad man and have broken other laws. Here I dissent from most upholders of the retributive theory—from Hegel, from Bradley, and from Dr. Ross. They maintain that the essential connection is one between punishment and moral or social wrong-doing.

My fundamental difficulty with their theory is the question of *status*. It takes two to make a punishment, and for a moral or social wrong I can find no punisher. We may be tempted to say when we hear of some brutal action "that ought to be punished"; but I cannot see how there can be duties which are nobody's duties. If I see a man ill-treating a horse in a country where cruelty to animals is not a legal offence, and I say to him "I shall now punish you," he will reply, rightly, "What has it to do with you? Who made you a judge and a ruler over me?" I may have a duty to try to stop him and one way of stopping him may be to hit him, but another way may be to buy the horse. Neither the blow nor the price is a punishment. For a moral offence, God alone has the *status* necessary to punish the offender; and the theologians are becoming more and more doubtful whether even God has a duty to punish wrong-doing.

Dr. Ross would hold that not all wrong-doing is punishable, but only invasion of the rights of others; and in such a case it might be thought that the injured party had a right to punish. His right, however, is rather a right to reparation, and should not be confused with punishment proper.

This connection, on which I insist, between punishment and crime, not between punishment and moral or social wrong, alone accounts for some of our beliefs about punishment, and also meets many objections to the retributive theory as stated in its ordinary form. The first point on which it helps us is with regard to retrospective legislation. Our objection to this practice is unaccountable on reform and deterrence theories. For a man who commits a wrong before the date on which a law against it is passed, is as much in need of reform as a man who commits it afterwards; nor is deterrence likely to suffer because of additional punishments for the same offence. But the orthodox retributive theory is equally at a loss here, for if punishment is given for moral wrong-doing or for invasion of the rights of others, that immorality or invasion existed as certainly before the passing of the law as after it.

My theory also explains, where it seems to me all others do not, the case of punishment imposed by an authority who believes the law in question is a bad law. I was myself for some time disciplinary officer of a college whose rules included a rule compelling attendance at chapel. Many of those who broke this rule broke it on principle. I punished them. I certainly did not want to reform them; I respected their characters and their views. I certainly did not want to drive others into chapel through fear of penalties. Nor did I think there had been a wrong done which merited retribution. I wished I could have believed that I would have done the same myself. My position was clear. They had broken a rule; they knew it and I knew it. Nothing more was necessary to make punishment proper.

I know that the usual answer to this is that the judge enforces a bad law because otherwise law in general would suffer and good laws would be broken. The effect of punishing good men for breaking bad laws is that fewer bad men break good laws. . . .

The view, then, that a judge upholds a bad law in order that law in general should not suffer is indefensible. He upholds it simply because he has no right to dispense from punishment.

The connection of punishment with law-breaking and not with wrong-doing also escapes moral objections to the retributive theory as held by Kant and Hegel or by Bradley and Ross. It is asked how we can measure moral wrong or balance it with pain, and how pain can wipe out moral wrong. Retributivists have been pushed into holding that pain *ipso facto* represses the worse self and frees the better, when this is contrary to the vast majority of observed cases. But if punishment is not intended to measure or balance or negate moral wrong then all this is beside the mark. There is the further difficulty of reconciling punishment with repentance and with forgiveness. Repentance is the reaction morally appropriate to moral wrong and punishment added to remorse is an unnecessary evil. But if punishment is associated with law-breaking and not with moral evil the punisher is not entitled to consider whether the criminal is penitent any more than he may consider whether the law is good. So, too, with forgiveness. Forgiveness is not appropriate to law-breaking. (It is noteworthy that when, in divorce cases, the law has to recognize forgiveness it calls it "condonation," which is symptomatic of the difference of attitude.) Nor is forgiveness appropriate to moral evil. It is appropriate to personal injury. No one has any right to forgive me except the person I have injured. No judge or jury can do so. But the person I have injured has no right to punish me. Therefore there is no clash between punishment and forgiveness since these two duties do not fall on the same person nor in connection with the same characteristic of my act. (It is the weakness of vendetta that it tends to confuse this clear line, though even there it is only by personifying the family that the injured party and the avenger are identified. Similarly we must guard against the plausible fallacy of personifying society and regarding the criminal as "injuring society," for then once more the old dilemma about forgiveness would be insoluble.) A clergyman friend of mine catching a burglar red-handed was puzzled about his duty. In the end he ensured the man's punishment by information and evidence, and at the same time showed his own forgiveness by visiting the man in prison and employing him when he came out. I believe any "good Christian" would accept this as representing his duty. But obviously if the punishment is thought of as imposed *by* the victim or *for* the injury or immorality then the contradiction with forgiveness is hopeless.

So far as the question of the actual punishment of any individual is concerned this paper could stop here. No punishment is morally retributive or reformative or deterrent. Any criminal punished for any one of these reasons is certainly unjustly punished. The only justification for punishing any man is that he has broken a law. . . .

It will be objected that my original question "Why ought X to be punished?"

is an illegitimate isolation of the issue. I have treated the whole set of circumstances as determined. X is a citizen of a state. About his citizenship, whether willing or unwilling, I have asked no questions. About the government, whether it is good or bad, I do not enquire. X has broken a law. Concerning the law, whether it is well-devised or not, I have not asked. Yet all these questions are surely relevant before it can be decided whether a particular punishment is just. It is the essence of my position that none of these questions is relevant. Punishment is a corollary of law-breaking by a member of the society whose law is broken. This is a static and an abstract view but I see no escape from it. Considerations of utility come in on two quite different issues. Should there be laws, and what laws should there be? As a legislator I may ask what general types of action would benefit the community, and, among these, which can be "standardized" without loss, or should be standardized to achieve their full value. This, however, is not the primary question since particular laws may be altered or repealed. The choice which is the essential *prius* of punishment is the choice that there should be laws. This choice is not Hobson's. Other methods may be considered. A government might attempt to standardize certain modes of action by means of advice. It might proclaim its view and say "Citizens are requested" to follow this or that procedure. Or again it might decide to deal with each case as it arose in the manner most effective for the common welfare. Anarchists have wavered between these two alternatives and a third—that of doing nothing to enforce a standard of behaviour but merely giving arbitrational decisions between conflicting parties, decisions binding only by consent.

I think it can be seen without detailed examination of particular laws that the method of law-making has its own advantages. Its orders are explicit and general. It makes behaviour reliable and predictable. Its threat of punishment may be so effective as to make punishment unnecessary. It promises to the good citizen a certain security in his life. When I have talked to business men about some inequity in the law of liability they have usually said "Better a bad law than no law, for then we know where we are."

Someone may say I am drawing an impossible line. I deny that punishment is utilitarian; yet now I say that punishment is a corollary of law and we decide whether to have laws and which laws to have on utilitarian grounds. And surely it is only this corollary which distinguishes law from good advice or exhortation. This is a misunderstanding. Punishment is a corollary not of law but of law-breaking. Legislators do not choose to punish. They hope no punishment will be needed. Their laws would succeed even if no punishment occurred. The criminal makes the essential choice; he "brings it on himself." Other men obey the law because they see its order is reasonable, because of inertia, because of fear. In this whole area, and it may be the major part of the state, law achieves its ends without punishment. Clearly, then, punishment is not a corollary of law. . . .

To return to the main issue, the position I am defending is that it is essential to a legal system that the infliction of a particular punishment should *not* be determined by the good *that particular punishment* will do either to the criminal or to "society." In exactly the same way it is essential to a credit system that the repayment of a particular debt should not be determined by the good that particular payment will do. One may consider the merits of a legal system or of a credit system, but the acceptance of either involves the surrender of utilitarian considerations in particular cases as they arise. This is in effect admitted by Ewing in one place where he says "It is the penal system as a whole which deters and not the punishment of any individual offender."[1]

To show that the choice between a legal system and its alternatives is one we do and must make, I may quote an early work of Lenin in which he was defending the Marxist tenet that the state is bound to "wither away" with the establishment of a classless society. He considers the possible objection that some wrongs by man against man are not economic and therefore that the abolition of classes would not *ipso facto* eliminate crime. But he sticks to the thesis that these surviving crimes should not be dealt with by law and judicature. "We are not Utopians and do not in the least deny the possibility and inevitability of excesses by *individual persons,* and equally the need to suppress such excesses. But for this no special machine, no special instrument of repression is needed. This will be done by the armed nation itself as simply and as readily as any crowd of civilized people even in modern society parts a pair of combatants or does not allow a woman to be outraged."[2] This alternative to law and punishment has obvious demerits. Any injury not committed in the presence of the crowd, any wrong which required skill to detect or pertinacity to bring home would go untouched. The lynching mob, which is Lenin's instrument of justice, is liable to error and easily deflected from its purpose or driven to extremes. It must be a mob, for there is to be no "machine." I do not say that no alternative machine to ours could be devised but it does seem certain that the absence of all "machines" would be intolerable. An alternative machine might be based on the view that "society" is responsible for all criminality, and a curative and protective system developed. This is the system of Butler's "Erewhon" and something like it seems to be growing up in Russia except for cases of "sedition."

We choose, then, or we acquiesce in and adopt the choice of others of, a legal system as one of our instruments for the establishment of the conditions of a good life. This choice is logically prior to and independent of the actual punishment of any particular persons or the passing of any particular laws. The legislators choose particular laws within the framework of this predetermined system. Once again a small society may illustrate the reality of these choices and the distinction between them. A Headmaster launching a new school must explicitly make both decisions. First, shall he have any rules at all? Second, what rules shall he have? The first decision is a genuine one and one of great importance. Would it not be better to have an "honour" system, by which public opinion in each house or form dealt with any offence? (This is the Lenin method.) Or would complete freedom be better? Or should he issue appeals and advice? Or should he personally deal with each malefactor individually, as the case arises, in the way most likely to improve his conduct? I can well imagine an idealistic Headmaster attempting to run a school with one of these methods or with a combination of several of them and therefore

[1] *The Morality of Punishment*, p. 66.

[2] *The State and Revolution* (Eng. Trans.), p. 93. Original italics.

without punishment. I can even imagine that with a small school of, say, twenty pupils all open to direct personal psychological pressure from authority and from each other, these methods involving no "rules" would work. The pupils would of course grow up without two very useful habits, the habit of having some regular habits and the habit of obeying rules. But I suspect that most Headmasters, especially those of large schools, would either decide at once, or quickly be driven, to realize that some rules were necessary. This decision would be "utilitarian" in the sense that it would be determined by consideration of consequences. The question "what rules?" would then arise and again the issue is utilitarian. What action must be regularized for the school to work efficiently? The hours of arrival and departure, for instance, in a day school. But the one choice which is now no longer open to the Headmaster is whether he shall punish those who break the rules. For if he were to try to avoid this he would in fact simply be returning to the discarded method of appeals and good advice. Yet the Headmaster does not decide to punish. The pupils make the decision there. He decides actually to have rules and to threaten, but only hypothetically, to punish. The one essential condition which makes actual punishment just is a condition he *cannot* fulfill—namely that a rule should be broken.

I shall add a final word of consolation to the practical reformer. Nothing that I have said is meant to counter any movement for "penal reform" but only to insist that none of these reforms have anything to do with punishment. The only type of reformer who can claim to be reforming the system of punishment is a follower of Lenin or of Samuel Butler who is genuinely attacking the *system* and who believes there should be no laws and no punishments. But our great British reformers have been concerned not with punishment but with its accessories. When a man is sentenced to imprisonment he is not sentenced also to partial starvation, to physical brutality, to pneumonia from damp cells and so on. And any movement which makes his food sufficient to sustain health, which counters the permanent tendency to brutality on the part of his warders, which gives him a dry or even a light and well-aired cell, is pure gain and does not touch the theory of punishment. Reformatory influences and prisoners' aid arrangements are also entirely unaffected by what I have said. I believe myself that it would be best if all such arrangements were made optional for the prisoner, so as to leave him in these cases a freedom of choice which would make it clear that they are not part of his punishment. If it is said that every such reform lessens a man's punishment, I think that is simply muddled thinking which, if it were clear, would be mere brutality. For instance, a prisoners' aid society is said to lighten his punishment, because otherwise he would suffer not merely imprisonment but also unemployment on release. But he was sentenced to imprisonment, not imprisonment *plus* unemployment. If I promise to help a friend and through special circumstances I find that keeping my promise will involve upsetting my day's work, I do not say that I really promised to help him and to ruin my day's work. And if another friend carries on my work for me I do not regard him as carrying out part of my promise, nor at stopping me from carrying it out myself. He merely removes an indirect and regrettable consequence of my keeping my promise. So with punishment. The Prisoners' Aid Society does not alter a man's punishment nor diminish it, but merely removes an indirect and regrettable consequence of it. And anyone who thinks that a criminal cannot make this distinction and will regard all the inconvenience that comes to him as punishment, need only to talk to a prisoner or two to find how sharply they resent these wanton additions to a punishment. . . .

I feel convinced that penal reformers would meet with even more support if they were clear that they were *not* attempting to alter the system of punishment but to give its victims "fair play." We have no more right to starve a convict than to starve an animal. We have no more right to keep a convict in a Dartmoor cell "down which the water trickles night and day" than we have to keep a child in such a place. If our reformers really want to alter the system of punishment, let them come out clearly with their alternative and preach, for instance, that no human being is responsible for any wrong-doing, that all the blame is on society, that curative or protective measures should be adopted, forcibly if necessary, as they are with infection or insanity. Short of this let them admit that the essence of prison is deprivation of liberty for the breaking of law, and that deprivation of food or of health or of books is unjust. And if our sentimentalists cry "coddling of prisoners," let us ask them also to come out clearly into the open and incorporate whatever starvation and disease and brutality they think necessary *into the sentences they propose*. If it is said that some prisoners will prefer such reformed prisons, with adequate food and aired cells, to the outer world, we may retort that their numbers are probably not greater than those of the masochists who like to be flogged. Yet we do not hear the same "coddling" critics suggest abolition of the lash on the grounds that some criminals may like it. Even if the abolition from our prisons of all maltreatment other than that imposed by law results in a few down-and-outs breaking a window (as O. Henry's hero did) to get a night's lodging, the country will lose less than she does by her present method of sending out her discharged convicts "charged with venom and hatred" because of the additional and uncovenanted "rubbing it in" which they have received.

I hope I have established both the theoretical importance and the practical value of distinguishing between penal reform as we know and approve it—that reform which alters the accompaniments of punishment without touching its essence—and those attacks on punishment itself which are made not only by reformers who regard criminals as irresponsible and in need of treatment, but also by every judge who announces that he is punishing a man to deter others or to protect society, and by every juryman who is moved to his decision by the moral baseness of the accused rather than by his legal guilt.

JUST v. UNJUST LAW*

Jerome Hall

Jerome Hall, professor of criminal law at Indiana University, is an articulate proponent of a necessary connection between morality and the law, specifically penal law. The selection below, taken from his popular General Principles of Criminal Law, *illustrates his sympathy with a retributivist defense of punishment challenging Mabbott's foregoing separation of law from morality. He asks whether punishment can justly follow the breach of all types of law, or merely of a morally valid law.*

The principle of punishment generalizes the distinctive character of all the punitive sanctions specified in the rules of criminal law. The sanctions of other legal rules relevant to the broad problem of social protection provide corrective treatment, *e.g.* for juvenile delinquents, alcoholics and drug addicts, or measures of security, *e.g.* the confinement of dangerous psychotics and the isolation of persons having contagious diseases. For the most part, the following discussion will be concerned with punishment.

What this presupposes may be indicated by locating the present discussion in the context of the principal meanings of "responsibility."[1] First, "responsibility" means competence to understand and to conform to relevant moral and legal obligations, *i.e.* that the accused is a normal adult. Second, "responsibility" means authorship, that a particular person *caused* the harm in issue, he is responsible, in that teleological sense, for its occurrence. Third, "responsibility" means accountability, *i.e.* that if he is convicted, having satisfied the first two meanings of "responsibility," he must be subjected to the prescribed sanction—in the present context, punishment.

Although the meaning of punishment and the purposes of punishment may be distinguished, the two are closely interrelated. Ordinarily, one would follow the logical order and discuss first the meaning or nature of punishment, and then its justification. The reverse order has been adopted in the following discussion because the justification of punishment concerns its ends and grounds; and the meaning of punishment cannot be understood apart from that knowledge. In addition, the wide perspective which theories of justification delineate provides a framework within which a more precise analysis of the nature of punishment is facilitated.

THE JUSTIFICATION OF PUNISHMENT

In a very thoughtful essay, Professor J. D. Mabbott presents what he calls

* Reprinted from HALL, GENERAL PRINCIPLES OF CRIMINAL LAW, second edition, copyright 1947 and 1960 by The Bobbs-Merrill Company, Inc.

[1] See Moberly, Responsibility (1956).

"a retributive theory of punishment"[2] which, however, rejects the retributive theories of Kant, Hegel and Bradley. Professor Mabbott's theory is "retributive" in the sense that he rejects the utilitarian theories of punishment—deterrence and reformation. He does this mainly because they justify the punishment of innocent persons. For example, the deterrent theory requires only the belief that those punished were guilty; moreover, false publicity, not the actual punishment of guilty persons, suffices to deter. On the other hand, the reformative theory justifies punishing (correcting?) a bad or dangerous man even though he is not a criminal. Professor Mabbott holds, "The only justification for punishing any man is that he has broken a law."[3] This is evidently an expression of the principle of legality.

The author's assertion that his theory is "retributive" has elicited the criticism that: "Surely a punishment which is legally correct may still be unjust . . .," for example, punishment on the basis of *ex post facto* enactment, punishment where a law requires a morally wrong action, such as ordering an officer to kill or torture civilians, and excessive punishment in relation to the gravity of the offense, such as the death penalty for stealing a loaf of bread.[4] Professor Mabbott does not deal with the issue raised in such cases; as stated, he treats punishment "as a purely legal matter."[5] The connection on which he insists is that "between punishment and crime, not between punishment and moral or social wrong. . . ."[6]

More important than his use of the term "retributive" are the grounds upon which Dr. Mabbott relies to reject "traditional" retributive theories, namely:

(1) Punishment implies that someone is legally authorized to impose it upon offenders.

(2) No more than do the reformative and deterrent theories can the traditional retributive ones account for the serious objections to retroactive penal legislation.

(3) None of the other theories can account for punishment imposed by an official who disapproves the law which he is enforcing. In Professor Mabbott's theory, the fact that a rule, *i.e.* any rule, was violated makes punishment "proper."[7]

(4) His theory escapes the retributionist's difficulty of measuring moral wrong and equating pain (punishment) with it.[8]

It is not possible here to defend the leading exponents of retributive theories from the criticism leveled against them, except to note that most, if not all, of them assumed the existence of a

[2] Mabbott, *Punishment,* 48 Mind (n. s.) 152 (1939).

[3] *Id.* at 158; also see *id.* at 154–157.

[4] Mundle, *Punishment and Desert,* 4 Philos. Quart. 225 (1954).

[5] Mabbott, *supra* note 2, at 154.

[6] *Id.* at 155.

[7] *Ibid.* The use of this term instead of "just" or even "justifiable" again indicates that Professor Mabbott's theory is a formal one. "A 'criminal' means a man who has broken a law, not a bad man. . . ." *Id.* at 154. "X has broken a law. Concerning the law, whether it is well-devised or not, I have not asked." *Id.* at 160.

Cf. Quinton, *On Punishment,* pub. in Philosophy, Politics and Society 83 (Laslett ed. 1956).

[8] While Professor Mabbott's theory "escapes" that difficulty, it contributes to the solution of the difficult cases noted above, *e.g.* a capital penalty for stealing a loaf of bread, only by saying: That is the law. *Cf.* "However—and this is the point which Mabbott's account ignores—the duty to obey one's State is not an unconditional duty." Mundle, *op. cit. supra* note 4, at 226. *Cf.* Flew, *"The Justification of Punishment,"* 29 Philosophy 291 (1954).

legal system and presented a retributive theory of punishment on that postulate.[9] Apparently, Professor Mabbott proceeded on the assumption that theories in justification of punishment are either utilitarian or retributive; and that since his theory (legality) was not utilitarian, it must be retributive. That, however, is hardly a satisfactory solution, as the above quoted criticism of his theory indicates. The fact is that the theory he espouses is that of formal legality, associated with the school of legal positivism. In any event, it is not a descriptive theory and therefore is not opposed to utilitarian and retributive theories. In other words, a formal theory, *e.g.* insistence on law, if it is to be justified, must find that justification in utilitarian or retributive theories or in both of them. Such justification as legality directly summons, *e.g.* certainty and uniformity, insofar as it is not explicitly resolved into intrinsic and instrumental values, at least presupposes the justification of what the officials do by reference to those theories of ethics.

The difficulty, it is respectfully submitted, which underlies Professor Mabbott's thesis lies in his formulation of the issues.[10] He narrows the choice to law or no law, *i.e.* to the problem of legality, whereas the pertinent issue is that between just law and unjust law.[11] That it is actually impossible to avoid this issue is shown by the fact that Professor Mabbott himself introduces proportionality into his legal system,[12] which seems hardly consistent with his earlier avowals that he is not interested in the quality of the law.[13]

If the principal issue is not that of merely formal law versus a purely ethical theory, but, instead, just law versus unjust law, there is a ready answer to Professor Mabbott's criticism of other theories of justification. Thus, the objections which he raises against "pure retribution," if they are restated as suggested, are better answered in terms of ethical positive law than they are in terms of merely formal law. The position of the latter is arbitrary as regards retroactive legislation and tautologous as regards the enforcement of a bad law ("because he has no right [*i.e.* legal right] to dispense from punishment"). For, unless a law has some value, is it any criticism of retroactive penal legislation to assert that there was no law at the time of the conduct in issue? The insistence that law

[9] *Cf.* "Juridical Punishment . . . must in all cases be imposed only because the individual on whom it is inflicted *has committed a Crime.*" Kant, The Philosophy of Law 195 (Hastie, trans. 1887).

[10] Some of the difficulty met in Professor Mabbott's essay seems to reflect Ross' discussion. Ross first rejects retribution on the ground that it requires a perfect assessment of the virtues and pleasures of everyone, which leads him to conclude that "the state has no duty of retributive punishment." Ross, The Right and the Good 60 (1930). Ross states that the alternative is not "a utilitarian view of punishment." The relevant duty, he says, is not to punish moral guilt but "to protect the most fundamental rights of individuals." *Ibid.* It is the failure to respect others' rights which extinguishes a person's own rights and thus makes him a proper subject of punishment. But the voluntary violation of other persons' rights is one way of describing moral guilt; hence it is difficult to see how retributive justice has been excluded. *E.g.* the state "is morally at liberty to injure him as he has injured others. . . ." *Id.* at 61.

[11] *Cf.* Mundle, *op. cit. supra* note 4, at 226.

[12] "But we can grade crimes in a rough scale and penalties in a rough scale, and keep our heaviest penalties for what are socially the most serious wrongs regardless of whether these penalties will reform the criminal or whether they are exactly what deterrence would require." *Op. cit. supra* note 2, at 162.

[13] See *supra* note 7.

exist at that time implies both that punishment is not just except on that condition and also that it is just if that condition is met. But whether it is just then does not depend on the existence of any law, regardless of its content. So, too, the legal duty of officials to enforce bad laws has limits imposed by ethical policy, as both legal history[14] and current practice abundantly attest. In any case, the official "obligation" to apply punitive sanctions cannot be defended or even explained on the sole ground that "that is the law." It rests equally upon the ethical quality of the legal order which must be "basically just," *i.e.* a defensible principle of legality is derived from legal rules that for the most part are substantially just. More directly, legality is not a value to be opposed to or contrasted with intrinsic or instrumental value. It is, instead, the essential condition of the uniform, sound, effective implementation of any values.

In sum, retributive ethics does not require that a *legal* sanction be applied against one who violated only a moral duty. Nor does the principle of legality, including the rule against retroactive penal legislation, oppose retributive ethics. On the contrary, it supports the principle which requires the moral guilt of those punished and proportions the punishment to the gravity of the harm. So, too, the principle of harm effects limitations which pure ethics, concerned only with subjective guilt, does not require. Thus, apart from exceptional situations concerning civil disobedience in a dictatorship and the grounds invoked in democratic societies for conformity, with freedom to take the legal steps necessary to change unjust or otherwise unsound laws, it is submitted that "the only justification for punishing any man [*i.e.* imposing a legal privation] is" not "that he has broken a law"[15] but that he has broken an ethically valid law. . . .

THE NATURE OF PUNISHMENT

As was suggested above, the nature of punishment is, in part, determined by reference to its purposes and functions. For example, if one purpose of punishment, in the sense of a reason for it, is that an offender deserves to be punished, punishment has a moral significance which is lacking or, at least, is quite different from that where it is viewed only as a painful experience imposed to deter potential offenders. So, too, the latent functions of punishment, *e.g.* the maintenance of the individual's "sense of justice" and the cohesion of the community's moral attitudes, are additional factors which determine the nature of punishment.

"Punishment" is, of course, a very ambiguous word;[16] but, it is believed, a substantial consensus can be obtained or, at least, the central issues can be drawn by reference to the following suggested char-

[14] Hall, Theft, Law and Society ch. 4 (2nd ed. 1952).

[15] *Supra* note 2, at 158.

[16] Even in the legal decisions there is considerable divergence in the definition of "punishment." *E.g.* in United States v. Lovett, 328 U. S. 303, 316, 90 L. Ed. 1252, 66 S. Ct. 1073 (1946) it was held that "permanent proscription from any opportunity to serve the Government is punishment, and of a most severe type." In Ex parte Garland, 71 U. S. (4 Wall.) 333, 18 L. Ed. 366 (1867), disqualifying persons for the practice of law because of their past conduct was held punishment and a violation of the *ex post facto* provision.

acteristics:[17] First, punishment is a privation (evil, pain, disvalue). Second, it is coercive. Third, it is inflicted in the name of the State; it is "authorized." Fourth, punishment presupposes rules, their violation, and a more or less formal determination of that, expressed in a judgment.[18] Fifth, it is inflicted upon an offender who has committed a harm, and this presupposes a set of values by reference to which both the harm and the punishment are ethically significant. Sixth, the extent or type of punishment is in some defended way related to the commission of a harm, *e.g.* proportionately to the gravity of the harm, and aggravated or mitigated by reference to the personality of the offender, his motives and temptation.[19]

It will be noticed that the first three criteria are equally applicable to civil sanctions. The fourth concerns legality, and its significance in penal law differs from that in civil law, *e.g.* the degree of precision required in penal law, strict interpretation of statutes and the bar on retroactivity. Again, there are important differences in procedure, such as the burden of proof, rules limiting the introduction of confessions, and so on. Non-legal scholars sometimes depreciate this characteristic of punishment, "to vindicate the law," as arbitrary. Without going into the issues thus raised concerning the principle of legality, it may be noted that the above view challenges the predominant meaning of "punishment," which implies the existence of a set of rules and their violation. Even in countries which abandoned the principle of legality some years ago, the "punishment" of persons who committed "anti-social" harms was defended by reference to the violation of an analogous penal law. So, too, those who administer the sanction are authorized officials, *e.g.* the injury inflicted by a mob upon an escaped convicted murderer is not punishment. In sum, punishment is for the transgression of rules; and it is inflicted by legally authorized persons.[20]

With reference to the sixth characteristic of punishment, it may be noted that while there is also a rational relation of compensation to damage, its significance differs in important respects from its analogue in penal law. Some of these differences have been previously suggested in the differentiation of tortious injuries and penal harms. The fuller significance of the differences may be developed in discussion of the fifth attribute of punishment, noted above.

The most pronounced disagreement regarding punishment concerns this criter-

[17] See Strömberg, *Some Reflections on the Concept of Punishment,* 23 Theoria 71 (1957). For a summary of present American tendencies, which stresses the institutional meaning of punishment, see Jeffery, *The Historical Development of Criminology,* 50 J. Cr. L. Crim. & Pol. Sci. 14–18 (1959) and the citations there given.

[18] *Cf.* "A punishment is an evill inflicted by publique authority on him that hath done or omitted that which is judged by the same authority to be a Transgression of the Law to the end that the will of men may thereby the better be disposed to obedience." Hobbes, Leviathan ch. 28, p. 161. See Givanovitch, *De la notion de la peine,* 27 Rev. Pen. Suisse 360 (1914).

[19] "There is no society where the rule does not exist that the punishment must be proportional to the offense. . . ." Durkheim, The Rules of Sociological Method 73 (Catlin ed. 1938). "The tendency of all conduct codes is to proportion to some extent the severity of the group's reaction to a violator, *i.e.* the punishment, to the severity of injury done to its moral values." Sellin, *The Law and Some Aspects of Criminal Conduct,* pub. in Conference on Aims and Methods of Legal Research 121 (Ed. Conard, 1957).

[20] Hobbes' Leviathan, ch. 28, reprinted in Vol. 23, Great Books of the Western World 145 (1952).

ion, especially, its ethical aspect. Within the correctionist schools, themselves, there is sharp disagreement, certain modern scholars holding that punishment is an unmitigated "absolute" evil, while Plato regarded it as having instrumental value as a necessary cure, no more evil than the bitter medicine which a physician might administer.[21] His views are compatible with St. Thomas Aquinas' theory of punishment as the privation of a "natural condition," for again, that is an evil only in a relative sense. In an "absolute" sense, punishment is good since it is corrective, deterrent and necessary for the public welfare.[22] There is thus in St. Thomas' theory a very important difference between the evil of a crime and the evil of punishment. Stubborn wilfulness, action in disregard of reason, is the essence of crime; but punishment is imposed on rational grounds and serves useful purposes.

Bentham views punishment in a very different perspective. For him, it is an empirical question of desire and of the infliction of sufficient pain to provide an effective deterrent.[23] He therefore saw no inherent difference between the evil of crimes and that of punishment except that the latter was "legal;" and he also held it had desirable consequences.[24] Accordingly, for Bentham, the offender's temptation—not his moral culpability or the gravity of the harm—determined the nature and extent of punishment. "The punishment," he said, "must be more an object of dread than the offence is an object of desire;"[25] and the fact that "temptation diminishes fault" is irrelevant. Thus, it is not sound to ask "whether a penal code be more or less severe. The only question is, whether the severity of the code be necessary or not."[26] Despite his literal and sometimes harsh language, Bentham showed much sensitivity for the welfare of the offender.[27]

---

[21] Plato is usually interpreted as a thoroughgoing utilitarian who stressed the educative influence of punishment but, in fact, he also espoused a retributive theory. He speaks frequently and favorably of punishment as "deserved" (Gor. 525; Laws 855), of being "rightly punished" (Gor. 525) and of "retribution" (*id.* at 509). In any case, it is certain that Plato viewed the pain of punishment as both beneficial and necessary. So, too, Kant, Critique of Practical Reason 148–163 (Abbott ed. 1883).

[22] Retribution is also recognized, *e.g.* De Malo, Q. 1. Art. 5. ad. 12; S. T. II II Q. 108, a. 4, I II Q. 21, a. 3; and see Rooney, Lawlessness, Law and Sanction 43 (1937).

[23] "If hanging a man in *effigy*, would produce the same salutary impression of terror upon the minds of the people, it would be folly or cruelty ever to hang a man *in person*." Bentham, Rationale of Punishment 29 (1830).

[24] "The same evil done by authority of the law, or in violation of the law, will constitute a punishment, or an offence. The nature of the evil is the same, but how different the effect! The offence spreads alarm; the punishment reestablishes security." Bentham, The Theory of Legislation 341 (Ogden ed. 1950). "The difference between punishments and offences is not then in their nature, which is, or may be, the same; . . ." *Op. cit. supra* note 23, at 17.

[25] Bentham, Theory of Legislation 325 (Ogden ed. 1950). Bentham goes into great detail and to great extremes in adapting the type of punishment to that of the harm committed. *Op. cit. supra* note 23, at chapter 8 and *cf. id.* at 65 and 68.

[26] Bentham, Theory of Legislation 345 (Ogden ed. 1950). *Cf. op. cit. supra* note 23, at 34 where he urges mitigation if the temptation shows "the absence of confirmed depravity, or the possession of benevolence. . . ." Bentham also advocated individualization adapted to "[a]ge, sex, rank, fortune, and many other circumstances. . . ." Theory of Legislation 327 (Ogden ed.). He preferred punishments which reformed offenders over those that only deterred. Rationale of Punishment 47–8 (1830).

[27] "It ought not to be forgotten, although it has been too frequently forgotten, that the delinquent is a member of the community, as well

Bentham also held that there is no substantive difference between punishment and compensation. All injuries are "offenses," all sanctions are punitive; and they were treated in his penal code.[28] Bentham even said that civil sanctions are sometimes more painful, and therefore more punitive, than criminal ones.[29] For Austin, who in the main adopted Bentham's ethics, the difference between criminal and civil sanctions was only a procedural one, namely, the civil sanction "is enforced at the discretion of the party whose right has been violated" while the criminal sanction "is enforced at the discretion of the Sovereign or State."[30]

Kelsen's discussion of criminal and civil sanctions resembles that of the Utilitarians except that he ignores the possibility of any "desirable consequences." He first states that civil and criminal sanctions are alike in being coercive; then, that there is a difference in their purpose, namely, while criminal law aims at retribution and deterrence, "civil law aims at reparation." But this, he quickly adds, is only a "relative" difference, *e.g.* the fine is like reparation since both consist of economic deprivations. The civil sanction, however, awards compensation to the plaintiff, while the criminal one transfers the fine to the community. Again, he state, this is hardly a significant difference and, concurring with Austin,[31] he notes that both criminal and civil sanctions deter. He also accepts Austin's view of the procedural difference. But this, too, states Kelsen, "is of minor importance." Hence, he concludes, there is only a "very relative difference between civil and criminal sanction. . . ."[32] This "relativity" must, of course, be interpreted in the context of Kelsen's naturalistic ethics.[33]

It is significant that writers who find no substantive difference between punishment and compensation also find no such difference between sanctions and harms. We have noted this, with a reservation as to consequences, in Bentham's theory. Going far beyond that, Kelsen states that "the coercive act of the sanction is of exactly the same sort as the act which it seeks to prevent [namely] . . . the delict; that the sanction against socially injurious behavior is itself such behavior. . . . Force is employed to prevent the employment of force in society."[34] That there is no doubt whatever about the "neutrality" of Kelsen's theory is shown in his rejection of "the usual assumption" that sanctions are applied *because* delicts (harms) are committed. That is "not correct," states Kelsen. "It is a delict *because* it

as any other individual—as well as the party injured himself; and that there is just as much reason for consulting his interest as that of any other. . . . It may be right [sic!] that the interest of the delinquent should in part be sacrificed to that of the rest of the community; but it never can be right that it should be totally disregarded." Rationale of Punishment 28–29 (1830).

[28] But there is considerable looseness. For example, Bentham discusses punishment separately from compensation and pecuniary satisfaction in relation to theft, peculation and extortion, (Theory of Legislation, 286 Ogden ed. 1950) while he here ignores injuries caused by torts and breach of contract.

[29] But Bentham also said—at least once—that "compensation" must be distinguished from "punishment." The Rationale of Punishment 4 (1830).

[30] 1 Austin, Lectures on Jurisprudence 518 (4th ed. 1879).

[31] *Id.* at 517.

[32] Kelsen, General Theory of Law and State 50–51 (1945).

[33] This is discussed in Hall, Living Law of Democratic Society, ch. 2 (1947).

[34] *Op. cit. supra* note 32, at 21.

entails a sanction."[35] In his theory, "there is no other critierion of the delict than the fact that the behavior [delict] is the condition of a sanction."[36] Thus, while natural law philosophers and laymen find important ethical differences between harms and legal sanctions, and utilitarians acknowledge that the two have very different consequences, Kelsen's theory culminates in a formality. Actually, however, Kelsen's insistence on efficacy as a criterion of law and the substantive character of the postulate of his theory (the *grundnorm*) imply an analogous relationship between sanction and delict. The general conclusion to which we are drawn is that for practically all writers, sanctions are meaningful in relation to harms. It follows that if there is an important difference between criminal harms and torts, punishment and compensation are correspondingly different.

Before further consideration of the relation of sanction to harm (always on the premise of legal rules by reference to which harm is a transgression and sanction a prescription), it is necessary to take account of the indicated dissenting view which is espoused by some ardent advocates of rehabilitation, who find no merit whatever in retributive and deterrent theories and characterize punishment simply and solely as the cruel, senseless infliction of suffering.[37] This rejection of any valid relationship of sanction to harm excludes the possibility of finding any rational quality of punishment. It obstructs any effort to distinguish civil from penal sanctions. And it raises other difficulties; for example, it becomes impossible to distinguish the imprisonment of a person for the commission of a crime from the detention of an arrestee or an alien pending deportation.

But the imprisonment of a witness surely has a very different meaning from that of a felon. So, too, hospitalization of psychotic persons and imprisonment of felons have very different meanings because they are related, respectively, to damage caused by natural forces and to harm deliberately inflicted by normal persons. Unlike punishment, neither educative nor safety measures presuppose culpability; they are not proportioned to the harm committed; and the privation, although intentional, is only a necessity. The recognition of more subtle differences, *e.g.* between very enlightened individualized punishment and corrective treatment depends even more on reference to the respective condition or prior harm which sets the perspective of interpretation.[38]

[35] *Id.* at 51, italics added.

[36] *Ibid.*

[37] The "fundamental character of [punishment] being a suffering that is a purpose in itself. . . ." Kinberg, *Punishment or Impunity?*, 21 Acta Psych. et Neur. 438 (1946).

Cf. "The essential element in so-called Retributive Punishment is not the infliction of pain or loss on the evil doer, as though that by itself were good, but the assertion of the good will of the community against his evil will. . . . But this action of the community must be painful, because its essential quality is antagonism to the criminal so far as he is criminal." Temple, The Ethics of Penal Action 31 (1934). "No society has ever approved suffering as a good thing in itself." Kluckhohn, pub. in Towards a General Theory of Action 418 (Parsons and Shils Eds. 1951).

[38] *Cf.* "The Prison Commissioners know that if prisons were made reasonably happy places, and thrown open to volunteers like the army, they might speedily be overcrowded." Shaw, Imprisonment 51 (1924).

There is no real danger "so long as the milder special treatment does not become such a commonplace that the potential criminal can count on it and behave accordingly." Andenaes, *General Prevention—Illusion or Reality?*, 43 J. Cr. L. and Criminol. 176 at 195–196 (1952).

If we therefore reject polemics which isolate the sanction, and recognize that its interrelatedness with the harm is basic, the relevant problems concern the significance of that relationship. Kelsen's theory offers very little assistance in such an inquiry; and the indiscriminate utilitarian thesis that all harms are evils excludes any substantive differentiation of sanctions. . . . A penal harm is not merely an illegal pain or the mere "condition" of a sanction. It is also, and much more significantly, an actual disvalue. So, too, the relationship of sanctions to these deviations has social significance which eludes concentration upon the sanctions. We thus return to the central fact regarding sanctions—their relation to relevant harms and, specifically, to the question of any consequent substantive difference between punitive and civil sanctions. The present position is that there are important substantive differences because the respective harms are substantively different and this is reflected in the nature and functions of the corresponding sanctions.

. . . The principal ground relied upon to distinguish torts and criminal harms is that the latter, defined in terms of certain principles, connote the actor's moral culpability whereas this is not essential in tortious injuries. This must also characterize the respective sanctions, *i.e.* punishment implies the criminal's moral culpability and is apt (fitting, correct) in light of that, while civil sanctions do not carry this significance but serve instead to discharge certain economic functions. These are the insights which guide the following further discussion of this problem.

With reference to the moot situation which involves voluntary injuries and the thesis that "the same act" is both a tort and a crime, we previously asked, do we really have "the same act" in a legally relevant sense? It was submitted that the thesis that there is "one act" prejudges the meaning of "the act" in a common sense way and ignores the relevant ideational factors. Here we must add that the different sanctions applied to "the act" also alter "its" significance. An intentional harm, viewed from tort law, means one for which it is just or expedient to require reparation; while, viewed from criminal law, it means one where punishment should be imposed upon the offender. To reply that this is "merely" applying different sanctions to "the same act" is to forget that sanctions are essential parts of the respective ideas which give any relevant act its meaning. In sum, one reason why civil injuries differ from penal harms is that they are rationally subjected to different sanctions. Surely, there is little warrant for restricting legal analysis to the external aspects of "acts"? What is paramount is their meaning.

It must follow from the premises here employed, which locate penal harm between conduct and punishment in an interrelated means-end figure, that the penal sanction is also distinctive by virtue of its relation to the penal harm. The salient difference is shown in the fact that punishment focuses primarily on the defendant as a person, while the civil sanction is oriented primarily to the reparation of the victim's economic loss. In other words, the punitive sanction is intimate, while civil sanctions lack that quality. Many persons are, of course, attached to their pocket-books, but the seizure of their property, though personal, falls so far short of the direct, intimate treatment of the person and personality of criminals—the so-called infliction of suffering—as to constitute a very different type of sanction. That is why a criminal cannot substitute another to undergo his punishment, but the reparation of economic damage does not entail any concern with the source of the repairs[39] In sum, punishment is a coercive deprivation intimately applied to an offender because of his voluntary commission of a harm forbidden by penal law and implying his moral culpability.

[39] Even a fine, viewed as this kind of personal deprivation, is different from money paid to repair damage. But the fine raises various questions. On the one hand, recent statutes providing a very wide range in fines and their administration by reference to the wealth of the defendant reflect its punitive import. So, too, permission to pay fines in installments over a long period of time also accords with its punitive significance. Sellin, The Protective Code—A Swedish Proposal 13 (1957). On the other hand, although an association formed to pay fines would be illegal (*Clubs for Fine Playing,* 84 J. P. 89 [1920]), no one really questions where the money comes from. See H. M. Treasury v. Harris (1957), 3 W. L. R. 12, 2 All E. R. 455.

CRIME AND PUNISHMENT*

Pope Pius XII

Possessor of both civil and canon law degrees, Pope Pius XII maintained a life-long interest in both law and punishment. In his 1954 speech to the Italian Association of Jurists he argues for a necessary relationship between "vindictive" punishment and rehabilitation. In the process, he reflects the close alliance between retribution and religion, specifically that of the Roman Catholic Church. The interested reader might well seek to distinguish the confessional, educational, and retributive threads woven into his argument.

The question which We shall examine today was suggested to Us by one of you, the illustrious Professor Carnelutti. It is: the function of punishment, the "redeeming of the criminal through repentance"; a question which We should like to formulate in this manner: crime and punishment in their reciprocal relationship. We should wish, that is, to indicate in broad outline the path of a man from the state of noncriminality, through the actual crime, to the state of criminal guilt and its punishment (*reatus culpae et poenae*); and vice versa, the return from this state, through repentance and expiation, to the state of liberation from the crime and punishment. We shall be able then to see more clearly what is the origin of punishment, what is its nature, what its function, what form it should take in order to conduct the criminal to his liberation.

It is necessary here to make two preliminary remarks.

Above all, the problem of crime and of punishment is a problem concerned with persons, and this under a double aspect. The path toward crime takes its beginning from the person of the one acting, from his "Ego." In the sum of the actions which proceed from the Ego as from a center of action, there is question here only of those which are based upon a conscious and voluntary determination; that is, acts which the Ego was able to perform or not perform, those which it performs because it has freely determined to do so. This central function of the Ego with regard to itself—even if operating under various influences of a different nature—is an essential element when there is question of true crime and true punishment.

The criminal act, however, is also always an opposition of one person against another, both when the immediate object of the crime is a thing, as in theft, and when it is a person, as in murder; further, the Ego of the person who becomes a criminal is directed against higher authority, and therefore in the end always against the authority of God. In this mat-

* Excerpted from Pope Pius XII, *Crime and Punishment*, 6 CATHOLIC LAWYER 92 (1960). Reprinted with permission.

ter We, Who have as Our aim the true problem of crime and punishment properly so-called, prescind from the merely juridical crime and from its consequent penalty.

It is also to be observed that the person and the function of the person who is the criminal form a strict unity, which in its turn presents different aspects. Simultaneously it concerns the psychological, juridical, ethical and religious fields. These aspects can certainly also be considered separately; but in true crime and punishment they are so closely related among themselves that only by taking them all together is it possible to form a correct concept about the criminal and the question of crime and punishment. It is not even possible, therefore, to treat this problem unilaterally, merely under its juridical aspect.

The path toward crime therefore is this: the spirit of a man is found in the following situation: it is faced with the performance or omission of an action, and this performance or omission is presented to it as simply obligatory, as an absolute "you must," an unconditional demand to be fulfilled by a personal decision. The man refuses to obey this demand: he rejects the good, accepts the evil. When the internal resolution is not terminated within itself, it is followed by the external action. Thus the criminal action is accomplished both internally and externally.

As far as the subjective side of the crime is concerned, in order to judge rightly it is necessary to take into account not only the external act, but also the influences, both internal and external, which have cooperated in the decision of the criminal, such as innate or acquired dispositions, impulses or obstructions, impressions from education, stimulations from persons or things in the midst of which the person lives, circumstantial factors, and in a particular way the habitual and actual intensity of the will-act, the so-called "criminal urge," which has contributed to the accomplishment of the criminal act.

Considered in the object affected by it, the criminal action is an arrogant contempt for authority, which demands the orderly maintenance of what is right and good, and which is the source, the guardian, the defender and the vindicator of order itself. And since all human authority cannot be derived ultimately except from God, every criminal act is an opposition to God Himself, to His supreme law and sovereign majesty. This religious aspect is inherently and essentially connected with the criminal act.

The object affected by this act is also the legally established community, if and in as far as it places in danger and violates the order established by the laws. Nevertheless not every true criminal act, as described above, has the character of a crime against the public law. Public authority must be concerned only with those criminal actions which injure the orderly society as established by law. Hence, the rule concerning a juridical crime: no crime where there is no law. But such a violation, if it is otherwise a true criminal act in itself, is also always a violation of the ethical and religious norm. It follows therefore that those human laws which are in contradiction to divine laws cannot form the basis for a true criminal act against the public law.

Connected with the concept of the criminal act is the concept that the author of the act becomes deserving of punishment (*reatus poenae*). The problem of punishment has its beginning, in an individual case, at the moment in which a man becomes a criminal. The punishment is the reaction, required by law and justice, to the crime: they are like a blow and a counter-blow. The order violated by the criminal act demands the restoration and re-establishment of the equilibrium which has been disturbed. It is the proper task of law and justice to guard and preserve the harmony between duty, on the one hand, and the law, on the other, and to re-establish this harmony if it has been injured. The punishment in itself touches not the criminal act, but the author of it, his person, his Ego, which with conscious determination has performed the criminal act. Likewise the punishing does not proceed, as it were, from an abstract juridical ordination, but from the concrete person invested with legitimate authority. As the criminal act, so also the punishment opposes person to person.

Punishment properly so-called cannot therefore have any other meaning and purpose than that just mentioned, to bring back again into the order of duty the violator of the law, who had withdrawn from it. This order of duty is necessarily an expression of the order of being, of the order of the true and the good, which alone has the right of existence, in opposition to error and evil, which represent that which should not exist. Punishment accomplishes its purpose in its own way, in as far as it compels the criminal, because of the act performed, to suffer, that is, it deprives him of a good and imposes upon him an evil. But in order that this suffering may be a punishment, the causal connection with the crime is essential.

We add that the criminal has brought about, by his act, a state which does not automatically cease when the act itself is completed. He remains the man who has consciously and deliberately violated a law which binds him (*reatus culpae*), and simultaneously he is involved in the penalty (*reatus poenae*). This personal condition endures, both in his relation to the authority on which he depends (or better, the human authority of public law in so far as this has a share in the corresponding penal process), and at all times also in his relation to the supreme divine authority. There is thus brought about an enduring state of guilt and punishment, which indicates a definite condition of the guilty party in the eyes of the authority offended, and of this authority with respect to the guilty party. (St. Thomas: *Sum. Theol.* III, q. 69, a.2, obj. 3 et ad 3.) . . .

What We have so far explained concerns the essence of the state of guilt and punishment. On the other hand, by virtue of the special prerogative of the higher authority, to which the culprit has refused due obedience and submission, its indignation and disapproval turn against not only the action, but its author, against his person on account of the action.

With the act of crime is immediately linked, as was just now indicated, not the punishment itself, but the guiltiness and punishability of the action. Nonetheless, there is not excluded a penalty, which, by virtue of a law, is incurred automatically at the moment of the criminal action. In Canon Law are recognized penalties (*"latae sententiae"*) liable to be incurred by the very fact of committing a sin. In civil law, such a penalty is rare, nay, in some legal systems, unknown. Always, moreover, this automatic incurring of a penalty supposes real and serious guilt.

Consequently, it is customary for the penalty to be imposed by a competent authority. That presupposes a penal law actually in force, a legal person invested with authority to punish, and in him certain knowledge of the act to be punished, as much from the objective standpoint, that is to say, concerning the actual commission of the crime contemplated by the law, as from the subjective standpoint, that is, from a consideration of the culpability of the guilty one, its gravity and extension.

This knowledge, necessary for pronouncing a penal sentence, is, before the court of God the Supreme Judge, perfectly clear and infallible, and to have called attention to it cannot be without interest to the jurist. God was present to the man in the internal resolve, and in the external execution of the criminal act, having all fully within His gaze down to the last detail; all is before Him now, as in the moment of the act. But this knowledge in absolute fullness and sovereign certainty, at every instant of life, and over every human act, is proper to God alone. Because of this, there belongs to God alone the final judgment on the value of a man, and the decision on his ultimate fate. He pronounces the judgment as He finds the man at the moment He calls him to eternity. Yet an infallible judgment of God exists also during life on earth, and not only taken as a whole, but over every sinful act, together with the corresponding penalty; yet, in spite of the ever-ready divine disposition to forgiveness and remission, in some cases He carries it into effect during the present life of the man.

The human judge, on the other hand, since he does not possess the omnipresence and omniscience of God, has the duty of forming for himself, before issuing a judicial sentence, a moral certainty —that is, one which excludes every reasonable and serious doubt about the external fact and the internal culpability. But he does not have immediate insight into the interior dispositions of the accused at the very moment of the crime; rather in most cases the judge is not in a position to reconstruct them with absolute clarity from the arguments offered in proof, nor, often enough, even from the confession of the delinquent. But this difficulty should not be exaggerated as though it were ordinarily impossible for a human judge to attain sufficient certainty, and therefore a solid foundation for a sentence. According to the cases, the judge will not fail to consult renowned specialists on the capacity and responsibility of the presumed criminal, and to take into consideration the findings of the modern sciences of psychology, psychiatry and characterology. If, despite all these precautions, there still remains a grave and serious doubt, no conscientious judge will proceed to pronounce a sentence of condemnation, all the more so when there is a question of an irrevocable punishment, such as the death penalty.

In most crimes external behavior is already sufficient manifestation of the internal motivation which was responsible for the crime. Therefore, ordinarily one can—and at times one even should—deduce a substantially sound conclusion from the exterior; otherwise juridical actions would be rendered impossible for mankind. On the other hand, one should not forget that no human sentence finally and definitely settles the fate of a man, but only the judgment of God, both for single acts and for those of a lifetime. Consequently, in every case where human judges have erred, the Supreme Judge will re-establish equilibrium, first of all, immediately after death with the definitive judgment on the whole life of a man, and then later and more fully in the final and universal judgment before all men. This is not to be understood as though it dispenses a judge from conscientious and exact efforts in ascertaining the facts. Still, there is something magnificent in the realization that there will be a final equation of guilt and punishment which will be absolutely perfect.

Whoever has the duty of guarding the accused person in protective custody should not fail to bear in mind the painful burden which the investigation itself inflicts upon the prisoner, even when those methods of investigation are not being employed which cannot be justified in any way. Ordinarily these sufferings are not taken into account when the penalty is finally inflicted, a consideration which would be difficult to realize. However they should not be lost sight of.

In external juridical matters the sentence of the court is definitive for all that concerns guilt and punishment. . . .

Up to a certain point it may be true that imprisonment and isolation, properly applied, is the penalty most likely to effect a return of the criminal to right order and social life. But it does not follow that it is the only just and effective one. What We said in Our discourse on international penal law, on Oct. 3, 1953, referring to the theory of retribution, is to the point here. Many, though not all, reject vindictive punishment, even if it is proposed to be accompanied by medicinal penalties. We then declared that it would not be just to reject completely, and as a matter of principle, the function of vindictive punishment. As long as man is on earth, such punishment can and should help toward his definitive rehabilitation, provided man himself does not raise barriers to its efficacy, which, indeed, is in no way opposed to the purpose of righting and restoring disturbed harmony, which, as We already pointed out, is an essential element of punishment.

The inflicting of punishment finds its natural complement in its being carried out as the effective privation of a good, or the positive imposition of an evil, by competent authority as a reaction to the criminal action. It is a weight placed to restore balance in the disturbed juridical order, and not aimed immediately at the fault as such. The criminal action has revealed in the guilty person an element that clashes with the common good and with well ordered life with others. Such an element must be removed from the culprit. The process of removing it may be compared with the intervention of a doctor in the body, an intervention which may be painful, especially when the cause of sickness, and not the symptoms, must be dealt with. The culprit's own good, and, perhaps, more so that of the community, demand that the ailing member become sound again. The meting out of punishment, however, no less than the healing of the sick, demands a clear diagnosis of causes, not merely of symptoms, a therapy adapted to the ailment, a cautious prognosis and a suitable prophylaxis.

The meaning and purpose of the punishment, and the intention of the punishing authority, which is usually in agreement with that purpose, indicate the attitude the culprit should have; it is that of acknowledgment of the evil done, which provoked the penalty; of aversion from, and repudiation of, the evil deed itself, of repentance, expiation and purification, and purpose of future amendment. That is the path the condemned man should follow. The problem, however, is whether he will really take it. Turning Our attention to such a question, it may be helpful to consider the suffering caused by the punishment, according to its various aspects: psychological, juridical, moral and religious.

though normally these various aspects are all closely united in the concrete.

Psychologically, nature spontaneously reacts against the physical evil in the penalty, her reaction being all the stronger in proportion to the suffering imposed on human nature as such, or on the individual temperament. Along with this, there is a fixing, likewise spontaneous, of the culprit's attention on the criminal action which caused his punishment, and whose connection is now vividly before his mind, or at least is now uppermost in his conscience.

Following such more or less involuntary attitudes, there appears the conscious and willed reaction of the Ego, the center and source of all personal actions. This higher reaction can be a voluntary, positive acceptance, as is shown by the good thief on the cross: "We receive what our deeds merit" (Luke; 23, 41). It may be mere passive resignation; or at times it may be a deep bitterness, a total interior collapse; then, too, it may be a proud resistance, which at times becomes a hardening in evil; finally it may be a complete revolt, savage but impotent. Such psychological reactions take differing forms, depending on whether there is question of a long punishment, or of a short punishment, short in time, but surpassing in height and depth all time-measure—the pain of death, for example.

Juridically, execution of the punishment implies the valid, effective action of the higher and stronger power of the juridical community (or rather, of the one possessing authority in this community) on the law-breaker, who, obstinately opposed to the law, has culpably violated the established juridical order, and now is forced to submit to the prescriptions of that order—for the greater good of the community and of the criminal himself. Thus the idea and necessity of penal law is clear.

On the other hand, justice demands that, in carrying out the provisions of penal law, any increase of those punishments provided for the case, as also any arbitrary harshness, annoyance or provocation, be avoided. Higher authority must see to the carrying out of the punishment, and give it a form which will correspond to its purpose, not in an unyielding fulfillment of minute prescriptions, but in adapting it, so far as possible, to the person to be punished. Indeed the gravity and dignity of the power to punish, and its exercise, naturally indicate that the public authority view as its main duty contact with the person of the guilty one. Judgment on him must be made, therefore, according to special circumstances, if the functioning of that office is to be fully taken care of through the proper channels. Very often, if not always, one aspect of punishment must be entrusted to others, especially the real and effective care of souls. . . .

The moral aspect of carrying out of punishment and the sufferings effected are in relation to the purpose and principles which should determine the dispositions of the condemned.

To suffer in this life means practically a turning of the soul within itself; it is a path which drives one from the superficial to deep within oneself. Considered in that light, suffering has great moral value. Presupposing a right intention, its free acceptance is a priceless act. *"Patientia opus perfectum habet,"* (Suffering makes a perfect work"), writes St. James (1, 4). That is true also of the sufferings caused by punishment, which can bring progress to one's interior life. By its nature it is a reparation and a restoration—

through and in the guilty person, and willed by him—of the culpably violated social order. The essence of the return to good consists more exactly in breaking away from the fault than in the free acceptance of suffering. Suffering, however, can lead to this break, and turning away from one's wrongdoing can, in its turn, be of great moral value, and facilitate and elevate its moral effectiveness. Thus, suffering can reach moral heroism, heroic patience and expiation.

In the area of moral reaction, however, contrary manifestations are not lacking. Often the moral value of punishment is not even recognized; often it is consciously and deliberately rejected. The criminal will neither recognize nor confess his guilt, will in no way submit to good, wills no expiation or repentance for his own crimes.

And now a few words on the religious aspect of the suffering which results from punishment.

Every moral transgression of man, even if materially committed only in the sphere of legitimate human laws and then punished by men according to positive human law, is always a sin before God and calls down upon itself from God a punitive judgment. Not to take this into account is contrary to the interest of public authority. Sacred Scripture (Romans 13, 2–4) teaches that human authority, within its own limits, is, when there is question of inflicting punishment, nothing else than the minister of divine justice. "For he is God's minister: an avenger to execute wrath upon him that doth evil."

This religious element in the infliction of punishment finds its expression and realization in the person of the guilty one, in so far as he humbles himself under the hand of God Who is punishing him through the instrumentality of men; thus he is accepting his sufferings from God, offering them to God as a partial payment of the debt which he has contracted before God. Accepted in this way, punishment becomes for the guilty person a source of interior purification on this earth, of complete conversion, of resolution for the future, a bulwark against possible relapse. Suffering thus accepted with faith, repentance and love is sanctified by the pains of Christ and supported by His grace. This religious and holy meaning of suffering due to punishment is impressed upon us by the words which the good thief addressed to his crucified companion: "We receive the due rewards of our deeds," and by his prayer to the dying Redeemer: "Lord, remember me when thou shalt come into thy kingdom"; a prayer which, when weighed upon the scales of God, brought to the repentant sinner the assurance of the Saviour: "This day thou shalt be with me in paradise" (Luke 23, 41–43); the first plenary indulgence, as it were, granted by Christ Himself.

May all who have fallen under the blows of human justice suffer the punishment inflicted upon them not in a spirit of duress, not without God and without Christ, not in revolt against God, not spiritually shattered by anguish; but may it open for them the way which leads to holiness.

It remains now to speak of the final section of the path which We wished to point out to you, that is, the return from the state of guilt and punishment to that of liberation.

Liberation from guilt and liberation from punishment are not necessarily identified, either in concept or in reality. Prescinding from the fact that, in the sight of God, the remission of eternal punishment is always connected with the remission of grave guilt—guilt may be remitted without necessarily implying the extinguishing of the penalty. On the other hand, the penalty may have been paid without the guilt having ceased to exist in the inner being of the culprit.

Now, the return to the juridical and ethical order consists essentially in the liberation from guilt, and not from punishment.

In the exposition of the first section of this path, We pointed out the internal and external character of the guilty act, that is, in relation to its author, as also in its relations to higher authority, which is, in the last analysis, the authority of God Himself, Whose majesty, justice and holiness are slighted and offended in every culpable act.

Liberation from guilt must, therefore, reintegrate the relations disturbed by the culpable act. If we are dealing with a simple real debt, that is, one that is concerned with purely material considerations, it may be fully extinguished by the handing over of the thing required, without the necessity of any personal contact with the other party. If, however, there is question of a personal offense (either by itself or connected with a real debt), then the culprit is bound to an obligation, in the strict sense, to the person of the creditor. It is from this strict obligation that he must be released. And because, as We have already said, this obligation has a psychological, juridical, moral and religious aspect, so his liberation must have a similar aspect.

Guilt, however, in its internal element, also implies in the culprit a state of enslavement and of bondage on his part to the object to which he has given himself in the performance of the culpable act; that is, in substance, an enslavement to a pseudo-ego whose tendencies, impulses and ends constitute in man a caricature of the genuine ego, intended by the Creator and by nature only for the good and the true. This contradicts those norms of the right path according to whose direction man, made in the image of God, should act and form himself. From this enslavement also must there be effected a psychological, juridical, moral and religious liberation.

In human law, we may speak of a sort of liberation from guilt when the public authority no longer proceeds against the culpable act; for example, even without regard to the actual internal dispositions of the culprit, by positive remission of the guilt on the part of authority, or because there has expired the period established by the law within which exclusively the same authority intends, under certain conditions, to bring before its tribunal, and to pass judgment upon, the violation of the law that has taken place. However, this way does not constitute an interior conversion, a metanoia, a liberation of the ego from its interior slavery, from its will to evil and to illegality. Now, it is only to this liberation from guilt in its proper meaning, to this metanoia (that is, change of mental attitude), that We would wish here to draw attention.

Psychologically considered, the liberation from guilt is the abandonment and retraction of the perverse will freely and consciously placed by the ego in the culpable act, and the renewed intention to will what is right and good. This change of will presupposes a return into oneself, and hence an understanding of the evil and culpability of the resolution formerly taken against the good recognized as obligatory. There is united to such understanding the reprobation of the evil done, repentance as directly willed sorrow, deliberate regretfulness in the soul for the evil perpetrated because it was wicked, contrary to law and, in fine, contrary to God. In this catharsis of the inner being, there is also accomplished and included a withdrawing from the false good to which man had turned in his guilty act. The culprit begins to submit himself to the order of justice and right, in obedience to its author and guardian, against whom he had rebelled.

This leads psychologically to the final step. Since the culpable act—as already mentioned—is not the offense directed against an abstract norm of law, but is, in substance, a stand against the person of the obligating or prohibiting authority, complete conversion tends, through psychological necessity in one form or another, toward the person of the offended authority with the explicit or implicit sorrowful confession of the fault, and with interior petition for remission and pardon. Holy Scripture gives us brief and classic examples of such repentance, like the words of the publican in the Temple: "O God, be merciful to me, a sinner." (Luke 18, 13); or the words of the prodigal son: "Father, I have sinned" (Luke 15, 21).

In spite of this, when considered under the purely psychological aspect, the perverse will expressed in the culpable act can end in another way without attaining release from guilt. The culprit no longer thinks of his act, but he has not actually retracted it; it has simply ceased to weigh upon his conscience. Now, it should be clearly stated that such a psychological process does not constitute a release from guilt, just as falling asleep in the evening does not signify or obtain the removal, much less the suppression, of the evil committed during the day. Nowadays, some will perhaps say that the guilt has been submerged in the subconscious or the unconscious. But it is still there.

Nor would any better result be obtained with the attempt to suppress the psychological awareness of guilt by means of autosuggestion or external suggestion, or even by means of clinical psychotherapy, or psychoanalysis. A real, free, guilty will cannot be psychologically corrected or suppressed by insinuating the persuasion that it has never existed. . . .

A final observation must yet be made on this question of psychological liberation from guilt. A single, fully conscious and free act can contain all the psychic elements of a true conversion; but its depth, firmness and extent can present defects which, if not essential, are at least appreciable. A profound, extended and lasting liberation from guilt is often a lengthy process which only gradually reaches maturity, particularly if the culpable act has been the fruit of an habitual disposition of the will. The psychology of relapses offers more than sufficient material for proof on this point, and the supporters of the purifying, educative and fortifying function of a somewhat lengthy imprisonment find in these experiences a confirmation of their theory.

Juridical liberation from guilt, as distinct from the psychological conversion that is accomplished in the intimate will of the culprit, is directed essentially to the higher authority, whose requirements for observance of established norms have been slighted or violated. Private violations of legal rights, if they have occurred in good faith or otherwise, do not prejudice the common good, are settled privately between the parties or by means of a civil action. They are not ordinarily the object of penal law.

In the analysis of the culpable act, We have already pointed out that it constitutes the withdrawal and the negation of due subordination, due service, due devotion, due respect and homage; that it is objectively an offense against the loftiness and majesty of the law, or rather of the law's Author, Guardian, Judge and Vindicator. The exigencies of justice, and hence juridical liberation from guilt, require that as much service, subordination, devotion, homage and honor be restored to authority as were taken from that authority by the delict.

This satisfaction may be performed freely; it may also, in the suffering endured because of the penalty inflicted, be to a certain degree forced; it may at one and the same time be forced and free. Law in modern nations does not attach much importance to voluntary reparation. It is content to have the will of the culprit, by means of the penalty suffered, submit to the powerful will of public authority, and to re-educate his will in this way to work, to social relations, to right action. It is not to be denied that such a method of procedure can, by reason of immanent psychological laws, lead to an interior reform, and hence to an interior liberation from guilt. But that this must happen, or regularly does happen, is still to be demonstrated. In any event, not to take into consideration, as a matter of principle, the will of the culprit to give satisfaction insofar as sound juridical sense and violated justice require, is a deficiency a lacuna, the bridging of which is earnestly demanded by the interests of doctrine and of fidelity to the fundamental principles of penal law.

However, juridical liberation from guilt comprises not only the will to perform the required reparation but the actual reparation itself. Here science and the circumstances of concrete life are frequently confronted by a difficult question: what should be the rule in the event of moral or physical inability to perform such reparation? Must we recur to a sort of compensation or substitution, or may the exigencies of violated law be left without reparation?

We have already indicated that man, by means of a culpable act committed with full responsibility, is capable of offending or of destroying certain goods and juridical obligations; but after the fact he is often no longer in a position to provide adequate satisfaction. This is true in the instance of murder, of privation of sight, of mutilation, of full sexual violation, of adultery, of definitive destruction of another's good name, of the declaration of an unjust war, of the betrayal of state secrets, of certain forms of *lèse majesté*, and of other like delicts.

The law of retaliation would inflict a proportionate evil on the culprit. However, by this alone, the one injured in his rights would not receive reparation nor have his rights restored. But, prescinding from the fact that adequate indemnity is not impossible in all cases, it should be noted that judgment on the guilt regards not so much the damaged good of the other party, but principally the person of the culprit and his perverse will exercised to his own advantage.

In opposition to this is the offering or reparation made by the culprit at his own expense, from his personal being, property and ability, for the benefit of another, that is, in every case, of the violated law, namely, of the superior authority. Thus active reparation, which includes the interior conversion of the will, is for the culprit who, at his own expense, performs the required satisfaction, the second of the two above-indicated elements which constitute liberation from guilt. The same cannot be said of purely passive reparation when the culprit is forced to bow beneath the suffering that this reparation implies. This purely passive satisfaction, from which any element of voluntary and repentant will is lacking, is thus deprived of the essential element of liberation from guilt. Consequently, the culprit remains in his culpable condition.

We have many times pointed out that every grave culpable act is in the last analysis an offense before God, Who has an absolute, because divine, right to obedience and submission, to service and praise, and Who as Author, Guardian, Judge and Avenger of the juridical order makes known to the culprit His exigencies with that unconditional absoluteness which is proper to the intimate manifestations of conscience. In the guilty resolution of the ego, man slights God Who thus reveals Himself, he leaves aside the infinite good, the absolute majesty, and in this way places himself by his action above God. But if man repents and returns to his proper subordination before the majesty of God, if, in conscious and complete surrender of his ego to the supreme infinite good, he separates himself from his culpable act in its deepest roots in order once again to be free in good and in his God, he nevertheless finds it impossible to make reparation by his own powers (that is, as derived from his own being, will and potency) in any proportionate fashion for that which he has committed in the sight of God by his act. He has offended and slighted an absolutely infinite good, an absolutely unlimited right, a supreme majesty. In the gravity of his fault there thus intervenes this absolute infinity, while anything that man might offer or actuate is essentially, intensively and extensively, finite. Even were such reparation to endure until the end of time, it can never reach a stage of equality—*tantum quantum*—between the exigency of God and the offering or reparation of man.

God has bridged this abyss; He has put into the hands of finite man an infinite price; He has accepted as an offering of reparation for guilty man the ransom offered by Christ, which is super-abundant because it is of infinite value in submission, honor and glorification, by reason of its derivation from the hypostatic union. As long as time will endure, this ransom remits for repentant man his guilt before God through the merits of Jesus Christ.

Let it not be said that these theological and religious considerations lie outside the field and the interests of science and juridical practice. Doubtless a sharp distinction of competencies is an advantage to life and to any true science; but in this self-limitation one must not reach the point of denying or ignoring explicitly inseparable connections which by intrinsic necessity are manifested on every side. In every real offense—in whatever material field it may have taken place—there is contained a relation with the ultimate requirement of all law and of all order. It is a characteristic or prerogative of the world of law that there is nothing in it which in its fundamental structure has been created without this supreme requirement, or which in its final analysis can be made intelligible without this transcendent relation. In this there is no debasement, but rather an elevation of law and of juridical science, for which total laicization is an impoverishment, not an enrichment.

The ancient Romans united law and right (*ius ac fas*), notwithstanding the difference in concepts, and they always conceived them as related to the divinity. If now modern depth-psychology is correct, there is in the innate dynamisms of the subconscious and the unconscious a tendency which draws toward the transcendent and makes the essence of the soul gravitate toward God. The analysis of the guilt-process and of liberation from guilt reveals the same tendency toward the transcendent. This analysis brings forward considerations and aspects which the science and practice of penal law do not of course have to treat of directly, but about which they should have sufficient knowledge in order that others may make them useful to the end of the execution of the penalty and apply them to the advantage of the culprit.

Moral liberation from guilt coincides substantially for the most part with what We have already said concerning psychological and juridical liberation. It is the reprobation and withdrawal of the positive contempt and violation of the moral order committed by the culpable act; it is the conscious and voluntary return of the penitent culprit to submission and conformity with the ethical order and its obligatory requirements. There are comprised in these positive acts the endeavor and the offering of the guilty one to satisfy the just demands of violated law of the ethical order, or better, of the Author, Lord, Guardian and Vindicator of that order. And there appèars the conscious will and resolution of the culprit to be faithful in future to the precepts of what is right and good. In its essential parts, then, this liberation consists in that interior disposition which has been indicated in the statement presented by you as the purpose and the fruit of the right fulfillment of the penalty, even though it is here considered and circumscribed under a slightly different viewpoint.

Finally, by religious liberation there is understood liberation from that interior guilt which burdens and binds the person of the culprit in the sight of God, that is to say, before the supreme and ultimate requirement and necessity of all law and of every moral obligation, Who with His infinity covers and protects His will and His law, which has come forth, either immediately from Himself, or mediately from some legitimate human authority within the area of its own competence.

How man can free himself or be freed from his offense against God has been already sufficiently explained in the second point concerning the juridical aspect. But if this final religious deliverance is not manifested to the culprit, or at least if the way to such is not pointed out or made smooth—if only by means of a long and severe penalty—then in such a case very little, not to say nothing, is offered to guilty "man" in his punishment, however much one may talk of psychic cure, of re-education, of social formation of the person, or emancipation from aberrations and from enslavement to himself.

Doubtless these expressions mean something that is good and important; but for all that, man remains in his guilt before the supreme necessity upon which his final destiny depends. This necessity can wait and often does wait at length, but in the end it consigns the culprit to the guilt from which he is unwilling to desist, and to the consequences of that guilt. It is indeed sorrowful to have to say about a man: "It were better for that man if he had not been born" (Matt. 26, 24).

Therefore, if someone or something

can contribute toward warding off such an evil, even though it be penal law or the execution of a lawful penalty, no effort should be spared. All the more since God during this life is always most willing to effect a reconciliation. He incites man to accomplish internally the psychic withdrawal from his senseless act; He offers to welcome him once again, if he repents, into His friendship and His love. May human penal law, in its judgments and in the execution of those judgments, never forget the man in the culprit and never omit to strengthen him and assist him to return to God!

The return from the state of guilt and of punishment necessarily includes liberation not only from the guilt, but also from the penalty; only thus is there obtained that *"restitutio in integrum,"* as it were, a restitution to the original state or condition of non-culpability and hence of nonpenalty. . . .

The final stage of man's road through guilt and punishment leads anew to the problem, already mentioned several times, of the highest aim or object of the penalty, and particularly about the sense, or according to some, the nonsense, of a purely vindictive penalty.

In Our discourse of October 3, 1953, to the 6th International Congress of Penal Law, and also on the present occasion, We called attention to the fact that many, perhaps the majority, of civil jurists reject vindictive punishment. We noted, however, that perhaps the considerations and arguments adduced as proof were being given a greater importance and force than they have in reality. We also pointed out that the Church in her theory and practice has maintained this double type of penalty (medicinal and vindictive), and that this is more in conformity with what the sources of revelation and traditional doctrine teach regarding the coercive power of legitimate human authority.

It is not a sufficient reply to this assertion to say that the aforementioned sources contain only thoughts which correspond to the historic circumstances and to the culture of the time, and that a general and abiding validity cannot therefore be attributed to them. The reason is that the words of the sources and of the living teaching power do not refer to the specific content of individual juridical prescriptions or rules of action (cf. particularly Rom. 13:4), but rather to the essential foundation itself of penal power and of its immanent finality. This, in turn, is as little determined by the conditions of time and culture as the nature of man and the human society decreed by nature itself. But whatever the attitude of positive human law on this problem, it is sufficient for Our present purpose to make clear that in any total or partial remission of punishment the vindictive penalties (no less than the medicinal) can and even should be taken into consideration.

Arbitrariness cannot prevail in the application of condonation. The good of the culprit, no less than that of the juridical community whose law he has culpably violated, must serve as a norm. Above both of these are the respect and excellence of the order established according to what is good and righteous. This norm requires, among other things, that, as is the case in the normal relations of men with one another, so also in the application of penal power, there be considered not only strict law and justice, but also equity, goodness and mercy. Otherwise there is danger that the *"summum ius"* be converted into *"summa iniuria."*

It is precisely this reflection which

gives rise to the thought that, in medicinal penalties, and also, within certain limits, in vindictive penalties, a remission of the punishment should be taken under consideration whenever there is moral certainty that the inherent purpose of the penalty has been obtained, that is, the true interior conversion of the guilty person, and a serious guarantee of its lasting character. . . .

EXPIATION*

Sir Walter Moberly

Sir Walter Moberly, author of a number of treatises on Christian, ethical, and legal issues, offers his Ethics of Punishment *as a moral defense of retributive punishment. Like Pius XII, Moberly believes that a religious position supports the moral issues involved in the experience of free choice. Yet two secular questions appear foremost: First, in what sense is punishment a privilege for the offender, and second, how does it achieve an expiation of the offense?*

δράσαντι παθεῖν. *Qui malum fecit, malum ferat. Qui casse, paie.* 'Be done by as you did.' Over and above protection of society, and over and above vindication of the Moral Law, advocates of retributive punishment constantly insist that a wrongdoer should be given his *due*. Here the wrongdoer is himself a centre of interest and his suffering is no mere incidental accompaniment of his removal from the scene. On the contrary, they want him to suffer and to know why he suffers, 'to rue his deed' and to feel ashamed of himself. Indeed many thinkers adhere to the retributive theory of punishment just because it seems the only theory which recognizes a wrongdoer's status as a responsible person. It is no accident that it is Kant who both laid down the principle 'Treat humanity whether in thy own person or in that of any other always as an end, never as a means only,' and who was also the uncompromising champion of punishment inflicted as retribution. If to punish a man in order to intimidate, is to treat him as a dog, and to punish in order to correct, is to treat him as a child; to give him the chastisement which is his due—simply because it is his due—is to treat him as a man and a responsible person.

This claim is based on the essential association between the idea of punishment and the idea of desert. Punishment has *two* essential attributes. It always purports to be inflicted, not only *for* a bad act, but also *upon* the guilty person or persons.

> If there is any opinion to which the man of uncultivated morals is attached, it is the belief in the necessary connection of punishment and guilt. Punishment is punishment only where it is deserved. We pay the penalty because we owe it and for no other reason; and if punishment is inflicted for any other reason whatever than because it is merited by wrong, it is a gross immorality, a crying injustice, an abominable crime and not what it pretends to be.[1]

'We pay the penalty because we owe it.' The metaphor by which wrongdoers

* Excerpted from MOBERLY, THE ETHICS OF PUNISHMENT (1968) by permission of Archon Books and Faber & Faber Ltd.

[1] F. H. Bradley, *Ethical Studies*, pp. 24–5.

are pictured as incurring a debt is persistent[2] and calls for further examination. It is insisted on in Bradley's discussion,

> To give an account to the tribunal means to have one's reckoning settled. It implies that, when the tribunal has done with us, we do not remain, if we were so before, either creditors or debtors. We pay what we owe; or we have that paid to us which is our due, which is owed to us (what we deserve). Further, because the court is no civil court between man and man, that which is owed to us is what *we pay* . . . In short, there is but one way to settle accounts; and that way is punishment, which is due to us, and therefore is assigned to us.[3]

This passage suggests the following reflections:

(a) A debt is something which cannot be ignored. Sooner or later, in a properly organized society, it must be paid. A man must meet his obligations.

(b) To ask for payment may be a mark of respect to the debtor. It is to assume that he is a responsible and honourable person, prepared to meet his liabilities. For a creditor to waive repayment, or to refuse to accept it, can sometimes be an insult.

(c) This is partly because repayment is a means of the debtor's quittance. He has settled his account and can retain his self-respect. If his punishment is viewed as exaction of a debt, it need not be an unfriendly act; it may even do him a service, while to refrain from punishing would be to do him a disservice; *nulla poena, quanta poena.*

(d) Here is the truth underlying Bradley's description of the debt as two-sided, which at first may seem merely fanciful. Punishment is not only owed to society *by* the criminal; it is also owed by society *to* the criminal. It is his 'due.'[4] To refrain from punishing would be to act like a complaisant moneylender, who encourages his victim to plunge deeper and deeper into debt. So far then, retributive punishment is conceived as a privilege of the criminal. When he has done wrong, he has a *right* to be punished as an alternative to a still worse fate.

The conception of the nature and grounds of retributive punishment here adumbrated needs further development.

(a) Such punishment presumes the offender's *guilt.* It is incurred only by a person who has done wrong and who is held to account for that wrong, because, as a person, he is held to be responsible for his actions. An infant, an idiot, or a beast of prey, cannot properly incur punishment, offensive and dangerous though the idiot or the beast may be and drastically though they may be treated. No doubt men may feel towards snakes an elemental antipathy and revulsion, deeper than any they can feel towards a fellow man; but snakes only act after their kind. It is only another person who can reasonably be blamed and can thus incur the particular kind of antagonism which retributive punishment expresses. Indeed only a blameworthy person can reasonably be punished, and he is punished for an evil deed which *ex hypothesi* was perverse and unnatural. It follows that, though he did it voluntarily, it is alien to his essential being.

[2] Cf. Winston Churchill, speaking as Home Secretary in the House of Commons, in 1910 of convicted criminals. 'Those who have paid their "due" in the hard coinage of punishment.' (Quoted by Sir Evelyn Ruggles-Brise, *The English Prison System,* Macmillan & Co., London, 1921, p. 4, 1912.)

[3] Op. cit., p. 54.

[4] Contrast Puffendorf, *The Law of Nature and of Nations,* Book viii, ch. 3. 'The obligation to punish is not to the offender but to the Commonwealth.'

(b) It is only a *traitor,* and not an alien enemy, who can reasonably be punished. Society's behaviour towards such an enemy and towards a delinquent citizen respectively may *seem* to be the same since, towards each, it is aggressive and militant. But the underlying temper is very different. Antagonism towards a delinquent citizen may be more sharp but it is less fundamental. The difference corresponds to a distinction which St. Thomas Aquinas draws between 'Hatred and Anger.'

> 'Hatred,' he says, 'is felt towards a whole class in virtue of some common quality; but Anger is felt only towards an individual who acts.'[5]

For rational anger at least—as distinct from non-rational animal anger—is only felt towards one who is himself animate and rational. So a man may hate snakes but he can reasonably be angry only with his fellow men. Anger is only felt towards those with whom we have relations of justice; it is evoked not by 'damage' but only by 'injury,' i.e. wrongful damage. Hence it implies some magnitude and arduousness in its object as well as in the degree of vengeance taken.[6] Again hatred aims at unmitigated evil for its objects, and ultimately at their destruction; but anger does not aim at evil without qualification. On the other hand, anger, unlike hatred, aims directly at causing pain to him who is its object and at opening his eyes to the cause of his pain. 'The worse thing is not always the more distressing' and, conversely, the more distressing is not always intrinsically the worse.

Unlike hatred, anger implies some interest in the individual who is its immediate object. For that reason it has about it a fire and energy which is lacking in hatred, but it is far less deadly. The one seeks to wound, the other to destroy. To stick pins into people merely for the sake of hurting, is no doubt sadistic and pathological. But to stick pins into a man who is far gone in a deadly coma, and so to sting him into some sense of his condition and into a strenuous effort to save himself, has no such sinister character. So with the evildoer, the pain which it is sought to induce in him is the salutary pain of ruing his deed and of being ashamed of himself. His best friend must desire him to 'suffer the particular pain of seeing the hideousness of his present self.'[7] But an intention to make a man ashamed of himself and an intention to destroy him are quite distinct, and they cannot rationally be directed at one and the same time against the same person.

(c) Though, when we punish, our immediate concern may be to inflict pain on the wrongdoer, it is here implied that our attitude to him is not unmitigatedly hostile. The wrongdoer has been our fellow-citizen and he may be so again; basically he is friend and not enemy,[8] and to recognize this must

[5] *Summa Theologiae,* ii, ii, question 158.

[6] We destroy a snake or a man-eating tiger with no compunction whatever; but it would be senseless to be angry with either. We blame, and perhaps we punish, a bully or a thief, because he ought to have known better; but we should not ordinarily feel justified in putting him to death. Aristotle had made the same point long before (*Politics,* iv, ch. 7, ss. 7 and 8). High-mettled and liberal-minded men only react with ferocity when they are despitefully used by their own familiar friends, i.e. by those from whom they had a right to expect goodwill.

[7] Edwyn Bevan, *Symbolism and Belief,* Allen & Unwin, London 1938, p. 233.

[8] This is the exact contrary of the attitude expressed and extolled by Dr. Frank, one of the

affect profoundly the way we are to treat him. The very same quality in him which makes it worth while to be indignant with him at all makes it wrong to allow indignation to monopolize our minds or even to dominate them.[9] Anyone who acts on an exclusively retributive principle is at fault. When punishing, he remembers that the wrongdoer is a man and a fellow-citizen, for the purpose of stoking his own wrath, but not for the purpose of transcending that wrath.

This is not a hostile criticism made against the retributive theory by opponents. It is inherent in the logic of the theory itself, as is abundantly illustrated in the works of Kant and Hegel, and of such English writers as Bradley and Bosanquet. This is seen in the constant recurrence of two ideas which, at first sight, are highly paradoxical. The first is that a criminal is *honoured* by being punished, since punishment is an implicit tribute to his status as a responsible person. The second is that he must be deemed, somehow, to have *consented* to his own punishment, and that this consent is one of the chief reasons why it is right to punish him. Both these ideas, I repeat, are highly paradoxical. They are frequently rejected as canting and hypocritical; as conventional pieces of pious humbug on a par with the cliché of odious memory—'this hurts me more than it hurts you'; in fact just the kind of comfortable make-believe with which pastors and masters, and persons in authority generally, are prone to delude themselves. But they are not the idiosyncrasy of any one thinker or school and they will repay closer examination.

'The criminal is honoured as reasonable,' says Hegel, 'because punishment is regarded as containing his own right.'[10] On the face of it, of course, punishment is a disgrace and, in being punished, a man is dishonoured.[11] Yet, to Hegel as to Plato, that is only part of the truth and it is the more superficial part. Rightly understood, a wrongdoer's punishment is a boon to him because the alternative is that he should continue to do wrong with impunity, and that would be his ruin. And this boon is one to which, as a man, a citizen and a brother, he has a claim. Hence, to punish him, is tacitly to recognize his status and, in this sense, is even to pay him a compliment. As a citizen he has the privilege of being punished for his misdoing instead of suffering a worse fate. If the community and its officers fail to punish him, they are neglecting a duty, and that duty is, in part at least, a duty to the wrongdoer himself. They are robbing him of something to which he has

---

Nazi Ministers, in an address to an international penal congress held in 1935.

'The National Socialist State knows no humanitarian scruples so far as the criminal is concerned. National Socialism stands in a position of war against criminal elements. The National Socialist journalist is a fanatical exponent of the principle of reprisal, yes of intimidation.' (Quoted in *The Times,* Aug. 19, 1935.) Here the criminal is apparently regarded as being, like a snake, both dangerous and repulsive.

[9] Thus Dr. A. C. Ewing argues from Kant's own principle, i.e. recognition of the offender's personality, that Reformation has as strong a moral claim on society as Retribution. 'Retributive justice may be a very good thing, but the saving of souls is a much better thing.' *The Morality of Punishment,* Kegan Paul, London 1929, p. 18.

[10] *Philosophy of Right,* Trans. S. W. Dyde, George Bell & Sons, London 1896, S. 100, p. 97.

[11] Every punishment, argues Kant, is an affront to the dignity of the person punished, for it contains a mere one-sided compulsion. *Philosophy of Law,* E. T. Hastie, T. Clark, Edinburgh 1897, p. 244.

a right.[12] On the other hand, if they punish him, they do something, not only to maintain the standards which he has transgressed, but also to promote his own deepest welfare. No doubt a criminal has forfeited some rights by his crime; but, short at least of a capital offence, he has not forfeited his basic human rights. Both in punishing him and in declining to allow its attitude to him to be penal and nothing more, society recognizes *Das Recht des Rechtsbrechers.*

In this region of thought ordinary values are reversed. On the face of it, the wrongdoing seems to have aggrandized the wrongdoer at the expense of other people; more truly, it has impoverished him. To remit his punishment would ostensibly be to his benefit; but, to a deeper insight and *sub specie aeternitatis,* it is seen to be an injury.

> Whom the Lord loveth He correcteth; even as a father the son in whom he delighteth.[13]

> If ye endure chastening, God dealeth with you as with sons . . . but if ye be without chastisement, whereof all are partakers, then are ye bastards, and not sons.[14]

This attempt to knit punishment to the will of the wrongdoer himself is most marked in Hegel and in writers influenced by him. At first sight nothing seems more unreal and doctrinaire. The average criminal so clearly does not will to be punished; he would so clearly evade punishment if he could. Indeed Kant says roundly:

> No one undergoes punishment because he has willed to be punished, but because he has willed a *punishable action.* It is in fact no punishment when anyone experiences what he wills, and it is impossible, for anyone to *will* to be punished.[15]

Thus any claim to base a culprit's punishment upon his own consent may seem to add insult to injury. It may seem only explicable as an upshot of some 'social-contract' theory of society run mad. Yet this doctrine, so often and so naturally ridiculed as preposterous, has some counterpart in the mind of the plain man when he says—as he sometimes does —not only 'it serves him right' but 'he has asked for it.' *'Vous l'avez voulu, Georges Dandin.'* This does not mean that, viewing the punishment in isolation, he has chosen to be punished or even that he may not furiously resent and resist punishment. It means that his punishment is a logical outcome of something which he did choose, and that the bond between the wrongdoing and the punishment is such that the wrongdoer did know it; or at least he should have known, and is to be treated as if he had done so.[16]

---

[12] So Bosanquet argues that—

(a) The conditions of true punishment only exist where some system of rights has been violated by one who shares in it.

(b) The authorities charged with the maintenance of the system react on him in the form of pain.

(c) This penal action upon him should be regarded as an expression of his own will since it is entailed in maintenance of a system to which he is himself a party and in which he has a vital interest.

In these conditions 'the punishment . . . is his right, of which he must not be defrauded'. (*The Philosophical Theory of the State,* p. 227.) N. B. Bosanquet claims that 'this is the theory of punishment as retributive'.

[13] Proverbs, iii, 12.

[14] Hebrews, xii, 7, 8.

[15] Op. cit., p. 201.

[16] Grotius denies that a criminal has a right to be punished. Yet he holds that a criminal's punishment arises indirectly out of his own will. He bases this view on the analogy of Contract. For he who contracts is held to have pledged himself,

So far then the moral quality of the punishment is derived partly from the will of the person punished, in the sense that in the past he has willed a punishable act and, as a citizen, must be presumed to have willed that punishable acts should be punished.[17] But this is not all. In such punishment there may be in fact, and there is always presumed to be in germ, some degree of acquiescence by the wrongdoer even at the moment of his punishment. So far as a wrongdoer has any sense that he is guilty and deserves to be punished, he may fairly be said to consent to his own punishment even while he is smarting under it. A man may say to himself, 'I have done wrong; I ought to be punished.' Where his conscience is exceptionally developed, he may even say to his fellows, 'I demand to be punished.'[18] This is possible in virtue of his dual personality. He is both Jekyll and Hyde; and, as Jekyll, he can approve and respect that moral order which, as Hyde, he has outraged.

He may even take some melancholy satisfaction in this self-condemnation, for he feels inarticulately that it is the way of hope. In assenting to society's verdict, which rejects and condemns his own wrongful act, he holds on to something by which he may assert and make good his continued membership. If he were left to himself, revolving in the vicious circle of his own rotten will, there would be little hope for him. By keeping contact, even at the cost of pain, with the unimpaired moral sense of the community, he is taking the best path to maintain his own threatened moral sanity and to further his own ultimate moral recovery.

Such a sense of guilt in the mind of the wrongdoer may be formulated in a series of propositions:

First, my misdeed is not only something which has happened to me like a misfortune of a disease; it is not only a horrid experience to look back on. I did it and I *chose* to do it.

Secondly, it is *mine*. I am the identical person who did it and it is still attached to me and still characterizes me. I cannot disclaim it. It is a personal liability which I can transfer to no one else.

Thirdly, however disagreeable the penalty and however much I shrink from it, it is *just* that I should pay it and my reason approves my doing so. I know it serves me right.

Fourthly, it is *well for me* that I should pay. That is the way of hope. It would be a misfortune for me to be excused, for that would be to relegate me to a lower grade, to treat me as a child and to deny me the responsibilities and privileges of an adult.

Lastly, given these wretched circumstances, I am even *glad* to pay. As *civis Romanus* I claim the privilege of so discharging my debt and purging my guilt.

But such a 'highbrow' conception of punishment is likely to be received with some contempt by the average man. If punishment is only to be inflicted with the consent of the person punished and

---

not only to what he specifically mentions, but tc whatever is logically bound up with that—*Omnia quae venditionis sunt naturalia. De Jure Belli ac Pacis,* vol. ii, p. 663, ch. xx, s. xxi.

[17] Puffendorf denies that a criminal strictly *consents* to his punishment; but he adds that the criminal did originally consent to the establishment of a social authority and, if that authority subsequently punishes him, he has no ground for complaint. *The Law of Nature and of Nations,* Book viii, ch. 3.

[18] For example Inspector Javert in Victor Hugo's *Les Miserables.*

as a form of disguised benevolence, it may be felt that there is implied an order of society so unlike any that we know and a human nature so remote from our experience that, however attractive, they have little or no pertinence to existing social facts. In Utopia, perhaps, an offender will be committed to prison only when he countersigns his own sentence. If any such limitations were observed in our own world, crime would continue and multiply, while prisons would soon be empty and law courts idle. Even if the demand for consent were abandoned, any suggestion that punishment should be imposed as a boon is generally felt to be too fine-spun to fit the facts.

> If we wish to remain on solid ground we shall have to avow that punishment means the infliction of evil upon the offender, and that it ceases to be punishment when it ceases to be an evil.[19]

This is a natural objection but it is not conclusive. Admittedly we are here concerned with ideals which are very imperfectly embodied in any existing penal system. But it does not follow that they are not embodied at all. It certainly sounds fanciful to talk of a wrongdoer as 'consenting' to his own punishment, but it need not be simply nonsensical as a rather trivial example may show. Voluntary societies have rules and often impose some penalty for non-observance of those rules. For example, such a society may have a Library, and if a member borrows books from the society's Library and fails to return them within the specified time, he may incur a fine. In that event he does not enjoy paying up; yet he may thoroughly approve the system of fines and, in spite of the personal annoyance, he may perfectly understand that the rule must be enforced. Having committed the offence, he is willing to pay the penalty as the price of retaining membership. His only alternative would be to resign.

Of course a State is not a voluntary society, but it is so far like a voluntary society that there are some implied conditions of membership. Communal life is only made possible by a certain amount of common understanding, it is based on certain conventional assumptions. At any given time and in any given community, the understanding may be incomplete and the conventions may frequently be disregarded. But if the facts entirely failed to bear out the assumption, civilized life would be impossible. So it is with punishment. Underlying the temporary conflict, there is assumed a certain community of moral standard and purpose between those who punish and him who is to be punished. A magistrate cannot be assured in advance that this assumption will be verified in regard to any particular delinquent. He can only act in hope and take the risk; and, in so acting, he at least gives the delinquent the benefit of the doubt.[20] But it is only in so far as the assumption is verified that the punishment has any kind of moral relation to the criminal. An offender believed to be utterly hardened might still be sent to prison or put to death; but that could

[19]Oppenheimer, *The Rationale of Punishment*, University of London Press, London 1913, Book II, Part II, p. 247.

[20] Hence the words used by Dr. Grünhut of welfare work in prisons can be applied even to the penal element in imprisonment. A prisoner's punishment should be 'what he himself, in so far as he is reasonable, will see is best for him even though he may fail to recognize it as such for the time being.' *Penal Reform*, Clarendon Press, Oxford 1948, p. 245.

only be in order to reduce him to impotence or to deter others from following his evil example, and the 'punishment' would lose its distinctively moral quality. When we turn from the particular sentence and the particular criminal to the penal system generally and its relation to public opinion or to the opinion of criminals, actual and potential, the same principle holds good. So long as penal law enjoys any moral prestige at all and inspires not only fear but some degree of respect, it is because some inchoate assent and recognition of its justice is genuinely to be found, even among those who are subject to it. Some 'Amen' to verdict and sentence is wrung even from those upon whom they are pronounced.

Of course such embryonic recognition and assent does not necessarily imply that a criminal will not evade his punishment if he can. Nevertheless it has in it the germ of consent, and it is likely to blunt the edge of the criminal resentment and resistance.

> It must be laid down that, in as far as any sane man fails altogether to recognize in any form the assertion of something which he normally respects in the law which punishes him (putting aside what he takes to be miscarriage of justice) he is outlawed by himself and the essentials of citizenship are not in him. Doubtless if an uneducated man were told, in theoretical language, that in being punished for an assault he was realizing his own will, he would think it cruel nonsense. But this is a mere question of language, and has really nothing to do with the essential state of his consciousness. He would understand perfectly well that he was being served, as he would say anyone should be served, whom he saw acting as he had done, in a case where his own passions were not engaged.[21]

At this point a suggestion of Fichte seems illuminating. He distinguishes between two different forms of punishment which he terms 'Outlawry' and 'Expiation.'[22] All society, he holds, is based on a tacit contract, and the logical result of violating this contract is expulsion. As a member of society I enjoy rights and privileges; for example, I have a claim on other people that they should allow me some opportunity of life, liberty and the pursuit of happiness. But any such claim on my part must clearly depend on my being prepared to respect the similar claims of my fellow-members. If I infringe their rights, or if I threaten the whole social order which makes peaceful life possible, I forfeit my own right to the countenance and protection of society.[23] Yet the question still remains whether that forfeiture need be complete or final. In some instances it may be allowable to substitute expiation by punishment as a more merciful alternative to outlawry, just as, in school discipline, a flogging may be a more merciful alternative to expulsion.

The distinction harmonizes with the account which some historians have given of the origin of punishment among Teutonic peoples. The first need of society, we are told, was to repress lawless violence. Crime was originally viewed as a breach of the Folk's Peace and the natural penalty was outlawry—to be put out of the Peace. This is like the doom of Cain—'I shall be a fugitive and a

[21] Bosanquet, *Philosophical Theory of the State*, p. 226.

[22] J. G. Ficte, *The Science of Rights*, trans. A. E. Kroeger, Trueber & Co., London 1889, pt. 2, Book 3, s. 2.

[23] *Merito sine lege perire debent, qui secundum legem vivere recusant.* Quoted Ives, *A History of Penal Methods*, Stanley Paul, London 1914, p. 99, from J. Selden's edition of *Fleta*, London 1647.

vagabond in the earth; and it shall come to pass that everyone that findeth me shall slay me.'[24] The criminal then loses his status as a man and becomes a wolf to be slaughtered as soon as may be, for every man's hand is against a wolf.[25] But the institution of 'afflictive' punishments, which hurt but do not destroy, is an ingenious way of averting the full logical consequences of lawlessness while still upholding the law.

These two ways of dealing with crime correspond roughly to the two different attitudes to wrongdoing, the impersonal and the personal, discussed in this chapter. Hence they may be regarded as alternatives, suitable to different classes of criminal. The utterly remorseless attitude (*Delenda est Carthago*) is appropriate only to the lowest class, the incorrigible; and, where it prevails, *ex hypothesi,* the offender's suffering no less than his soul's welfare, must be disregarded. On the other hand, conscious suffering or shame are essential attributes of expiatory punishment; but such punishment is not inflicted simply as an evil.

As Fichte presents it, 'Outlawry' would seem to be the original norm of punishment, 'Expiation' to be derivative and, at first, exceptional. But in a modern civilized State, these proportions are reversed. Ordinary punishments are provisional and not final; they leave room for an eventual return to normal life. Capital punishment and life-long imprisonment are exceptions. In a criminal's trial and sentence his moral sanity is ordinarily assumed. He is still assumed to be 'one of us' and to have some understanding of the difference between right and wrong and some recognition of the moral authority of the tribunal. *Ex hypothesi* he is fit to plead, he has in him the essentials of moral citizenship. If, with any individual criminal, the hypothesis breaks down, this only means that he is not a fitting subject either for ordinary civic rights or for ordinary penal treatment, and that his proper destination is Broadmoor.

In both these forms retributive punishment is designed to restore the status *quo ante.* Its advocate holds that 'evil calls and cries for obliteration,' and he will not surrender the hope that, in some sense, the wrong can be annulled and set right by some vigorous counteraction of a penal character. Of course, such a hope may be a vain delusion; that we shall consider later. Here it is enough to note that this insistence on annulment is an essential feature of the retributive theory of punishment. But, if so, it is only the personal form of retributive justice that can really satisfy, and if retribution is to be consummated, it must include the reformation of the wrongdoer. Resentment itself demands that the offender's will shall cease to be offensive.[26] If the evil of the misdeed consists not only in its harmful social consequences, but in the perversion of the wrongdoer's own character, it cannot be fully annulled until 'the wicked man turneth away from his wickedness that he hath committed, and doeth that which is lawful and right.'[27]

[24] Genesis, iv, 14.

[25] *Caput gerat lupinum,* Pollock and Maitland, *History of English Law,* The University Press, Cambridge 1895 ii, p. 449. 'Outlawry was a very terrible punishment, little better than the gallows.' (If the outlaw returns) 'It is the duty of every man to hunt him down like a wild beast.' Austin Lane Poole, writing on Plantagenet England, *Essays in honour of James Tait,* Manchester 1933, p. 246.

[26] Westermarck, *The Origin and Development of Moral Ideas,* Macmillan, London 1906, vol. i, p. 105.

[27] Ezekiel, xviii, 27.

Thus all punishment by courts of law has some analogy with two other types of penal discipline. The one is the educational punishment of children by parents or teachers; here the child's own welfare is always the primary concern and some appeal is made to the child's own conscience. The other is the penitential discipline of the Christian Church; here any penance imposed is directed to the welfare of the contrite soul, its effectiveness depends on the penitent's co-operation, and a spiritual director's power to enforce any penance at all depends, from first to last, on the penitent's voluntary submission.

When analysed then, the kernel of the Retributive Theory turns out to be this. Evildoing must be counteracted and stamped out, whether by expiation or by outlawry. But, so long as the way of expiation remains possible, it should always be preferred; to resort to outlawry would be a confession of failure. No doubt it may be less disastrous to expunge evil by banishing or executing the evildoer than to condone it, but the only victory which can be won in that way is a marred victory. It follows that retributive punishment can only give full satisfaction if it takes the form of expiation and not of outlawry. Expiation then is the true norm of retributive punishment, and it is to this that we must next direct our attention. For the other form—suppression by expulsion or outlawry—is, at best, a *pis aller*. In short, retribution, when fully understood, includes the moral amendment of the wrongdoer. Where there is no such amendment, retribution remains incomplete and unsatisfying.

VARIETIES OF RETRIBUTIVISM*

Nigel Walker

One of England's leading criminologists and a professor at Oxford University, Nigel Walker used the honored occasion of his Seth Lecture (1966) at Edinburgh University to discuss the aims of the penal system. Toward the end of the lecture he classifies various retributive positions. His classification illustrates the particular problems which each formulation of retribution solves—only, in so doing, to create problems anew elsewhere. Of especial interest is his discussion of the "sophistication" of distributive retribution.

In its unsophisticated form, penal retributivism asserts:

> *that the penal system should be designed to ensure that offenders atone by suffering for their offences.*

This must be clearly distinguished from Montero's aim, as well as from reductivism and humanitarianism. The genuinely retributive penologist believes that the enforcement of atonement is a proper aim of penal systems whether or not this enforcement reduces the incidence of the offences in question, and whether or not it protects the offender against unofficial retaliation. Indeed, if he is both consistent and courageous the retributivist must be prepared to argue that the penal system should enforce atonement even if by doing so it *increases* the frequency of the offence in question (as imprisoning some homosexuals is said to do), or even if it renders the offender *more* exposed to unofficial retaliation (as the pillory did).

The relationship between penal retributivism and humanitarianism is not easy to analyse logically. It would be unfair to point to the fact that in other centuries or other countries retributivists have supported punishments which here and now would be labelled 'inhuman' or even 'sadistic.' A civilised retributivist would probably accept that certain punishments are too inhuman to be regarded as just atonement, no matter what the crime. If so, he would of course have to give up the idea that every offender must suffer as much as his victim.

Most penal retributivists seem prepared to compromise . . . by claiming only:

> *that the penal system should be designed to exact atonement for offences in so far as this would not impose excessive unofficial retaliation, or inhumane suffering on the offender, and in so far as it would not increase the incidence of offences.*

I shall call this 'compromising retributivism.'

It is a curious fact that people who lay a great deal of stress on atonement as an aim of secular penal measures are

* Excerpted from WALKER, THE AIMS OF THE PENAL SYSTEM (Edinburgh: Edinburgh University Press, 1966). Reprinted with permission.

usually people whose religion promises that atonement for wrong-doing will be arranged by a supernatural authority. The two beliefs are not necessarily inconsistent. For example, one may think that God uses human beings as agents for enforcing atonement, although if this is the case he must be assumed to tolerate something less than perfect justice or efficiency in his agents. Or one may believe that the secular penal system enforces atonement for some sorts of behaviour, God for others: but this view is plausible only if one holds the unusual view that no crime is a sin and *vice versa*. Or one may simply see nothing objectionable in the possibility that many sinners will atone twice—once under a fallible secular system and once under an infallible supernatural justice.

Atheists, agnostics, and people whose religion is not pre-occupied with morals can be penal retributivists with less difficulty. If *no* supernatural authority enforces atonement, and if atonement *ought* to be enforced, it is natural to assume that the obligation rests on human shoulders. In fact, most atheists and agonistics would probably disown the retributive aim. But even so, they are likely to accept several essentially retributive assumptions about the way in which the penal system ought to operate.

Consistency. The best example is the assumption that similar acts must be dealt with by similar measures. Although Parliament, judges, and other sentencers have accepted the notion that the measures which are applied to this or that offender should be 'individualised' (so as to fit assessments either of his culpability or of his prospects of reform, according to one's interpretation of 'individualisation'), in practice great efforts are made to achieve consistency. The lengths to which they can be carried are illustrated by the case of *Regina versus Reeves*.[1] Reeves and another man had been convicted of receiving twenty stolen pitch-fibre pipes. The other man, who had been tried summarily, had been fined £25; but Reeves, who had elected to be tried by a higher court, was sentenced to nine months' imprisonment. When he appealed, the Court of Criminal Appeal did not consider this sentence excessive; on the contrary, they criticised the other man's fine as too lenient. But such was their respect for consistency that they felt obliged to reduce Reeves' sentence by an amount which ensured his immediate release. In other words, although it was within their power to ensure that at least one of the pair received what they considered the right[2] sentence, they considered it more important to ensure that both received the same sentence, and therefore reduced Reeves' sentence to one which they considered inadequate.

Legal Realism. This veneration of consistency sometimes combines with another phenomenon to produce a particularly unfortunate result. There is a tendency (which is very hard to resist unless one is constantly on guard) to regard acts which have the same legal name as being to some extent equally culpable. It is the persuasive effect of a legal name which makes some people so reluctant to accept the idea that some 'murderers' need not be imprisoned. Such is the power of what might be called 'legal realism' that one way of weakening their objections is to reclassify some forms of murder as 'manslaughter,' 'cul-

[1] Reported in *London Times*, Nov. 20, 1963.

[2] It is not clear whether they had in mind retributive or reductive rightness.

pable homicide,' 'child destruction,' or 'infanticide.' Again, people who use the word 'murder' to support the present prohibition on abortion are exploiting our legal realism.

Irrevocability. Another retributive aspect of sentences is their theoretical irrevocability. It is true that this can be explained historically (hanging, mutilation, branding, and whipping could not be undone); and that the principle of irrevocability has been modified to a considerable extent by expedients such as the appeal against sentence, the use of the prerogative of mercy, and remission of prison sentences and release on licence. But expedients such as these serve to emphasise the difficulty which we have in ridding ourselves of the assumption that the sentence of the court is not to be interfered with later. One can try to justify this on the grounds that the possibility of later modification would weaken the deterrent effect of sentences (although, if so, it is inconsistent of us to allow courts to remove disqualifications from driving). But the real justification is certainly the assumption that the sentence is retributively appropriate, and that what is retributively appropriate today cannot cease to be so at a later date.

Harm. Another assumption which is built upon a retributive foundation is that the severity of the sentence should be related to the amount of harm done by the offence. This assumption is embodied in statutes which provide lesser maximum penalties for unsuccessful attempts than for successful attempts. Even offences which are committed unintentionally are sometimes distinguished in this way: the maximum penalty for dangerous driving is two years' imprisonment, but for causing death by dangerous driving it is five years. Statutes apart, sentencers are often moved to leniency by the argument that the offender has undone, or partially undone, the harm resulting from his offence. The petty embezzler who is able to say that he has paid back most of the money often earns a favourable comment and a lighter sentence from the court.

It is true that some retributivists would repudiate these naive distinctions, and would argue that the amount of blame and therefore the severity of the penalty should be governed by the offender's intentions and not by the actual result. The view that the severity of punishment should depend upon the harm done is thus only a natural and not a necessary inference from the retributive view of penal measures.

But the greater the emphasis which the retributivist places on the offender's state of mind the harder it is to be sure that penal measures are achieving the aim of enforcing atonement. For if the atonement must be appropriate not to the harm done, but to the state of mind in which the offender did it, the task of ensuring that the severity of the punishment shall be fairly adjusted becomes very difficult indeed. So obvious is this difficulty that at least one religion assumes (or used to assume) the existence of a full-time angel for the purpose, endowed with complete insight into the minds and hearts of men, and known as 'The Recording Angel.'

It is true that the impossibility of complete accuracy is not a conclusive objection. Rough justice is usually considered better than no justice. But even a penal system whose *sole* objective was the enforcement of appropriate atonement would be very rough indeed; and if other objectives are accepted as proper it is very doubtful whether it can be regarded as achieving even the roughest sort of retributive justice. The reduction of the frequency of certain types of behaviour may necessitate prolonged detention of the very offenders who are least able to control their behaviour, and therefore, on retributive principles, the least culpable.

Doli Capax. Another example of this paradox is the legal maxim which—in theory always and in practice occasionally—guides English courts in deciding whether a child between his tenth and fourteenth birthdays should be 'found guilty' of an offence. Scottish courts seem to have abandoned the principle some time in the nineteenth century. But in England, even if it is clear that the child performed an act prohibited by the criminal law, it is presumed that he did not know that he was doing 'wrong'[3] unless evidence is given which makes it probable that he did know; and if no such evidence is given he should be acquitted. If this principle were conscientiously applied, the result would be that the young thief who did not know that stealing is wrong would be exempt from interference by the penal system, while the young thief who did could be dealt with. Yet if anything the one who did not know that stealing is wrong or illegal would be in greater need of intervention, since a boy of ten or eleven who does not know this must either be very abnormal or have had a very abnormal upbringing. It is this sort of paradox which the Kilbrandon Committee's approach (1964) will eventually abolish.

But perhaps the hardest question which the retributivist has to answer is 'How should we decide the form or degree of suffering which is appropriate to the offence?' (a question which must be answered whether the offence consists of the harm done or the harm attempted). This question is least difficult to answer if one takes the unsophisticated view that the punishment which is retributively most appropriate is that which most closely resembles the offence. It is on this view that capital punishment is the right way to enforce atonement for murder, although in civilised societies it is not carried to the logical extreme at which the murderer's choice of weapons is imitated. Imitation is recognised to be either too inhumane or too impracticable, depending on the circumstances; but once it is abandoned retributivists find it difficult to suggest any *objective* measure of appropriateness. Some seem to appeal to a kind of intuition, which seems to be stronger in the case of those with strong moral or religious convictions. Others seem to appeal to a consensus of opinion: if they are judges they consult their colleagues; so do criminals. Legislators consult a wider variety of people and organisations, short of actually holding plebiscites. In any case, one logical consequence of the appeal to consensus is that a sentence which was retributively right in 1966 could become excessive or inadequate as opinions change—a position which retributivists as well as others would find uncomfortable.

On the other hand, the reductivist who wants to eliminate retribution as a penal aim has to overcome at least one practical difficulty. This is the impossibility of exercising complete control over the considerations which influence the agents in the penal system. No doubt

[3] It is not entirely clear whether 'wrong' means 'morally wrong' or 'against the criminal law,' although the same ambiguity has long since been cleared up so far as the M'Naghten Rules are concerned.

it would be possible to declare explicitly in a statute what the aims of a sentencer may or may not be. Something of this sort has been attempted in the Children and Young Persons Acts, which say that in dealing with a child or young person the court 'shall have regard to his welfare,' although it is noteworthy that they do not actually *forbid* the court to 'have regard' to other considerations. It would be possible to enact that in sentencing any offender the court should have regard *only* to his correction and the protection of society, so that it would at least be possible for the offender to appeal against a court whose decision was explicitly or demonstrably influenced by retributive reasoning; but since a fine or a sentence of imprisonment can be imposed either for reductivist reasons or for retributive reasons it would be impossible to infer the intentions behind most sentences.

It would be equally out of the question to ensure that the penal system was *invoked* only for reductivist purposes. Most of the victims who report an offence which has affected them personally do so in order to retaliate against the offender. Consequently even if it were possible to devise a penal system in which the aims of all the official agents were non-retributive it would be impossible to prevent the public from using it for retributive purposes.

These practical limitations, however, are not arguments in favour of an official retributive aim. At most the retributivist can argue that, since penal systems require human agents and since human agents are vindictive or at best moralistic, it is inevitable that a penal system should often be invoked or manipulated for retributive reasons. To which the reductivist can reply that it is at least possible to design a system so that its penalties, even if invoked for retributive reasons, are justifiable by reductivist aims and are used in accordance with a reductivist policy.

If the retributivist tries to go further and argue that the penalties of a penal system should be designed with his aim in view, neither he nor his reductivist opponent can produce conclusive arguments. What the reductivist can argue is that attempts to achieve the retributive aim as well as other aims lead to difficulties, and that even if no attempt is made to achieve other aims it is impossible to tell how accurately one is achieving the retributive aim.

At this stage in the argument the retributivist might retort that the reductivist is no better able to tell when *he* is succeeding in *his* aim of reducing the frequency of the behaviour of which the penal system takes notice. It is true that the difficulties of measuring the success of reductivist measures are all too great. But this is a debating point rather than a genuine *tu quoque*. In the first place, the difficulties of assessing reductive efficacy are practical rather than theoretical, and are therefore not impossible to overcome, as some recent research has shown; whereas the difficulties of assessing retributive accuracy are theoretical, fundamental, and insuperable. Secondly, even if this difference did not exist, the reductivist is aiming only at efficacy, whereas the retributivist is aiming at accuracy. In other words, reductivists' mistakes at worst make them less effective than they would like to be, but retributivists' mistakes have consequences which, on their own assumptions, are moral 'injustices,' and therefore more serious.

I must now repeat a point which I

made at the outset. Since I have been discussing *penal* retributivism—that is, the view that retributive justice in some form should be an aim or principle of penal systems—I am not saying anything about retributivism in its other aspects. For example, I am not condemning either the morality or the logic of the view that there are acts which, as 'sins,' call for atonement. It seems to me inevitable that at our present early stage in our cultural evolution most people should feel vindictive towards someone who has harmed them or their friends or kin; inevitable, too, that some people should feel a slightly more disinterested vindictiveness when someone whom they do not know is harmed; and inevitable that this feeling should be promoted to the status of morality—divinely approved or otherwise—by the notion of retribution. Private feelings of this sort are not to be abolished by rational argument. Moreover, the same person can quite consistently feel vindictive or retributive towards people who have infringed the criminal code, and yet believe that his private feelings are irrelevant to the question 'What should be the aims of the penal system?'

But these observations allow the penal retributivist to fire two more shots. Private feelings of this sort, he can argue, may be *consistent* with a pure reductivism in the penal system, but will they tolerate it? Must not the penal policy-maker ensure that his system satisfies the retributive demands of a man in the street, especially if the latter no longer has sufficient confidence in the existence of a retributively efficient deity? And since modern penal policy-makers cannot share Bentham's hope that the public can be deceived by making penal measures *appear* to be retributive when they are not, penal measures must be at least partly retributive in aim. Otherwise, the retributivist might add, Montero's aim, the protection of the offender against unofficial retaliation, might be frustrated.

This argument, which asserts in effect that even if retributive aims are undesirable in a penal system it must embody them in order to avoid being destroyed, would be more formidable if penal policy-makers were faced with a genuine choice between pleasant and unpleasant measures. In concrete terms, a system which *prescribed* a free holiday on the Costa Brava for bankrobbers (instead of merely failing to prevent it now and then) would certainly be so unpopular that it could hardly survive. But, since virtually all penal measures which we seriously contemplate for mentally normal adults are unpleasant (although in varying degrees), it is possible for the man in the street (or on the bench) who thinks that penal measures should be retributive to reassure himself that they are, and indeed to accept an imperceptibly decreasing degree of unpleasantness. What is more, when it is a question of measures for the very young or the mentally disordered, he is prepared even to accept the notion that unpleasantness is not always essential; and it is a fact of penal history that principles which one generation applies to the immature and the insane are sooner or later applied to the mature and sane.

The last shot left in the retributivist's locker is the argument that retribution is after all not an end in itself but one of the means by which we improve offenders. I am not sure that many retributivists would take this line but I have heard some do so. If they believe that it improves secular conduct, then retribution becomes merely another corrective technique in the repertoire of the reductivist. But is this really retributivism? After all, those who argue in this way have to concede that if it is to have this beneficial effect the punishment must be seen and accepted as just retribution by the offender himself. This could have paradoxical consequences. Is the severity of the penalty to be regulated by the offender's conscience? If so, is the man with the tenderer conscience to suffer a more severe penalty than the man who does not admit that he deserves his punishment?

If, on the other hand, the retributivist is arguing that punishment is justified by spiritual improvement, he is asking that the penal system should do the work of the Church. He is certainly entitled to ask that it should not make the work of the Church impossible (for example by placing obstacles in the way of contact between offender and priest). But if he asks that it should adjust the nature of the penalty to assist in the work of the Church he is raising awkward questions. For example, would this justify longer (or shorter) prison sentences for Christians than for atheists? But I do not think that genuine retributivists regard retribution as a means in this way. For them it is an end in itself.

The Limiting Retributivist. There are, however, more sophisticated forms of penal retributivism which must be discussed. It can be maintained that, while penal measures should not be designed or applied with atonement in view, their severity should be *limited* by retributive considerations.[4] On this view, what is done to offenders can be planned with a view to reducing the frequency of repetitions of their offences so long as the principle is observed that

> *the unpleasantness of a penal measure must not exceed the limit that is appropriate to the culpability of the offence.*

In concrete terms, the length of imprisonment imposed on a burglar should be such as to maximise his prospects of reform (or protect society against him for a substantial time if his prospects of reform are small), *so long as it is not too heavy a price to pay for burglary.* A principle of this sort can be used to justify a system which—like the English, and to a lesser extent the Scottish system—fixes the maximum penalties for offences but leaves the court free to impose less than the maximum.

Retribution as a limiting principle must be clearly distinguished from the strong form of humanitarianism, which asserts that there are some forms or degrees of suffering that should not be imposed, however effective they may be from the point of view of prevention. For example, assuming that detention until the age of sixty is the only effective means of preventing a violent recidivist aged thirty from committing further injuries to other people, a retributivist would ask whether the injuries he had so far committed were so bad as to justify thirty years of custody, whereas a humanitarian would ask whether so long a sentence should be permissible in *any* circumstances.

This sort of retributivist—who might be called a 'limiting retributivist'—is less likely to find himself in conflict with reductivists. True, the lower the limits which he sets the more likely the reductivist is to object that he is not being allowed to achieve *his* aim. And when

[4] Longford proposes this in *The Idea of Punishment* (1961).

faced with an offender who is very likely to do serious and irremediable harm for the rest of his active life the limiting retributivist (whose principle allows him to have regard only to the harm which the offender has already done or attempted) is almost bound to want to release the offender before reductivists would. In any case, he must still try to answer the very awkward question 'How do you tell what is a retributively appropriate maximum?' and his answers are no less lame than those of the ordinary retributivist.

Retribution in Distribution. The third and most refined sort of retributivist surrenders not only the idea that penal measures should be designed with an eye to atonement, but also the idea that there should be a retributively appropriate limit to their severity (although he can consistently appeal to the humanitarian principle that some forms of penalty are too severe to be applied to anyone). This retributivist points out that so long as we confine penal measures to people who have committed a criminal offence and do not allow penal measures to be applied to someone who has not, we are honouring a retributive principle —the principle that

> *society has no right to apply an unpleasant measure to someone against his will unless he has intentionally done something prohibited.*

Kant was probably the first moral philosopher to enunciate it, but Professor Hart[5] was the first to discuss it fully, and he has called it the principle of 'retribution in distribution.'

[5] "Prolegomenon to the Principles of Punishment" (Presidential Address to the Aristotelian Society) London, 1959; *Punishment and the Elimination of Responsibility* (Hobhouse Memorial Trust Lecture) London, 1962.

The distributive retributivist is in a much stronger position than his less sophisticated brethren, the ordinary, compromising or limiting retributivists. He does not have to answer the question 'How do you know what penalty—or maximum penalty—is appropriate to this offence or that?' He is not in conflict with reductivists over offenders who seem to need very long periods of detention. For he leaves both the nature and the duration (or severity) of the penal measures entirely to the reductivist (with or without a humanitarian at his elbow); and he concerns himself entirely with the question 'Who is to be liable to whatever measures the reductivist thinks necessary (and the humanitarian considers permissible)?' To which his answer is 'Only those people who have intentionally committed acts prohibited by the penal system.'

Two forms of distributive retributivism have to be distinguished. One asserts that this is the only principle on which a workable penal system *can* be founded. This could be called the 'practical' form, to distinguish it from the 'moral' form which asserts that this is a principle which *ought* to be honoured by any penal system, even if it were practicable to do without it.

The moral version is on the whole harder to maintain than the practical version. Imagine a situation in which it is as certain as it can be that a man will commit serious and irreparable harm—such as murder or mutilation—to another person (he may, for instance, be a jealous and violent husband whose wife has eloped with another man). The only method of ensuring that the harm is not done may well be to put him in custody for a while. Strictly speaking, the moral kind of distributive retributivist is bound to object to this, on the grounds that the man has not yet done something to justify his detention. Or suppose that the man is paranoid, that his murderous intentions are uncontrollable and based on delusion. Here again, if Hart is thinking in moral terms, we have no right to impose detention on him. Yet in both cases we feel, somehow, that it would be wrong to do nothing to prevent murder being done. It is in such cases that the conflict between the philosophy of retributivism and the philosophy of social defence or reductivism seems irreconcilable.

At the moment we side-step this conflict by double-think of one sort or another. If the man is mentally abnormal we expect a psychiatrist to arrange for his compulsory admission to a mental hospital, and we keep our retributive consciences quiet by pointing out that the mental hospitals are not part of the penal system. If he is too sane for this expedient, we expect the police to keep an eye on him until he does something which can be regarded as a 'breach of the peace'—for example, prowling around the house where his wife and her paramour are living. He can then be brought before a court and 'bound over to keep the peace,' although he has really committed no breach of the criminal law. As a manual written by a police officer for policemen says 'this charge is useful where the breach of the peace does not amount to any other [sic] offence. . . .'[6] Another expedient is to select an easily definable and testable circumstance which is often associated with the future commission of an offence and to enact that this shall in itself be a crime. An example is the carrying of an offensive weapon.

[6] J. Daniel Devlin, *Police Charges,* London (1961).

All these represent efforts to avoid the admission that we are officially intervening in a manner objectionable to the person concerned merely on the strength of a probability that he will commit an offence. Our reason for wanting to avoid this is that it would be an admission that Hart's principle of retribution in distribution is sometimes contrary to common sense. To admit this directly seems a dangerous step onto a slippery slope.

Neither of these forms of double-think, however, will salve our consciences in a much more frequent type of situation. Many modern statutes penalise behaviour which is not intentionally harmful, but merely negligent, and do so even if the negligence has caused no actual harm. An everyday example is the offence of driving without due care and attention. Indeed we sometimes go further, and apply the criminal law to situations in which it can hardly be argued that negligence is involved. A shopkeeper who sells adulterated food may be convicted of an offence under the Food and Drug Acts even if he had no means of knowing whether it was adulterated, for example because it was tinned. Such cases worry not only Hart but practising lawyers as well, and they try to salve their consciences in several ways. If negligence is an element of the offence, they insist that it should be greater than is necessary in a civil action, so that it can be called 'gross' or 'criminal' negligence, or in extreme cases 'recklessness.' What they are trying to do is to reassure themselves that, even if the accused did not intend harm, he is to some extent morally culpable. They ask 'Did he know that he was likely to cause it, but without caring?' or (accepting a lesser degree of culpability) '*Ought* he (presumably in a moral sense) to have given the matter sufficient thought to realise what might happen?' (Many academic lawyers, of course, are unhappy about these subterfuges and their objective.) If not even negligence is required to satisfy the statute, so that what is often called 'strict liability' is involved, courts are willing to entertain unusual defences—for instance, that the driver of a car who ignored traffic lights was not 'driving' because he had had a blackout. Or they may convict the offender but discharge him if he does not appear to have acted intentionally or with a culpable degree of negligence.

Our laws for preserving public order, for dealing with the dangerously insane, and for discouraging certain kinds of inadvertence demonstrate that, however much Hart's principle appeals to our moral sense, we are prepared to modify it in the interests of expediency, if three conditions are satisfied:

1. that the danger thus avoided is a *serious* one;
2. that there is some fairly objective and not too crude way of *defining* circumstances in which the probability that the danger will materialise is much greater than usual;
3. that the preventive measures which are permitted are not *drastic.*

Thus while no one would accept a system which imposed death on people who were suspected of hanging around Woolworth's in order to shoplift, it is not intolerable to contemplate the prevention of serious violence and sexual molestation of unwilling victims by measures which involve tactful and unobtrusive supervision of persons who can be shown to be likely to behave in this way.

Another kind of conflict between the reductivist and the distributive retributivist arises when the former considers it essential to deal with an offender in a way which imposes hardship or distress on his family (as a heavy fine or a prison sentence may do). The man who upholds the principle that it is morally wrong for penal measures to fall on the innocent is bound to worry about this. We salve our consciences in several ways. The State provides material assistance to families rendered destitute by the imprisonment of the wage-earner. Judges sometimes mitigate their sentence because of its probable effect on dependents, especially if the convicted person is a mother. The man in the street simply tells himself that the offender should have thought of his family before risking their happiness.

On the whole, however, it is easier to reconcile vicarious punishment with distributive retributivism when the latter is regarded not as a *morally binding* principle, but simply as a *practically desirable* one. If one adopts this practical justification one is prepared to tolerate exceptions in cases of expediency so long as the principle governs most of the operations of the penal system. Otherwise a man could not order his life rationally, and would go about in fear and trembling lest he be locked up because his wife has run away with his best friend. Certainly a penal system which operated in this way with great frequency would arouse so much opposition that it would not be tolerated. *But it is important to realise that the strongest case for this sophisticated form of retributivism is not that to breach it occasionally is unthinkable or morally insupportable, but that to abandon it completely is politically out of the question.*

CHAPTER THREE

DETERRENCE

Deterrence can be defined as the restraint which fear of criminal punishment imposes on those likely to commit crime. As a doctrine, it is hard to find a more fundamental justification for our system of criminal laws. We pass criminal legislation in order to denounce what we as a society abhor. We attach a penalty to performance of the prohibited act in order to threaten those contemplating doing it. The fear generated by this threat supposedly inhibits potential criminals, and society is thereby protected from harmful acts. Nothing more or less than prevention of crime by threat is the norm we use to justify criminal punishment.

It will be noted that punishment is not itself the threat but a consequence of failure of the threat. Only when the threat has failed in a particular case do we apply punishment. When we do so, we say that in order to keep the threat credible we must punish those who break the law. This does not say that we *have* to punish all lawbreakers. Rather it says that we punish in order to threaten. What one suffers is unimportant to the system as long as the suffering of wrongdoers is known to other potential wrongdoers. Thus the principle of *selection* is at the base of this system of deterrence, since its purpose is not to punish but only to prevent by threatening. But selection seems to cut across a traditional and fundamental notion of justice: that all like cases (criminals) should be treated alike (punished). This, in essence, is the frustration which a future-oriented prevention system experiences when it rationalizes its punishment approach.

Other moral dilemmas of deterrence exist. First, the classic case of punishment of the innocent can be raised. A utilitarian scheme of things seems to justify punishing an innocent man in order to improve the threat quality of the criminal justice system. There are several answers offered to this charge: First, the logical answer is that we can't *punish* the innocent, since we have defined punishment as directed only against *wrongdoers.* Needless to say, this doesn't satisfy most critics, who will insist that whatever you call inflicting criminal penalties on the innocent, the dilemma stands. Second, the severity argument points to cases where deterrence is achieved at the price of punishing minor crimes with major penalties, viz., public flogging for parking violations. The answer may be that this type of severity violates the principle of utility, which is a judgment of economy, i.e., the punishment should cause *less* evil than it prevents. It is clear that parking violations are more tolerable than flogging. Another, more sophisticated, riposte is that deterrence justifies no single act of punishment but only serves to justify the institution of punishment. In the case of parking violations it is necessary to question the particular judgment on this criminal sanction from the point of view of the institution as a whole. Third, isn't a system of criminal law which is based upon crass fear-conformity really morally degenerating? The answer to this can be positive, saying that—yes, it is—and that is why we should use criminal law only where we absolutely have to, and use other means of social control instead. The other answer says that criminal law is really a much more subtle product than we think. Deterrence is really much more than just fear-conformity. It includes a whole series of socializing factors which result in law-abidance. To call this deterrence is probably to oversimplify. Punishment is a moral pedagogue as well as—or much more than—an inspirer of fear.

But all of these arguments operate at the ethical level. The real thrust against deterrence as a justification of both the system and particular laws is its failure to produce results. Many will concede the moral argument and say that criminal punishment can be justified by the prevention of crime, but only if it is actually preventing it. This is a factual argument and is best illustrated in the capital punishment debate. Those against capital punishment argue that the death penalty as a deterrent doesn't work. Therefore, its continued imposition is unjustified. There are statistics bearing this assertion out. On the other hand, defenders take one of several tacks. First, one can debate the statistics and say that they are really not comparable, or at least not conclusive. Second, one can argue that much more is accomplished by the death penalty than mere fear-deterrence, i.e., it is hazardous to argue from cases of failure where the threat didn't work to total ineffectiveness. Finally, one can concede that the death penalty is a special case and deny the validity of arguing from it to other cases of deterrence.

But the fact remains that in order to justify imposing any punishment in a utilitarian scheme of things, one has to depend on empirical proof that the system is working. This will explain, naturally enough, the continuous call for research to determine the effectiveness of actual criminal penalties.

A final classification seems in order. It will be evident from the readings that the two dominant schools of doctrinal justification of criminal punishment are utilitarian and retributivist. Classically, the debate has placed the retributivist into the posture of asserting that punishment for crime is a good in itself, since (moral) evil "deserves" to be repaid with evil (punishment). The utilitarian argues that punishment is indeed an evil and can only be justified when it outweighs the good generated by its use. Inveighing against the moral absolutism of retributivists, the utilitarian argues his case on "facts." But one quickly sees that the facts entailed are often the very moral qualities which ground the retributivist argument: respect for authority, public denunciation of wrongdoing, law-abidance, all become "facts" to be calculated by the utilitarian in weighing the gains and losses of the penal system.

The reader will find Professors Benn and Peters' exposition of the philosophical case for deterrence clear and concise, though at a crucial point the authors seem to hesitate. Does utilitarian ethics really justify punishing the innocent? No unambiguous answer emerges. The next case made for deterrence is so muted that one may suspect that Herbert Packer is really half retributivist. His point seems to be a defense of a utilitarian justification of punishment in the context of a traditional retributivist (and moral) explanation of common law criminal jurisprudence.

Utilitarians, it is said, have asserted far more than they have proved. This point is both admitted and denied by the well-known Norwegian jurist Johannes Andenaes, whose defense of deterrence as the best rationale for punishment is internationally known. For this author the very term *deterrence* has unfortunately reduced the field of inquiry to the question of the fear generated by the threat of punishment. Calling for more research, he directs attention to the broader aspects of "general prevention," which, besides fear, involve other socializing factors which may bring about habitual law-abidance.

A final selection is devoted to a pursuit of the tantalizing subjects broached by Professor Andenaes. In it Professor Gordon Hawkins adopts a sympathetic but critical view of the "moralizing" potential of deterrence. He attempts to show that while the presence of punishment in society may well clarify a sense of right and wrong, it is a morality that is no broader than the criminal laws of that society. While this interpretation takes us beyond the crude model of deterrence as creating conformity through fear, it is a good way off from an ethic of right and wrong on which retributivists would base their explanation of punishment.

THE UTILITARIAN CASE FOR DETERRENCE*

Stanley I. Benn and Richard S. Peters

Professors Stanley I. Benn and Richard S. Peters, both British philosophers, argue in their book Social Principles and the Democratic State *for an ethic of social utility. In the excerpt given below, they defend punishment on grounds that, as an institution, punishment creates less evil than it causes and thus fulfills Bentham's principle of utility. In so doing, the authors attempt to answer the hard case raised by utilitarianism: the punishment of the innocent person for purposes of social gains. Their success in meeting the arguments against such a position depends heavily on an acceptance of rule-utilitarianism, which may appear more a postponement of the question than an answer.*

Bentham's case is that punishment is a technique of social control which is justified so long as it prevents more mischief than it produces. At the point where the damage to the criminal outweighs the expected advantage to the rest of society, it loses that justification. As a technique, it operates advantageously in three ways (though these need not exhaust the possibilities): by reforming the criminal, by preventing him (e.g. by death or imprisonment) from repeating the offence, and by deterring others from like offences.

i. Reformation. Not all theories dealing with the reform of criminals are theories of punishment, in our sense. We must distinguish theories dealing with reformative measures to *accompany* the punishment from those which hold that the suffering intrinsic to the idea of punishment is itself reformative. Detention in a mental hospital may not be in itself an essential part of the process of curing mental disorders, though it may provide a convenient opportunity for psychotherapy. Similarly, prison reformers concerned with the moral re-education of criminals are offering theories of punishment in a strict sense only if they expect the suffering involved in loss of liberty, prison discipline, etc. itself to lead to reformation. This is important, for though reformative treatment might cure criminal inclinations by relaxing the rigours of punishment, it might still defeat the ends of punishment, if it reduced the deterrent effects for others.

'Reformation' is in any case ambiguous. A prison sentence may persuade a man that 'crime does not pay'; but in that case he is as much deterred by example as anyone who learns the lesson at second hand. He would be a 'reformed character' only if he showed remorse for his past misdeeds, and resolved not to re-

* Reprinted with permission of The Macmillan Company and George Allen & Unwin Ltd. from Social Principles and the Democratic State by Stanley L. Benn and Richard S. Peters.

peat them, not through fear of further punishment, but simply because they were wrong. It is questionable whether punishment produces this sort of moral reformation in very many cases. Some offenders may be shaken by imprisonment into reflecting on their behaviour and resolve to do better; it is at least as likely, however, that the blow to self-respect, and criminal associations, may lead to moral deterioration. We attempt to reform first offenders by passing them over to the probation officer, rather than to the prison warder. There is, however, the further point that, no matter how humane the intentions of the officials providing reformative treatment, it will almost certainly be accompanied by some compulsion and carry some elements of stigma and rebuke, which would tend to act as deterrents.

This is not to say that punishment is never justifiable as reformative; but it is questionable, on utilitarian grounds, whether the reformative benefits alone of the institution would justify it.

ii. Prevention. Similarly, though we should not regard it as the *main* purpose of punishment to prevent crime by removing or otherwise disabling the potential criminal, this aim is recognized, in long terms of 'preventive detention' for hardened criminals, and in sentences of transportation and deportation. The death penalty is thought by some to be similarly justified. It is clear, however, that the case for punishment as prevention is convincing only for criminals with several convictions; for in other cases we are not entitled to assume that the offender would repeat his crime.

iii. Deterrence. The strongest utilitarian case for punishment is that it serves to deter potential offenders by inflicting suffering on actual ones. On this view, punishment is not the main thing; the technique works by threat. Every act of punishment is to that extent an admission of failure, and we punish only that the technique may retain some effectiveness in the future. The problem of justifying punishment arises only because the technique is not completely effective; if it were, there would be nothing to justify.

Retributivists do not of course deny that punishment can act in these ways, nor that it has these advantages. They maintain only that they are incidental, and that a system of punishment devised solely on these principles would lead to monstrous injustices, which we shall consider in the next section. However that may be, it is evident that while the utilitarian can provide *some* sort of justification, the retributivist is either offering utilitarian arguments in disguise, or virtually denying that punishment in general needs any justification at all. Of course there is no arguing with him if he *consistently* takes his stand on the intuition that there ought to be punishment. If a retributivist just insists that it is morally repugnant that a man should do an injury to another man without suffering injury himself there is little more to be said. For by standing on such an 'intuition' he is claiming that there are no further reasons for his principle. The utilitarian can only point out to the retributivist that a great many people think that punishment requires some justification; that he can provide good reasons for punishing people; and that, though it is intolerable that there should be murder, rape, and dope-peddling, punishment is just one way of reducing the incidence of such admitted evils. He sees nothing intrinsically fitting about this particular way, which itself involves increasing the misery in the world. The strength of the retributivist position lies, however, in his approach to the justification of the particular act of punishment, which we must now consider.

JUSTIFYING PARTICULAR PUNISHMENTS

i. Retributivist criticisms of utilitarianism. Critics of the utilitarian approach contend that it would justify punishing not only the guilty but the innocent too. For if punishment is justified solely by its effects, would it not be permissible to manufacture evidence against an innocent man, in order to provide an example to others? If there were an outbreak of crimes particularly difficult to detect, and if people generally could be persuaded that an innocent man had in fact committed such a crime, would not the utilitarian conditions for punishment be adequately satisfied? Alternatively, if the advantages of deterrence could be achieved by merely *seeming* to punish a criminal, would it not be wrong to do more than pretend to punish him, since the advantages could then be had without the disadvantages?[1] Again, to the extent that the utilitarian relies on reformative or preventive benefits, would he not seem justified in punishing before a crime had been committed? If a man were thought to be contemplating, or even capable of, an offence, might he not be sent to prison and a crime thereby prevented, with the prospect of a reformed character thrown in for good measure?

If utilitarianism could really be shown to involve punishing the innocent, or a false parade of punishment, or punishment in anticipation of an offence, these criticisms would no doubt be conclusive. They are, however, based on a misconception of what the utilitarian theory is about. We said at the beginning of this chapter that 'punishment' implied, in its primary sense, not the inflicting of *any* sort of suffering, but inflicting suffering under certain specified conditions, one of which was that it must be for a breach of a rule. Now if we insist on this criterion for the use of the word, 'punishment of the innocent' becomes a logical impossibility. For it follows from the definition of 'punishment' that suffering inflicted on the innocent cannot be '*punishment.*' It is not a question of what is morally justified, but of what is logically possible.[2]

When we talk of 'punishing the innocent,' we may mean: (i) 'pretending to punish,' in the sense of manufacturing evidence or otherwise imputing guilt, while knowing a man to be innocent. This would be to treat him *as if* he were guilty, and involve the lying assertion that he was. It is morally objectionable,

[1] This criticism is prompted by Bentham's assertion: 'It is the idea only of the punishment (or, in other words, the *apparent* punishment) that really acts upon the mind . . . It is the apparent punishment, therefore, that does all the service, I mean in the way of example, which is the principal object' *(Introduction to the Principles of Morals and Legislation* [ed. W. Harris, 1948] Ch. XV, 9, p. 303). Some 'indirect utilitarians' have maintained that rules must be observed, and punishments inflicted, even when the immediate effects are not on balance beneficial, in order that the over-all advantage of respect for law shall be preserved. J. D. Mabbott contends that this argument could always be met by the injunction to 'keep the exception dark' ('Punishment,' in *Mind*, Vol. 48, 1939, pp. 155–7).

[2] An analogous relation between 'guilt' and 'pardon' accounts for the oddness of 'granting a free pardon' to a convicted man later found to be innocent.

not only as a lie, but because it involves treating an innocent person differently from others without justification, or for an irrelevant reason, the reason offered being falsely grounded.[3] (ii) We may mean, by 'punish,' 'cause to suffer'; we might use it, for example, of a case in which suffering is inflicted where there is no offence in question, and so where no guilt, actual or pretended, is implied. Further, suffering might not be the main intention, but only incidental to some other aim. In that case, it could not be said that as a matter of *logical necessity,* it is wrong to punish the innocent. To imprison members of a subversive political party, treating them *in that respect* like criminals, though no offence had been proved or even charged, would not necessarily be immoral, especially if the intention were not primarily that they should suffer, but to prevent them causing mischief. Persons believed by the Secretary of State 'to be of hostile origin or association' were detained, under war-time Defence Regulation 18b, though technically guiltless of an offence. Critics of the Regulation might have attacked this as 'punishment of the innocent'—but they would have been borrowing implications of the primary sense of 'punishment' to attack a type of action to which these did not apply. For it is only *necessarily* improper to 'punish the innocent' if we pretend they are guilty, and if suffering is essential to the intention, i.e. if we accept all the primary usage criteria. If we use the word in some looser sense, there might be a case for acting in this way in special circumstances.

We are arguing that in exceptional conditions it may be legitimate to inflict suffering as a technique of social control or policy, without relation to offences under rules, just as we detain lunatics or enemy aliens. Such suffering is not, however, in the primary sense of the word, 'punishment,' and is not *therefore* objectionable as 'punishment of the innocent' (though it may be on other grounds). It is only when it is deliberately inflicted on the pretext of guilt that it is open to the retributivist objections. The short answer to the critics of utilitarian theories of punishment, is that they are theories of 'punishment,' not of *any* sort of technique involving suffering.

It might be objected that we are seeking to answer a moral objection with a definition. For why should we stop short at inflicting suffering on *offenders?* Supposing we could protect society yet further by having a rule that authorised inflicting suffering on, say, the relatives of offenders, if the actual offenders had vanished or escaped abroad? Though it might be strictly inaccurate to describe such a system as 'punishment' it might well serve the same purpose as punishment. Such a system would be highly objectionable, at any rate in any ordinary circumstances; but could it not be justified by the utilitarian procedure of appealing to the net advantage of having such a system?

On a crude understanding of utilitarianism, it could; but it would leave out of account the considerations of impartiality and respect for persons which we have argued are as necessary to the idea of morality as regard for consequences. It is not inconsistent with regarding a man as a source of claims, with ends of his own deserving of respect, to have a system of punishment which lays it

[3] A. Quinton, 'On Punishment,' in *Philosophy, Politics, and Society* (ed. P. Laslett, 1956).

down that people who choose to break rules suffer penalties. In a sense, to have *rules* forbidding certain types of conduct commits us to doing *something* to discourage people from breaking them. As a responsible person, the potential offender can decide whether to put himself in the class of persons liable to punishment. But this is not the case if the victims of the suffering to be inflicted are not themselves offenders. They would be made to suffer only as instruments for inflicting suffering on the real offender. Their own claims would have received no consideration at all; nor would they have *put themselves* in the class of people liable to punishment. They would be passive levers employed by society to bring pressure to bear upon potential offenders, without themselves being offenders. This would be morally intolerable.[4]

ii. The retributive theory. We are now able to examine the strength and the weakness of the retributive position itself.

> 'If there is any opinion to which the man of uncultivated morals is attached' (wrote F. H. Bradley) 'it is the belief in the necessary connection of punishment and guilt. Punishment is punishment, only where it is deserved. We pay the penalty, because we owe it, and for no other reason; and if punishment is inflicted for any other reason whatever than because it is merited by wrong, it is a gross immorality, a crying injustice, an abominable crime, and not what it pretends to be.'[5]

What is misleading in this way of putting the case, is that it overlooks the extent to which this is a definition of 'punishment.' The 'necessary connection of punishment and guilt' is a logical connection. It would be more accurate to write 'Punishment is "punishment," only when it is deserved'—for the inverted commas indicate that the sentence is about the way a word is to be used, not about the qualities of the act. A. M. Quinton has put this point succinctly: 'It is not, as some retributivists think, that we *may* not punish the innocent and *ought* only to punish the guilty, but that we *cannot* punish the innocent and *must* only punish the guilty . . . The infliction of suffering on a person is only properly described as punishment if that person is guilty. The retributivist thesis, therefore, is not a moral doctrine, but an account of the meaning of the word "punishment." '[6] This is strictly true, but it presupposes the moral principle, which we have already allowed, that inflicting suffering on *offenders* is the only systematic way of inflicting suffering to maintain law which is morally defensible in most circumstances.

So long, then, as the retributive thesis is limited to saying that no act of punishment is justified that is not the consequence of a breach of law, it is unobjectionable—but its truth depends on the meaning of the words used. This is

[4] It might be, however, that in very exceptional conditions one might take the claims of such people into account, but decide, nevertheless, that it was so important that the law should be upheld that they must be put aside. It is impossible to say, without reference to any particular context, that such a choice would be wrong. But it would have to be a *choice:*—maintaining the law would have to be quite deliberately chosen as more important than the claims of the innocents not to be made to suffer without having committed an offence. On occasion, a schoolmaster may feel justified in punishing a whole class of boys, if he cannot find the actual offenders and feels that it is vital for discipline that the guilty shall not escape unpunished.

[5] *Ethical Studies* [2nd edn., 1927], pp. 26–27.

[6] Quinton, *op. cit.* p. 96.

not however the only interpretation that could be put on retributive theory. For it might be held that the theory points to a close connection between punishment and *moral* guilt.[7] The connection however cannot be very close. For moral guilt is not a *sufficient* condition of punishment, there being many offences like lying, which are moral offences, but which are not dealt with as punishable offences, like making false declarations of income to the Inspector of Taxes. It is difficult to maintain even that moral guilt is a *necessary* condition for punishment. For since it is the duty of the judge to apply law as it is, not to question its morality, from his point of view at least it would be right to punish a purely legal offence. It would also be open to the utilitarian to argue that, though one might be morally guiltless in disobeying a mischievous law, punishment would be unjustifiable, not because of the absence of moral guilt, but because no mischievous law could justify the further mischief of punishment. It is not a question of what conditions a particular act of punishment must satisfy, but of the conditions that a *rule* must satisfy if punishment is to be properly attached to a breach of it.

[7] Cf. C. W. K. Mundle: *Punishment and Desert*, in Philosophical Quarterly, Vol. 4, 1954: 'the retributive theory implies that punishment of a person by the State is morally justifiable, if and only if he has done something which is both a legal and a moral offence, and only if the penalty is proportionate to the moral gravity of his offence' (p. 227).

[8] Cf. Hume, in App. III to *Enquiry concerning the Principles of Morals.*

It remains, however, to consider how the utilitarian approach should deal with the question of justifying the particular act of punishment. To ask, in respect of every particular case, that it be justified as preventing more mischief than it causes would be to miss the point of punishment as an institution. Once we agree that rules are desirable, and that they ought to take a particular form, there is always a *prima facie* case for applying them whenever appropriate occasions arise. For there would be no point in having rules if, on every separate occasion, we were required to balance the probable consequences of keeping them or ignoring them. Such a process would defeat the very purpose of the rule, which is to introduce regularity and predictability into human intercourse.[8] It would be especially self-defeating in respect of punishment. Punishment would not be an effective deterrent unless it could be relied upon to follow every breach of law, except in circumstances sufficiently well-understood for the exceptions not to constitute a source of uncertainty, diminishing the effectiveness of the threat. This is not to say that guilt should be a sufficient condition, nor even that no discretion should be permitted to judges in deciding whether a particular case called for punishment or not. It means only that guilt once established, there is a case for punishment which has to be defeated. Proof of an offence is sufficient to overcome the initial utilitarian presumption against causing suffering, and the onus of proof then rests on whoever would set the punishment aside.

THE PRACTICAL LIMITS OF DETERRENCE*

Herbert L. Packer

Herbert Packer, a member of the Stanford University law faculty, has written many articles on criminal law and jurisprudence. In the present selection, he defends deterrence as the only acceptable general rationale of criminal punishment, but he qualifies this with a limiting principle of culpability. What he says is that we may only punish in order to prevent others from crime, but that in punishing we must choose our victim from among criminals. His principle of utility, oddly enough, seems to be the very principle of retributivism: blameworthiness.

The position that I propose to elaborate and defend in this chapter can be stated summarily as follows:

(1) It is a necessary but not a sufficient condition for punishment that it is designed to prevent the commission of offenses.

(2) It is a necessary but not a sufficient condition of punishment that the person on whom it is imposed is found to have committed an offense under circumstances that permit his conduct to be characterized as blameworthy.

To locate this position among the various justifications for punishment that we have been examining: it rejects the retributive position insofar as that position views the infliction of punishment on a blameworthy offender as a sufficient justifying condition; it rejects the behavioral branch of the utilitarian theory insofar as that position views the tendency of punishment to prevent crime by reforming or incapacitating the offender as a sufficient justifying condition; it accepts the classical utilitarian theory as the proper starting point for a justifying theory; it views utilitarianism as inadequate to serve all the purposes that ought to be served by an integrated theory of punishment.

My reasons for adopting this position may well start with a reiteration of the point made at the end of the last chapter: punishment is a necessary but lamentable form of social control. It is lamentable because it inflicts suffering in the name of goals whose achievement is a matter of chance. It may be useful at this point to sum up briefly the reasons why the achievement of those goals is a matter of chance.

Deterrence is the only utilitarian goal of punishment that affords a generalized *a priori* justification for the infliction of punishment. It is the only goal we can accept in advance for punishing all crimes committed by all persons, without scrutinizing the facts of the particular case in which punishment may be imposed. Yet acceptance of its existence,

* Reprinted from The Limits of Criminal Sanction by Herbert L. Packer with the permission of the publishers Stanford: Stanford University Press; London: Oxford University Press.

let alone its efficacy, involves a leap of faith. In contrast, intimidation, incapacitation, and rehabilitation are all partial and fragmentary goals, and their relevance in any given case is always at issue. Although it is easier to make an empirical assessment of their effectiveness than to do the same for deterrence, they involve difficult moral puzzles, central among which is: what is the calculus by which one determines whether punishment in their name serves or disserves even the limited goals of crime prevention, let alone the range of goals that a legal system is designed to achieve?

If we could be sure that the threat of criminal punishment averts more harm than is caused by the infliction of even that minimum of punishment needed to keep the threat credible, or if we could be equally sure about the outcome of the same calculus applied to the claims for individualized measures of intimidation, incapacitation, or rehabilitation, we might—I do not say that we would—be able to assert that the prevention of crime is a sufficient justification for the infliction of criminal punishment. But we cannot be sure. Instead, we are forced to recognize the moral ambiguity of punishment even when taken on its own terms for the narrow utilitarian objective of reducing the incidence of criminal behavior. And for that reason, limits need to be placed on the adoption of the utilitarian stance, whether in its classical form of reliance on deterrence or in its modern, behavioral form of reliance on individualized measures of intimidation, incapacitation, and reform. There are other reasons, which we shall come to shortly, for skepticism about the utilitarian stance, reasons having to do with values that transcend the goal of crime prevention. The point being made here meets the utilitarian crime prevention argument on its own ground: if the utilitarian calculus yielded a clear answer, it might be justifiable to ignore the issue of moral blameworthiness or culpability in setting forth the rationale, and hence the limiting doctrines, of the criminal law. But it does not, and we cannot.

I shall not try to define culpability, but shall merely identify what kind of thing or quality is meant by it in this discussion. It is, in any event, better described than defined. By culpability, I mean those aspects of human conduct, as defined by the legal system, that serve, or ought to serve, as excuses for exemption from criminal punishment. These include, as is conventionally recognized, states of mind. They also include the interaction between conduct as it occurs in human events and conduct as a legal construct. . . . Up to a point, of course, the absence of such aspects may also, although it need not, satisfy the utilitarian that a particular instance of human conduct does not call for punishment in the interest of preventing crime. That is particularly true of the individualized measures of punishment applied after the fact. A man who is shown to have committed a homicide through an accident for which he was not at fault does not present a case for social protection through measures of incapacitation or reform. But when we consider the *a priori* justification for punishment—its propensity to deter others from committing offenses—it is far from clear that a willingness to entertain such excuses serves the end of crime prevention.

The argument runs as follows. If people are to be deterred from engaging in criminal conduct by the punishment of those who have done so in the past, it is important that the imposition of punishment be as nearly certain as possible. An important source of uncertainty arises when persons who have engaged in criminal conduct are allowed to present excuses, because it is possible that false excuses may be presented and believed. The prospect that this holds out to others who may be contemplating criminal conduct results in "utilitarian losses"; therefore, the demands of utility require that excuses not be entertained. The idea of strict liability in the criminal law, to the extent that it has any coherent intellectual basis, rests on notions of this kind.

So long as deterrence is viewed in the narrow, crude, *in terrorem* sense employed by Bentham and still prevalent in utilitarian thought, the argument has considerable force. If all that is at stake is the propensity of punishment to scare people, if our image of man is exclusively that of the rational hedonist who will do anything that promises to enhance his well-being if he thinks he can get away with it, then it is hard to answer the argument that permitting excuses weakens the deterrent efficacy of the criminal law. But if deterrence (or prevention) is more broadly conceived as a complex psychological phenomenon meant primarily to create and reinforce the conscious morality and the unconscious habitual controls of the law-abiding, then the flank of the old argument may be turned. Punishment of the morally innocent does not reinforce one's sense of identification as a law-abider, but rather undermines it. A society in which excuses were not allowed would be a society in which virtue would indeed have to be its own reward. What could be more certain to undermine one's sense that it is important to avoid the intentional or reckless or negligent infliction of harm upon others than the knowledge that, if one inflicts harm, he may be punished even though he cannot be blamed for having done so? If we are to be held liable for what we cannot help doing, there is little incentive to avoid what we can help doing. One may as well be hanged for a sheep as a lamb.

Losses may and will occur through the acceptance of false excuses. But the calculus cannot end there. These losses must be weighed against the damage that will be done to the criminal law as carrier of our shared morality unless its reach is limited to blameworthy acts. Unjust punishment is, in the end, useless punishment. It is useless both because it fails to prevent crime and because crime prevention is not the ultimate aim of the rule of law.

Law, including the criminal law, must in a free society be judged ultimately on the basis of its success in promoting human autonomy and the capacity for individual human growth and development. The prevention of crime is an essential aspect of the environmental protection required if autonomy is to flourish. It is, however, a negative aspect and one which, pursued with single-minded zeal, may end up creating an environment in which all are safe but none is free. The limitations included in the concept of culpability are justified not by an appeal to the Kantian dogma of "just deserts" but by their usefulness in keeping the state's powers of protection at a decent remove from the lives of its citizens.

The case for an essentially preventive view of the function of criminal law is unanswerable; anything else is the merest savagery. But a purely preventive view, reinforced as that view is today by a scientific and deterministic attitude toward the possibilities for controlling human conduct, carries the danger that single-minded pursuit of the goal of crime prevention will slight and in the end defeat the ultimate goal of law in a free society, which is to liberate rather than to restrain. Human autonomy is an illusion if we make it conditional on human perfection. As Holmes once observed, law, like other human contrivances, has to take some chances. I see an important limiting principle in the criminal law's traditional emphasis on blameworthiness as a prerequisite to the imposition of punishment. But it is a *limiting* principle, not a justification for action. It is wrong to say that we should punish persons simply because they commit offenses under circumstances that we can call blameworthy. It is right to say that we should not punish those who commit offenses unless we can say that their conduct is blameworthy. . . .

The rationale that I have sketched is a transitional one. As we find ourselves gaining more nearly exact knowledge about the sources and control of deviant behavior, the pressure from the behavioral position upon this rationale will become very strong and may prove to be irresistible. The more confidently we can predict behavior and the more subtly we can control it, the more powerful will be the temptation to relax the constraints that inhibit us at present from aggressively intervening in the lives of individuals in the name of crime prevention. But the millennium will not announce itself with unmistakable clarity. And skeptics about its advent may then as now find some merit in a limiting rationale for the criminal sanction.

In this survey of the general justifying aims of criminal punishment I have taken a somewhat skeptical attitude toward the claim that the rehabilitation of offenders is a sufficient justification for imposing punishment. My skepticism is based on two distinct but related grounds: first, the great uncertainty, indeed ignorance, that presently attends our efforts to reform offenders; second, the injustices, greatly increased by our uncertainty and ignorance, that may be done to offenders who are treated differently because of assumed differences in the needs to which their penal treatment is supposed to respond. I should make it clear, if I have not already done so, that my skepticism is limited to reliance on rehabilitation as an *a priori* justifying aim of punishment; it does not extend to questions about how particular offenders should be dealt with once we have determined on other grounds that the institution of criminal punishment is morally justifiable. The place for operation of the rehabilitative ideal is not in determining whether punishment is justified; neither is it in determining what kinds of conduct should be made criminal. However, once a decision to punish has been made and justified on other grounds, the rehabilitative ideal should be fully used in deciding what kinds of punishment should be imposed. To put it another way, the rehabilitative ideal deserves consideration in evaluating not the propriety of punishment but its severity.

It seems desirable to make clear also the extent of the difference between the views I have been setting forth and what I conceive to be the essence of the retributive position. That position views the imputation of blame or culpability to the offender as in itself a sufficient justification for the imposition of criminal punishment. This view is sometimes expressed forthrightly; at other times it is masked by assertions that punishment on the basis of moral fault strengthens the moral fiber of the individual being punished, or constitutes education for good citizenship, or something of that sort. That kind of assertion has a pharisaical ring to it made less attractive, if anything, by its Pollyanna-ish overtones. Punishment is not a virtue, only a necessity.

The view I take of the role of culpability in the justification for punishment is an instrumental one. I see this limitation on the utilitarian position as desirable not for any inherent quality that it possesses but because it serves ends that I think require attention in a criminal system. It does so in several different ways. First, it establishes a firm basis for resisting the attenuation of the offense as a component in the definition of punishment. Without an offense—a more or less specifically defined species of conduct—there can be no basis for imputing blame. A man may be a danger to others, or in need of help, or any other equivalent in the current cant that denotes an inconvenient human being whom we would like to get out of the way; but unless he has committed an offense, unless he has done something rather than merely been something, we cannot say that he has been culpable. And, it follows from the view taken of culpability as a necessary condition, that he cannot be found guilty through the criminal process and subjected to criminal punishment. A strictly preventive view would rightly see this limitation to offenses actually committed as nonsense. If we have solid grounds for thinking that a person is disposed to the commission of offenses, why wait until he has done so to punish (i.e., rehabilitate and/or restrain) him? The instrumental use of culpability through the ascription of legal guilt prevents this dissolution of the nexus between offense and punishment. Of course, the important practical question is not whether the nexus is to be dissolved, but rather how far and in what ways it may be relaxed. . . . It is enough . . . to note that there are solid arguments for keeping the offense in sharp focus, and the culpability restriction is a good means of doing this.

Another aspect of this instrumental case for culpability is that there is a rough correspondence between the dictates of the culpability limitation and aspects of the desirable operation of the criminal sanction. People ought in general to be able to plan their conduct with some assurance that they can avoid entanglement with the criminal law; by the same token the enforcers and appliers of the law should not waste their time lurking in the bushes ready to trap the offender who is unaware that he is offending. It is precisely the fact that in its normal and characteristic operation the criminal law provides this opportunity and this protection to people in their everyday lives that makes it a tolerable institution in a free society. Take this away, and the criminal law ceases to be a guide to the well-intentioned and a restriction on the restraining power of the state. Take it away is precisely what you do, however, when you abandon culpability as the basis for imposing punishment. While it may often serve the state's purposes not to interfere with its citizens unless they have acted with foresight on many occasions their foresight or lack of it may seem immaterial. If we leave to a purely utilitarian calculus the decision whether a man's innocence or ignorance shall count for him, the answer on any given occasion will be uncertain. Only by providing the shield of a culpability requirement can this desirable aspect of the criminal law be preserved.

Finally, the singular power of the criminal law resides, as I have argued, not in its coercive effect on those caught in its toils but rather in its effect on the rest of us. That effect, I have tried to show, is a highly complex one. It includes elements of coercion and of terror: if I do as he did, I too shall suffer for it. But it also includes conscious and unconscious moralizing and habit-forming effects that go far beyond the crassness of a narrowly conceived deterrence. If it is not thought enough of a justification that the law *be* fair, the argument may seem appealing that a criminal law system cannot attract and retain the respect of its most important constituents—the habitually law-abiding—unless it *is seen to be* fair. And whatever fairness may be thought to mean on the procedural side, its simplest (if most neglected) meaning is that no one should be subjected to punishment without having an opportunity to litigate the issue of his culpability. Even imagining a system in which, once forbidden physical conduct has taken place, no excuses are listened to is enough to show the importance of making culpability a necessary condition of liability to punishment.

I have emphasized in these pages the moral ambiguity of punishment as well as its inevitability. We cannot avoid punishment, nor can we ever feel entirely happy about it. One virtue of the criminal law is that it brings the problem of punishment out into the open. Alternative sanctions that involve many of the same pitfalls may appear superficially attractive because they seem to permit avoidance of the issues of punishment. The issues are still there, although in a less direct and therefore less striking form. Even if by a stroke of the pen we could wipe out the criminal law as a legal institution, we would sooner or later have to confront the triad of Crime, Guilt, and Punishment, and to decide whether we wanted to make them part of a sanctioning system.

It is to the ambiguity, rather than the inevitability, that I want to return in a final word. What should we conclude from this effort to expose the ambiguity that lies at the heart of the case for punishment? If this social institution is indeed necessary but lamentable, what does this mean to the rational legislator, that mythical reader of these words? First, it suggests that he pay careful attention to the limits imposed by the rationale of the criminal law, that he understand them and accept them, not grudgingly as a nuisance or an interference with important practical goals, but willingly as a means of preventing this human agency from becoming tyrannical and in the end destructive. Second, it suggests the need for careful scrutiny of the institutions and processes of criminal justice, and in particular, an assessment of their strengths and weaknesses as modes of crime prevention. Finally, it suggests that the rationale of the criminal law conceals important clues to the central issue with which our rational legislator is concerned: what are the criteria that he should take into account in determining what kinds of behavior should be treated as "criminal."

GENERAL PREVENTION: A BROADER VIEW OF DETERRENCE*

Johannes Andenaes

Johannes Andenaes has been active as a lawyer, teacher, and judge in his native Norway, where he is Director of the Institute of Criminology and Criminal Law at the University of Oslo. His defense of deterrence as the primary rationale of criminal law has been a frequent theme of his writing and has given him an international reputation among scholars. In this recent article, prepared for American audiences, he answers critics of deterrence by showing that the conception is considerably more subtle than Bentham had initially envisioned. But in developing nuances the author seems to so broaden the base of a deterrent justification of punishment that it encroaches on the moral grounds underlying retribution. It is clear, however, that fear of punishment alone is too narrow a view of the preventive effects of punishment.

THE CONCEPT OF GENERAL PREVENTION

In continental theories of criminal law, a basic distinction is made between the effects of punishment on the man being punished—individual prevention or special prevention—and the effects of punishment upon the members of society in general—general prevention. The characteristics of special prevention are termed "deterrence," "reformation" and "incapacitation," and these terms have meanings similar to their meanings in the English speaking world. General prevention, on the other hand, may be described as the *restraining influences emanating from the criminal law and the legal machinery.*

By means of the criminal law, and by means of specific applications of this law, "messages" are sent to members of a society. The criminal law lists those actions which are liable to prosecution, and it specifies the penalties involved. The decisions of the courts and actions by the police and prison officials transmit knowledge about the law, underlining the fact that criminal laws are not mere empty threats, and providing detailed information as to what kind of penalty might be expected for violations of specific laws. To the extent that these stimuli restrain citizens from socially undesired actions which they might otherwise have committed, a general preventive effect is secured. While the effects of special prevention depend upon how the law is implemented in each individual case, general prevention occurs as a result of an interplay between the provisions of the law and its

* Excerpted from Andenaes, *The General Preventive Effects of Punishment,* 114 UNIVERSITY OF PENNSYLVANIA LAW REVIEW 949 (1966).

enforcement in specific cases. In former times, emphasis was often placed on the physical exhibition of punishment as a deterrent influence, for example, by performing executions in public. Today it is customary to emphasize the *threat* of punishment as such. From this point of view the significance of the individual sentence and the execution of it lies in the support that these actions give to the law. It may be that some people are not particularly sensitive to an abstract threat of penalty, and that these persons can be motivated toward conformity only if the penalties can be demonstrated in concrete sentences which they feel relevant to their own life situations.

The effect of the criminal law and its enforcement may be *mere deterrence*. Because of the hazards involved, a person who contemplates a punishable offense might not act. But it is not correct to regard general prevention and deterrence as one and the same thing. The concept of general prevention also includes the *moral* or *socio-pedagogical* influence of punishment. The "messages" sent by law and the legal processes contain factual information about what would be risked by disobedience, but they also contain proclamations specifying that it is *wrong* to disobey. Some authors extend the concept of deterrence so that it includes the moral influences of the law and is, thus, synonymous with general prevention.[1] In this article, however, the term deterrence is used in the more restrictive sense.

The moral influence of the criminal law may take various forms. It seems to be quite generally accepted among the members of society that the law should be obeyed even though one is dissatisfied with it and wants it changed. If this is true, we may conclude that the law as an institution itself to some extent creates conformity. But more important than this formal respect for the law is respect for the values which the law seeks to protect. It may be said that from law and the legal machinery there emanates a flow of propaganda which favors such respect. Punishment is a means of expressing social disapproval. In this way the criminal law and its enforcement supplement and enhance the moral influence acquired through education and other nonlegal processes. Stated negatively, the penalty neutralizes the demoralizing consequences that arise when people witness crimes being perpetrated.

Deterrence and moral influence may both operate on the conscious level. The potential criminal may deliberate about the hazards involved, or he may be influenced by a conscious desire to behave lawfully. However, with fear or moral influence as an intermediate link, it is possible to create unconscious inhibitions against crime, and perhaps to establish a condition of habitual lawfulness. In this case, illegal actions will not present themselves consciously as real alternatives to conformity, even in situations where the potential criminal would run no risk whatsoever of being caught.

General preventive effects do not occur only among those who have been informed about penal provisions and their applications. Through a process of learning and social imitation, norms and taboos may be transmitted to persons who have no idea about their origins—in much the way that innovations in Parisian fashions appear in the clothing of country girls who have never heard of Dior or Lanvin.

[1] See, *e.g.*, TAPPAN, CRIME, JUSTICE AND CORRECTION 247 (1960).

Making a distinction between special prevention and general prevention is a useful way of calling attention to the importance of legal punishment in the lives of members of the general public, but the distinction is also to some extent an artificial one. The distinction is simple when one discusses the reformative and incapacitative effects of punishment on the individual criminal. But when one discusses the deterrent effects of punishment the distinction becomes less clear. Suppose a driver is fined ten dollars for disregarding the speed limit. He may be neither reformed nor incapacitated but he might, perhaps, drive more slowly in the future. His motivation in subsequent situations in which he is tempted to drive too rapidly will not differ fundamentally from that of a driver who has not been fined; in other words a general preventive effect will operate. But for the driver who has been fined, this motive has, perhaps, been strengthened by the recollection of his former unpleasant experience. We may say that a general preventive feature and special preventive feature here act together.

Let me hasten to point out here that so far I have only presented a kind of conceptual framework. Determination of the extent to which such general preventive effects exist, and location of the social conditions that are instrumental in creating them, are empirical problems which will be discussed in this paper. . . .

SOME ERRONEOUS INFERENCES ABOUT GENERAL PREVENTION

Certain untenable contentions are frequently introduced in various forms into discussions of general prevention, and it might be helpful to clear them away before we proceed.

(1) *"Our knowledge of criminals shows us that the criminal law has no deterrent effects."*

The fallacy of this argument is obvious. If a man commits a crime, we can only conclude that general prevention has not worked *in his case.* If I interview a thousand prisoners, I collect information about a thousand men in whose cases general prevention has failed. But I cannot infer from this data that general prevention is ineffective in the cases of all those who have *not* committed crimes. General prevention is more concerned with the psychology of those obedient to the law than with the psychology of criminals.

(2) *"The belief in general prevention rests on an untenable rationalistic theory of behavior."*

It is true that the extreme theories of general prevention worked out by people like Bentham and Feuerbach were based on a shallow psychological model in which the actions of men were regarded as the outcome of a rational choice whereby gains and losses were weighed against each other. Similar simplified theories are sometimes expressed by police officials and by authors of letters to newspaper editors asking for heavier penalties. But if we discard such theories, it does not follow that we have to discard the idea of general prevention. Just as fear enters the picture when people take a calculated risk in committing an offense, fear may also be an element in behavior which is not rationally motivated. As mentioned earlier, modern theories of general prevention take into account both deterrence and moral influence, and they concede that the effects involved may be "unconscious and emotional, drawing upon deep rooted fears and aspirations."[2] This does not mean that one's general theory of motivation is of no consequence in assessing the effect of general prevention. The criminologist who believes that a great many people walk about carrying an urge for punishment which may be satisfied by committing crimes is likely to be more skeptical about the value of penal threats than is another who believes that these cases are rare exceptions. Similarly, a man who views human nature optimistically, is less inclined to advocate repressive measures than a person who believes that man is ruthless and egoistic by nature and kept in line only by means of fear.

(3) *"Legal history shows that general prevention has always been overestimated."*

It is true that in the course of history there have been contentions about general prevention which seem fantastic today. There was a time when distinguished members of the House of Lords rose to warn their countrymen that the security of property would be seriously endangered if the administration of justice were weakened by abolition of capital punishment for shoplifting of items having a value of five shillings.[3] Even today, one might find people with exaggerated conceptions of what can be accomplished by means of strong threats of punishment. But the fact that the general preventive effects of punishment might have been exaggerated does not disprove the existence of such effects.

(4) *"Because people generally refrain from crimes on moral grounds, threats of penalty have little influence."*

The premise contains a large measure of truth, but it does not justify the conclusion. Three comments are necessary. (a) Even if people on the whole do not require the criminal law to keep them from committing more serious offenses, this is not true for offenses which are subject to little or no moral reprobation. (b) Even though moral inhibitions today are adequate enough to prevent the bulk of the population from committing serious crimes, it is a debatable question whether this would continue for long if the hazards of punishment were removed or drastically minimized. It is conceivable that only a small number of people would fall victim to temptation when the penalties were first abolished or greatly reduced, but that with the passage of time, crime would attract the weaker souls who had become demoralized by seeing offenses committed with impunity. The effects might gradually spread through the population in a chain reaction. (c) Even though it be conceded that law abiding conduct in certain areas predominantly depends upon nonlegal conditions, this does not mean that the effects of the legal machinery are not extremely valuable from a community point of view. Let us imagine a fictitious city which has a million adult male inhabitants who commit a hundred rapes annually. Suppose, then, that abolishing the crime of rape led to an increase in the number of rape cases to one thousand. From a social psychological point of view one might conclude that the legal measures were quite insignificant: 999,000 males do not commit rape even when the threat of penalty is absent. If observed from the view point

[2] Tappan, *op. cit. supra* note 1, at 246.

[3] Koestler, Reflections on Hanging 30 (1957) (with extracts of the speech of Chief Justice Ellenborough on May 30, 1810). See also 1 Radzinowicz, A History of English Criminal Law 231–59 (1948) (on "the doctrine of maximum security").

of the legal machinery, however, the conclusion is entirely different. A catastrophic increase of serious cases of violence has occurred. In other words, the increase in rape has demonstrated the tremendous social importance of general prevention.

(5) *"To believe in general prevention is to accept brutal penalties."*

This reasoning is apparent in Zilboorg's statement that "if it is true that the punishment of the criminal must have a deterrent effect, then the abolition of the drawing and quartering of criminals was both a logical and penological mistake. Why make punishment milder and thus diminish the deterrent effect of punishment?"[4]

Here we find a mixture of empirical and ethical issues. It was never a principle of criminal justice that crime should be prevented at all costs. Ethical and social considerations will always determine which measures are considered "proper." As Ball has expressed it: "[A] penalty may be quite effective as a deterrent, yet undesirable."[5] Even if it were possible to prove that cutting off thieves' hands would effectively prevent theft, proposals for such practice would scarcely win many adherents today. This paper, however, is primarily concerned with the empirical questions.

SOME BASIC OBSERVATIONS ABOUT GENERAL PREVENTION

There are other varieties of error about general prevention, but the five types discussed are the basic ones. I shall now state in greater detail some facts we must bear in mind when considering general prevention. While most of these points seem fairly self evident, they nevertheless are frequently overlooked.

(1) *Differences between types of offenses.* The effect of criminal law on the motivation of individuals is likely to vary substantially, depending on the character of the norm being protected. Criminal law theory has for ages distinguished between actions which are immoral in their own right, *mala per se,* and actions which are illegal merely because they are prohibited by law, *mala quia prohibita.* Although the boundaries between these two types of action are somewhat blurred, the distinction is a fundamental one. In the case of *mala per se,* the law supports the moral codes of society. If the threats of legal punishment were removed, moral feelings and the fear of public judgment would remain as powerful crime prevention forces, at least for a limited period. In the case of *mala quia prohibita,* the law stands alone; conformity is essentially a matter of effective legal sanctions.

But there are variations within each of these two main groups. Let us take the ban on incest and the prohibition of the theft, as examples. As a moral matter, the prohibition of incest is nearly universal, but violations are not legally punishable everywhere. I doubt that the absence of a threat of punishment seriously influences the number of cases of incest. The moral prohibition of incest is so closely integrated with family structure that there is little need for the support of the criminal law. Stealing, however, is an entirely different matter. As Leslie Wilkins puts it: "The average normal housewife does not need to be deterred from poisoning her husband, but possibly does need a deterrent from

[4] ZILBOORG, THE PSYCHOLOGY OF THE CRIMINAL ACT AND PUNISHMENT 78 (1954).

[5] Ball, *The Deterrence Concept in Criminology and Law,* 46 J. CRIM. L., C. & P.S. 352 (1955).

shoplifting."[6] And what applies to stealing applies even more to tax dodging. In this field, experience seems to show that the majority of citizens are potential criminals. Generally speaking, the more rational and normally motivated a specific violation may appear, the greater the importance of criminal sanctions as a means of sustaining lawfulness.

Any realistic discussion of general prevention must be based on a distinction between various types of norms and on an analysis of the circumstances motivating transgression in each particular type.[7] This is a fact easily overlooked, and authors often discuss general prevention as if all norms were the same. Probably they have certain basic types of offenses in mind—for instance murder or property violations—but they fail to make this limitation explicit.

(2) *Differences between persons.* Citizens are not equally receptive to the general preventive effects of the penal system. The intellectual prerequisites to understanding and assessing the threat of punishment may be deficient or totally absent. Children, the insane and those suffering from mental deficiency are, for this reason, poor objects of general prevention. In other cases, the emotional preconditions are missing; some people more than others are slaves of the desires and impulses of the moment, even when realizing that they may have to pay dearly for their self-indulgence. In addition, psychiatrists claim that some people have feelings of guilt and consequent cravings for penance that lead them to commit crimes for the purpose of bringing punishment upon themselves.

Just as intellectual and emotional defects reduce the deterrent effects of punishment, they may also render an individual more or less unsusceptible to the moral influences of the law. While most members of the community will normally be inclined to accept the provisions and prohibitions of the law, this attitude is not uniform. Some people exhibit extreme opposition to authority either in the form of indifference or overaggression and defiance.

(3) *Differences between societies.* The criminal laws do not operate in a cultural vacuum. Their functions and importance vary radically according to the kind of society which they serve. In a small, slowly changing community the informal social pressures are strong enough to stimulate a large measure of conformity without the aid of penal laws. In an expanding urbanized society with a large degree of mobility this social control is weakened, and the mechanisms of legal control assume a far more basic role.[8]

[6] Wilkins, *Criminology: An Operational Research Approach,* in SOCIETY—PROBLEMS AND METHODS OF STUDY 322 (Welford ed. 1962).

[7] See Andenaes, *General Prevention—Illusion or Reality?,* 43 J. CRIM. L., C. & P.S. 176–190 (1952). Six types of violations are discussed: Police offenses, economic crimes, property violations, moral offenses, murder and political crimes.

[8] Military forces waging war in enemy territories might be regarded as constituting separate societies in which the pressure toward violations of law and the pressure toward conformity are both especially powerful. "There have been armies having no disciplinary punishments, no dungeons or execution platoons," says Tarde; "in every instance they soon became a horde." TARDE, PENAL PHILOSOPHY 480 (1912). The statement may contain some exaggeration, but there is a substantial measure of truth in it. In occupation armies characterized by strict discipline, as for example the German army in Norway during World War II, plunder and rape are practically unknown, while such encroachments may assume great proportions when the discipline is weak. See RUSSELL, THE SCOURGE OF THE SWASTIKA 132–33 (1959).

Even in countries which have reached equivalent stages of economic development, the cultural atmosphere may differ. After a visit to the United States in the 1930's, two leading European criminologists found that the American attitude toward the law was different from the attitude in the more tradition bound European societies. The Austrian criminologist Grassberger spoke of the lack of a legal conscience (Rechtsbewusstsein) in the European sense.[9] The Swedish psychiatrist Kinberg emphasized

> the apparently slight influence exercised by the penal laws on the public opinion of morals. The legislative mill grinds as it does in European countries, but the average American cares little what comes out of it. His own behavior-patterns are but slightly affected by the fact that the penal law disapproves of a certain behavior-pattern, but so much the more by the opinion of his own social group, *i.e.*, the people with whom his psychological relations are more or less personal, *e.g.*, his family, friends, fellow workers, acquaintances, clubs, etc.[10]

(4) *Conflicting group norms.* The motivating influences of the penal law may become more or less neutralized by group norms working in the opposite direction. The group may be a religious organization which opposes compulsory military service, or it may be a criminal gang acting for the sake of profit. It may be organized labor fighting against strike legislation which they regard as unjust, or it may be a prohibited political party that wants to reform the entire social and political order of the day. It may be a subjugated minority using every means available in its struggle for equality, or the dominating group of society which employs every means available to prevent the minority from enjoying in practice the equality it is promised in law. Or perhaps it may be an ethnic or social group whose traditional patterns of living clash with the laws of society.

In such cases, the result is a conflict between the formalized community laws, which are expressed through the criminal law, and the counteracting norms dominating the group. Against the moral effects of the penal law stands the moral influence of the group; against the fear of legal sanction stands the fear of group sanction, which may range from the loss of social status to economic boycott, violence and even homicide.

(5) *Law obedience in law enforcement agencies.* The question of general prevention is normally treated as a matter of the private citizen's obedience of the law. However, a similar question may be raised about law enforcement agencies. All countries have outlawed corruption and neglect of duty within the police and the civil service, but in many places they are serious problems. In all probability, there are few areas in which the crime rates differ so much from country to country. Laxity and corruption in law enforcement in its turn is bound to reduce the general preventive effects of criminal law.

VARIATIONS IN GENERAL PREVENTION WITH CHANGES IN LEGISLATION AND ENFORCEMENT

It is a matter of basic interest, from a practical point of view, to determine how general prevention varies according to changes in legislation or legal machin-

[9] Grassberger, Gewerbs-und Berufsverbrechertum in den Vereinigten Staaten von Amerika 299 (1933).

[10] Kinberg, Basic Problems of Criminology 168–69 (1935).

ery. Such changes may be classified into four different categories.

(1) *The Risk of Detection, Apprehension and Conviction.* The efficiency of the system could be changed, for example, by intensifying or reducing the effort of the police or by altering the rules of criminal procedure so as to increase or lower the probabilities that criminals will escape punishment. Even the simplest kind of common sense indicates that the degree of risk of detection and conviction is of paramount importance to the preventive effects of the penal law. Very few people would violate the law if there were a policeman on every doorstep. It has even been suggested that the insanity of an offender be determined by asking whether he would have performed the prohibited act "with a policeman at his elbow."[11]

Exceptions would occur, however. Some crimes are committed in such a state of excitement that the criminal acts without regard to the consequences. In other cases the actor accepts the penalty as a reasonable price for carrying out the action—we may think of the attitude a busy salesman has toward parking regulations. Further a political assassin may deliberately sacrifice his life to his cause. But there is good reason to believe that certainty of rapid apprehension and punishment would prevent *most* violations.[12]

On the other hand there is evidence that the lack of enforcement of penal laws designed to regulate behavior in morally neutral fields may rapidly lead to mass infringements. Parking regulations, currency regulations and price regulations are examples of such laws.[13] The individual's moral reluctance to break the law is not strong enough to secure obedience when the law comes into conflict with his personal interests.

There is an interesting interplay between moral reprobation and legal implementation. At least three conditions combine to prevent an individual from perpetrating a punishable act he is tempted to perform: his moral inhibitions, his fear of the censure of his associates and his fear of punishment. The latter two elements are interwoven in many ways. A law violation may become known to the criminal's family, friends and neighbors even if there is no arrest or prosecution. However, it is frequently the process of arrest, prosecution and trial which brings the affair into the open and exposes the criminal to the censure of his associates. If the criminal can be sure that there will be no police action, he can generally rest assured that there will be no social reprobation. The legal machinery, therefore, is in itself the most effective means of mobilizing that kind of social control which emanates from community condemnation....

The decisive factor in creating the deterrent effect is, of course, not the objective risk of detection but the risk as it is calculated by the potential criminal. We know little about how realistic these calculations are. It is often said that criminals tend to be overly optimistic—they are confident that all will work out well. It is possible that the reverse occurs among many law abiding people; they are deterred because of an over-estimation of the risks. A faulty estimate in one direction or the other may consequently

[11] See, *e.g.*, Model Penal Code § 4.01, comment at 158, appendix C at 184 (Tent. Draft No. 4, 1955).

[12] The time element is important. Threats of punishment in the distant future are not as a rule as important in the process of motivation as are threats of immediate punishment.

[13] See Andenaes, *supra*, note 7 at 182–187.

play an important part in determining whether an individual is to become a criminal. If fluctuations in the risks of detection do not reach the potential offender, they can be of no consequence to deterrence. If, on the other hand, it were possible to convince people that crime does not pay, this assumption might act as a deterrent even if the risks, viewed objectively, remained unchanged.

Popular notions regarding the risks of convictions are also likely to have a bearing on the moral effects of the criminal law. The law's moral influence on the citizen is likely to be weakened if the law can be violated with impunity. The law abiding citizen who has subdued his anti-social inclinations might become frustrated when he observes others follow their desires without experiencing disagreeable consequences. He will not be able to confirm that his sacrifice was worthwhile.[14] Violations unknown to him, of course, will not produce similar results. . . .

(2) *The Severity of Penalties.* At least since the time of Beccaria, it has been commonly accepted that the certainty of detection and punishment is of greater consequence in deterring people from committing crimes than is the severity of the penalty. This notion has undoubtedly contributed significantly to the abolition of brutal penalties, and there is certainly a large measure of truth in it. Part of the explanation is that one who ponders the possibility of detection and punishment before committing a crime must necessarily consider the total social consequences, of which the penalty is but a part. A trusted cashier committing embezzlement, a minister who evades payment of his taxes, a teacher making sexual advances towards minors and a civil servant who accepts bribes have a fear of detection which is more closely linked with the dread of public scandal and subsequent social ruin than with apprehensions of legal punishment. Whether the punishment is severe or mild thus appears to be rather unimportant. However, in cases of habitual criminals or juvenile delinquents from the slums the situation may be quite different.

Even if we accept Beccaria's position, it does not follow that the severity of penalties is without importance. It is difficult to increase the likelihood of detection and punishment because the risk of detection usually depends on many conditions beyond the reach of the authorities, and because improvement of police effectiveness requires money and human resources. Accordingly, when the legislators and courts attempt to check any apparent rise in the crime rate they generally increase the severity of penalties. On the other hand, for those who wish to make the criminal law more humane the problem is one of determining how far it is possible to proceed in the direction of leniency without weakening the law's total preventive effects. It is impossible to avoid the question of how important a change in the severity of the punishment may be under standard conditions of detection, apprehension and conviction. For the judge this is the only form in which the problem presents itself.

A potential criminal who reflects upon the possibilities of punishment may pay attention to the severity of the penalty to which he exposes himself, as well as to the risks of detection. He may be willing to run the risk of a year's im-

[14] See Toby, *Is Punishment Necessary?*, 55 J. Crim. L., C. & P.S. 332, 333–34 (1964).

ing to Marxist ideology, this condition will be attained when the final Communist society has been established. The theory assumes that everyone will perform his duty willingly and habitually so that it will not be necessary to use punishment or other means of coercion, and consequently the state will wither away. But as we look at the actual developments within Communist countries we see no obvious signs that the state is withering away or that the police or punishment have been eliminated. Nearly half a century after the Russian Revolution, we find capital punishment used in the Soviet Union not only for treason but for economic crimes as well.

There may be fields where a sufficient degree of conformity could be reached without any sanction, by appealing to the citizens and making it easy for them to conform. But it does not seem probable that such techniques will be widely applicable. If it is felt necessary to interfere through legislation, it will normally also be felt necessary to put a sanction behind the rules. A threat of punishment is the traditional means of enforcement. Perhaps greater imagination should be used to develop alternatives to punishment.

It seems fairly safe to predict that no society will experiment in these matters to the extent of abolishing the basic penal provisions protecting life, bodily safety or property. The involuntary experiments created by police strikes or similar conditions support the notion that a highly urbanized industrial society can scarcely exist without police and criminal courts or a state power apparatus with similar functions. However, outside the basic areas protected by the criminal law the direction is much less certain. The regulation of economic activities through the use of criminal sanctions has varied from country to country. Religious offenses constitute another field in which there have been great fluctuations in the penal approach. Similarly, there currently is a great degree of uncertainty concerning the legal treatment of many activities rooted in or related to sex, such as prostitution, homosexuality, *crimen bestialitatis* and pornography. Abortion constitutes still another category which is subject to differing legal evaluations. Political crimes also deserve to be mentioned. In some countries there is nearly boundless freedom for verbal attacks on the government and the prevailing social order, while in others any kind of criticism is considered a dangerous crime against the state.

Just an enumeration of some of these categories of crimes conveys the hopelessness of treating them as a single unit. Any discussion of the possibility—and desirability—of making citizens conform by means of the penal law must treat each category separately, and it must be based on detailed information about the activity being discussed. "Motivation" and "detection risks" are necessary key words in such a discussion. Prohibition laws in the United States and in some European countries after World War I are horrendous examples of miscalculation on the part of legislators. The experiments illustrate how difficult it is to evoke respect for penal provisions regarded by the bulk of the population as an undue interference with their freedom.

PUNISHMENT AS A MORAL EDUCATOR*

Gordon Hawkins

Gordon Hawkins is a criminologist with a broad background in prison administration and philosophy. As senior lecturer at the University of Sydney's Institute of Criminology, his interest in punishment has led him to expand on a theme struck by Professor Andenaes: that punishment prevents crime by instilling a moral sense of right and wrong. Sympathetic though he is to such a broader view of deterrence, Hawkins believes that there are some sharp distinctions to be drawn between the "morality" generated by punishment and an ethic of conscience developed by reason and insight. One may still wonder where social utility begins and morality ends.

It is a welcome sign that in more recent discussions of deterrence its conceptual aspect has been brought to the forefront. This may constitute one of the most significant advances since deterrence theory was first formulated and elaborated in the writings of Beccaria, Bentham, Blackstone, Romilly, Pailey, and Feuerbach. Indeed, it is probably the most significant advance; for prior to this development, discussion of deterrence has been almost exclusively in terms of the simple conceptual model of the classical theorists.

That model was conceived in terms of man as "a lightning calculator of pleasures and pains," to use Veblen's phrase, directly responsive to systematic intimidation by threat of punishment designed to outweigh any pleasure to be derived from crime. It is a model which plainly fails to fit all the facts. Yet, most critics would agree that the existence of the institution of punishment exerts some control over some types of crime. This conceptual scheme appears to be compatible with some aspects of experience and yet incompatible with others.

To conceive the preventive effects of punishment as simply a matter of deterrence or intimidation is to miss more subtle points which are fundamental; the whole thing is considerably more complex than the classical theory suggests. Classical theory is misleading in that it neglects what is called variously "the educative-moralizing function of the law," "the moral or socio-pedagogical influence of punishment," or the "educative, and habituative effects of our penal sanctions."[1]

* Excerpted from Hawkins, *Punishment and Deterrence: The Educative, Moralizing, and Habituative Effects*, 1969 WISCONSIN LAW REVIEW 550. Reprinted with permission.

[1] "Educative-moralizing function of the law," P. TAPPAN, CRIME, JUSTICE AND CORRECTION 247 (1960); "the moral or socio-pedagogical influence of punishment," Andenaes, *The General Preventive Effects of Punishment*, 114 U. PA. L. REV. 949, 950 (1966); "educative and habituative effects of our penal sanctions," Morris, *Impediments to Penal Reform*, 33 U. CHI. L. REV. 631 (1966).

It has been noted (1) that to the extent to which punishment has moral or educative effects, and (2) that the location of the social conditions instrumental in creating them are empirical problems answerable through empirical research.[2] Empirical investigation requires that we have some idea of the character of the phenomena to be investigated.[3] Yet, both those who assert and those who deny that deterrence is an important aspect of punishment and that the threat and infliction of punishment provide a powerful means of social control, do not provide more than alternative slogans or catch words. And assertions to the effect that punishment has educative, moralizing, and habituative effects have to be formulated in ways that make it clear what such statements mean in terms of practical implications. Only then can there be the possibility of their being tested in experience and by observation. So it is necessary to attempt to identify the empirical referents involved and clarify the issues under consideration.

As a preliminary point, the way in which these educative, moralizing, and habituative functions of punishment relate to the traditionally recognized deterrent function must be considered. Sometimes it is made clear that these functions are regarded as something distinct from mere deterrence.[4] But this is not always the case.

One suggested redefinition of deterrence occurs in the following passage from Professor Tappan's *Crime, Justice and Correction:*

> One difficulty with the classical theory was its implication that prevention occurred merely through repression by fear. Deterrence may be and, indeed, it commonly is defined in this limited sense. . . . General prevention is also served, however, by the educative-moralizing function of the law in strengthening the public's moral code. . . . We would define deterrence as the term is generally used here today as "the preventive effect which actual or threatened punishment of offenders has upon potential offenders."[5]

Unfortunately, this solution of the "difficulty with the classical theory" presents some difficulties itself. It may be true that the classical theorists overestimated the efficiency of "repression by fear" as a means of social control and oversimplified the process of crime prevention or control. It is a different matter, however, to imply that they were mistaken in defining deterrence in the "limited sense" of discouraging action through fear of unpleasant consequences. This not only conforms with ordinary usage but also refers to a familiar pattern of action and reaction. The proposed redefinition does neither for it is unclear what is included within the re-

---

This approach is most clearly and fully expounded in the writings of Professor Johannes Andenaes with whose name it is most widely associated. This commentary is largely responsive to the text of his two well known articles, *General Prevention—Illusion or Reality?*, 43 J. CRIM. L., C. & P.S. 176 (1952), and *The General Preventive Effects of Punishment, supra,* and with the treatment of these topics in his book, THE GENERAL PART OF THE CRIMINAL LAW OF NORWAY 66–79 (1956).

[2] Andenaes, *The General Preventive Effects of Punishment,* 114 U. PA. L. REV. 949, 951–78 (1966).

[3] "To understand a proposition means to know what is the case if it is true." L. WITTGENSTEIN, TRACTATUS-LOGICO-PHILOSOPHICUS 41 (1961).

[4] *See* text accompanying notes 11–13 *infra.*

[5] P. TAPPAN, *supra* note 1, at 247.

drawn boundaries or what is involved in the new concept.[6]

Yet it is clear that something quite different from, and independent of, deterrence as ordinarily understood is involved. For the situation of an individual deterred from offending by conscious fear of punishment is basically dissimilar to that of one refraining because of the operation of some unconscious controls. In one instance, he may still wish to commit the offense "but he no longer dares to do it."[7] In the other, presumably there will be no conscious fear of punishment present and possibly even no awareness of the law or the relevant penal sanctions.

Similar contradictions would seem to apply to some of the other behavior patterns mentioned. Habit, for example, specifically implies a doing unconsciously or without premeditation. When settled patterns of conduct are established, deterrence is no longer relevant, for we need not discourage persons through fear from actions they do not wish to take in the first place.

This is not to say that the suggestion that punishment has general preventive effects other than deterrence is mistaken. But, it seems unwise to formulate a theory of punishment so that those not consciously conforming to a legal prohibition because of the penalty threat are said to be deterred by it. To subsume such varied behavior patterns within one process not only obscures basic distinctions but also begs fundamental etiological questions; indeed, questions which "meaningful empirical research . . . directed toward discovering the effectiveness of punishment"[8] cannot ignore.

Professor Andenaes specifically distinguishes these other effects from "the mere frightening or deterrent effect of punishment."[9] Moreover, he also provides some descriptive detail. "We can say that punishment has three sorts of general preventive effects: it may have a *deterrent* effect, it may strengthen *moral inhibitions* (a *moralizing* effect), and it may stimulate habitual *law-abiding conduct*."[10] In another place, he distinguishes "the *moral* or *socio-pedagogical* influence of punishment,"[11] the establishment of a "condition of habitual lawfulness,"[12] and "*mere deterrence*,"[13] as the three principal general preventive effects of punishment. . . .

Professor Andenaes has written that

> [i]n Swedish discussion, the *moralizing*—in other words the *educational*—function has been greatly stressed. The idea is that punishment as a concrete expression of society's disapproval of an act helps to form and strengthen the public's moral code and thereby creates conscious and unconscious inhibitions against committing crime.[14]

[6] It is true that Professor Tappan says that the "moralizing task of the penal law" is one which "involves the introjection of conscious and unconscious controls against violations." He also says that "the criminal and penal law, in providing standards of conduct and penalties, stimulates the habit of law-abiding conduct: it aids in the conditioning of accepted norms." But the processes of introjection, habit formation and conditioning are not further described; nor is the way which penal law functions so as to stimulate or aid them. *Id.*

[7] 1 J. Bentham, *Principles of Penal Law in* Works 396 (1843).

[8] P. Tappan, *supra* note 1, at 252.

[9] Andenaes, *General Prevention—Illusion or Reality?*, 43 J. Crim. L., C. & P.S. 176, 179 (1952).

[10] *Id.* at 180.

[11] Andenaes, *supra* note 2, at 950.

[12] *Id.* at 951.

[13] *Id.* at 950.

[14] Andenaes, *supra* note 9, at 179.

> It may be said that from law and the legal machinery there emanates a flow of propaganda which favors such respect. Punishment is a means of expressing social disapproval. In this way the criminal law and its enforcement supplement and enhance the moral influence acquired through education and other non-legal processes.[15]

Of course, the idea that the enforcement of punishment expresses society's moral condemnation and, at the same time, helps to form and strengthen the public's moral code is not novel. It is not clear either. But the *Report of the Royal Commission on Capital Punishment 1949–53* not only embodies this idea but also provides a concrete example of how it is supposed to operate in practice.

> We think it reasonable to suppose that the deterrent force of capital punishment operates not only by affecting the conscious thoughts of individuals tempted to commit murder but also by building up in the community, over a long period of time, a deep feeling of peculiar abhorrence for the crime of murder. "The fact that men are hung for murder is one great reason why murder is considered so dreadful a crime." This widely diffused effect on the moral consciousness of society is impossible to assess but it must be at least as important as any direct part which the death penalty may play as a deterrent in the calculations of potential murderers.[16]

[15] Andenaes, *supra* note 2, at 950.

[16] Report of Royal Commission on Capital Punishment 1949–1953, at 20 (1953). Professor Andenaes also discusses this point. "The moral effects of capital punishment also must be considered. It may be said that capital punishment for murder exerts a moral influence by indicating that life is the most highly protected value." Andenaes, *supra* note 2, at 967.

But, what the Royal Commission put forward as a "reasonable" supposition is not entirely convincing. While it may be true that it is "impossible to assess" the "widely diffused effect on the moral consciousness of society," it is reasonable to question whether, if it exists, it can be of the kind suggested. Indeed, over 200 years ago, Beccaria used the same example to draw the opposite conclusion.

> The death penalty cannot be useful, because of the example of barbarity it gives men. If the passions or the necessities of war have taught the shedding of human blood, the laws, moderators of the conduct of men, should not extend the beastly example, which becomes more pernicious since the inflicting of legal death is attended with much study and formality. It seems to me absurd that the laws, which are an expression of the public will, which detest and punish homicide, should themselves commit it. . . .[17]

It might seem, at first glance, that, because of its unique character, the death penalty belongs in a different category from all other penalties and that, therefore, discussion of the moral effect of that penalty is not really relevant to consideration of the educative-moralizing function of other penalties. But the doctrine we are considering might be viewed as little—if at all—more plausible when seen in relation to any other penalty.

For, as Professor Kenny pointed out in explaining the "special attractiveness" of the criminal law both for students and ordinary readers, "the vivid and violent nature of the events which criminal courts notice and repress" is matched by the character "of those by which they effect the repression." He continues:

[17] C. Beccaria, On Crimes and Punishments 50 (Bobbs-Merrill ed. 1963).

> Forcible interferences with property and liberty, with person and life, are the causes which bring criminal law into operation; and its operations are themselves directed to the infliction of *similar acts of seizure, suffering, and slaughter.*[18]

There seems to be no obvious reason to think that any other item from this collection of threats is more likely to engender respect for values than the threat of the death penalty. Indeed, it could be argued that the only sort of respect which systems of compulsion commonly inspire is precisely that which is implied in the concept of mere deterrence and no more.

Yet, this line of argument, which seems to suggest that punishment has no effect, apart from deterrence, which could be described as educative or moralizing, is not only not probative, but also doubtfully relevant to the point at issue. This is because what is called the educative-moralizing function of punishment is largely independent of the nature of the penalties employed. It is true that some penalties may be regarded as poetically appropriate (castration for dangerous sex offenders) or inappropriate (imprisonment in a wholly male institution for male homosexuals) for particular types of offenders and offenses. However, there is nothing in the intrinsic nature of any punishment which makes it either fitting or unfitting. Extrinsic factors deriving from the context in which punishment is used are determinative.

The argument we have been considering fails to meet the point that the educative-moralizing function of punishment derives simply from the fact that "[p]unishment is a means of expressing social disapproval."[19] In other words, punishment is a ritualistic device designed to influence persons by intimating symbolically social disapproval and society's moral condemnation. In this connection, some methods may be regarded as preferable on aesthetic or humanitarian grounds but this is independent of the ritual function. The essential point is that, whatever their nature, "penal provisions may symbolize values which various groups within the populace cherish."[20]

When both this ritualistic aspect of punishment and the way in which the machinery of the traditional criminal legal process achieves "the dramatization of evil"[21] is recognized, it is evident that it is not inappropriate to talk of punishment as in some sense educational. That punishment is effective in conveying social reprobation is clearly reflected in the stigmatization and the loss of social status commonly involved in criminal

[18] C. S. Kenny, Outlines of Criminal Law 2 (13th ed. 1929) (emphasis added). "Criminal law is itself a system of compulsion on the widest scale. It is a collection of threats of injury to life, liberty, and property if people do commit crime." J. F. Stephen, History of the Criminal Law of England 107 (1883).

[19] Andenaes, *supra* note 2, at 950. "Punishment is the way in which society expresses its denomination of wrong-doing." Royal Commission on Capital Punishment, Minutes of Evidence 207 (1953).

[20] J. Andenaes, The General Part of the Criminal Law of Norway 78 (1956). It is, of course, perfectly legitimate to ask why the punishment of offenders should be regarded as an appropriate way of expressing moral condemnation. *See* H.L.A. Hart, Law, Liberty and Morality 66 (1963). But the fact is that such ritualistic procedures have long been used in the sphere of education to foster commitment to values. *See* Berstein, Peters, & Elvin, *The Role of Ritual in Education,* Proceedings of the Royal Society (1965).

[21] F. Tannenbaum, Crime and the Community 19 (1938)

punishment. That ex-prisoners have severe problems re-establishing themselves in society may be regarded as empirical evidence of the stigma's effectiveness.[22]

From this point of view, a criminal trial followed by conviction and sentence can be seen as a public degradation ceremony in which the public identity of the convicted individual is lowered on the social scale. It has been maintained that "only in societies that are completely demoralized, will an observer be unable to find such ceremonies, since only in total anomie are the conditions of degradation ceremonies lacking."[23] Such ceremonies are described as "a secular form of communion" which help to "reinforce group solidarity" and "bind persons to the collectivity."[24] Although all societies do not have "degradation ceremonies [which] are carried on in accordance with publicly prescribed and publicly validated measures" *we* have "our professional degraders in the law courts." For, in our society, it is said, "the arena of degradation . . . has been rationalized, at least as to the institutional measures for carrying it out. The court and its officers have something like a fair monopoly over such ceremonies, and there they have become an occupational routine."[25]

It is, moreover, a mistake to say as was said above that the only sort of respect inspired by the criminal law is that which is implied in the concept of mere deterrence and no more.[26] The criminal law is more than a neutral system of compulsion; respect for legal authority is different from mere response to threats. To ignore this confuses authority with coercive power. Although coercive power may sometimes be a necessary condition for the exercise of authority and for securing obedience, respect for authority depends on recognition of its legitimacy.

It is not necessary to consider here the various principles of legitimacy upon which authority is said to depend, nor to discuss their sociological and ideological bases. It is sufficient to note that in any society, if it is to continue in existence, there must be general acceptance of authoritative regulation as a means of achieving social control. This affirmative attitude toward obedience to rules is probably a more powerful factor than the fear of punishment in securing conformity. Moreover, the respect, or deference, which the law attracts makes it possible for the law to exercise a socializing influence by securing the acceptance by members of society of rules and regulations in areas where custom, tradition, morality, or religion provide no guidance.

That punishment can be and is used

---

[22] *See* J. P. MARTIN, OFFENDERS AS EMPLOYEES 39 (1962); McSally, *Finding Jobs for Released Offenders*, 24 FED. PROBATION 12 (June 1960); Schwarts & Skolnick, *Two Studies of Legal Stigma*, 10 SOCIAL PROBLEMS 133 (1962). *See also* E. GOFFMAN, STIGMA (1963); Freidson, *Disability as Social Deviance* in SOCIOLOGY AND REHABILITATION 71–79 (M. Sussman ed. 1966).

Because it relates to conduct, such evidence is more convincing than evidence derived from attitude studies, the results of which are derived from verbal responses: Walker & Argyle, *Does the Law Affect Moral Judgments?*, 4 BRIT. J. CRIM. 570 (1964). This article reports an attitude survey, the results of which suggest that knowledge that a form of conduct or type of action is criminal appears to have little bearing on peoples' moral attitude toward the behaviour in question.

No matter how much people may disclaim censorious feelings, their conduct is apt to belie their professions.

[23] Garfinkel, *Conditions of Successful Degradation Ceremonies*, 61 AM. J. SOC. 420 (1956).

[24] *Id.* at 421.

[25] *Id.* at 424.

[26] *See* text following note 18 *supra*.

as an educational technique is, of course, recognized even by those dubious about its value as an instrument of moral education. Thus, it is significant that Hart says "there is very little evidence to support the idea that morality is *best* taught by fear of legal punishment."[27] Similarly, R. S. Peters says of the argument that punishment might "help to mark out what is right and wrong and . . . help to stamp in desirable habits which will later make a solid foundation for a rational moral code," that "whether punishment *often* has this effect on individuals is an empirical question."[28] Nevertheless, he goes on to say that "isolated punishments of the 'sharp shock' variety . . . may function in a beneficial way by focusing awareness on social realities";[29] and he also suggests that punishment which brings home to offenders "imaginatively the consequences of actions as they affect other people" may have some "effectiveness . . . in moral education."[30]

These statements do not constitute evidence that punishment does operate in the manner suggested, but they represent acknowledgment that it makes sense to suggest that it might and in some circumstances does. The extent to which it does is, of course, an empirical question.

However, it may be unwise to use the term "moralizing" in reference to this aspect of the law's functioning. There are a number of reasons why this term may be inappropriate.

In the first place, the criminal law is designed to secure conformity in response to sanctions. But the notion of morality, both in ordinary usage and in philosophical and psychological literature, refers to action in accordance with internalized standards or rules as opposed to mere response to sanctions. "Rules are said to be internalized if they are conformed to in the absence of situational incentives or sanctions, *i.e.,* if conformity is intrinsically motivated."[31] Thus, the concept of morality implies internalized values which may call for behavior which conflicts with self-interest whereas the threat of punishment depends for its effectiveness on an appeal to self-interest. And as Professor Andenaes points out, "while the law certainly serves to strengthen the moral inhibitions against crime in general, it is not very successful in pressing upon the public its own evaluation of various types of conduct."[32] Certainly an affirmative attitude toward obedience to rules does not imply even agreement with, much less the internalization of, the content of particular rules. Nevertheless, if this were the only argument against the use of the term "moralizing" it would not in itself constitute a very powerful objection.

Secondly, morality implies more than a behavioral response to psychological conditioning, so that it is something of a contradiction to speak of a "threat-induced conscience."[33] Whether we think

[27] H.L.A. Hart, *supra* note 20, at 58 (emphasis added).

[28] R. S. Peters, Ethics and Education 274 (1966) (emphasis added).

[29] *Id.* at 275.

[30] *Id.* at 279.

[31] Kohlberg, *Moral Development and Identification, in* Child Psychology 277 (H. Stevenson ed. 1963).

[32] Andenaes, *supra* note 2, at 966.

[33] Schwartz & Orleans, *On Legal Sanctions,* 34 U. Chi. L. Rev. 274, 292 (1967). This article reports the results of a field experiment on motivational factors affecting compliance with federal income tax laws conducted at Northwestern University. It is stated that interviews "aimed at inducing sanction threat" produced an increase in "normative sentiments" on the part of upper and middle class Americans. *Id.* at 286 n.45.

of conscience as merely the "exercise of the ordinary judgment on moral questions"[34] or as some kind of internal oracle, we ordinarily distinguish between actions in accordance with moral scruples and response to threats. The antimony is reflected in the fact that conscientious offenders, such as conscientious objectors to military service, are commonly unresponsive to threats. Indeed, by referring to such persons as conscientious we mean that their conduct is governed by considerations of principle rather than material interest. It is significant that, both in respect of conscientious offenders and others, the process of status degradation and stigmatization, which may well be of value as a means of reinforcing group solidarity and social cohesion, relies on an emotive response rather than an exercise of moral judgment.

Moreover, although punishment may in some degree facilitate the process of moral learning, its moralizing role is essentially accessory. This hypothesis can never be entirely proved empirically; for morality transcends the law in the sense that moral considerations belong to a more fundamental level of discourse than juristic ones. Indeed, it has been said that "critical rejection or acceptance of custom or law is what is distinctive of morality. . . . Moral philosophy . . . presupposes a critical attitude to rules and the refusal to equate what is right with what is laid down by custom, law or any other authoritative source."[35]

An illustration may serve to demonstrate this point and indicate the paradoxical consequences of failure to draw the relevant distinction. In Bruno Bettelheim's eye witness account of the behavior of political prisoners in two German concentration camps, the author comments:

> In their behavior became apparent the dilemma of the politically uneducated German middle classes when confronted with the phenomenon of National socialism. They had no consistent philosophy which would protect their integrity as human beings. . . . They had obeyed the law handed down by the ruling classes, without ever questioning its wisdom. . . . They could not question the wisdom of law and of the police, so they accepted the behavior of the Gestapo as just. What was wrong was that *they* were made objects of a persecution which in itself *must* be right, since it was carried out by the authorities.[36]

Some relatives of those in the camps

> just would not believe that the prisoners in the camps had not committed outrageous crimes since the way they were punished permitted only this conclusion.[37]

Working or upper lower class individuals showed a decline in such sentiments following threat, however, and in neither case are the authors able "to report changes in payment in relation to . . . attitudinal responses." *Id.* at 294. Consequently the study is somewhat inconclusive even in regard to tax-paying, which as the authors point out differs significantly "from other forms of legal compliance." *Id.* at 284 n.37. Schwartz and Orleans also point out that "[A]n appeal to conscience could, of course, heighten the determination to *resist* taxes," for there are those "for whom reflection on the intended use of taxes might *decrease* the tendency to comply." *Id.* at 288 n.47 (emphasis added). They cite in this connection, E. Wilson, The Cold War and the Income Tax: A Protest (1963).

[34] 2 The Oxford English Dictionary 845 (1893).

[35] S. Benn & R. S. Peters, Social Principles and the Democratic State 26–28 (1959).

[36] Bettelheim, *Individual and Mass Behaviour in Extreme Situations,* 38 J. Ab. & Soc. Psych. 417, 426 (1943). The two camps were Dachau and Buchenwald.

[37] *Id.* at 441.

These examples illustrate not only the way in which respect for legal authority may help to secure social control but also why it is important not to confuse acceptance of, and submission to, authorthority with morality: To identify morality with social or behavioral conformity ignores that morality "implies that fully internalized moral norms should determine behavior, not only when they conflict with impulse or ego-interest but also when they conflict with external authority."[38]

The essential point is that because the constraints set by the criminal law are designed to achieve social control rather than moral improvement, "socializing" rather than "moralizing" better describes their nature and purpose, and better indicates the criteria by which their success or failure can be measured. De Tocqueville's skepticism about the possibility of reforming the morals of an individual by using the penal system reflects the distinction I am making. Although "radical reformation" was an almost illusory objective "another kind of reformation, less thorough than the former, but yet useful for society" was possible. For one might hope, in regard to the offender "leaving the prison" that

> if he is not more virtuous, he has become at least more judicious; his morality is not honor, but interest. . . . [H]is mind has contracted habits of order, and he possesses rules for his conduct in life; . . . if he has not become in truth better, he is at least more obedient to the laws, and that is all which society has the right to demand.[39]

This distinction is reflected also in Nigel Walker's statement that we "learn prudentially, not ethically, to abstain from traffic offenses."[40]

The significance of the distinction from the viewpoint of research lies in the fact that, as was indicated at the start,[41] identification of the phenomenon to be investigated is a necessary preliminary to empirical investigation. Of course, it may be that in practice this distinction will have no specific research implications. And certainly the fundamental point that criminal punishment has educative or socializing effects which are clearly distinguishable from its deterrent effects is in no way invalidated, nor is its importance diminished, by any of the qualifications suggested above. . . .

---

[38] Kohlberg, *supra* note 31, at 324. We must recognize that the kinds of behavior forbidden by the criminal law are not necessarily regarded as morally wrong; especially in a pluralistic democratic society, they may sometimes be seen as morally neutral, morally acceptable, or even morally desirable.

[39] G. de Beaumont & A. de Tocqueville, On the Penitentiary System in the United States, and its Application in France 89–90 (Lantz ed. 1964).

[40] N. Walker, Crime and Punishment in Britain 79 (1965).

[41] *See* text accompanying and following notes 2-3 *supra*.

CHAPTER FOUR

SOCIAL DEFENSE

As Marc Ancel has noted in the selection below, social defense is a theory that fits almost any system of punishment. It holds that criminals are to be punished to protect society, a thesis that most reasonable people would accept. Thus it may appear that social defense, deterrence, and rehabilitation, as justifying grounds for criminal punishment, are indistinguishable. But as one reads further, a distinctive element specifying social defense as a theory begins to emerge.

The point of view of social defense is quite clearly collectivistic. It views the offender as dangerous to society as a whole. While deterrence also views society at large, its focus is on the individual potential wrongdoers and their calculation of risk. Social defense is not interested in the individual except insofar as he presents a danger to the community. He is not even dignified with much status as a criminal; he is identified as a man with dangerous tendencies. It is not what he did that interests us, but using what he did to predict what he might do in the future. Prediction, then, becomes the vital key to understanding—and justifying—social defense.

While utilitarian explanation "looks to the future" for its justification, it does so on the basis of a prediction different from that used in social defense. Deterrence is justified by the prediction that others in society will commit crimes similar to those committed by the criminal unless they are deterred by fear of punishment made effective by actual imposition in this case. This prediction is vague and general, true, but grounded on the fact that every society has its potential wrongdoers and that they will commit crimes unless prevented. On the other hand, social defense predicts that *this* man will commit certain acts unless prevented. The obvious difficulty with such pinpoint prediction is hedged by social defense advocates, who claim great powers of accuracy for "science." But, as appear in the essays below, there are huge gaps in our knowledge of the human personality which none of the social or medical sciences has begun to fill. The justification for coercively preventing this individual from committing future crimes is based on society's need for protection and the ability to forecast his future acts.

A further feature of social defense is its repugnance toward punishment. It is not the coercive features of criminal punishment which bother the social defense theorist, since he believes in restraining the dangerous person. Rather, it is the condemnatory aspects of punishment which repel. From this perspective there is either no crime or crime is irrelevant. What is of concern is the danger which a man presents to others. The assumption is that the dangerous man is really not able to control his actions and so must be restrained. This quasi-medical model leads its advocates to substitute neutral terms, such as *measure, consequence, provision,* for the word *punishment.* By not condemning a person, by not attempting to hold him responsible, social defense is able to take a position of objectivity that is ethically neutral. In the end, punishment needs no other justification than the need of society to be protected from an imminent danger.

It may seem that in many aspects social defense is really nothing more than another version of rehabilitationism. But this is misleading for several reasons. First of all, rehabilitation looks to the good of the individual and not of society. Risks can be taken where it will benefit the individual's recovery. Not so with social defense theory. Further, rehabilitation is concerned with restoring the individual to social health. Although social defense is not opposed to this approach, incapacitation rather than restoration now becomes primary. Finally, though most rehabilitationists are not strong on using punishment as *the* means of helping the individual, they do not exclude it from their thinking. On the other hand, punishment fits very poorly with social defense's view of control.

After distinguishing social defense as sharply as we can from other theories, let us see how much it really is a part of all criminal law. Were we to ask any practicing lawyer familiar with the criminal courts of the United States why a certain criminal received an extended prison sentence, he would reply that the judge wanted to "send him away." Such a statement means that the judge felt that this man, having (probably) committed many crimes in the past and being presently convicted of another, was likely to commit still others in the future and that being placed in confinement was the easiest and best way to prevent future crimes—at least for a while. This familiar sense of preventive detention is implied in much, if not most, of our criminal law. Trying to sort it out has proven difficult, in concept as well as practice. In countries which have tried to give matching sentences of punishment for the present crime and of protective detention against the danger of future crimes, there has been a great deal of dissatisfaction. Criminals don't mind serving time for what they did, but feel sinned against when held for what they might (would?) do in the future. The obvious peril in allowing such distinctions to be drawn is the misuse of criminal law to control social or political undesirables, as witnessed in Nazi Germany.

The selections on this interesting theme come from several nations. Marc Ancel, a French jurist, attempts most valiantly to bring social defense into alignment with the dictates of justice which criminal law implies. Ancel refers to the vigorous critique of the shortcomings of criminal law made by Professor Fillipo Gramatica, an Italian, who would replace criminal law with his theory of social defense. In this theory punishment would give way to the scientific prediction of danger to society and the taking of preventive measures. Helen Silving gives the reader an overview of several European countries which have adopted a "dual-track" system of law, where punishment and social defense lie side by side. Her report is objective, but no one will miss the point made in her account of the history which such laws had in the hands of the National Socialists under Hitler. Turning to American practice, the "Guides to Sentencing the Dangerous Offender" and a part of the Model Sentencing Act are set out to illustrate the language problems inherent when one attempts to draft a law which allows for detention of dangerous criminals. Professors Morris and Hawkins are critical of the Model Act's attempt and have some sensible, if harsh, things to say about the state of the art of predicting future criminal acts. It seems an unavoidable conclusion from their piece that we have a long way to go before we begin applying freely such will-o'-the-wisp terms as *dangerousness*.

Finally, Lady Barbara Wootton, an English social scientist and magistrate, gives her version of the proper blend of social defense and criminal law. By displacing responsibility from the determination of guilt, Lady Wootton clearly precludes the possibility of punishment in any sense of retribution. Her prediction that corrective institutions will be both medical and penal points up the full effect which the "withering away" of criminal responsibility would have on our present system.

NEW SOCIAL DEFENSE*

Marc Ancel

Marc Ancel sits as a judge of the Supreme Court of France and still finds time to pursue an academic career of teaching and writing in the area of criminal law and criminology. In his influential book Social Defense *he combines the best features of earlier schools of penal thought, with special debt to the positivists of the nineteenth century. Ancel is anxious to demonstrate that social defense leaves room for true criminal law. As one moves through the selection given below, he will detect signs of conflict between the neutral process of prevention and the traditional process of guilt-finding in criminal justice.*

For a very long time, even, we may say, for centuries, it was never questioned that pitiless punishment of the offence was the only means of controlling the phenomenon of crime. Of course, this over-simplified notion has varied much in content from Plato to Beccaria, as will be shown in the next chapter. Moreover, as everyone knows, the object of such punishment has been—successively or concurrently—vengeance, expiation, retribution, reparation for the harm inflicted, intimidation, reformation, satisfaction of the public conscience, or the prevention of new offences. In all these cases, however, the social reaction against crime was primarily thought out in terms of punishment: the criminal must 'pay,' and the other purposes of the penalty were secondary. The classical criminal law which emerged in the late eighteenth century, while rejecting the brutalities of the former régime, itself established a system of retributive punishment. To a large extent, this consisted in fitting the means of dealing with crime into a rigid legal framework: this, then, was the system of law responsible for ensuring the protection of society against crime and hence was 'social defence.'

Now in its modern connotation, social defence appeared first of all as a reaction against this exclusively retributive system. That is why the term acquired a scope—or if we prefer, an autonomy—which was new; that is why, again, it came to imply a renewed conception of the struggle against delinquency; that is why, finally, it came to presuppose the existence of a deliberate penal policy founded on data provided by the social sciences and by criminology. Such modern penal policy is based on the essential premise that, because crime is a social fact and a human act, the process of dealing with crime is not completed once the offence has been legally defined

* Reprinted by permission of Schocken Books Inc. and Routledge & Kegan Paul Ltd. from SOCIAL DEFENSE: A MODERN APPROACH TO CRIMINAL PROBLEMS by Marc Ancel.

and equated with a penalty imposed by law: there remains the need to understand the crime as a social and individual phenomenon; the need to prevent its commission or repetition; the need, finally, for asking oneself what attitude is to be adopted towards the criminal, over and beyond the legal qualification of the offence.

The history of these ideas thus confronts us with two main interpretations of the notion of 'social defence,' fundamentally different from one another: first the old interpretation, which still has many supporters, who would limit the notion to the protection of society by the repression of crime; and secondly the *modern* conception, which finds expression in the excellent formula adopted by the United Nations Organization when its social defence section was set up in 1948: 'The prevention of crime and the treatment of offenders.' Prevention and treatment, it may be said, are the two dimensions that were lacking in the traditional interpretation, which likewise failed to place the reaction against crime in proper perspective: whereas in the traditional interpretation this reaction consisted wholly in the precise determination of a body of legal rules, the modern tendency is to envisage the problem in a social and criminological context. To arrange the system of protection of society with due regard to criminological facts, but bearing in mind the need to perfect a true system of criminal law—this is what we understand by the implementation of a 'penal policy.' In its modern meaning, social defence thus appears simultaneously as a new approach to the problem of crime and as a new trend in the practical decision-making which organizes the means of controlling crime.

It is essential to have a thorough understanding of the fundamental antithesis between the old and the new conceptions of social defence, and constantly to bear this antithesis in mind, for only thus can serious confusion be avoided and the precise significance of the notion of social defence, in its modern dynamic force, be appreciated. It goes without saying that the modern conception alone will engage our attention from now on.

Furthermore, it will be seen that this modern conception is not unitary or uniform, but has at least two very different aspects, which will be discussed in greater detail. . . . In the opinion of Gramatica, for instance, social defence is definitely to be visualized as a reaction against repressive criminal law, and would even envisage substituting for the criminal law, *stricto sensu*, a non-punitive system of reaction against anti-social behaviour. Such a system would then aim at establishing a coherent body of remedies chosen with a view to the attainment of social harmony.[1]

From this point of view, social defence might even be considered in the context of political philosophy as a conception in which the State did not simply exercise the utilitarian and beneficient function attributed to it by Bentham, of ensuring the greatest happiness of the greatest number, but would go further than the mere *protection* of the citizen and organize a system designed to *ameliorate* both society and the citizens. Some time ago, Saldana also worked out the idea of a similarly perfectionist crim-

[1] 'Criminologia e difesa sociale,' *Riv. di Difesa sociale,* 1950, pp. 113 ff., esp. pp. 127, 129. Cf. the same author's *Principi di difesa sociale,* Padua, 1961.

inal law.[2] This writer, in a vision more enthusiastic than convincing and less precise than generous, even wished to project his scheme on to the world scale and to have it administered by an international tribunal. He was thus led to envisage a system of 'universal social defence' which would replace the existing penal law by a 'law of insurance' consisting of reciprocal means of protection and safeguards.[3] Gramatica, for his part, has asserted on many occasions that such an undertaking would involve fundamental changes in the structure of the legal system and even in that of society itself.

We are here confronted with what may be termed the 'extremist interpretation' of social defence. Later on, we shall see what reservations and even opposition this interpretation has aroused, because—as may be imagined—it has provoked bitter controversy.

Whatever we may think of these discussions, which are not always free from mere verbosity but which at least illustrate the topical importance and the vitality of the concept of social defence, the fact remains that, quite apart from the extreme view just referred to, the modern concept of social defence is often considered to be a synonym for action of a non-penal nature, or at any rate for a treatment of the offender in a way that is not merely repressive. A Danish criminologist has adopted the notion of the struggle against punishment, but without giving this the negative significance favoured by Gramatica.[4] Again, as the latter very properly observed, it is impossible to overlook the great reputation and inspiring work in this field of the great Swedish specialist, Karl Schlyter, whose celebrated slogan 'Empty the prisons!' could well be adopted as a rallying-cry by the partisans of social defence. Schlyter remained within the logic of his system and his work in expressing the wish that the term 'criminal code' should be replaced by 'social defence code' or 'code of protection.'[5] Here the concept of social defence covers an active and preventive social policy which aims at the protection of society by protecting the offender as well, and is designed to ensure that the latter should receive the treatment which is appropriate to his individual case, within a legal framework and by legal methods. Thus conceived, social defence is largely based on the substitution of treatment for retributive punishment. It need hardly be emphasized that this approach in no way denies the value of criminal law, since it is the approach which the United Nations Organization adopted and has undertaken to develop, with the consent and active participation of all its member states. In the Council of Europe, the same work has been undertaken by the European Committee on Crime Problems, since it was set up in 1957.[6] In

[2] This system is derived, in particular, from pragmatic penology (*Nueva penologia,* 1931). Cf. J. Masaveu, *Nueva dirección española en filosofia del derecho penal,* pp. 53 ff.

[3] *La Défense sociale universelle,* Paris, 1925; cf. 'Peine et mesures de sûreté', *Rev. int. de droit pénal,* 1927, pp. 7 ff.

[4] Louis Le Maire, *Kampen mod Straffen,* Copenhagen, 1952, who considers that crime is the expression of an abnormality requiring purely therapeutic treatment. See, for conclusive objections to this kind of approach, S. Hurwitz, *Den danske kriminalret,* Copenhagen, 1950, pp. 111–112.

[5] Stephan Hurwitz, *op. cit.,* pp. 102–103; cf. Thore Engströmer, *Festskrift tillägnad Karl Schlyter,* Stockholm, 1949, p. 10. On Karl Schlyter, see *Rev. de Science crim.,* 1959, p. 916; 1960, p. 134.

[6] On this Committee, see *Rev. de Science crim.,* 1958, p. 922.

the same spirit, the Twelfth (and last) International Penal and Penitentiary Congress—a memorable event—expressly raised the question 'of the measures which are appropriate substitutes for punishment, taking into account the necessities of a humane social defence.'[7]

Does it then follow that the concept of social defence necessarily involves the rejection of all repressive measures, and a final separation from the notion of punishment? Is it necessary to make a choice, here again, between criminal law and social defence? On the contrary, many determined advocates of social defence believe that criminal law *and* social defence should be brought together in a fresh perspective.[8] Stefan Hurwitz, indeed, sees social defence as a doctrine that would give greater weight to the repression of crime than to its prevention, and he would prefer the expression 'punishment' to be abandoned altogether, so as better to stress the fact that penal sanction is no longer associated with ignominious suffering: he considers such a change advantageous not only from the technical standpoint but also as 'the expression of a sound programme of penal policy.'[9] Yet he does not forget that in public opinion the idea of sanction still retains its vitality, and that the necessary social reaction may still involve depriving certain persons of their freedom or inflicting fines on them. I. Strahl, for his part, while supporting the elaboration of a system of social defence measures and a procedural reform which would make possible a more satisfactory individual approach to the situation of the particular person accused, has no intention of doing away altogether with the criminal trial as such or with the possibility of inflicting punishment.[10] The *Nordisk Kriminalistik Års-bok* (Yearbook of the Northern Associations of Criminalists), which never fails to concern itself in a sound and genuine manner with problems of social defence, contains many examples of this tendency to make room for punishment in a rational system of social defence. So Graven, who played a major and unforgettable part in the first social defence Congresses, did not hesitate on occasion to declare himself in favour of the death penalty, arguing for the necessity of its retention and even—in the case of Switzerland—its reintroduction.[11]

[7] See Marc Ancel, 'Security Measures Appropriate to a Humane System of Social Defence', in *Proceedings of the Twelfth International Penal and Penitentiary Congress,* Berne, 1951, vol. II, pp. 503–515. The same approach is to be found in the paper submitted to this Congress by Paul Cornil, on the problem of applied penal law in the light of new relevant tendencies, *ibid.,* vol. II, pp. 476 ff., and *Rev. de droit pénal et de criminologie,* Brussels, February 1951.

[8] Cf. the study by E. R. Frey already cited, 'Strafrecht oder soziale Verteidigung', *Rev. pénale suisse,* 1953, pp. 405 ff.; cf. also Marc Ancel, 'Droit pénal et défense sociale', *Rev. de Science crim.,* 1953, pp. 144 ff. See especially the conclusive reply of J. Graven in *Rev. Pénale suisse,* 1955, pp. I ff., and cf. the discussion with Frey at the International Society for Criminology, *Bulletin* of that society, 1956, pp. 119 ff.

[9] Report of the San Remo Congress, 1947, in *Respekt for Mennesket,* Copenhagen, 1951, pp. 217 ff.

[10] I. Strahl, 'La Réforme du droit pénal en Suède', *Rev. de Science crim.,* 1952, pp. 359 ff., also the same author's *Brotten och brottspåföljderna* ('The Offence and its consequences'), Stockholm, 1952. J. Andenaes, in his study of social defence in Norway (same *Revue,* 1953, pp. 273 ff.) seems to accept an identical point of view as legitimate; cf. his 'General Prevention, Illusion or Reality?', *Journal of Criminal Law, Criminology, and Police Science,* Jul.-Aug. 1952, pp. 176 ff.

[11] 'Le Problème de la peine de mort et sa réapparition en Suisse', *Rev. int. de criminologie et de police technique,* Special issue, Jan.-Mar. 1952, pp. 3 ff.

The expression 'social defence' is therefore subject to a great variety of uses and interpretations. As has already been observed, some writers have sought to compare—if not to assimilate—social defence both to penology and to criminology, whereas other specialists have tried to give the notion the scope of a genuine political philosophy. Again, some have asserted that social defence should postulate the criminal problem 'from a higher standpoint which would be derived from first principles, would acquire an ever-increasing ascendancy over the Criminal Code as the idea and the reality of society as such gained strength, and would command increasing attention from man considered as an individual.' The concept of social defence would therefore involve consideration of 'the problem of man and society, of their respective natures and of their relation.' This philosophical and social problem would be resolved with the help of the social sciences. With regard to the legal aspects of the problem, social defence would require above all that 'the progress accomplished in the social sciences and particularly in sociology should be amply integrated in the law.'[12] There is also a new affinity between the respective fields of social defence, criminology, and political philosophy. Still another author, in a report expressing certain extreme opinions that are characteristic of a particular interpretation of social defence, even concludes with a reference to brotherly love and the vision of this particular concept of social defence as the philosophical system where the individual and society are harmoniously inter-related for the social well-being of all.[13]

This certainly takes us a long way from a criminal policy applied solely with a view to the rational prevention of crime and the scientific treatment of offenders. Will social defence therefore get lost among these well-meaning generalizations, in which non-lawyers feel more at home than academic lawyers or practitioners concerned with criminal law? Some non-specialists may occasionally have been responsible for such pseudo-philosophical attitudes and a certain facile dogmatism. It does not necessarily follow that the term 'social defence' may not have a content and a significance which one is compelled to link up with the general system of thought that dominates the rules of law actually applied. This proposition could be demonstrated, if need be, not so much by scattered references culled from the works of recent theoreticians of social defence, but rather by the significant discussions that have taken place ever since June 1953 on the occasion of the *Journées de Défense sociale* which are arranged annually by the Comparative Law Institute of the University of Paris, with the assistance of the various university law faculties in France.[14]

[12] See the first 'Chronique de défense sociale' ('Avertissement') in *Rev. de Science crim.*, 1948, pp. 119 ff.; cf. Piprot d'Alleaume, *ibid.*, 1948, p. 801.

[13] De Vincentiis, General Report to the San Marino session (1951), *Riv. di difesa sociale,* 1951, pp. 86 ff., esp. p. 160. T. Collignon, *Rev. int. de criminologie et de police technique,* 1949, p. 80, writes that 'social defence tends to suppress the need for repression, by doing away with the cause thereof'.

[14] On these *Journées,* see *Rev. de Science crim.,* 1953, p. 540; 1954, pp. 172, 809; 1955, pp. 578, 724; 1956, pp. 162, 200, 650, 872; 1957, pp. 700, 835; 1958, p. 805; 1959, pp. 41, 125, 898; 1960, pp. 41, 125, 595, 702; 1961, p. 843; 1962, pp. 574, 801; 1963, pp. 751, 774, 779, 855; 1964, pp. 721, 801, 898.

The first of these meetings[15] considered the particularly important problem of the relation between social defence and individual freedom. Gradually, irresistibly so to speak, there emerged the idea that not only was the concept of social defence not opposed—or no longer opposed—to individual freedom, but, on the contrary, presupposed such freedom, the latter being redefined in terms of a social action ultimately providing genuine safeguards for the individual. The concept of social defence thus leads to a true judicial humanism which, while avoiding any violent rejection of the existing criminal law, aims in a consistent and resolute fashion to transform the administration of criminal justice itself. It then becomes possible to envisage social defence less as an objective doctrine than as a *commitment,* in the most modern sense of the word, meaning the deliberate acceptance of a particular approach to criminal justice, marked both by respect for the human person and by a concern to redeem for society those who must inevitably be affected by the social reaction against their acts. Of course, this generous conception goes beyond the province of criminal law envisaged as a particular kind of legal technique. However, it will be seen that this 'social penal policy' (for such, perhaps, might be the true definition of the new social defence) has no intention of disregarding either the inescapable exigencies of a legal system or the requirements of legal science.

So it is that the term 'social defence,' founded on a certain idea of the social reaction against the phenomenon of crime, may be given a very wide meaning, which is ultimately suggestive of a new penal philosophy while remaining closely and necessarily bound up with the organization of a system of criminal law. The term may likewise be given meanings that are narrow, more restricted, and more strictly technical. As we have observed, it has even been used in opposite senses and has on occasion, here and there, been the object of distortions that were not always merely unintentional.

These several interpretations of the term 'social defence' have been mentioned simply in order to emphasize the many shades of meaning that could variously or in turn be attributed to this expression, which is today in general use. A little later, it may not be very difficult to show that many of these shades of meaning can in fact be reconciled in a single broad conception, destined to give way to distinct tendencies emanating, if truth be told, from the one basic idea. Without in any way professing to give a lapidary definition of social defence at this point—for in the light of the foregoing pages it is well to bear in mind the maxim *omnis definitio periculosa*—but after surveying, however briefly, most of the valid uses of the notion and the expression 'social defence,' it appears possible to give at least a provisional answer to the question raised at the head of this chapter: what is meant by social defence?

From the unquestionable confusion of the different doctrines, as well as from the undeniable rivalry of the authors, we can already draw both a lesson and an encouragement. In effect, the term 'social defence,' through all the ways in which it is used, even though they be empirical or fortuitous, emerges from the foregoing brief survey with certain salient features that enable us to place it in perspective

[15] See the full report of these *Journées* in the *Rev. de Science crim.,* 1954, pp. 172 ff.

with regard to the traditional, classical criminal law. We would recall once again, at this point, that it is intended to consider the *modern* concept of social defence, as contrasted with the older notion of the protection of society by way of repressive punishment alone. It may easily be perceived that this modern concept of social defence immediately calls to mind a few very simple ideas. In order to formulate the problem with sufficient precision in this preliminary chapter, these may now be enumerated. For the sake of brevity, it is proposed to set forth the ideas that follow in a schematic fashion, giving a summary in a synthetic form: at a later stage, perhaps, it will be necessary to draw attention to certain points needing greater elaboration or more specific treatment.

1. In the first place, social defence presupposes that the means of dealing with crime should be generally conceived as a system which aims not at punishing a fault and sanctioning by a penalty the conscious infringement of a legal rule, but at protecting society against criminal acts. There is no doubt that in this respect—which must engage our attention later—social defence recalls the positivist revolt against the traditional criminal law.

2. The intention of social defence is to carry such social protection into effect, quite naturally, by means of a body of measures that are generally outside the ambit of the criminal law as such and are designed to 'neutralize' the offender, either by his removal or segregation, or by applying remedial or educational methods. Here again there is clearly a connexion between the ideas of social defence and the notion of 'dangerousness' which has been worked out, in particular, by the International Union of Criminal Law.

3. Social defence thus leads to the promotion of a penal policy which naturally favours the individual rather than the collective approach to the prevention of crime, and endeavours to ensure 'the prevention of crime and the treatment of offenders.' Consequently, this rational penal policy aims at the systematic *resocialization* of the offender, and the importance of this term must be stressed from the very beginning.

4. Nevertheless, such a process of resocialization can take place only by way of an ever-increasing *humanization* of the new criminal law, which will have to call upon all the resources of the person concerned, seeking to restore not only his self-confidence but also his sense of personal responsibility (or more precisely, the awareness of his freedom in society) and the sense of human values. Moreover, this conception will endeavour to safeguard the offender's inherent rights as a human being, whether he is charged with an offence or actually convicted.

5. Such a humanization of criminal law and the criminal trial will not just be the result of a merely humanitarian or sentimental movement. On the contrary, the process will be based as firmly as possible on scientific understanding of the phenomenon of crime and the offender's personality. Moreover, the humanization of criminal law presupposes a humanist philosophy and a moral ideal which naturally go far beyond the boundaries of materialistic determinism. In this sense, and in this sense only, it may be said that social defence impinges directly upon the essential problem of the relations between the individual and the State. It is in this sense also that social defence differs fundamentally from totalitarianism, in so far as it considers

that society can exist only through man and for man. In short, it is based on a political philosophy which tends to what may be described as social individualism.

These are the basic factors that enable us to define, tentatively at any rate, the admittedly complex notion of social defence. It should be understood at once that these several factors make their appearance in the historical context outlined above and in this ascending order. *New* social defence, the spirit of which we should like to bring into the open, precisely involves becoming aware of these factors in their essential sequence and their natural order. To this extent also it may be said that social defence today implies, above all, a way of reflecting upon, approaching, and reconsidering the fundamental problems of criminal law in the light of a few essential ideas which form the philosophical basis of the whole system.

THE DUAL-TRACK SYSTEM: PUNISHMENT AND PREVENTION*

Helen Silving

Helen Silving is a professor of criminal law at the University of Puerto Rico and author of many essays and articles. Her concern, as we will see expressed in our last chapter, is for the rule of law: nulla poena sine lege. *In examining here the penal law of Germany, she discusses the dual-track system in which both punishment and preventive detention are explicitly combined as sanctions for the violation of a single statute. This procedure raises questions as to the purpose which criminal law serves and whether multiple goals are not frequently contradictory in theory as well as practice.*

The . . . "dual-track" system (*Zweispurigkeit*),[1] . . . consists in a systematic differentiation and separation of legal reactions to the delinquent individual. His freedom and self-direction is emphasized in his responsibility for his freely committed illegal acts, a responsibility expressed in liability to punishment. His lack of freedom, if any, expressed in irresponsiblity and consequent dangerousness, is met by a distinctive sanction, the "measure," which implies no censure but aims at cure and community protection. The advantage of this system, prevailing in many civil law countries, when adequately supported by "criminal law science," lies in its compelling awareness of the distinctive functions of each state intervention, thus suggesting the proper limits of each, facilitating development in each area of safeguards of due process appropriate to it. In a "dual-track system" punishment must not be used for protective purposes, and "measures" must not serve punitive ends. The system of punishment is governed by conventional "legality" of the "law of the act." The system of "measures" is governed by distinctive safeguards against abuse.[2] I shall deal first with the puni-

* Excerpted from Silving, *Rule of Law in Criminal Justice*, in ESSAYS IN CRIMINAL SCIENCE, ed. Gerhard Mueller (South Hackensack, N.J.: Rothman, 1961). Reprinted with permission.

[1] I am using this term to describe systems in which the dualism of punishment and measures is in principle maintained, even though on special policy grounds application of both punishment and measure in the same case may be excluded by legal mandate or in the exercise of judicial discretion. The latter situation is not referred to in the terminology of civil law countries as one of "dual-track."

[2] The separation of punishment and measures has been variously challenged, particularly during the Sixth International Criminal Law Congress held in Rome in 1953. French and Belgian jurists pointed out that in practice there is no difference between punishment and measures. Jiménez de Asúa, with his usual vigor, answered the challenge by saying that (1) if the differentiation is theoretically justified, it is the function of law to make practice conform to theoretical requirements; (2) the practical consequences of

tive scheme, and thereafter discuss the scheme of "measures."[3]

Ethical "personalism" combined with a "sense of guilt" pervading German post-war reality are reflected in a "guilt-oriented criminal law" (*Schuldstrafrecht*).[4] According to it, "guilt" is the exclusive basis of punitive responsibility.[5] "Guilt" is "blameworthiness" and consists in accountability for a wrong legal-ethical decision freely made.[6] Obviously, the legal response to such "guilt" is retribution. The idea of "reformation," which is concerned with the "character" of man, is conceptually alien to the punitive scheme of criminal law. Indeed, within that scheme, reformation is reminiscent of "responsibility based on character" (*Charakterschuld*) of National Socialist ideology. After a thorough debate, "accountability for a life conduct" (*Lebensführungsschuld*)—a continued course of antisocial conduct, resulting in a man's having become insensitive to the dictates of law and morality—has been rejected by the Draft of a German Penal Code of 1958.[7] In the prevailing view, no one should be held punitively responsible for "*being thus*" or for having permitted himself to become "*thus*." Nevertheless, within the limits of "guilt-adequate punishment," pursuit of other criminal law ends, particularly reformation and deterrence, is considered admissible.[8] But German writers emphasize that consideration of social protection, in contrast to reformation, even if confined within the limits of the "guilt-adequate," is highly dubious.[9]

What of man's uniqueness, his atypical response to punitive state intervention? The solution, accepted without hesitation in our law, of keeping the incidence of responsibility within the confines of the "law of the act" while permitting the sentence and execution phase to be dominated by a "law of the actor" has been thoroughly discussed in German legal literature. The question has been posed

confusing the two notions have proved to be dangerous to human liberty (citing an instructive Spanish example). See Jiménez de Asúa, "Las Medidas de seguridad," in *El Criminalista*, 2nd series, Vol. II, 219–221 (1958). In our law we may find similarly instructive examples of the effects of confusing criminal law goals. For further criticism of the "dual-track system" and replies to such criticism see *infra*.

[3] The "law of guilt," as basis of the punitive scheme, has been most consistently elaborated by German doctrine. I shall hence present the latter scheme mainly against the background of German law. The law of "measures" will be considered against a broader comparative law background.

[4] Of course, the notion of "guilt" as basis of criminal responsibility is very old. But the logical conclusions from the limitation of punitive responsibility to accountability for guilt have been drawn only recently. The process is by no means concluded.

[5] It should be noted that the idea of responsibility based on "guilt" is conceived exclusively as a limitative notion. It does not require punishment to be imposed in all cases of "guilt," but merely prohibits punishment beyond guilt. See Draft of new German Penal Code, 1958, *Entwurf des Allgemeinen Teils eines Strafgesetzbuchs* (Bonn, 1958), hereinafter cited as German Draft, 1958, at 4–5.

[6] On this see Ryu and Silving, "Error Juris: A Comparative Study," 24 U.Chi.L. Rev. 421 at 451. On the ethical basis of this approach see *ibid.* at 449.

[7] German Draft, 1958, at 63. But see Eb. Schmidt, "Strafzweck und Strafzumessung in einem künftigen Strafgesetzbuch," in I *Materialien zur Strafrechtsreform, Gutachten der Strafrechtslehrer,* 9, 26 (1954). (Hereinafter cited as *Materialien.*)

[8] See particularly Decision of the Bundesgerichtshof in Criminal Matters (V. Strafsenat), November 10, 1954, g. H., 7 B.G.H.St. 28 (1955). See also decisions cited in Eb. Schmidt, *supra,* note 7.

[9] On this see Würtenberger, "Die unbestimmte Verurteilung," I *Materialien,* 89 at 96.

whether it makes sense to follow the ritual of adjudication for the purpose of establishing "guilt" for a particular act, if the end-result of such adjudication is assumption of an entirely new standard, that of the personality of the actor. Clearly in such scheme the incidence of responsibility is judged by retributive standards geared to an act which lies in the past and for which the accused is now called to account although he is entirely unable to undo it, whereas consequences drawn from the establishment of "guilt," the sentence and execution, follow preventive or reformative standards. Von Liszt and his disciples, when accused of inconsistency for suggesting such solution, had defended it by presenting it as a functional compromise between the demand of "legality" and teleological needs. Bockelmann has recently rejoined that the inconsistency cannot be thus eliminated unless a necessary constant relationship can be shown to exist between the act and the character of the actor. Since, in general, no particular "actor type" in terms of preventive or reformative needs is discernible as a "natural" performer of definite crime types, it is impossible either to formulate statutory types with a view to deterring particular types of actors or to adjust sentencing in such manner as to do justice both to the social significance of the crime and the individuality of each actor.[10]

Stress on "guilt" marks the return of German law to principles of the "law of the act" and basic "legality." In fact, during the post-war era, the "guilt principle" was elaborated into a consistent system based upon the element of independence in personality. Some survivals of vicarious and collective responsibility have been eliminated earlier.[11] *Versari in re illicita* has been now reduced to a minimum.[12] True, many objectionable innovations of the National Socialist régime, particularly those based on its voluntaristic approach punishing attitudes rather than social harm, have been preserved in present law.[13] But the "law of the actor" elements have been considerably modified. In the law of "homicide," the figures of "murderer" and "manslayer" have been judicially held

[10] Bockelmann, "Wie würde sich ein konsequentes Täterstrafrecht auf ein neues Strafgesetzbuch auswirken?" in I *Materialien*, 29 at 32–34.

[11] Civil law countries have never in principle admitted such concepts as responsibility of corporations for acts of their agents, conspiracy as a separate crime figure. But see a recently appearing contrary trend, evidenced by such cases as (on corporate responsibility), *Hervillard et autres*, Decision of the Cour de cassation (French) (Chambre criminelle), Oct. 14, 1953, [1954] Dalloz Jurisprudence 47; *Ministère public* v. *Faugères*, Cour de cassation (French) (Chambre criminelle), March 6, 1958, [1958] Dalloz Jurisprudence 465; Decision of the Bundesgerichtshof (Federal Republic of Germany) in Criminal Matters (V. Strafsenat), Oct. 27, 1953, 5 B.G.H.St. 28 (1954).

The statement in the text refers specifically to § 50, German Penal Code, reformulated by Ordinance of May 29, 1943, R.G.Bl. I S. 339, providing that where "several persons participate in one act, each is responsible in accordance with his own guilt and without regard to the guilt of another," and that where "the law provides that special personal qualities or circumstances aggravate, mitigate or exclude punishment, this applies only to that principal or accomplice in whose person they occur."

[12] See as to crimes qualified by consequences (§ 56, German Penal Code, inserted by Act of August 4, 1953, B.G.Bl. I S. 735), Silving, *Euthanasia: A Study in Comparative Criminal Law*, 103 U. Pa. L. Rev. 350 at 361, note 40 (1954). For discussion of the provision see Silving, "Psychoanalysis and the Criminal Law," 51 J.Crim.L., Criminology & Pol.Sc., 19, at 26 (1960).

[13] See particularly the highly questionable § 49a, German Penal Code, amended only partially. For criticism see 1 Kohlrausch, *Strafgesetzbuch*, 165 *et seq.* (41st ed., Lange, 1956).

to refer not to permanent "actor types" but to typified motives and manners of crime commission.[14] A significant remnant of the "actor orientation" of the National Socialist era in the sphere of punishment is aggravation of punishment in the case of the "actor type" of "habitual offender." But the provision is felt to be alien to the "guilt principle" and the Draft of a new German Penal Code has entirely eliminated this ominous figure from the punitive scheme.[15]

The purity of the punitive scheme, that is, its exclusive orientation to "guilt," is believed to be guaranteed by the availability of the scheme of "measures," which serves other than punitive criminal law ends.[16] Of course, except in theory,[17] the separation of "punishment" and "measures" has not been carried out to such degree as to entirely exclude reformative and preventive goals from the punitive scheme. Strictly speaking, any state intervention aimed at such goals is a "measure." But most legal orders assume the punitive scheme to pursue, in addition to retribution, other concurrent goals,[18] particularly reformation.[19] Nevertheless, as seen, these goals in German law are not admissible within the scheme of punishment unless they can be fitted into that which is "guilt-adequate." In other respects, the "law of guilt" has been maintained reasonably pure of elements appropriate to "measures." The idea of such purity, stressed on the ground of the desirability of preserving to the utmost possible degree the "legal-

[14] For illustration of case law see Silving, *Euthanasia, supra,* note 12, at 364–365, note 53. Since this note was written, German courts have completely freed the law of homicide of all "actor type" elements. See Decision of the Bundesgerichtshof (Great Senate in Criminal Matters), December 2, 1957, reported in 11 *Neue Juristische Wochenschrift* (hereinafter cited as NJW), 309 (1958).

[15] See German Draft, 1958, at 4, 63.

[16] See German Draft, 1958, at 84.

[17] In Welzel's view, the "realistic reason for punishment by the state is that it is an essential requisite of the maintenance of the community order." The "measure," on the other hand, pursues the aim of securing the community against "dangerousness of the actor," which transcends his guilt. Welzel, *Das Deutsche Strafrecht,* 201, 205 (6th ed., 1958).

[18] That so-called "general prevention," that is, deterrence of others than the actor himself, is incompatible with the Kantian concept of human dignity, implying that man must never be used as a means to ends extraneous to himself, has been repeatedly emphasized in German ethical philosophy and in a number of recent decisions. But there are also decisions which reverse judgments below on the ground of their failure to consider such deterrence. For citations see Eb. Schmidt, *supra,* note 7, at 17–18. Kohlrausch, in an often-quoted statement, "We need not worry about general deterrence," for it is sufficiently secured by the statutory provisions for punishment, has actually thereby accepted such deterrence as a valid legal goal, eliminating it merely as a special ground to be considered in meting out a sentence. Whether or not statutory punishment provisions "deter" in fact, has never been ascertained. But neither has the deterrent effect of a sentence imposition been tested. There can be no doubt that it is the purpose of criminal laws to "deter," in the sense of preventing crime. The real issue would seem to be whether a law which is never enforced can conceivably act as a "deterrent," and if the answer to this question is negative, the ultimate problem is reduced to one of selecting those to be used as "deterrent examples." Thus, the Kantian ideal of human dignity can be realized only within a doctrine of retribution concerned with the individual, the question still remaining unanswered whether the incidental deterrent effect upon others is taken for granted, accepted, accepted with approval, or what other place it may be assigned in the scheme of criminal law goals.

[19] See particularly Art. 37, Federal Swiss Penal Code, 1937, which specifically states the purpose of executing imprisonment to be "to exercise an educational influence upon the prisoner and to prepare him for re-entry into civic life."

ity principle" governing the "law of the act" as well as the newly emphasized "law of guilt," is importantly reflected in the approach of civil law countries generally to the problems of "punishment scales," of sentencing methods, of the indeterminate sentence and of probation. In all these areas over which the "law of the actor" approach has assumed practically full control in this country, civil law countries have preserved an attitude of moderation. . . .

The "measure" is a concept derived from the vocabulary of the positivist school of criminal law. The latter school denies the existence of responsibility based on "guilt" freely incurred and hence the justification of "punishment." It predicates state intervention into the individual sphere upon the "social necessity" of community protection against danger emanating from the delinquent individual. Such protection, in its view, is afforded by reformation of the reformable and confinement of the unreformable. The ensuing policy is "actor-oriented." The adherents of the opposing view, though insisting on assumption of basic human freedom of choice and hence responsibility based on "guilt," admit that man's freedom varies with personalities and with circumstances. Relative reduction of freedom is in part considered within the "guilt system" itself in institutions such as diminished responsibility, mitigating circumstances, necessity, inexigibility of law abidance in certain situations. In those cases, however, where psychic freedom is wholly lacking, as in states of insanity or of total drunkenness, and to the extent that such freedom is relatively diminished, as in diminished responsibility, the individual may be more dangerous than is a fully responsible person, precisely because he possesses no full capacity of self-direction. "Measures" are used within the "dual-track system" in situations of danger arising outside of the limits of punitive responsibility.

The characteristic feature of a "measure," as distinct from punishment, consists in its being determined as to kind and duration by its reformative, curative or protective goal rather than by the graveness of the crime in issue.[20] In contrast to punishment, measures are flexible. As soon as it appears that the goal pursued by a measure is either achieved or cannot be reached, the measure must be terminated. At times one measure may be substituted for another.

Since measures are non-retributive and based on a present state of danger, the pertinency of a conviction as requisite of their application has been questioned. In fact, there has developed in civil law countries the concept of "pre-delictual measures," among which those applied in Spanish and in Latin American legislation to "vagrants" (*vagos y maleantes*) figure prominently and which also include the ominous Italian Law of December 27, 1956, on Preventive Measures.[21]

[20] In the case of habitual offenders, the number and character of the crimes committed are often deemed as particularly symptomatic of danger. On this see *infra.*

[21] On the Spanish *Ley de Vagos y Maleantes* of August 4, 1933, see Del Rosal, *La Personalidad del delincuente en la tecnica penal* (2nd ed., 1953), 121–129. The Cuban Code of Social Defense specifically divides "measures" into (A) "Medidas de Seguridad post-delictivas" and (B) "Medidas de Seguridad pre-delictivas." Art. 582, "Código de Defensa Social de Cuba," in I *Códigos Penales Iberoamericanos,* edited by Jiménez de Asúa and Carsï Zacarés, 855 at 989 (1946). For collection of Latin American "pre-delictual measures" see Jiménez de Asúa, "Las Medidas de seguridad," in *El Criminalista,* 2nd series, Vol. II, 219, 226 (1958). A pre-delictual measure has been introduced for alcoholics in France. See Décret

In principle, however, in civil law countries of Continental Europe application of measures is predicated upon conviction for crime commission, upon a particular type of acquittal, *e.g.*, acquittal on the ground of insanity, or upon unfitness to plead. Precautions against danger arising otherwise than in context with crime are referred to branches of law administration other than criminal. There are, in addition, certain exceptional instances of pre-delictual measures provided for in penal codes. Thus, *e.g.*, there are only two such instances in the Italian Penal Code.[22] The substantive legality requirement is deemed satisfied in these instances by the fact that the situation to which the measure is applied as well as the measure itself must be defined by statute.[23]

On the other hand, as regards the most significant group raising the issue of separating punishment and measures, habitual offenders, the problem to be resolved has been the number and types of convictions that ought to be required for classification within the group. Von Liszt suggested that one conviction is sufficient to show a "tendency" toward crime in the case of the "offender of status" (chronic state) (*Zustandsverbrecher*). Since the standard for applying a "measure" is a quality of the offender, that is, his dangerousness, it would seem that for this purpose crime repetition is not an indispensable requirement.[24] While it is to some extent deemed symptomatic of danger, it is mainly demanded because it affords a certain objective guarantee of legality. As regards the type of crime that may be committed "habitually," some provisions require "intentionality,"[25] some also identity or similarity of the crimes committed, etc. The Italian Code recognizes as distinctive types the "habitual" and "professional misdemeanant"—*contravventore abituale*[26] and *contravventore professionale*.[27] Jiménez de Asúa suggested that the problem of habitual "negligence" ought to be given more serious consideration,[28] and this suggestion is significant in the light of the psychoanalytic discovery of danger inherent in unconsciously intentional acts, which in law might qualify as either inadvertently negligent or accidental.[29] There is also another intermediate group between the category of "pre-delictual measures" and that of measures predi-

du' 8 février 1955, in Dalloz, *Code pénal* (53rd ed., 1956), at 341. The Italian law mentioned in the text is the law of December 27, 1956, n. 1423, "concerning measures of prevention as regards persons dangerous for public safety and for public morality," in force since January 15, 1957. On this law see Velotti, "Le Misure di prevenzione nel primo anno della loro applicazione," in *Conferenze, Secondo Corso di Perfezionamento per Uditori Giudiziari,* Ministero di Grazia e Giustizia, Academia della Magistratura, Milano, 1959, 567–581.

For measures similar to the "vagrants" laws, cited *supra,* in England and in the United States, see Dession, *Criminal Law, Administration and Public Order,* 153 (1948).

[22] See provisions on putative crime (Art. 49, Penal Code) and agreement to commit crime (Art. 115, *ibid.*).

[23] Arts. 199 and 202 (2), Italian Penal Code.

[24] In fact, the Italian "criminal by tendency" (*delinquente per tendenza*) of Art. 108, Penal Code, as distinguished from the "habitual criminal" (*delinquente abituale*), Arts. 102–103, and the "professional criminal" (*delinquente professionale*), Art. 105, is not a recidivist.

[25] Arts. 102, 103, Italian Penal Code.

[26] Art. 105, *ibid.*

[27] Art. 104, *ibid.*

[28] "El Delinquente habitual y el 'recidivismo,' " in *El Criminalista,* 2nd series, Vol. II, 253 at 255 (1958).

[29] Notice the phenomenon of "accident-proneness."

cated upon "intentionality" and graveness of the crime involved. To this group belong measures imposed where the precipitating crimes are minor but of a type mostly committed "habitually," such as prostitution, begging. The variations of precipitating crimes and situations are given consideration in the variety of applicable measures, hospitalization, security commitment, the "workhouse," supervision, etc., and of the permissible periods of detention.

A corollary of the principle of "guilt-adequacy" in the law of punishment is what might be called "danger-adequacy" in the law of measures. It is a principle akin to that governing the law of "necessity." The measure must not be out of proportion to the danger. According to the German Draft, serious measures, *e.g.*, protective detention in a mental hospital of those acquitted on the ground of mental incapacity or of those less severely punished on the ground of diminished capacity, may not be applied unless the danger to the community or to particular individuals is "considerable."[30] They are not admissible where commission of insignificant crimes is anticipated. Similarly, compulsory placement of alcoholics and drug addicts in institutions for the cure of alcoholism or addiction may be ordered only to prevent commission of "considerable crimes."[31] Significantly, "dangerousness," upon which declaration of a person as an "actor by tendency" (*Hangtäter*)—this is the Draft's equivalent of the present concept of "dangerous habitual criminal"—is predicated, requires the "tendency to be directed to considerable crimes" and the actor to be, "because of that tendency, dangerous to the community or to particular individuals."[32] As will be later shown, time limitations and proof requirements are also differentiated to meet the demand for proportionality of the restriction to the danger involved.

Proportionality to danger is also required in the case of measures not involving "freedom deprivation," such as withdrawal of licences, prohibition to exercise a profession or trade, confiscation. Some of these restrictions, particularly those involving freedom to engage in a profession or trade, might be of questionable constitutionality in principle when applied as punitive devices. Even as measures, they have been challenged when their scope appeared not to be proportionate to the precipitating crimes. Decisions upholding their validity rely on proportionality of the measure to the danger to the community.[33]

A noteworthy feature of the new development is introduction of probation into the law of measures. The German Draft regards institutionalization of persons acquitted on the ground of insanity and those declared "actors by tendency" as not a subsidiary measure, meaning that it must be imposed even though other methods of coping with the subject are available. Instead, the Draft permits the court to release the subject on

30 § 86, German Draft, 1958, at 18.

31 § 87, *ibid.*

32 § 88, *ibid.*, and comment at 89. The "*Hangtäter*" or "criminal by tendency" of the German Draft must not be confused with the Italian "*delinquente per tendenza*," Art. 108, Italian Penal Code, though it bears the same name.

33 It has thus been held that where a person has committed crimes in only one section of his trade, prohibition of the exercise of the trade may be, nevertheless, imposed without limitation, if this is necessary for the protection of the public. Decision of the Bundesgerichtshof in Criminal Matters (Federal Republic of Germany) (I. Strafsenat), July 8, 1958, relying on a decision of the Reichsgericht (R.G.St. 71, 69), reported in 11 NJW 1404 (1958).

probation, in which event, however, the court must provide for supervision and probation aid.[34] Thus, probation aid is being made available to the mentally ill requiring no institutionalization.

In a system combining measures with punishment, problems of conflict present major difficulties. Where the grounds justifying punishment concur with those calling for measures, the solutions of the conflicting claims of the two schemes vary in different countries; and even within the same country, they vary from issue to issue. These solutions have been cumulation of punishment and measure or substitution of one by the other. In the case of cumulation, priority of execution varies and methods are being developed of permitting the judge to dispense with execution of the device last to be applied.

The central problem of the described systems has been the complex issue of recidivism and habitual criminality, in which punitive demands concur with the need of averting danger. An important contribution of the dual approach consists in affording a basis for elaboration of the distinctiveness of the two terms, recidivism and habitual criminality, that have been often used interchangeably. As pointed out by Jiménez de Asúa, recidivism is a purely punitive category, and thus not to be confused with habitual criminality. In the author's view, however, the distinctive feature of "recidivism" cannot be anything but dangerousness. For this reason, he advocates eliminating the punitive concept of "recidivism" and preserving solely the notion of habitual offender, characterized by dangerousness, to be treated within the law of measures.[35] But the German Draft, as will be shown, finds sufficient grounds, other than danger, for justifying aggravation of punishment for recidivism. Dean Ryu has correctly pointed out that a repeated crime constitutes a *sui generis* crime category.[36] Thus, only the "habitual offender," presumably both guilty and dangerous, presents a problem of conflict of treatment methods.

The German law, as now in force, draws the consequence from the combination of guilt and dangerousness in the habitual offender by applying to him a "dual-track system" of pure form. The punishment of such offender is aggravated, and after serving the punitive sentence, the convict is subject to an "indeterminate security detention" which is deemed a measure.[37] In other countries, the reverse procedure is followed. The offender is first subject to a measure and thereafter punished. The combination of punishment and measure has been vigorously criticized.[38] Kohlrausch pointed out that the detainee sees no difference between having his freedom restrained under the label of punishment and being detained under the label of measure.[39] Welzel answered that the difference lies not in the method of execution but in the bases of detention and the standards of release.[40] The latter part of his argument must appeal even to the most prac-

[34] §§ 86, 90, 100–106, German Draft, 1958, and comments at 86–87, 90–91.

[35] "El Delinquente habitual y el 'recidivismo,'" *supra*, note 28, at 254–256.

[36] Ryu, *Korean Culture and Criminal Responsibility*, Yale thesis 1958, on file in Yale Law School Library, p. 82.

[37] §§ 20a, 42e, German Penal Code.

[38] For a thorough discussion of the varieties of approach see Lang-Hinrichsen, "Das Strafensystem," in 2 —*Materialien zur Strafrechstreform, Rechtsvergleichende Arbeiten, Allgemeiner Teil*, 33 at 38–44 (Bonn, 1954).

[39] Cited in Würtenberger, *supra*, note 9, at 97.

[40] Welzel, *op. cit., supra*, note 17, at 207–208.

tically minded critics. But they also question the psychological soundness of applying the measure after execution of the punishment. On the other hand, the reverse procedure of sending a man to jail after he has been presumably reformed by a measure has been criticized as awkward. Finally, the Swiss solution, which substitutes the measure for the punishment,[41] has been challenged on the ground that it grants the habitual offender a preference over the situational offender. German professors consulted by the Ministry of Justice as to the proper solution to be adopted in the new code project advocated the one-track system for such cases—the punitive one in the form of indeterminate sentence.[42] The Draft, however, adopted a different approach. The concept of "dangerous habitual offender" has been abandoned. Its substitute, the "actor by tendency," does not appear in the punitive scheme at all, for this "actor type" is deemed incompatible with the idea of responsibility based on "guilt" except in the form of "responsibility for life conduct"; but, as mentioned before, the latter concept has been rejected. The punitive scheme attaches aggravation to recidivism, the ground of aggravation being an increased responsibility for commission of repeated "acts" based on blame of the actor for "not having let the prior convictions be a warning to him."[43] The "actor by tendency," whose "actor type" quality lies in his being personally "dangerous" in addition to having committed several "acts" of crime, figures only in the part of the Draft dealing with "measures." The measure applied to the "actor by tendency," that is, "security detention," is executed after punishment for recidivism, provided that the "court in charge of execution" (*Vollstreckungsgericht*) then finds that the "purpose of the measure still calls for detention."[44]

In the case of other measures of freedom deprivation, such as placement in an institution of cure, the workhouse, the court may order that the measure be applied prior to execution of punishment if the reformation and resocialization goal prevails over the retributive one. It may also order the period of measure application deducted from the time of punishment.[45]

[41] Art. 42, Swiss Federal Criminal Code.

[42] Würtenberger, *supra*, note 9.

[43] § 63, German Draft, 1958, and see comment at 63.

[44] § 94, German Draft, 1958. The wisdom of the draft solution is doubtful.

[45] § 93, German Draft, 1958. Special institutions for sociopaths following the Danish pattern being provided for within the treatment plan for the mentally ill and for persons of diminished responsibility, authority to transfer detainees from penal to such special institutions is under consideration. See comment to § 86 at 87.

DANGEROUSNESS AND SANCTION*

National Council on Crime and Delinquency

The National Council on Crime and Delinquency has sparked professional interest in a whole range of subjects on the treatment and control of offenders. Their influential Model Sentencing Act of 1963 (a part of which is reprinted here as Appendix A) is the product of a distinguished group of judges working with the staff of the Council. In that Model Act the Council proposes an extended term for dangerous offenders. In a more recent report the Council of Judges supplies practical guidelines for implementing the norm of "dangerousness." The reader is directed to a careful reading of these practical guidelines to see if there is any connection between the crime committed and the sentence imposed.

At the point of sentence, how is the judge to know whether the defendant before him is homicidal, assaultive, or otherwise violent?

In every criminal case, two elements enter the sentencing decision—(1) the nature of the offense; (2) the nature of the offender.

The crimes that most agitate the community are crimes of personal violence, such as rape, serious assault, and armed robbery. With this general view in mind, the Model Sentencing Act proposes that only for a serious crime against the person can a long term of incarceration (over five years) be imposed.[1] But whether or not a jurisdiction has such a sentencing statute, every criminal court judge about to pass sentence must face the question: Is the defendant before me dangerous? The test recommended above—"a serious crime against the person"—is generally applicable. Thus the United States Court of Appeals, in passing on the Maryland Defective Delinquent Act, said:

> Many of the inmates of Patuxent are there by reason of offense against property rights. Many jurists and laymen would seriously question the wisdom of the practice of indefinitely confining young men under these circumstances.[2]

In sentencing for a serious crime against the person, the judge must be informed on the character and mental makeup of the offender. Merely to know that the crime was armed robbery is not enough; it may have been committed under the pressure of circumstances not likely to be repeated. An assault may

* Excerpted from National Council on Crime and Delinquency, *Guides to Sentencing the Dangerous Offender* (1969).

[1] It also provides that a defendant convicted of murder in the second degree, arson, forcible rape, robbery while armed with a deadly weapon, or any one of several other crimes may be committed for a term of ten years without meeting the criteria of the dangerous offender. NCCD, Council of Judges, Model Sentencing Act (1963), Optional § 8. See Appendix A.

[2] Sas v. Maryland, 334 F.2d 506 (4th Cir. 1965).

have been the outcome of an argument; on the other hand, it may have been an unprovoked attack by a mentally disturbed person. If the defendant is seriously disturbed and the disturbance is of a kind that may produce a repetition of the "serious crime against the person" under ordinary circumstances, then public safety requires that he be sentenced to a fairly long maximum term of incarceration, in an institution which, ideally, can provide therapeutic treatment.

Those who are dangerous offenders, as defined in the Model Act, constitute only a small part of today's prison population. The Act visualizes the confinement of the dangerous offender in institutions much different from and smaller than the typical maximum-security prison. Rehabilitation of disturbed offenders can be achieved only in an institution whose size permits the application of psychiatric and other forms of therapeutic treatment as needed.

Because of its pervasiveness, its corruption of government, its ruthless use of violence, and the improbability of reformation of its members, organized crime is also included in the Model Sentencing Act as a type of offense that calls for long maximum terms of incarceration for the protection of the public. . . .

If the defendant is one who, because of the nature of his crime, may be dangerous, the judge requires more information than he would need for sentencing an offender whose crime did not involve serious violence. First of all, therefore, he must be alert to certain situations in the defendant's history and in the circumstances surrounding the particular crime which suggest the possibility that the defendant may be suffering from a mental or emotional disorder indicating a propensity toward continuing criminal activity of a dangerous nature. If these indicia are present, he would call for a diagnostic work-up or pursue other leads to significant information.

What are some preliminary indications? Although there are no rules of thumb,[3] some common-sense signs may be noted. For example, a violent sex crime, such as a forcible rape under a threat of stabbing, calls for further study. So also would a serious assault in which the offender was armed. (However, if the assault was committed by a person in or from a neighborhood where, say, carrying a knife was a common characteristic, the court must determine whether the defendant possessed the weapon to commit the assault or was merely conforming to his culture.) A serious assault by a person under the influence of alcohol may indicate the need for further investigation to determine whether the defendant has exhibited a persistent pattern of violence when intoxicated. Com-

[3] Studies of personality patterns produce many criteria that are useful to a clinic in evaluating a violent offender, but there are no simple rules of thumb. "Many people assume that prediction has become a precise science. In practice, this assumption takes the form of a belief that if 'someone' had given the proper tests to Whitman, Speck, or Oswald, the tragedies connected with each of them could have been averted. Nothing in the realm of 'Might Have Been' is certain. What is certain is that Whitman saw a psychiatrist shortly before his rampage, and the psychiatrist was not unduly alarmed. Speck had been in and out of prisons on a variety of lesser offenses, and none of the officials rated him a greater release risk than any other prisoner. Oswald had had psychiatric tests in the Marine Corps, and these, along with considerable other data, were available to the Secret Service. The Secret Service thought he was a political eccentric, nothing more."—California Legislature, Assembly Interim Committee on Ways and Means, Subcommittee on Mental Health Services, The Dilemma of Mental Commitments in California 149 (1967).

munity concern over a violent crime is, by itself, sufficient reason for further study, but not, by itself, sufficient reason for a severe sentence; only a careful study of the defendant would determine whether a severe sentence is justified. A soldier may have committed a violent crime. What is his background? What were his battlefield experiences and reactions? Information on the nature of his behavior off the battlefield, too, would be significant.

The Model Sentencing Act calls for a presentence investigation in all felony cases and in any misdemeanor case involving moral turpitude. The presentence report, which gives the basic facts for a sentence, may contain material alerting the judge to the need for fuller information, or it may explicitly recommend further study, but the probation department does not always have the resources to make such a further investigation, and the information needed may be of some other kind that the probation department does not have access to. For example, the judge may have to contact a commanding officer for details of the soldier's background that might not have been given to the probation officer (but which should then be incorporated in the report). Or, community leaders may be asked for their knowledge of a defendant about whom others will not give information because they fear his power and regard him as being beyond the reach of customary law enforcement.

Often the further information needed can be supplied in a diagnostic work-up. (The special sentencing provisions of sexual psychopath statutes typically require referral for diagnostic work-ups.) The Model Sentencing Act requires that before sentencing a defendant (other than a racketeer) as a dangerous offender, the judge must remand him to a diagnostic facility[4] for study and report as to whether he is suffering from a "mental or emotional disorder indicating a propensity toward continuing criminal activity of a dangerous nature."[5] The expertise that psychiatric and psychological knowledge is best equipped to provide in the report will focus not merely on diagnosis, but also on analysis of the defendant's "life style" and experiences. The essence of the dangerous offender classification is not one specific diagnosis, but any significant mental or emotional disorder or disturbance—a lay concept; the important material is the explanation of past behavior and particularly the current crime.

Thus, the information on which the sentence of a dangerous offender will be based—the presentence investigation report and the report of the clinic or diagnostic facility—comprises a *life history,* one in which the elements that will clarify past and probable future criminal behavior are adequately stated. . . . A brief report based principally on psycho-

[4] In the federal system the judge may call for a diagnostic work-up either before sentencing or after imposing a maximum sentence subject to revision. It seems more desirable to call for the examination before the sentence, as part of the entire presentence study process.

[5] The wording in the first edition of the Model Sentencing Act, published in 1963, is slightly different: "severe personality disorder indicating a propensity toward criminal activity." The second edition of the MSA, in preparation, will revise this language to the words used in the text. The change was adopted because a number of psychiatrists had pointed out that the term "personality disorder" might be mistakenly construed as the classification of a specific type of disorder, whereas this is not what was intended. The intention was to refer to defendants who, in the terms of laymen, were suffering from some mental or emotional disorder and not to limit the disordered state to any one specific diagnosis.

logical tests of the defendant would not be acceptable. A diagnostic service of the kind visualized here would report to the judge not only on the particular defendant, but on general psychological and behavioral patterns that have been discovered from numerous cases that might shed light on this defendant.

Present understanding of violence in personality patterns is quite limited, but we expect that knowledge of it will accumulate if a diagnostic referral service, whether this be housed in an institution or in a court clinic, is established, or if existing resources are given such a mission. For an understanding of such patterns, the individual reports are not sufficient. It is important for the judge to become acquainted with the literature. With a new focus on the issue of violent behavior, new materials are likely to be forthcoming.

The judge should not merely make a general referral; rather, he should specify whatever clues or questions he has. A general referral is acceptable if the clinic knows, from past experience with the judge, specifically what he desires. If some element in the crime or some facet of the defendant's history puzzles the judge, he should make his query specific. Details of the crime should be made known to the clinic, and whatever denial of the facts is made by the defendant should also be presented.

The sentence should be based on the judge's evaluation of all the information gathered, not exclusively on the clinical diagnosis. A psychiatric report that is couched in a jargon the judge cannot understand or that states conclusions drawn from unrevealed facts is not usable. The judge should, when necessary, call for the psychiatric or psychological work-ups on which the report to the court was based.

Under the Model Sentencing Act a long term may be imposed on the defendant found to be dangerous. In such cases, the Act requires that "the judge shall make the presentence report, the report of the diagnostic center, and other diagnostic reports available to the attorney for the state and to the defendant or his counsel or other representative upon request. Subject to the control of the court, the defendant shall be entitled to cross-examine those who have rendered reports to the court."[6] This more than meets the procedural due process requirements of the Supreme Court pronouncement on the subject.[7] The defendant may also submit his own report and may offer witnesses.

> If the judge is to have the responsibility, as he does, to render the important and discriminating judgment as to the nature of the offender, a substantial hearing of the type outlined by this model statute is essential for the judge to obtain an adequate sense of the defendant, his past record, and the studies made.[8]

The defendant being committed to examination should also be told by the judge that he has a right to remain silent. If he does remain silent, the report can still be made; it will be based on an examination of the various reports on the defendant and observations of him by nurses, clinicians, and attendants. Guides for conducting examinations of uncooperative patients are available.[9]

Having obtained the expanded report on a defendant who may be subject to a long term as a dangerous offender, the

[6] *Op. cit. supra* note 1, § 4.

[7] Specht v. Patterson, 386 U.S. 605, 87 Sup. Ct. 1209, 18 L. Ed. 326 (1967), invalidating the Colorado sexual psychopath statute.

[8] Murrah, *The Dangerous Offender under the Model Sentencing Act,* Fed. Prob., June 1968, p. 3.

[9] Davidson, Forensic Psychiatry (2nd ed. 1965).

judge must evaluate it. He must consider, for example, the defendant's relationship to the victim. Was the victim a stranger who had no role in provoking the crime? Did the defendant act alone? Was he encouraged or incited by a codefendant, by the victim, or by someone else? Was the violence incidental or did the defendant intend to inflict serious harm?

Should a repeater be sentenced differently from a first offender? Statutes in all states say he should, enunciating as policy that a repeater may receive greater punishment than a first offender. Unfortunately, they are useless in distinguishing dangerous from nondangerous offenders; most defendants committed under the repeated offender statutes are nondangerous property offenders.[10] Judges and prosecutors are well aware of this, and most offenders who might be more severely sentenced under the recidivism statutes are not so punished; rather, the threat of the increased sentence is used to persuade defendants to plead guilty to lesser charges.

Categorical use of the criminal record should be avoided. A defendant convicted as a first offender may be, in fact, a dangerous person who previously committed one or more serious crimes without being apprehended; it may be that the occasion of the crime leading to his first conviction was merely the first time that a previously suppressed compulsion was not controlled. The judge should search for the facts that will serve as a guide to the defendant's likely behavior in the future.

The Model Sentencing Act makes these principles operative by providing that (1) a first offender convicted of a serious crime against the person may be committed for a long term as a dangerous offender and (2) a repeater whose crimes are not of this type may not be committed for more than a five-year term despite their repetition.[11] A dangerous offender, it says, is one who "is being sentenced for a felony in which he inflicted or attempted to inflict serious bodily harm, and the court finds that he is suffering from a mental or emotional disorder indicating a propensity toward continuing criminal activity of a dangerous nature" or "the defendant is being sentenced for a crime which seriously endangered the life or safety of another, has been previously convicted of one or more felonies not related to the instant crime as a single criminal episode, and the court finds that he is suffering from a mental or emotional disorder indicating a propensity toward continuing criminal activity of a dangerous nature."[12] The second of these concepts allows the court to sentence the defendant to a long term by taking his previous criminal and personal history into account even though the instant crime itself—e.g., arson—may not have shown clearly that he intended bodily harm to persons.

One of the clichés in penal codes and sentencing is the presumed dangerousness of sex offenders. A majority of the states have one or another version of a sexual psychopath statute. The definitions are unsatisfactory and unscientific.[13]

[10] RUBIN, WEIHOFEN, EDWARDS, & ROSENZWEIG, THE LAW OF CRIMINAL CORRECTION 391-403 (1963).

[11] Except for "atrocious crimes," *op. cit. supra* note 1.

[12] *Op. cit. supra* note I, rev. ed. § 5.

[13] The unscientific and confusing nature of the definitions is well illustrated by the opinions—majority and dissenting—of the U.S. Supreme Court in Boutilier v. Immigration and Naturalization Service, 387 U.S. 118, 87 Sup. Ct. 1563 (1967). The outcome of the case is itself an illustration of the point, the court saying in effect that a psychopath is what Congress says he is.

The statutes authorize or require a diagnostic work-up of defendants who come within their terms. At present this diagnostic service is inadequate and usually authorizes an increased term of commitment for the purpose of treatment. In many places the treatment of sexual psychopaths or sociopaths is minimal or nonexistent.[14]

It is important to note that some sexually disturbed persons commit violent crimes without sexually molesting the victim. The sexual psychopath statutes fail to differentiate between violent and nonviolent acts, and they are usually applied to persons who have committed a nonviolent act such as exhibitionism or sodomy with a consenting adult partner. At best, these statutes are ineffectual and give the public only the illusion of protection. The Model Sentencing Act would repeal the sexual psychopath statutes; by emphasizing instead the *dangerousness* of *any* offender whose crime is seriously assaultive, it would provide broader protection to the community.

The key to the MSA definition of dangerousness is not exclusively a finding of "mental or emotional disorder" but rather the finding of "a mental or emotional disorder indicating a propensity toward continuing criminal activity of a dangerous nature." The objective is prevention of future serious crime, carefully avoiding use of the criminal process to commit to penal institutions those mentally ill offenders whose abberations are not of the assaultive type.[15]

The diagnostic report should help the court determine the persistency of assaultive patterns. If the defendant's violence arises out of an irrational response to situations that will occur frequently in his lifetime or when he is under the influence of alcohol or drugs, or even if he is likely to strike out physically at others when he has had an argument, he is probably one who comes within the concept of dangerousness. But it must be borne in mind that not every shorttempered person who gets into fights readily is a serious threat; relatively few are "dangerous" in the sense considered in the Model Sentencing Act. If a seriously disturbed person commits a crime which the diagnostic study indicates he is not likely to repeat, either because the circumstances were unusual and not likely to reoccur or because the mental illness had nothing to do with the criminal act, a long term is probably not needed to protect the public. The focus should be not on heinousness but on the danger of repetition.

Conversely, a person who has all the outward attributes generally regarded as

---

14 Slovenko & Phillips, *Psychosexuality and the Criminal Law*, 15 VAND. L. REV. 797, at 822 (1962).

15 As a group the mentally ill are not more assaultive than others. "In a previous paper [*Dangerousness—Arrest Rate Comparisons of Discharged patients and the General Population*, 121 AM. J. PSYCHIAT. 776-83 (1965)] we compared the arrest rates of male discharged patients and the general population. Our findings indicated that of five serious offenses—murder, manslaughter, rape, robbery, and aggravated assault—only robbery showed a higher incidence among males with a psychiatric hospital experience. Taken over-all, we found that our male psychiatric population reflected the trends of criminality of the general male population, and did not show a lower rate of arrests as had been previously reported by others. We also noted that alcoholics and schizophrenics accounted for the largest percentage of those contributing to these statistics because they represented the majority of the hospitalized patients."—Rappeport & Lassen, *The Dangerousness of Female Patients: A Comparison of the Arrest Rate of Discharged Psychiatric Patients and the General Population*, 123 AM. J. PSYCHIAT. 413 (1966).

praiseworthy may commit a "senseless" crime, like the mass killing of several unrelated persons a few years ago by a young man who had been regarded as an average American youth—he had been an Eagle Scout and an altar boy, had taken piano lessons, had a satisfactory record as a Marine, was a good student at college. But he was seriously disturbed and, if released without treatment, would be likely to repeat the crime. In short, an unsavory-appearing defendant may be a good risk; a superficially "nice" defendant may be a bad risk.

Judges have always longed for reliable knowledge that would enable them to sentence with assurance. They have had to be satisfied with their own insight into human behavior, general understanding of offenders, and general knowledge of the success or failure of one or another form of disposition. When sentencing a defendant whose violence is so far beyond customary reactions to stress that surely it must indicate a mental aberration, judges turn with great expectations to the field of psychiatry.

Here too, unfortunately, present knowledge does not provide the means for confidently predicting future behavior. Research is needed to provide more precise guidance than is presently available. Judges are aware of the currently limited state of knowledge, and they know that the responsibility for understanding the defendant and formulating the sentence is, ultimately, theirs.[16]

The clinician, however, can help the judge distinguish between violent and nonviolent persons. Dr. Seymour Halleck writes:

> The psychiatrist has few more important functions in criminology than evaluating the probability that a given offender is likely to do violence to his fellow man. It must be reluctantly admitted that there is little science to be brought to this most sensitive task. Research in the area of dangerous behavior (other than generalizations from case material) is practically nonexistent. Predictive studies which have examined the probability of recidivism have not focused on the issue of dangerousness. If the psychiatrist or any other behavioral scientist were asked to show proof of his predictive skills, objective data could not be offered. The most a psychiatrist can say is that he has had considerable experience in dealing with disturbed people who commit dangerous acts, that he has been designated by society to diagnose and treat such individuals, and that his skill in treating dangerous behavior in those diagnosed as mentally ill has generally been appreciated.[17]

On the other hand, Dr. Guttmacher has said that a thorough social, psychological, and psychiatric study of a burglar, for example, can determine "with a great degree of accuracy" whether his antisocial behavior is caused by his dissocial orientation or whether it springs from deep, complex emotional factors. The first condition, says Dr. Guttmacher, may be amenable to ordinary corrective measures, whereas the latter would re-

[16] "There is very little in the literature of psychiatry about dangerousness of persons toward others. . . . Only a very limited number of psychiatric centers have dealt with problems of criminality . . . in this extremely serious area. . . . Very little study has gone into systematizing our knowledge of abnormal offenders so that they may be identified and subjected to timely preventive detention."—Dr. Harry Kozol, remarks on "Recognizing and Sentencing the Dangerous Offender," at National Conference of State Trial Judges, Aug. 6, 1966, pp. 37, 38.

[17] Halleck, Psychiatry and the Dilemmas of Crime 313–14 (1967); all of ch. 20, "Evaluating the Offender," is of interest.

quire special therapeutic techniques.[18]

Although the diagnostic labels "psychopath" and "sociopath" have been generally discredited as meaningless, they may still be found in many psychiatric reports to the court, which cannot tell from such a diagnosis whether the examined offender is violent. Other conventional diagnoses like "schizophrenia" and "paranoia" also do not tell the court whether the defendant so labeled is likely to be violent.

What the judge needs, rather, is a report giving information on the defendant's history with particular reference to violent behavior—assaultive or homicidal acts, reckless use of weapons or tools, etc. Projective tests administered by psychologists that may measure such things as "aggressiveness" cannot be used alone, though of course they are useful in weighing the psychiatrist's or psychologist's reasons for his opinion. A mere conclusion that the defendant is "not safe to be at large" is insufficient. The specific danger likely to occur under certain circumstances should be stated. The Model Sentencing Act provision for a specialized diagnostic facility reflects the need for special attention to the problem of violence and the reasonable assumption that psychiatry has the expertise to provide meaningful information when it turns to the study of violence. It is for the clinic to explain the medical significance of the diagnosis and for the judge to evaluate the report.

The principle purpose of the foregoing is to focus attention on the dangerous offender, one who is likely to commit a serious crime against the person. Since the primary objective in sentencing such a defendant is the protection of society, the Model Sentencing Act recommends a long term, up to a maximum of thirty years. What the specific maximum shall be for any given dangerous offender is for the court to decide. Not all offenders categorized as dangerous are the same; the maximum term of the sentence should reflect the judgment of the court as to the defendant's relative dangerousness, his age, and any other factors that would indicate the length of time his dangerousness is liable to persist.

If the defendant is not dangerous but is mentally disturbed, the judge should be cautious about committing him to prison. Penal commitment of a nonassaultive sex offender may worsen his aberration. In such a case, probation with psychiatric treatment or with outpatient service at a psychiatric clinic should be used. If no psychiatric service is available, then probation supervision alone, by knowledgeable officers competent to deal with disturbed offenders, should be the preferred disposition.

The Model Sentencing Act provides that no commitment shall have a minimum term of parole eligibility; and, where possible under the statute, the sentence should not state a minimum. A minimum term might conceivably be justified if precise prediction were a reality; since it is not, the time of release is best left to the releasing authority without the restriction of a minimum term.

The severe sentence imposed on the dangerous offender assures protection of the public against the violent repeater, but security does not rule out the penal system's need for therapeutic resources. It is the obligation of both the psychiatrist who is working in a penal institution and the judge who is committing offenders to it to exercise leadership so that the necessary treatment resources will be provided.

[18] Guttmacher, *Dangerous Offenders*, 9 CRIME & DELIN, at 385 (1963).

APPENDIX A

MODEL SENTENCING ACT

Advisory Council of Judges of the National Council on Crime and Delinquency

§ 5. DANGEROUS OFFENDERS

Except for the crime of murder in the first degree, the court may sentence a defendant convicted of a felony to a term of commitment of thirty years, or to a lesser term, if it finds that because of the dangerousness of the defendant, such period of confined correctional treatment or custody is required for the protection of the public, and if it further finds, as provided in section 6, that one or more of the following grounds exist:

(a) The defendant is being sentenced for a felony in which he inflicted or attempted to inflict serious bodily harm, and the court finds that he is suffering from a severe personality disorder indicating a propensity toward criminal activity. (b) The defendant is being sentenced for a crime which seriously endangered the life or safety of another, has been previously convicted of one or more felonies not related to the instant crime as a single criminal episode, and the court finds that he is suffering from a severe personality disorder indicating a propensity toward criminal activity. (c) The defendant is being sentenced for the crime of extortion, compulsory prostitution, selling or knowingly and unlawfully transporting narcotics, or other felony, committed as part of a continuing criminal activity in concert with one or more persons.

The findings required in this section shall be incorporated in the record.

§ 6. PROCEDURE AND FINDINGS

The defendant shall not be sentenced under subdivision (a) or (b) of section 5 unless he is remanded by the judge before sentence to diagnostic facility for study and report as to whether he is suffering from a severe personality disorder indicating a propensity toward criminal activity; and the judge, after considering the presentence investigation, the report of the diagnostic facility, and the evidence in the case or on the hearing on the sentence, finds that the defendant comes within the purview of subdivision (a) or (b) of section 5. The defendant shall be remanded to a diagnostic facility whenever, in the opinion of the court, there is reason to believe he falls within the category of subdivision (a) or (b) of section 5. Such remand shall not exceed ninety days, subject to additional extensions not exceeding ninety days on order of the court.

The defendant shall not be sentenced under subdivision (c) of section 5 unless the judge finds, on the basis of the presentence investigation or the evidence in the case or on the hearing on the sentence, that the defendant comes within the purview of the subdivision. In support of such findings it may be shown that the defendant has had in his own name or under his control substantial income or resources not explained to the satisfaction of the court as derived from lawful activities or interests.

DANGEROUSNESS AND PREDICTION*

Norval Morris and Gordon Hawkins

Norval Morris and Gordon Hawkins have recently given their extensive learning in criminology an innovative twist with the publication of The Honest Politician's Guide to Crime Control, *(1970). Its thesis is that crime control depends on an effort to eliminate wastage from the system so that police, courts, and prisons are more single-mindedly engaged in protecting life and property. In the course of their pragmatic review of the criminal justice system, they give a critique of prediction and dangerousness from which one may draw the warning that the rights of persons are being jeopardized by a pseudo-certainty parading as science. Norval Morris is Julius Kreeger Professor of Law and Criminology and director of the Center for Studies in Criminal Justice at the University of Chicago. Gordon Hawkins is a criminologist as well as a philosopher.*

The policeman, the prosecutor, the jury, the judge, the probation officer preparing a presentence report, the clinician in the diagnostic and classification center, the correctional officer planning the inmate's treatment and custody, the parole board and the parole officer—all, like it or not, must make predictions about the possible social dangerousness of the offender they confront. This is frequently a complex and difficult task to which psychiatric insights are often relevant. It involves at least two interacting issues: what kinds of behavior are sufficiently threatening to be called "dangerous" and with what degree of certainty must the prognosis establish the likelihood of recurrence of the kind or kinds of behavior designated "dangerous" and over what period of time?

The task of conceptualizing and providing methodologically sound processes for reaching decisions on these twin aspects of "dangerousness" is of central importance to the development of the criminal law. It is critical at every level of the criminal justice system. The report of the President's Crime Commission stresses the

> necessity for identifying those dangerous or habitual offenders who pose a serious threat to the community's safety. They include those offenders whose personal instability is so gross as to erupt periodically in violent and assaultive behavior, and those individuals whose long-term exposure to criminal influences has produced a thoroughgoing commitment to criminal values that is resistive of superficial efforts to effect change. . . .
>
> Clearly indicated is the need for an improved capability in the information gathering and analysis process and contin-

* Reprinted from THE HONEST POLITICIAN'S GUIDE TO CRIME CONTROL by Norval Morris and Gordon Hawkins by permission of the University of Chicago Press. © 1970 by the University of Chicago.

ued experimental development to improve the predictive power of the information gathered. These needs point to increased manpower and the training requisite for the development of sophistication and skill in the investigative-diagnostic process.

There is another reason, relevant to developments in the field of corrections which we have dealt with at some length in chapter 5, why we must move toward more sophisticated definitions of dangerousness. Certain goals and broad methods of correctional treatment are increasingly accepted. Following the lead of psychiatry we develop community-based corrections emulating the community psychiatry movement. We design an armamentarium of alternatives to prisons, all of which try to treat criminals in the community; specifically, we move toward halfway houses, work-releases, furloughs, and community treatment centers. And the leaders in the correctional field struggle to reduce the duration of the social isolation we call prison in those cases in which it is used. Our attitude to the mega-prison matches the psychiatrist's concern about the continued survival of the mega-asylum, the gross and pervasive state mental hospital. This aspect of the evolution of treatment processes is clear, and we have made it clear that we favor this development; yet the evolutionary pace is inhibited by a mixing of prisoners who are social nuisances with those who are social threats —the poacher with the predator, the sneak thief with the sadist. This Gresham's Law, this principle of the lowest common denominator, limits treatment processes to the needs of the least easily treated. It also besets the police and the courts as well as the correctional system. It is necessary better to discriminate and more meaningfully to diversify our processes.

There are various legal approaches to this task of separating dangerous criminals from less serious offenders. Let us briefly mention several of these in order to sharpen the focus on the challenging psychiatric tasks that remain:

Habitual criminal laws are widespread and long established. "The consensus," writes the director of the American Law Institute, Professor Herbert Wechsler, "is that they are a failure, productive of chaotic and unjust results when they are used, and greatly nullified in practice." They have swept up the persistent social nuisances while leaving the dangerous and serious offenders untouched.

Sexual psychopath laws have spread like a rash of injustice across this country, unjustly commingling the inadequate and aberrant with the dangerous and brutal. Their social and legislative psychopathology is clear; their contribution to the problem of the dangerous offender is slight.

Wherever discretion in sentencing exists, and this is now ubiquitous, the judge may and frequently does fix the sentence at least partly in relation to his view (guided by such advice as he has received) of the future danger the criminal presents to the community.

Wherever discretion in paroling exists, and this is now ubiquitous, the parole board may and frequently does defer the criminal's release if (guided by such advice as it has received) it regards him as a continuing and serious danger to the community. In making this decision, many parole boards are helpfully assisted by parole prediction tables developed for this purpose.

Special quarantine-type legislation, protracting custodial banishment, is also frequently used for persistent petty offenders, professional criminals, multiple offenders, vagrants, prostitutes, alcoholics, and narcotic addicts.

None of these techniques has brought us to grips with the various classifications of dangerous offenders we must reach if our criminal justice system is to have any chance of becoming socially protective. Two major recommendations for this purpose have been made—one by the American Law Institute, the other by the Advisory Council of Judges of the National Council on Crime and Delinquency.

The American Law Institute's Model Penal Code authorizes a trial judge, when sentencing a person convicted of a felony, to extend the term of imprisonment beyond the maximum provided for that category of felon when "the defendant is a dangerous, mentally abnormal person whose commitment for an extended term is necessary for protection of the public." Psychiatric examination "resulting in the conclusion that his mental condition is gravely abnormal; that his criminal conduct has been characterized by a pattern of repetitive or compulsive behavior or by persistent aggressive behavior with heedless indifference to consequences; and that such condition makes him a serious danger to others" is a precondition to the judicial imposition of the extended sentence.

The Model Sentencing Act of the Advisory Council of Judges of the NCCD has as a pivotal classification the distinction between "dangerous offenders" and all others. The former are defined as those who have committed or attempted certain crimes of physical violence and who the court finds to be "suffering from a severe personality disorder indicating a propensity towards criminal activity." Again psychiatric diagnosis and advice to the judge are a precondition to the exercise of this power. Unlike the Model Penal Code, however, a psychiatric recommendation in favor of the longer sentence is not required for such a sentence to be imposed. Furthermore, such a "dangerous offender" may be sentenced to a term of thirty years' imprisonment!

Under these two systems, pouring meaning into the definition of the "dangerous offender" would become an obligation of psychiatrists and lawyers. A third example of the need for this type of definition merits mention. The benevolence of the Durham rules has led to the compulsory hospitalization in the District of Columbia of those found not guilty by reason of insanity until such time as the court concurs in the certification of the superintendent of Saint Elizabeth's Hospital that the detained person "has recovered his sanity, . . . and will not in the reasonable future be dangerous to himself or others." It is a serious moral question whether the power to detain the "no longer insane" in a mental hospital because of his predicted future danger to himself or others is a fertile source of gross injustice; but whether or not it is, here too can be seen the urgent need for psychiatric and legal definition of an operable concept of dangerousness.

To take power over the lives of others on predictions of their future criminality, in particular of the likelihood of future physical injury they may inflict on others, is no light assumption of competence. Those who cautiously and modestly assess their abilities would, it might seem, hesitate in the face of such awesome authority; but neither lawyers nor psychiatrists seem to have been unduly disturbed by such reflections. The distressing moral problem inherent in this situation can be stated as: Whom shall we trust? Our reply, for the time being, is: Nobody. We believe that we can construct an effective and just system of criminal justice without relying on increasing our power over offenders on the grounds of their predicted dangerousness. Within the ambit of power defined by other purposes, mostly retributive, we must frequently relate sentences and parole decisions to our best judgments of the offender's dangerousness; but we should not rely on such inadequate judgments to increase our power over him, to raise the limits of punishment. This rejection of increased power based on predictions of the criminal's dangerousness does not mean that such predictions are irrelevant. Quite the contrary; they can be essential to rational decision making, from arrest to final discharge from parole, but only if we are sincere in our protestations of community protection without injustice to the offender.

The path before us is lengthy and passes through many thickets, clinical and jurisprudential. We wish here to consider only two: the myth of individual clinical judgments and the failure to develop methodologically acceptable means of predicting dangerousness. We must escape that mythology and design morbity tables appropriate to assisting us in predicting the criminal's dangerousness. It is surely clear, without argument, that neither a merely diagnostic classification nor one which is only a synonym for types of symptoms can suffice for purposes of such predictions. In 1958 Dr. Ralph Brancale argued that "an improved methodology in psychiatric work should, in time, dispel the popular notion that psychiatric conclusions are, for the most part, inferential guesses." Eleven years later, so far as predictions of the future danger of an offender are concerned, we are no closer to dispelling that popular notion. In 1966, Dr. Brancale himself wrote (and he and his staff of thirty full-time clinicians at the Menlo Park Diagnostic Center, New Jersey, have vast experience in this work): "Psychiatrically, our course of development has been slow and laborious. The insights which we believe we have gained are not readily confirmed by research methods and the judgments that are made are not always sustained by scientific formulations." We offer these quotations by Dr. Brancale as witness to the need for "research methods" and "scientific fomulations"; without them, our emotional reactions to the actualities and threats of crimes of violence will lead us to inflict injustice on individuals and to tolerate superficial and discordant concepts in our system of criminal justice; currently a myth of individual clinical psychiatric judgment, using a complex diagnostic taxonomy together with a primitive treatment nosology, bedevils psychiatry. Let us clarify that opaque condemnation by analogy.

Many readers will remember the heroic days when the weather forecaster would boldly aver a prediction of "no rain tomorrow." He is more cautious today. The proposition now is that "within a defined geographic area, there is a 10 percent chance of measurable rain." The forecaster does not thereby reveal that he has succumbed to the modern epidemic of pretentious circumlocution; rather, he is making a laudable effort more precisely to state his knowledge. And what is that knowledge? We assume that a fuller statement of his prediction would read, "The configuration of dynamically interacting meteorological processes within a given region which, to the best of our knowledge, create the weather conditions we now see and have observed over the past days and hours, giving these factors the weight which experience and our understanding of their operation leads us to allot to them, most closely resembles a category of weather experience in the past on which, during the immediately subsequent day, it rained measurably in another defined region in one in ten cases." And few people today would plan any outdoor activity on the advice of a weather predictor who, fresh for each case and judging only by his own vast experience and deep intuition, looked at those factors which he believed most significantly affected the weather and struck what he asserted to be an individual, personalized weather prediction.

The same is, we believe, true of psychiatric predictions of dangerousness. If, of course, a hurricane is marching steadily in one's direction, it requires no great prescience to predict tomorrow's weather. There are cases of equal obviousness in predicting serious criminality; but they are rare. The usual case demands, it seems to us, prediction in terms of probability based on existing categories of experience. These categories should not be expressed only in a multiplicity of lengthy case histories; they should also be reduced to a summarization of experience in a more precise and quantified form.

One should not place great reliance on psychiatric predictions of social dangerousness until they have been expressed in the form of prediction tables, which are really only "experience tables," and which are available for critical testing by other than the predictor. The raconteurs, the narrators of the individual case history, may greatly contribute to our understanding of the dynamic interaction of individual and social processes, but such solitary insights can only in the most exceptional cases form the basis of predictions of social dangerousness on which the law should rely. Control over another man's life is too serious a matter to be posited on other than tested, evaluated, refined experience—on carefully validated prediction tables.

The mechanics of the preparation of prediction tables are well established. There have been some false leads in criminology but, overall, the movement from prediction tables to base expectancy rates and the testing of alternative treatments in relation to those rates is the most promising methodological tool we have developed. It is no substitute for clinical judgment; it is rather a necessary precondition of clinical judgment. Until this hard work has been done, we would most strenuously oppose any sentencing or paroling process structured around psychiatric predictions of dangerousness. To this extent, we regard the provisions which we have discussed in the Model Penal Code and Model Sentencing Act as based on false assumptions of knowledge; accordingly, they should be vehemently resisted.

Such an approach to predicting dangerousness does not, of course, grapple with the quite separate and equally important question of defining "danger." For this purpose: danger of what type of criminal behavior? What *types of risk* should the community bear? But it does lead us to the central policy issue thereafter: what *degree of risk* should the community bear in relation to the countervailing values of individual freedom? It leads to the determinative and difficult policy question: how many "false positive" predictions (he will prove to be a danger, but does not) are justified for the sake of avoiding the "true positive" predictions? This is a sociolegal question, not one within the psychiatrist's particular competence. We cannot, however, even reach that question, let alone answer it, until psychiatry has more amply contributed the data within its competence relevant to posing the question for diverse categories of offenders. Psychiatrists must do the hard statistical work; they cannot slough it off by superficial assumptions of the sufficiency of clinical insights; nor can they rely on those in other disciplines to do that hard statistical work for them.

To put the argument in a slightly different form, we are submitting that, just as it is impossible to consider an individual case in a social vacuum, so it is impossible to make "individual" predictions. Every consideration of the individual is inevitably a consideration of the ways in which and the extent to which he conforms to and varies from a class or classes of people about whom we have defined experience. So guided, if our experience is ample and quantified, and our perceptions of his similarities to and differences from that class precise, we may be able to state that "this offender belongs to a group of whom X in every hundred commit a crime of defined gravity within Y months or years." Of course, even such knowledge, validated and refined, does not provide individual prediction. It leaves open the question, already referred to in chapter 3, whether he is a "false positive." Any individual who falls within a predictably dangerous group may be among the ten in one hundred who do not act out their dangerous potentialities rather than among the ninety who do.

Nevertheless, his "risk category" properly remains of importance to our many unavoidable decisions of how and for how long (within existing powers) to treat him. We can state probabilities based on experience and go slightly further by explaining our reasons for attributing this particular offender's qualities to those of the groups which make up the categories of experience which we are bringing to bear on this predictive task. The psychiatric literature has not, to our knowledge, supplied this necessary basic data for categorizing offenders as dangerous for purposes of sentencing, of allocating our sparse treatment resources, and of determining release procedures. The value of such an effort is clear, not only will it improve our capacity within our existing powers better to protect the community from violent recidivists but also it will set us free better to treat other offenders. Further, we will less frequently segregate the harmless on a false unity that sees the violent criminal as the prototypical criminal and assimilates the treatment of all to the treatment of the prototype.

CRIME, RESPONSIBILITY, AND PREVENTION*

Lady Barbara Wootton

Lady Barbara Wootton, Baroness of Abinger, is a noted social scientist and essayist in criminal law. Through her many years as a lay magistrate she has gained a depth of practical insights that few academic peers enjoy. Her significant Hamlyn Lectures of 1963, published under the title Crime and the Criminal Law *stress the preventive rather than the punitive work of criminal courts. Her most startling conclusion, that criminal responsibility should be allowed to "wither away," highlights the fresh look she takes at traditional criminal concepts. Her observations throw much light on a mixed system of punishment and prevention, and one must conclude that Lady Wootton distinctly prefers the latter for the future correctional system.*

Proposals for the modernisation of the methods by which the criminal courts arrive at their verdicts do not . . . raise any question as to the object of the whole exercise. Much more fundamental are the issues which arise after conviction, when many a judge or magistrate must from time to time have asked himself just what it is that he is trying to achieve. Is he trying to punish the wicked, or to prevent the recurrence of forbidden acts? The former is certainly the traditional answer and is still deeply entrenched both in the legal profession and in the minds of much of the public at large; and it has lately been reasserted in uncompromising terms by a former Lord Chief Justice. At a meeting of magistrates earlier this year Lord Goddard is reported to have said that the duty of the criminal law was to punish—and that reformation of the prisoner was not the courts' business.[1] Those who take this view doubtless comfort themselves with the belief that the two objectives are nearly identical: that the punishment of the wicked is also the best way to prevent the occurrence of prohibited acts. Yet the continual failure of a mainly punitive system to diminish the volume of crime strongly suggests that such comfort is illusory; and it will indeed be a principal theme of these lectures that the choice between the punitive and the preventive[2] concept of the criminal process is a real one; and that, according as that choice is made, radical differences must follow in the courts' approach to their task. I shall, moreover, argue that in recent years a perceptible shift has occurred away from the first and towards the second of these two con-

* Excerpted from CRIME AND THE CRIMINAL LAW by Lady Barbara Wootton, published by Stevens and Sons, London, 1963. Reprinted with permission.

[1] *The Observer*, May 5, 1963.

[2] I use this word throughout to describe a system the primary purpose of which is to prevent the occurrence of offences, whether committed by persons already convicted or by other people.

ceptions of the function of the criminal law; and that this movement is greatly to be welcomed and might with advantage be both more openly acknowledged and also accelerated.

First, however, let us examine the implications of the traditional view. Presumably the wickedness which renders a criminal liable to punishment must be inherent either in the actions which he has committed or in the state of mind in which he has committed them. Can we then in the modern world identify a class of inherently wicked actions? Lord Devlin, who has returned more than once to this theme, holds that we still can, by drawing a sharp distinction between what he calls the criminal and the quasi-criminal law. The distinguishing mark of the latter, in his view, is that a breach of it does not mean that the offender has done anything morally wrong. "Real" crimes, on the other hand, he describes as "sins with legal definitions"; and he adds that "It is a pity that this distinction, which I believe the ordinary man readily recognises, is not acknowledged in the administration of justice." "The sense of obligation which leads the citizen to obey a law that is good in itself is," he says, "different in quality from that which leads to obedience to a regulation designed to secure a good end." Nor does his Lordship see any reason "why the quasi-criminal should be treated with any more ignominy than a man who has incurred a penalty for failing to return a library book in time."[3] And in a personal communication he has further defined the "real" criminal law as any part of the criminal law, new or old, which the good citizen does not break without a sense of guilt.

[3] Devlin, Sir Patrick (now Lord), *Law and Morals* (University of Birmingham) 1961, pp. 3, 7, 8, 9.

Nevertheless this attempt to revive the lawyer's distinction between *mala in se* and *mala prohibita*—things which are bad in themselves and things which are merely prohibited—cannot, I think, succeed. In the first place the statement that a real crime is one about which the good citizen would feel guilty is surely circular. For how is the good citizen to be defined in this context unless as one who feels guilty about committing the crimes that Lord Devlin classifies as "real"? And in the second place the badness even of those actions which would most generally be regarded as *mala in se* is inherent, not in the physical acts themselves, but in the circumstances in which they are performed. Indeed it is hard to think of any examples of actions which could, in a strictly physical sense, be said to be bad in themselves. The physical act of stealing merely involves moving a piece of matter from one place to another: what gives it its immoral character is the framework of property rights in which it occurs. Only the violation of these rights transforms an inherently harmless movement into the iniquitous act of stealing. Nor can bodily assaults be unequivocably classified as *mala in se;* for actions which in other circumstances would amount to grievous bodily harm may be not only legal, but highly beneficial, when performed by competent surgeons; and there are those who see no wrong in killing in the form of judicial hanging or in war.

One is indeed tempted to suspect that actions classified as *mala in se* are really only *mala antiqua*—actions, that is to say, which have been recognised as criminal for a very long time; and that the tendency to dismiss sundry modern offences as "merely quasi-crimes" is simply a mark of not having caught up with the realities of the contemporary world. The criminal calendar is always the expression of a particular social and moral climate, and from one generation to another it is modified by two sets of influences. On the one hand ideas about what is thought to be right or wrong are themselves subject to change; and on the other hand new technical developments constantly create new opportunities for anti-social actions which the criminal code must be extended to include. To a thorough-going Marxist these two types of change would not, presumably, be regarded as mutually independent: to the Marxist it is technical innovations which cause moral judgments to be revised. But for present purposes it does not greatly matter whether the one is, or is not, the cause of the other. In either case the technical and the moral are distinguishable. The fact that there is nothing in the Ten Commandments about the iniquity of driving a motor-vehicle under the influence of drink cannot be read as evidence that the ancient Israelites regarded this offence more leniently than the contemporary British. On the other hand the divergent attitudes of our own criminal law and that of most European countries to homosexual practices has no obvious relation to technical development, and is clearly the expression of differing moral judgments, or at the least to different conceptions of the proper relation between morality and the criminal law.

One only has to glance, too, at the maximum penalties which the law attaches to various offences to realise how profoundly attitudes change in course of time. Life imprisonment, for example, is not only the obligatory sentence for non-capital murder and the maximum permissible for manslaughter. It may also be imposed for blasphemy or for the destruction of registers of births or baptisms. Again, the crime of abducting an heiress carries a potential sentence of fourteen years, while that for the abduction of a child under fourteen years is only half as long. For administering a drug to a female with a view to carnal knowledge a maximum of two years is provided, but for damage to cattle you are liable to fourteen years' imprisonment. For using unlawful oaths the maximum is seven years, but for keeping a child in a brothel it is a mere six months. Such sentences strike us today as quite fantastic; but they cannot have seemed fantastic to those who devised them.

For the origins of the supposed dichotomy between real crimes and quasi-crimes we must undoubtedly look to theology, as Lord Devlin's use of the term "sins with legal definitions" itself implies. The links between law and religion are both strong and ancient. Indeed, as Lord Radcliffe has lately reminded us, it has taken centuries for "English judges to realise that the tenets and injunctions of the Christian religion were not part of the common law of England"[4]; and even today such realisation does not seem to be complete. As recently as 1961, in the "Ladies Directory" case, the defendant Shaw, you may remember, was convicted of conspiring to corrupt public morals, as well as of offences against the Sexual Offences Act of 1956 and the Obscene Publications Act of 1959, on account of his publication of a directory in which the ladies of the town advertised their services, sometimes, it would seem, in considerable detail. In rejecting Shaw's appeal to the House of Lords on the charge of conspiracy, Lord Simonds delivered himself of

[4] Radcliffe, Lord, *The Law and Its Compass* (Faber) 1961, p. 12.

the opinion that without doubt "there remains in the courts a residual power to . . . conserve not only the safety but also the moral welfare of the state"; and Lord Hodson, concurring, added that "even if Christianity be not part of the law of England, yet the common law has its roots in Christianity."[5]

In the secular climate of the present age, however, the appeal to religious doctrine is unconvincing, and unlikely to be generally acceptable. Instead we must recognise a range of actions, the badness of which is inherent not in themselves, but in the circumstances in which they are performed, and which stretches in a continuous scale from wilful murder at one end to failure to observe a no-parking rule or to return on time a library book (which someone else may be urgently wanting) at the other. (Incidentally a certain poignancy is given to Lord Devlin's choice of this last example by a subsequent newspaper report that a book borrower in Frankfurt who omitted, in spite of repeated requests, to return a book which he had borrowed two years previously was brought before a local magistrate actually—though apparently by mistake—in handcuffs.[6]) But however great the range from the heinous to the trivial, the important point is that the gradation is continuous; and in the complexities of modern society a vast range of actions, in themselves apparently morally neutral, must be regarded as in varying degrees anti-social, and therefore in their contemporary settings as no less objectionable than actions whose criminal status is of greater antiquity. The good citizen will doubtless experience different degrees of guilt according as he may have stabbed his wife, engaged in homosexual intercourse, omitted to return his library book or failed to prevent one of his employees from watering the milk sold by his firm. Technically these are all crimes; whether or not they are also sins is a purely theological matter with which the law has no concern. If the function of the criminal law is to punish the wicked, then everything which the law forbids must in the circumstances in which it is forbidden be regarded as in its appropriate measure wicked.

Although this is, I think, the inevitable conclusion of any argument which finds wickedness inherent in particular classes of action, it seems to be unpalatable to Lord Devlin and others who conceive the function of the criminal law in punitive terms. It opens the door too wide. Still the door can be closed again by resort to the alternative theory that the wickedness of an action is inherent not in the action itself, but in the state of mind of the person who performs it. To punish people merely for what they have done, it is argued, would be unjust, for the forbidden act might have been an accident for which the person who did it cannot be held to blame. Hence the requirement, to which traditionally the law attaches so much importance, that a crime is not, so to speak, a crime in the absence of *mens rea*.

Today, however, over a wide front even this requirement has in fact been abandoned. Today many, indeed almost certainly the majority, of the cases dealt with by the criminal courts are cases of strict liability in which proof of a guilty mind is no longer necessary for conviction. A new dichotomy is thus created, and one which in this instance exists not merely in the minds of the judges but is actually enshrined in the law itself—

[5] *Shaw* v. *Director of Public Prosecutions* [1961] 2 W.L.R. 897.

[6] *The Times,* November 11, 1961.

that is to say, the dichotomy between those offences in which the guilty mind is, and those in which it is not, an essential ingredient. In large measure, no doubt, this classification coincides with Lord Devlin's division into real and quasi-crimes; but whether or no this coincidence is exact must be a question of personal judgment. To drive a car when your driving ability is impaired through drink or drugs is an offence of strict liability: it is no defence to say that you had no idea that the drink would affect you as it did, or to produce evidence that you were such a seasoned drinker that any such result was, objectively, not to be expected. These might be mitigating circumstances after conviction, but are no bar to the conviction itself. Yet some at least of those who distinguish between real and quasi-crimes would put drunken driving in the former category, even though it involves no question of *mens rea*. In the passage that I quoted earlier Lord Devlin, it will be remembered, was careful to include new as well as old offences in his category of "real" crimes; but generally speaking it is the *mala antiqua* which are held to be both *mala in se* and contingent upon *mens rea*. . . .

The conclusion to which this argument leads is, I think, not that the presence or absence of the guilty mind is unimportant, but that *mens rea* has, so to speak—and this is the crux of the matter—*got into the wrong place*. Traditionally, the requirement of the guilty mind is written into the actual definition of a crime. No guilty intention, no crime, is the rule. Obviously this makes sense if the law's concern is with wickedness: where there is no guilty intention, there can be no wickedness. But it is equally obvious, on the other hand, that an action does not become innocuous merely because whoever performed it meant no harm. If the object of the criminal law is to prevent the occurrence of socially damaging actions, it would be absurd to turn a blind eye to those which were due to carelessness, negligence or even accident. The question of motivation is *in the first instance* irrelevant.

But only in the first instance. At a later stage, that is to say, after what is now known as a conviction, the presence or absence of guilty intention is all-important for its effect on the appropriate measures to be taken to prevent a recurrence of the forbidden act. The prevention of accidental deaths presents different problems from those involved in the prevention of wilful murders. The results of the actions of the careless, the mistaken, the wicked and the merely unfortunate may be indistinguishable from one another, but each case calls for a different treatment. . . .

The problem of the mentally abnormal offender raises in a particularly acute form the question of the primary function of the courts. If that function is conceived as punitive, mental abnormality must be related to guilt; for a severely subnormal offender must be less blameworthy, and ought therefore to incur a less severe punishment, than one of greater intelligence who has committed an otherwise similar crime, even though he may well be a worse risk for the future. But from the preventive standpoint it is this future risk which matters, and the important question to be asked is not: does his abnormality mitigate or even obliterate his guilt? but, rather, is he a suitable subject for medical, in preference to any other, type of treatment? In short, the punitive and the preventive are respectively concerned the one with culpability and the other with treatability.

In keeping with its traditional obsession with the concept of guilt, English criminal law has, at least until lately, been chiefly concerned with the effect of mental disorder upon culpability. In recent years, however, the idea that an offender's mental state might also have a bearing on his treatability has begun to creep into the picture—with the result that the two concepts now lie somewhat uneasily side by side in what has become a very complex pattern. . . .

All these modifications in the criminal process in the case of the mentally abnormal offender thus tend (with the possible exception of the 1948 Act) to treat such abnormality as in greater or less degree exculpatory. Their purpose is not just to secure that medical treatment should be provided for any offender likely to benefit from this, but rather to guard against the risk that the mentally disordered will be unjustly punished. Their concern with treatability, where it occurs, is in effect consequential rather than primary: the question—can the doctors help him? follows, if at all, upon a negative answer to the question: is he really to blame?

Nowhere is this more conspicuous than in section 2 of the Homicide Act; and it was indeed from a study of the operation of that section that I was led nearly four years ago to the conclusion that this was the wrong approach; that any attempt to distinguish between wickedness and mental abnormality was doomed to failure; and that the only solution for the future was to allow the concept of responsibility to "wither away" and to concentrate instead on the problem of the choice of treatment, without attempting to assess the effect of mental peculiarities or degrees of culpability. That opinion was based on a study of the files of some seventy-three cases in which a defence of diminished responsibility had been raised,[7] which were kindly made available by the Home Office. To these have since been added the records of another 126 cases, the two series together covering the five and a half years from the time that the Act came into force down to mid-September 1962. . . .

The most important development of the past few years lies, however, in the fact that the impossibility of keeping a clear line between the wicked and the weak-minded seems now to be officially admitted. In the judgment of the Court of Criminal Appeal on Byrne's appeal, from which I have already quoted, the Lord Chief Justice frankly admitted that "the step between 'he did not resist his impulse,' and 'he could not resist his impulse' " was one which was "incapable of scientific proof. *A fortiori*," the judgment continues, "there is no scientific measurement of the degree of difficulty which an abnormal person finds in controlling his impulses. These problems which in the present state of medical knowledge are scientifically insoluble the jury can only approach in a broad commonsense way."

Apart from admiration of the optimism which expects common sense to make good the deficiencies of science, it is only necessary to add that the problem would seem to be insoluble, not merely in the present, but indeed in any, state of medical knowledge. Improved medical knowledge may certainly be expected to give better insight into the origins of mental abnormalities, and better predictions as to the probability that particular types of individuals will in fact "control their physical acts" or make "ra-

[7] Wootton, Barbara, "Diminished Responsibility: A Layman's View," (1960) *Law Quarterly Review* 244.

tional judgments"; but neither medical nor any other science can ever hope to prove whether a man who does not resist his impulses does not do so because he cannot or because he will not. The propositions of science are by definition subject to empirical validation; but since it is not possible to get inside another man's skin, no objective criterion which can distinguish between "he did not" and "he could not" is conceivable.

Logic, experience and the Lord Chief Justice thus all appear to lead to the same conclusion—that is to say, to the impossibility of establishing any reliable measure of responsibility in the sense of a man's ability to have acted otherwise than as he did. After all, every one of us can say with St. Paul (who, as far as I am aware, is not generally suspected of diminished responsibility) "the good that I would I do not: but the evil which I would not, that I do."

I have dealt at some length with our experience of diminished responsibility cases under the Homicide Act because taken together, the three facts, first, that under this Act questions of responsibility have to be decided before and not after conviction; second, that these questions fall to be decided by juries; and, third, that the charges involved are of the utmost gravity, have caused the relationship of responsibility to culpability to be explored with exceptional thoroughness in this particular context. . . .

At the same time the proposal that we should bypass, or disregard, the concept of responsibility is only too easily misunderstood; and I propose, therefore, to devote the remainder of this lecture to an attempt to meet some of the criticisms which have been brought against this proposal, to clarify just what it does or does not mean in the present context and to examine its likely implications.

First, it is to be observed that the term "responsibility" is here used in a restricted sense, much narrower than that which it often carries in ordinary speech. The measure of a person's responsibility for his actions is perhaps best defined in the words that I used earlier in terms of his capacity to act otherwise than as he did. A person may be described as totally irresponsible if he is wholly incapable of controlling his actions, and as being in a state of diminished responsibility if it is abnormally difficult for him to control them. Responsibility in this restricted sense is not to be confused with the sense in which a man is often said to be responsible for an action if he has in fact committed it. The questions: who broke the window? and could the man who broke the window have prevented himself from doing so? are obviously quite distinct. To dismiss the second as unanswerable in no way diminishes the importance of finding an answer to the first. Hence the primary job of the courts in determining by whom a forbidden act has actually been committed is wholly unaffected by any proposal to disregard the question of responsibility in the narrower sense. Indeed the only problem that arises here is linguistic, inasmuch as one is accustomed to say that X was "responsible" for breaking the window when the intention is to convey no more than that he did actually break it. Another word is needed here (and I must confess that I have not succeeded in finding one) to describe "responsibility" for doing an action as distinct from the capacity to refrain from doing it. "Accountable" has sometimes been suggested, but its usage in this sense is often awkward. "Instrumental" is perhaps better, though one could still wish for an adjective such perhaps as "agential" derived from the word "agent." However, all that matters is to keep firmly in mind that responsibility in the present context has nothing to do with the authorship of an act, only with the state of mind of its author.

In the second place, to discard the notion of responsibility does not mean that the mental condition of an offender ceases to have any importance, or that psychiatric considerations become irrelevant. The difference is that they become relevant, not to the question of determining the measure of his culpability, but to the choice of the treatment most likely to be effective in discouraging him from offending again; and even if these two aspects of the matter may be related, this is not to be dismissed as a distinction without a difference. The psychiatrist to whom it falls to advise as to the probable response of an offender to medical treatment no doubt has his own opinion as to the man's responsibility or capacity for self-control; and doubtless also those opinions are a factor in his judgment as to the outlook for medical treatment, or as to the probability that the offence will be repeated. But these are, and must remain, matters of opinion, "incapable," in Lord Parker's words, "of scientific proof." Opinions as to treatability, on the other hand, as well as predictions as to the likelihood of further offences can be put to the test of experience and so proved right or wrong. And by systematic observation of that experience, it is reasonable to expect that a body of knowledge will in time be built up, upon which it will be possible to draw, in the attempt to choose the most promising treatment in future cases.

Next, it must be emphasised that nothing in what has been said involves acceptance of a deterministic view of human behaviour. It is an indisputable fact of experience that human beings do respond predictably to various stimuli—whether because they choose to or because they can do no other it is not necessary to inquire. There are cases in which medical treatment works: there are cases in which it fails. Equally there are cases in which deterrent penalties appear to deter those upon whom they are imposed from committing further offences; and there are cases in which they do not. Once the criminal law is conceived as an instrument of crime prevention, it is these facts which demand attention, and from which we can learn to improve the efficiency of that instrument; and the question whether on any occasion a man could or could not have acted otherwise than as he did can be left on one side or answered either way, as may be preferred. It is no longer relevant.

Failure to appreciate this has, I think, led to conflicts between psychiatry and the law being often fought on the wrong ground. Even so radical a criminologist as Dr. Sheldon Glueck seems to see the issue as one between "those who stress the prime social need of blameworthiness and retributive punishment as the core-concept in crime and justice and those who, under the impact of psychiatric, psycho-analytic, sociological, and anthropological views insist that man's choices are the product of forces largely beyond his conscious control . . ."[8] Indeed Dr. Glueck's discussion of the relation of psychiatry to law is chiefly devoted to an analysis of the exculpatory effect of psychiatric knowledge, and to the changes that have been, or should be, made in the assessment of guilt as the result of the growth of this knowl-

[8] Glueck, Sheldon, *Law and Psychiatry* (Tavistock Publications) 1962, p. 6.

edge. In consequence much intellectual ingenuity is wasted in refining the criteria by which the wicked may be distinguished from the weak-minded. For surely to argue thus is to argue from the wrong premises: the real difference between the psychiatric and the legal approach has nothing to do with free will and determinism. It has to do with their conceptions of the objectives of the criminal process, with the question whether the aim of that process is punitive or preventive, whether what matters is to punish the wrongdoer or to set him on the road to virtue; and, in order to take a stand on that issue, neither party need be a determinist.

So much for what disregard of responsibility does not mean. What, in a more positive sense, is it likely to involve? Here, I think, one of the most important consequences must be to obscure the present rigid distinction between the penal and the medical institution. As things are, the supposedly fully responsible are consigned to the former: only the wholly or partially irresponsible are eligible for the latter. Once it is admitted that we have no reliable criterion by which to distinguish between those two categories, strict segregation of each into a distinct set of institutions becomes absurd and impracticable. For purposes of convenience offenders for whom medical treatment is indicated will doubtless tend to be allocated to one building, and those for whom medicine has nothing to offer to another; but the formal distinction between prison and hospital will become blurred, and, one may reasonably expect, eventually obliterated altogether. Both will be simply "places of safety" in which offenders receive the treatment which experience suggests is most likely to evoke the desired response.

Does this mean that the distinction between doctors and prison officers must also become blurred? Up to a point it clearly does. At the very least it would seem that some fundamental implications for the medical profession must be involved when the doctor becomes part of the machinery of law enforcement. Not only is the normal doctor-patient relationship profoundly disturbed, but far-reaching questions also arise as to the nature of the condition which the doctor is called upon to treat. If a tendency to break the law is not in itself to be classified as a disease, which does he seek to cure—the criminality or the illness? To the medical profession these questions, which I have discussed at length elsewhere,[9] must be of primary concern. But for present purposes it may be more relevant to notice how, as so often happens in this country, changes not yet officially recognised in theory are already creeping in by the back door. Already the long-awaited institution at Grendon Underwood is administered as an integral part of the prison system: yet the régime is frankly medical. Its purpose has been described by the Prison Commission's Director of Medical Services as the investigation and treatment of mental disorder generally recognised as calling for a psychiatric approach; the investigation of the mental condition of offenders whose offences in themselves suggest mental instability; and an exploration of the problem of the treatment of the psychopath. Recommendations for admission are to come from prison medical officers, and the prison itself is under the charge of a medical

[9] Wootton, Barbara. "The Law, The Doctor and The Deviant," *British Medical Journal*, July 27, 1963.

superintendent with wide experience in psychiatry.[10]

Grendon Underwood is (unless one should include Broadmoor which has, of course, a much narrower scope) the first genuinely hybrid institution. Interchange between medical and penal institutions is, however, further facilitated by the power of the Home Secretary to transfer to hospital persons whom, on appropriate medical evidence, he finds to be suffering from mental disorder of a nature or degree to warrant their detention in a hospital for medical treatment. Such transfers have the same effect as does a hospital order, and they may be (and usually are) also accompanied by an order restricting discharge. It is, moreover, of some interest that transfers are sometimes made quite soon after the court has passed sentence. Out of six cases convicted under section 2 of the Homicide Act in which transfers under section 72 were effected, three were removed to hospital less than three months after sentence. Although it is, of course, always possible that the prisoner had been mentally normal at the time of his offence and had only suffered a mental breakdown later, transfer after a relatively short period does indicate at least a possibility that in the judgment of the Home Secretary some mental abnormality may have been already present either at the time of sentence or even when the crime was committed.

The courts, however, seem to be somewhat jealous of the exercise of this power, which virtually allows the Home Secretary to treat as sick persons whom they have sentenced to imprisonment and presumably regard as wicked. Indeed it seems that, if a diagnosis of mental disorder is to be made, the courts hold that it is, generally speaking, their business, and not the Home Secretary's, to make it. So at least it would appear from the judgments of the Court of Criminal Appeal in the cases of Constance Ann James[11] and Philip Morris,[12] both of whom had been found guilty of manslaughter on grounds of diminished responsibility and had been sentenced to imprisonment. In the former case, in which the evidence as to the accused's mental condition was unchallenged, the trial judge apparently had misgivings about the public safety and in particular the safety of the convicted woman's younger child whose brother she had killed. He therefore passed a sentence of three years' imprisonment, leaving it, as he said, to the appropriate authorities to make further inquiries so that the Secretary of State might, if he thought fit, transfer the prisoner to hospital under section 72 of the Mental Health Act. The appeal was allowed, on the ground that there was obviously no need for punishment, and that there were reasonable hopes that the disorder from which the woman suffered would prove curable. In the circumstances, though reluctant to interfere with the discretion of the sentencing court, the Court of Criminal Appeal substituted a hospital order accompanied by an indefinite restriction.

In Philip Morris' case, in which, however, the appellant was unsuccessful, the matter was put even more clearly. Again the trial judge had refused to make a hospital order on grounds of the public safety and, failing any vacancy in a secure hospital, had passed a sentence of

[10] Snell, H. K. (Director of Medical Services, Prison Commission), "H.M. Prison Grendon," *British Medical Journal,* September 22, 1962.

[11] *R.* v. *James* [1961] Crim.L.R. 842.

[12] *R. v. Morris* [1961] 45 Cr.App.R. 233.

life imprisonment. But on this the Court of Criminal Appeal commented as follows: "Although the discretion . . . is very wide indeed, the basic principle must be that in the ordinary case where punishment as such is not intended, and where the sole object of the sentence is that a man should receive mental treatment, and be at large as soon as he can safely be discharged, a proper exercise of the discretion demands that steps should be taken to exercise the powers under section 60 and that the matter should not be left to be dealt with by the Secretary of State under section 72."

These difficulties are, one may hope, of a transitional nature. They would certainly not arise if all sentences involving loss of liberty were indeterminate in respect of the type of institution in which the offender is to be detained: still less if rigid distinctions between medical and penal institutions were no longer maintained. The elimination of those distinctions, moreover, though unthinkable in a primarily punitive system which must at all times segregate the blameworthy from the blameless, is wholly in keeping with a criminal law which is preventive rather than punitive in intention.

CHAPTER FIVE

REHABILITATION

When persons with mental disorders come into the hands of the criminal courts today, the increasingly prevalent preference is to avoid disposing of them by punitive sentence in favor of seeking to rehabilitate them by one or another variety of treatment.

By "mentally ill" the courts refer to those whom lawyers and laymen usually call *insane,* a word with no precise and unambiguous meaning. The term usually indiscriminately conveys either of two meanings: (1) any type of mental disorder or defect, or (2) such a degree of disorder or defect as to entail legal consequences (e.g., to require commitment to a mental hospital, to annul a will, or to relieve from criminal responsibility). Lawyers tend to use the term in the first sense: they consider it a medical term meaning mental disorder as such. Doctors, however, consider it a legal term and tend to use it to convey the second meaning above. This ambiguity of cross-referential contexts often leads to the testimonial confusion evidenced by such sensational trials as those of Sirhan Sirhan and Richard Speck.

In addition to various types of truly mental disorders of a physiological nature, sociologists and most behavioral psychologists increasingly suggest a deterministic relationship between the external environment and individual action. It is becoming commonplace today to hear the assertion that social conditions such as slum housing, poverty, bad companions, congestion, and unemployment are responsible for criminality. Masking behind this ready explanation is the assumption that individuals in such social settings are bereft of their freedom to choose from among alternative courses of acceptable behavior. Their social conditions force them to acquiesce to antisocial behavior.

Thus, in addition to mental disease as such, there is a second causal agency in rehabilitative theory—environmental determinism—which, though different in origin from physiological and genetic disorders, nonetheless has much the same result: conduct is a product of factors beyond one's control. Both forms of determinism, medical and sociological, suggest the same legal consequence: irresponsibility for one's criminality.

To some, the notion of irresponsibility strikes a death blow to the ideas of desert and merit enshrined in *mens rea*. If the responsible person deserves the rewards of his good acts and the evils of his bad ones, by the same token one incapable of control over his actions cannot be said to deserve either reward or punishment for his good or bad acts. Thus many humanistic penologists insist that the punishment of an incompetent person (often extended to include any criminal) is itself a crime, analogous to the absurdity of punishing someone for a headache or a runny nose.

Many penologists and criminologists of a therapeutic bent emphasize the rehabilitation of the offender and the protection of society by measures specifically aimed at preventing recidivism. Originally the impetus in this direction was humanitarian, motivated in large part by a steadily growing repugnance in the last century to the debasing modes of corporeal punishment then in use. To this humanistic motivation there are now joined the allies of psychology and sociology, especially those schools of these and related fields which emphasize the reality of external determinants of behavior. Among these schools, two seem foremost: behaviorism and psychoanalysis.

The variety of behaviorism proposed by Dr. Eysenck and other followers of Clark Hull and B. F. Skinner is often taken as one of the best analyses not only of the origins of crime but also of the successful mode of treating it. In Skinnerian terms, criminal behavior is "socially unacceptable" activity stemming from an imbalance between paired pleasures and pains. Thus Skinner distinguishes two varieties of conditioning: classical and operant, both seeking to control behavior by the methodological programming of stimuli and/or anticipations of reward and pain.

Joined to the Skinnerian behaviorism and occasionally complementing it is the Freudian theory of psychoanalysis, with its many contemporary varieties, one of which is espoused by Dr. Karl Menninger in the selection below. The Freudian view of human consciousness emphasizes that the psyche has a threefold structure: the rampaging instincts (id), the rational censor of restraint (the ego), and the pressures of social conformity (the superego). In such an analysis, criminal action is but a "leakage" of the id which the ego cannot plug up.

The Freudian approach to rehabilitation insists that whereas the tensions of the id do need to be released, they can be released in manifold ways. Thus the doctrine of sublimation suggests that the ego can channel the raw energy of the id away from its directly intended, socially unacceptable manifestations toward disguised, acceptable outlets. Thus, in theory, the instincts operative in sex offenses or kleptomania, for example, could be redirected by psychoanalysis into such acceptable social expressions as, for example, art or mail delivery.

On the other hand, some, like Dr. Shoham, would see the rehabilitative ideal as at best a mixed blessing, at worst a device for forcing men to do good at the expense of doing it freely. In his essay, English literary pundit C. S. Lewis invokes humanistic arguments to support his contention that rehabilitation is an affront to the human dignity located in the capacity for responsible choice. As Lewis sees it, rehabilitation implies that prisons become hospitals, crime becomes disease, and criminals cease to be the authors of their own acts.

In a less critical view, Dean Francis Allen maintains that the rehabilitative ideal has been debased in practice to such an extent that therapeutic language has disguised but not eliminated many of the vindictive practices of corporeal punishment. Whereas court sentences for "normal" offenders are becoming shorter and more individualized, Allen observes that the rehabilitative ideal tends to encourage increasingly long periods of incarceration. Allen's remarks raise such critical questions as, first, should rehabilitative "punishment" pretend to "fit" the crime, especially if the crime is less severe than the disease it reflects, and secondly, what is to be done to an individual who, perhaps because of his own voluntary refusal, cannot or will not be rehabilitated?

Finally, Professor Toby expands some of the reservations outlined by Lewis and Allen. While punishment may serve to prevent crime and sustain the morale of conformists, rehabilitation may be ultimately successful only if preceded by more traditional forms of punishment, much in the way that shock treatment makes certain types of psychotics accessible to psychotherapy. Like the other writers in this section, Toby suggests that paramount questions are still to be answered about rehabilitative treatment in theory and practice.

THE CRIME OF PUNISHMENT*

Karl Menninger

Dr. Karl Menninger, prominent psychiatrist of the Menninger Foundation in Topeka, Kansas, is author of Man Against Himself *and* Love Against Hate, *among other works. The article excerpted below is adapted from his widely read* The Crime of Punishment, *which suggests that it is imperative to achieve a shift from a vengeful to a rehabilitative-therapeutic concept of punishment. Of especial importance here are two issues: First, to what extent is crime a product of mental disturbance? And second, what sorts of techniques are best suited for therapeutic treatment?*

Few words in our language arrest our attention as do "crime," "violence," "revenge," and "injustice." We abhor crime; we adore justice; we boast that we live by the rule of law. Violence and vengefulness we repudiate as unworthy of our civilization, and we assume this sentiment to be unanimous among all human beings.

Yet crime continues to be a national disgrace and a world-wide problem. It is threatening, alarming, wasteful, expensive, abundant, and apparently increasing! In actuality it is decreasing in frequency of occurrence, but it is certainly increasing in visibility and the reactions of the public to it.

Our system for controlling crime is ineffective, unjust, expensive. Prisons seem to operate with revolving doors—the same people going in and out and in and out. *Who cares?*

Our city jails and inhuman reformatories and wretched prisons are jammed. They are known to be unhealthy, dangerous, immoral, indecent, crime-breeding dens of iniquity. Not everyone has smelled them, as some of us have. Not many have heard the groans and the curses. Not everyone has seen the hate and despair in a thousand blank, hollow faces. But, in a way, we all know how miserable prisons are. *We want them to be that way*. And they are. *Who cares?*

Professional and big-time criminals prosper as never before. Gambling syndicates flourish. White-collar crime may even exceed all others, but goes undetected in the majority of cases. We are all being robbed and we know who the robbers are. They live nearby. *Who cares?*

The public filches millions of dollars worth of food and clothing from stores, towels and sheets from hotels, jewelry and knick-knacks from shops. The public steals, and the same public pays it back in higher prices. *Who cares?*

Time and time again somebody shouts

* Excerpted from THE CRIME OF PUNISHMENT by Dr. Karl Menninger, published by Viking Press, 1968.

about this state of affairs, just as I am shouting now. The magazines shout. The newspapers shout. The television and radio commentators shout (or at least they "deplore"). Psychologists, sociologists, leading jurists, wardens, and intelligent police chiefs join the chorus. Governors and mayors and Congressmen are sometimes heard. They shout that the situation is bad, bad, bad, and getting worse. Some suggest that we immediately replace obsolete procedures with scientific methods. A few shout contrary sentiments. Do the clear indications derived from scientific discovery for appropriate changes continue to fall on deaf ears? Why is the public so long-suffering, so apathetic and thereby so continuingly self-destructive? How many Presidents (and other citizens) do we have to lose before we do something?

The public behaves as a sick patient does when a dreaded treatment is proposed for his ailment. We all know how the aching tooth may suddenly quiet down in the dentist's office, or the abdominal pain disappear in the surgeon's examining room. Why should a sufferer seek relief and shun it? Is it merely the fear of pain of the treatment? Is it the fear of unknown complications? Is it distrust of the doctor's ability? All of these, no doubt.

But, as Freud made so incontestably clear, the sufferer is always somewhat deterred by a kind of subversive, internal opposition to the work of cure. He suffers on the one hand from the pains of his affliction and yearns to get well. But he suffers at the same time from traitorous impulses that fight against the accomplishment of any change in himself, even recovery! Like Hamlet, he wonders whether it may be better after all to suffer the familiar pains and aches associated with the old method than to face the complications of a new and strange, even though possibly better way of handling things.

The inescapable conclusion is that society secretly *wants* crime, *needs* crime, and gains definite satisfactions from the present mishandling of it! We condemn crime; we punish offenders for it; but we need it. The crime and punishment ritual is a part of our lives. We need crimes to wonder at, to enjoy vicariously, to discuss and speculate about, and to publicly deplore. We need criminals to identify ourselves with, to envy secretly, and to punish stoutly. They do for us the forbidden, illegal things we *wish* to do and, like scapegoats of old, they bear the burdens of our displaced guilt and punishment—"the iniquities of us all."

We have to confess that there is something fascinating for us all about violence. That most crime is not violent we know but we forget, because crime is a breaking, a rupturing, a tearing—even when it is quietly done. To all of us crime seems like violence.

The very word "violence" has a disturbing, menacing quality. . . . In meaning it implies something dreaded, powerful, destructive, or eruptive. It is something we abhor—or do we? Its first effect is to startle, frighten—even to horrify us. But we do not always run away from it. For violence also intrigues us. It is exciting. It is dramatic. Observing it and sometimes even participating in it gives us acute pleasure.

The newspapers constantly supply us with tidbits of violence going on in the world. They exploit its dramatic essence often to the neglect of conservative reporting of more extensive but less violent damage—the flood disaster in Florence, Italy, for example. Such words as crash, explosion, wreck, assault, raid, murder, avalanche, rape, and seizure evoke pictures of eruptive devastation from which we cannot turn away. The headlines often impute violence metaphorically even to peaceful activities. Relations are "ruptured," a tie is "broken," arbitration "collapses," a proposal is "killed."

Meanwhile on the television and movie screens there constantly appear for our amusement scenes of fighting, slugging, beating, torturing, clubbing, shooting, and the like which surpass in effect anything that the newspapers can describe. Much of this violence is portrayed dishonestly; the scenes are only semirealistic; they are "faked" and romanticized.

Pain cannot be photographed; grimaces indicate but do not convey its intensity. And wounds—unlike violence—are rarely shown. This phony quality of television violence in its mentally unhealthy aspect encourages irrationality by giving the impression to the observer that being beaten, kicked, cut, and stomped, while very unpleasant, are not very painful or serious. For after being slugged and beaten the hero rolls over, opens his eyes, hops up, rubs his cheek, grins, and staggers on. The *suffering* of violence is a part both the TV and movie producers *and* their audience tend to repress.

Although most of us *say* we deplore cruelty and destructiveness, we are partially deceiving ourselves. We disown violence, ascribing the love of it to other people. But the facts speak for themselves. We do love violence, all of us, and we all feel secretly guilty for it, which is another clue to public resistance to crime-control reform.

The great sin by which we all are tempted is the wish to hurt others, and this sin must be avoided if we are to live and let live. If our destructive energies can be mastered, directed, and sublimated, we can survive. If we can love, we can live. Our destructive energies, if they cannot be controlled, may destroy our best friends, as in the case of Alexander the Great, or they may destroy supposed "enemies" or innocent strangers. Worst of all—from the standpoint of the individual—they may destroy us. . . .

My colleague, Bruno Bettelheim thinks we do not properly educate our youth to deal with their violent urges. He reminds us that nothing fascinated our forefathers more. The *Iliad* is a poem of violence. Much of the Bible is a record of violence. One penal system and many methods of child-rearing express violence—"violence to suppress violence." And, he concludes [in the article "Violence: A Neglected Mode of Behavior"]: "We shall not be able to deal intelligently with violence unless we are first ready to see it as a part of human nature, and then we shall come to realize the chances of discharging violent tendencies are now so severely curtailed that their regular and safe draining-off is not possible anymore."

When a psychiatrist examines many prisoners, writes [Seymour] Halleck [in *Psychiatry and the Dilemmas of Crime*], he soon discovers how important in the genesis of the criminal outbreak is the offender's previous *sense of helplessness or hopelessness.* All of us suffer more or less from infringement of our personal freedom. We fuss about it all the time; we strive to correct it, extend it, and free ourselves from various oppressive or retentive forces. We do not want others to push us around, to control us, to dominate us. We realize this is bound to happen to some extent in an interlocking, interrelated society such as ours. No one truly has complete freedom. But restriction irks us.

The offender feels this way, too. He does not want to be pushed around, controlled, or dominated. And because he often feels that he is thus oppressed (and actually is) and because he does lack facility in improving his situation without violence, he suffers more intensely from feelings of helplessness.

Violence and crime are often attempts to escape from madness; and there can be no doubt that some mental illness is a flight from the wish to do the violence or commit the act. Is it hard for the reader to believe that suicides are sometimes committed to forestall the committing of murder? There is no doubt of it. Nor is there any doubt that murder is sometimes committed to avert suicide.

Strange as it may sound, many murderers do not realize whom they are killing, or, to put it another way, that they are killing the wrong people. To be sure, killing anybody is reprehensible enough, but the worst of it is that the person who the killer thinks should die (and he has reasons) is not the person he attacks. Sometimes the victim himself is partly responsible for the crime that is committed against him. It is this unconscious (perhaps sometimes conscious) participation in the crime by the victim that has long held up the very humanitarian and progressive-sounding program of giving compensation to victims. The public often judges the victim as well as the attacker.

Rape and other sexual offenses are acts of violence so repulsive to our sense of decency and order that it is easy to think of rapists in general as raging, oversexed, ruthless brutes (unless they are conquering heroes). Some rapists are. But most sex crimes are committed by undersexed rather than oversexed individuals, often undersized rather than oversized, and impelled less by lust than by a need for reassurance regarding an impaired masculinity. The unconscious fear of women goads some men with a compulsive urge to conquer, humiliate, hurt, or render powerless some available sample of womanhood. Men who are violently afraid of their repressed but nearly emergent homosexual desires, and men who are afraid of the humiliation of impotence, often try to overcome these fears by violent demonstrations.

The need to deny something in oneself is frequently an underlying motive for certain odd behavior—even up to and including crime. Bravado crimes, often done with particular brutality and ruthlessness, seem to prove *to the doer* that "I am no weakling! I am no sissy! I am no coward. I am no homosexual! I am a tough man who fears nothing." The Nazi storm troopers, many of them mere boys, were systematically trained to stifle all tender emotions and force themselves to be heartlessly brutal.

Man perennially seeks to recover the magic of his childhood days—the control of the mighty by the meek. The flick of an electric light switch, the response of an automobile throttle, the click of a camera, the touch of a match to a skyrocket—these are keys to a sudden and magical display of great power induced by the merest gesture. Is anyone already so blasé that he is no longer thrilled at the opening of a door specially for him by a magic-eye signal? Yet for a few pennies one can purchase a far more deadly piece of magic—a stored explosive and missile encased within a shell which can be ejected from a machine at the touch of a finger so swiftly that no eye can follow. A thousand yards away something falls dead—a rabbit, a deer, a beautiful mountain sheep, a sleeping child, or the

President of the United States. Magic! Magnified, projected power. "Look what I can do. I am the greatest!"

It must have come to every thoughtful person, at one time or another, in looking at the revolvers on the policemen's hips, or the guns soldiers and hunters carry so proudly, that these are instruments made for the express purpose of delivering death to someone. The easy availability of these engines of destruction, even to children, mentally disturbed people, professional criminals, gangsters, and even high school girls is something to give one pause. The National Rifle Association and its allies have been able to kill scores of bills that have been introduced into Congress and state legislatures for corrective gun control since the death of President Kennedy. Americans still spend about $2 billion on guns each year.

Fifty years ago, Winston Churchill declared that the mood and temper of the public in regard to crime and criminals is one of the unfailing tests of the civilization of any country. Judged by this standard, how civilized are we?

The chairman of the President's National Crime Commission, Nicholas de B. Katzenbach, declared recently that organized crime flourishes in America because enough of the public wants its services, and most citizens are apathetic about its impact. It will continue uncurbed as long as Americans accept it as inevitable and, in some instances, desirable.

Are there steps that we can take which will reduce the aggressive stabs and self-destructive lurches of our less well-managing fellow men? Are there ways to prevent and control the grosser violations, other than the clumsy traditional maneuvers which we have inherited? These depend basically upon intimidation and slow-motion torture. We call it punishment, and justify it with our "feeling." We know it doesn't work.

Yes, there *are* better ways. There are steps that could be taken; some *are* taken. But we move too slowly. Much better use, it seems to me, could be made of the members of my profession and other behavioral scientists than having them deliver courtroom pronunciamentos. The consistent use of a diagnostic clinic would enable trained workers to lay what they can learn about an offender before the judge who would know best how to implement the recommendation.

This would no doubt lead to a transformation of prisons, if not to their total disappearance in their present form and function. Temporary and permanent detention will perhaps always be necessary for a few, especially the professionals, but this could be more effectively and economically performed with new types of "facility" (that strange, awkward word for institution).

I assume it to be a matter of common and general agreement that our object in all this is to protect the community from a repetition of the offense by the most economical method consonant with our other purposes. Our "other purposes" include the desire to prevent these offenses from occurring, to reclaim offenders for social usefulness, if possible, and to detain them in protective custody, if reclamation is *not* possible. But how?

The treatment of human failure or dereliction by the infliction of pain is still used and believed in by many nonmedical people. "Spare the rod and spoil the child" is still considered wise counsel by many.

Whipping is still used by many secondary schoolmasters in England, I am informed, to stimulate study, attention, and the love of learning. Whipping was long a traditional treatment for the "crime" of disobedience on the part of children, pupils, servants, apprentices, employees. And slaves were treated for centuries by flogging for such offenses as weariness, confusion, stupidity, exhaustion, fear, grief, and even overcheerfulness. It was assumed and stoutly defended that these "treatments" cured conditions for which they were administered.

Meanwhile, scientific medicine was acquiring many new healing methods and devices. Doctors can now transplant organs and limbs; they can remove brain tumors and cure incipient cancers; they can halt pneumonia, meningitis, and other infections; they can correct deformities and repair breaks and tears and scars. But these wonderful achievements are accomplished on *willing* subjects, people who voluntarily ask for help by even heroic measures. And the reader will be wondering, no doubt, whether doctors can do anything with or for people who *do not want* to be treated at all, in any way! Can doctors cure willful aberrant behavior? Are we to believe that crime is a *disease* that can be reached by scientific measures? Isn't it merely "natural meanness" that makes all of us do wrong things at times even when we "know better"? And are not self-control, moral stamina, and will power the things needed? Surely there is no medical treatment for the lack of those!

Let me answer this carefully, for much misunderstanding accumulates here. I would say that according to the prevalent understanding of the words, crime is *not* a disease. Neither is it an illness, although I think it *should* be! It *should* be treated, and it could be; but it mostly isn't.

These enigmatic statements are simply explained. Diseases are undesired states of being which have been described and defined by doctors, usually given Greek or Latin appellations, and treated by long-established physical and pharmacological formulae. Illness, on the other hand, is best defined as a state of impaired functioning of such a nature that the public expects the sufferer to repair to the physician for help. The illness may prove to be a disease; more often it is only vague and nameless misery, but something which doctors, not lawyers, teachers, or preachers, are supposed to be able and willing to help.

When the community begins to look upon the expression of aggressive violence as the symptom of an illness or as indicative of illness, it will be because it believes doctors can do something to correct such a condition. At present, some better-informed individuals do believe and expect this. However angry at or sorry for the offender, they want him "treated" in an effective way so that he will cease to be a danger to them. And they know that the traditional punishment, "treatment-punishment," will not effect this.

What *will*? What effective treatment is there for such violence? It will surely have to begin with motivating or stimulating or arousing in a cornered individual the wish and hope and intention to change his methods of dealing with the realities of life. Can this be done by education, medication, counseling, training? I would answer *yes*. It can be done successfully in a majority of cases, if undertaken in time.

The present penal system and the existing legal philosophy do not stimulate or even expect such a change to take place in the criminal. Yet change is what medical science always aims for. The prisoner, like the doctor's other patients, should emerge from his treatment experience a different person, differently equipped, differently functioning, and headed in a different direction than when he began the treatment.

It is natural for the public to doubt that this can be accomplished with criminals. But remember that the public *used* to doubt that change could be effected in the mentally ill. No one a hundred years ago believed mental illness to be curable. Today *all* people know (or should know) that *mental illness is curable* in the great majority of instances and that the prospects and rapidity of cure are directly related to the availability and intensity of proper treatment.

The forms and techniques of psychiatric treatment used today number in the hundreds. No one patient requires or receives all forms, but each patient is studied with respect to his particular needs, his basic assets, his interests, and his special difficulties. A therapeutic team may embrace a dozen workers—as in a hospital setting—or it may narrow down to the doctor and the spouse. Clergymen, teachers, relatives, friends, and even fellow patients often participate informally but helpfully in the process of readaptation.

All of the participants in this effort to bring about a favorable change in the patient—i.e., in his vital balance and life program—are imbued with what we may call a *therapeutic attitude*. This is one in direct antithesis to attitudes of avoidance, ridicule, scorn, or punitiveness. Hostile feelings toward the subject, however justified by his unpleasant and even destructive behavior, are not in the curriculum of therapy or in the therapist. This does not mean that therapists approve of the offensive and obnoxious behavior of the patient; they distinctly disapprove of it. But they recognize it as symptomatic of continued imbalance and disorganization, which is what they are seeking to change. They distinguish between disapproval, penalty, price, and punishment.

Doctors charge fees; they impose certain "penalties" or prices, but they have long since put aside primitive attitudes of retaliation toward offensive patients. A patient may cough in the doctor's face or may vomit on the office rug; a patient may curse or scream or even struggle in the extremity of his pain. But these acts are not "punished." Doctors and nurses have no time or thought for inflicting unnecessary pain even upon patients who may be difficult, disagreeable, provocative, and even dangerous. It is their duty to care for them, to try to make them well, and to prevent them from doing themselves or others harm. This requires love, not hate. This is the deepest meaning of the therapeutic attitude. Every doctor knows this; every worker in a hospital or clinic knows it (or should).

There is another element in the therapeutic attitude. It is the quality of hopefulness. If no one believes that the patient can get well, if no one—not even the doctor—has any hope, there probably won't be any recovery. Hope is just as important as love in the therapeutic attitude.

"But you were talking about the mentally ill," readers may interject, "those poor, confused, bereft, frightened individuals who yearn for help from you doctors and nurses. Do you mean to imply that willfully perverse individuals, our criminals, can be similarly reached and rehabilitated? Do you really believe that effective treatment of the sort you visualize can be applied to people *who do not want any help,* who are so willfully vicious, so well aware of the wrongs they are doing, so lacking in penitence or even common decency that punishment seems to be the only thing left?"

Do I believe there is effective treatment for offenders, and that they *can* be changed? *Most certainly and definitely I do.* Not all cases, to be sure; there are also some physical afflictions which we cannot cure at the moment. Some provision has to be made for incurables—pending new knowledge—and these will include some offenders. But I believe the majority of them would prove to be curable. The willfulness and the viciousness of offenders are part of the thing for which they have to be treated. These must not thwart the therapeutic attitude.

It is simply not true that most of them are "fully aware" of what they are doing, nor is it true that they want no help from anyone, although some of them say so. Prisoners are individuals: some want treatment, some do not. Some don't know what treatment is. Many are utterly despairing and hopeless. Where treatment is made available in institutions, many prisoners seek it even with the full knowledge that doing so will not lessen their sentences. In some prisons, seeking treatment by prisoners is frowned upon by the officials.

Various forms of treatment are even now being tried in some progressive courts and prisons over the country—educational, social, industrial, religious, recreational, and psychological treatments. Socially acceptable behavior, new work-play opportunities, new identity and companion patterns all help toward community reacceptance. Some parole officers and some wardens have been extremely ingenious in developing these modalities of rehabilitation and reconstruction—more than I could list here even if I knew them all. But some are trying. The secret of success in all programs, however, is the replacement of the punitive attitude with a therapeutic attitude.

Offenders with propensities for impulsive and predatory aggression should not be permitted to live among us unrestrained by some kind of social control. *But the great majority of offenders, even "criminals," should never become prisoners if we want to "cure" them.*

There are now throughout the country many citizens' action groups and programs for the prevention and control of crime and delinquency. With such attitudes of inquiry and concern, the public could acquire information (and incentive) leading to a change of feeling about crime and criminals. It will discover how unjust is much so-called "justice," how baffled and frustrated many judges are by the ossified rigidity of old-fashioned, obsolete laws and state constitutions which effectively prevent the introduction of sensible procedures to replace useless, harmful ones.

I want to proclaim to the public that things are not what it wishes them to be, and will only become so if it will take an interest in the matter and assume some responsibility for its own self-protection.

Will the public listen?

If the public does become interested, it will realize that we must have more facts, more trial projects, more checked results. It will share the dismay of the President's Commission in finding that no one knows much about even the incidence of crime with any definiteness or statistical accuracy.

The average citizen finds it difficult to see how any research would in any way change his mind about a man who brutally murders his children. But just such inconceivably awful acts most dramatically point up the need for research. Why should—how can—a man become so dreadful as that in our culture? How is such a man made? Is it comprehensible that he can be born to become so depraved?

There are thousands of questions regarding crime and public protection which deserve scientific study. What makes some individuals maintain their interior equilibrium by one kind of disturbance of the social structure rather than by another kind, one that would have landed him in a hospital? Why do some individuals specialize in certain types of crime? Why do so many young people reared in areas of delinquency and poverty and bad example never become habitual delinquents? (Perhaps this is a more important question than why some of them do.)

The public has a fascination for violence, and clings tenaciously to its yen for vengeance, blind and deaf to the expense, futility, and dangerousness of the resulting penal system. But we are bound to hope that this will yield in time to the persistent, penetrating light of intelligence and accumulating scientific knowledge. The public will grow increasingly ashamed of its cry for retaliation, its persistent demand to punish. This is its crime, *our* crime against criminals—and, incidentally, our crime against ourselves. For before we can diminish our sufferings from the ill-controlled aggressive assaults of fellow citizens, we must renounce the philosophy of punishment, the obsolete, vengeful penal attitude. In its place we would seek a comprehensive constructive social attitude—therapeutic in some instances, restraining in some instances, but preventive in its total social impact.

In the last analysis this becomes a question of personal morals and values. No matter how glorified or how piously disguised, vengeance as a human motive must be personally repudiated by each and every one of us. This is the message of old religions and new psychiatries. Unless this message is heard, unless we, the people—the man on the street, the housewife in the home—can give up our delicious satisfactions in opportunities for vengeful retaliation on scapegoats, we cannot expect to preserve our peace, our public safety, or our mental health.

CRIME AND CONDITIONING*

H. J. Eysenck

Prolific author of many treatises on psychology, Dr. H. J. Eysenck is a committed behaviorist both in psychological theory and in rehabilitative practice. His articulate Crime and Personality *proposes, in the main, that the social conscience is itself a product of conditioning and the wrong sort of this conditioning leads to running afoul of the law. Of particular interest in the selection below is the author's application of the behavioral model to the issues of motivation and cure.*

. . . Prisoners and criminals generally tend to have a rather high level of emotionality. It would seem to follow that this emotionality would potentiate the antisocial habits which they have developed, to such an extent that they would find it far more difficult than normal, non-emotional people to supplant these with a proper set of habits. Punishment, presumably by greatly increasing the degree of emotion present, would, therefore, have a negative rather than a positive effect; it would lead to still greater rigidity in the reactions of the prisoner, rather than leading to any kind of change. This general conclusion seems particularly apposite in view of the fact that little effort is made by society to inculcate proper social or moral habits in the prisoner. Punishment is supposed to be sufficient for this purpose, making formal training or reconditioning unnecessary. Under these circumstances, it is perhaps not surprising that punishment does not have the effect which society so confidently expects of it.

We may perhaps draw a comparison between the case of the prisoner in the dock and an experimental demonstration frequently made in the laboratory of stereotyped or fixated behaviour. Among the earliest studies of this was an experiment carried out by an American animal psychologist, G. V. Hamilton, in 1916. He used an apparatus from which animals could escape by choosing the correct exit door from a choice of four. The correct exit door was varied in random order and, under these conditions, his rats showed various kinds of adaptive or non-adaptive behaviour, including repetitive or stereotyped reactions. These may be defined as instances of persistent re-entrance of an alley during a given trial, when as many as ten successive punishments therein failed to direct the subjects' activities, away from that alley, and towards the untried alleys. This stereotyping was particularly likely to occur when the rats became very emotional. . . .

. . . Punishment may itself constitute

* Excerpted from Eysenck, Crime and Personality (Boston: Houghton Mifflin, 1964). Reprinted with permission.

a frustrating situation, in which case it will either increase the strength of any frustration-instigated behaviour already present, or transform the motivated state into a frustrated one. As he [N. R. F. Maier] puts it: 'Punishment can only serve as a negative incentive when the organism is in a motivated state and when its intensity is not great enough to excite the frustration process and cause it completely to dominate over the motivation process.'[1]

We need only note here that Maier's conclusions are in good agreement with those of other experimental psychologists as far as the effects of punishment are concerned. These effects always tend to be extremely variable and unpredictable. Punishment may produce the desired end, that is, the elimination of a certain type of conduct, but on the other hand, it may have exactly the opposite effect, stamping in the undesirable conduct even more strongly than before and making it a stereotyped pattern. Sometimes punishment may have no effect at all, one way or the other, and it is not even possible to say that strong and weak punishments differ in their effects in any predictable way. It is not surprising, therefore, that empirical studies of the effects of punishment on criminals have led to more confusion, so that no positive statements of any kind can be made. It is suggested that the old lag, the recidivist with many crimes behind him, and no prospect of any change in his pattern of behaviour, very closely resembles the frustrated rat with its stereotyped behaviour pattern, self-punishing and maladaptive as it may be. By repeatedly sending him to prison and punishing him for each criminal episode, society merely stamps in this type of conduct and does nothing to convert him into a useful, law-abiding citizen. Perhaps a different approach is required to achieve this aim.

What are the social purposes of punishment? There are essentially three purposes. Perhaps the first, in order of time, is simply vengeance. The criminal has offended society; he must be punished and made to feel on his own body the evil effects of what he has done, the principle of 'an eye for an eye and a tooth for a tooth.' Few people nowadays would endorse punishment simply from the point of view of vengeance; at least in our society, the rational tendency would be to accept the biblical exhortation, 'Vengeance is mine, saith the Lord.' However, at a less rational, more personal level, vengeance probably contributes a share to the motives behind punishment.

A second purpose of punishment is protection of the law-abiding public. What better method of protecting the public from the ravages of a criminal than by locking him up, thus making it impossible for him to commit crimes, at least while he is incarcerated? The sentence of preventive detention, for instance, places maximum emphasis on the protection of the public from the dangerous criminal in insisting on his removal from society for an indefinite period, without regard for rehabilitation. The indeterminate sentence, so popular in America, is similarly based largely on public protection, although it possibly lays greater stress on rehabilitation.

The third aim is that of deterrence, both as far as the criminal himself is concerned, and as far as others are concerned. Punishment, it is assumed, should deter the criminal from further crimes, and his punishment should deter others from following in his footsteps.

[1] Summarized in Yates, FRUSTRATION AND CONFLICT (1962).

As we have seen before, it is doubtful whether punishment acts as a very effective deterrent; certainly there is little evidence to show that the methods currently in use are very effective. Nevertheless, at least in theory, a good deal of the rationale behind punishment is based on this notion. These have been the aims and these have been the methods of penal philosophy for the last two thousand years. Perhaps it would not be too impertinent to say that very little improvement has taken place during this time. Our methods are still as primitive and as unsuccessful as they were in the days of Socrates or in the days of the Roman Empire. What has gone wrong?

Samuel Butler, the English novelist, in his book, *Erewhon,* posed the problem in a paradoxical form. In this country of Erewhon, he wrote, people who were suffering from diseases were sent to prison and treated harshly, whereas those who committed crimes were sent to the doctor and given medicines to cure them of their disease; in other words, he posited an exact reversal of the kind of thing that goes on in our society. Is there any reason to take this suggestion seriously and adopt a curative, rather than a deterrent point of view, in relation to our criminals? At first sight the prospects are not particularly good. . . .

We may deduce from [the Cambridge-Somerville Youth Study][2] and from other studies that have been carried out, in which psychotherapy has been used with criminals or potential criminals, that there is little reason to believe these methods of treatment can effect any cure or amelioration, or can serve in a preventive manner. This is not surprising; as we have seen before, even in relation to neurosis, as they were originally developed, these methods fail to have any demonstrable effect.

Must we conclude that there is no way we can change the behaviour of people, either for the better or for the worse? Fortunately, the outlook is not as bad as it may seem from looking at such studies as the Cambridge-Somerville Youth Study mentioned above. Recent work on behaviour therapy with neurotics has shown that considerable improvement can be effected in a relatively short time, and perhaps this work can be extended to the treatment of criminals. To introduce this new type of investigation, let us return to our discussion of little Albert and his conditioned phobia of white rats.

The reader will recall our discussion of the autonomic system and its two branches, the sympathetic and the parasympathetic. What we have done was condition a sympathetic response in little Albert to the conditioned stimulus, the sight, the feel and the smell of rats. What can we do to eliminate this conditioned sympathetic response? One answer was given by Watson in an original paper, which has since been developed into a method of treating neurotic disorders in human beings, both children and adults, by Professor J. Wolpe,[3] originally from South Africa, now living in the United States. He calls this the method of 'reciprocal inhibition,' and its principle is based on the fact that the two parts of the autonomic nervous system, the sympathetic and the parasympathetic, are mutually antagonistic in their action. For example, when the sympathetic system accelerates the heart beat rate, the parasympathetic slows it down. Watson and Wolpe argue that a

[2] Powers and Witmer, AN EXPERIMENT IN THE PREVENTION OF DELINQUENCY (1951).

[3] Wolpe, PSYCHOTHERAPY BY RECIPROCAL INHIBITION (1958).

conditioned sympathetic response to a given stimulus, can be eliminated by conditioning a parasympathetic response to the same stimulus. The parasympathetic response, being antagonistic to the sympathetic one, will inhibit it reciprocally and, in that way, will cancel it out, leaving the individual very much as he was before the original conditioning took place. How can this be done?

In the case of Albert, we might do something like this. We know that the sympathetic system inhibits digestion and that digestion is aided by the activity of the parasympathetic system. We might try giving little Albert some chocolate to produce a parasympathetic response. But since he is so afraid of the rats when they are right in front of him that he will simply refuse to take the chocolate, we must introduce an important variation into the experiment, the so-called distance gradient. . . . What is signified by this phrase is that the strength of fear experienced when we encounter a particular object which we fear is roughly proportional to the distance of that object from us: the nearer the object, the greater the fear. . . . It is possible to measure the amount of fear experienced by taking polygraph recordings of the activity of the autonomic system, demonstrating that the closer Albert is to the rats, the greater the sympathetic arousal in him.

The amount of sympathetic arousal in our subject can be minimized by simply putting the rats at the far end of the room, as far away from little Albert as possible; under these conditions, although hesitant, he will consent to take the chocolate. With the conditioned stimulus present, and the unconditioned stimulus, the chocolate, producing digestive (parasympathetic) activity, parasympathetic conditioning to the presence of the rats can take place. The parasympathetic activity, being incompatible with sympathetic activity, will decrease, to some degree, the effective strength of sympathetic conditioning still present. . . . We can now bring the rats a little nearer and repeat the experiment of feeding chocolate to Albert, adding another increment of parasympathetic conditioning. This increment subtracts still more from the strength of the original conditioned sympathetic response . . . enabling us to bring the rats still nearer. We can continue this process until, after a few repetitions of the experiment, we have achieved sufficient parasympathetic conditioning to cancel out the original sympathetic conditioning, and reciprocal inhibition has reached an equilibrium. The infant will now play happily with the rats, his conditioned fear having been eliminated. . . .

Wolpe and others have applied these principles to random samples of neurotics suffering from a variety of disorders, from anxiety states and reactive depressions to hysterical and obsessive-compulsive symptoms. They have shown that, under these conditions, a success rate of over ninety per cent can be achieved in relatively few sessions; in the majority of cases, twenty to thirty sessions are required for a cure. Wolpe has also shown that the cure, once achieved, is permanent; neither does a symptom return, nor is there any other symptom likely to take its place. . . . It is possible, therefore, to achieve a degree of success well beyond the rate of spontaneous remission in relation to the amelioration of neurotic disorders. We may take this as support for the possibility of treating criminal and delinquent disorders in a similar manner.

When we turn to these types of disorders, however, we must reverse the application of the principle of reciprocal inhibition. This reversal can be clearly demonstrated in certain neurotic disorders which border on the criminal and occasionally overstep the mark. The neurotic disorders we have been talking about so far are essentially ones which disturb the individual who is suffering from them. A person who experiences strong anxiety, strong depressive tendencies, or obsessive-compulsive reactions, is very upset and worried by these experiences and may seek help desperately. But we also find frequent cases where the opposite is true, where what has been conditioned, through some quirk of fate, is a parasympathetic response; that is to say, a reaction which, on the whole, gives him pleasure, and which he would be reluctant to abandon. Examples of this, for instance, are homosexuality, or attachment to a member of the same sex and the derivation of pleasure from such an attachment; fetishism, or the substitution of some normally neutral object for the normal sexual object, or at least the addition of such an object to the normal sex outlet; and transvestism, or the derivation of sexual pleasure from dressing up in clothing appropriate to the opposite sex. In these cases what is required is the conditioning of a sympathetic response to stimuli which, in the normal run of things, produce conditioned parasympathetic responses in our subjects. The unconditioned stimuli are, respectively, members of the same sex, of the opposite sex, or the objects of fetishes, whatever they may be. There are many ways of accomplishing this conditioning, but the two most frequently used are either electric shock used in connection with objects of this type, or an injection with apomorphine, a drug which produces sickness and vomiting after a short period of time. . . .

[N]o one would argue for a moment that the success of this particular method of treatment, which has been duplicated with many similar cases as well as with transvestites, homosexuals and others, can necessarily be expected with the typical kinds of criminals and delinquents we have in our prisons. What it demonstrates, however, is that by a suitable experimental conditioning regime we can decondition a very powerful impulse to perform a certain act . . . and that, therefore, the theory on which the treatment is based holds considerable promise, even in regard to other types of criminal conduct, to which it has not yet been applied.

Criminals and delinquents pose two problems, of which the elimination of certain conditioned responses is only one. The other, and possibly more urgent one, is the creation of new conditioned responses of a more desirable, socially acceptable nature. Is there anything in the literature to suggest that learning theory could help us in doing this? It may be instructive to look at one particular symptom which has been treated very effectively by behaviour therapy. The symptom in question is that of enuresis or bedwetting, which is so very frequent in children and which has always been extremely difficult to deal with by orthodox medical treatment or by psychotherapy. Essentially, what seems to happen in the case of the child suffering from enuresis is that a conditioned reflex has not been established between the conditional stimulus, the enlargement of the bladder beyond a certain point, and the beginning of urination, on the one hand, and waking up, stopping the urination, and going to the toilet, on the other. Failure to build up such a conditioned response we would expect to be more pronounced in extraverts and in people who, in general, condition poorly. Many investigators have found that juvenile delinquents and criminals generally tend to show a much higher incidence of enuresis than do normal people. This is, of course, precisely what we would have predicted in terms of our theory.

What can we do to produce the missing conditioned response? The answer to this problem was first given by O. H. Mowrer of the University of Illinois, who made use of the 'bell and blanket' method. In this method, the patient is made to sleep on a blanket which has on it a number of electrical contacts. These are linked to a battery and a bell. Whenever the subject begins to urinate in his sleep the urine, which is electrolytic, makes a contact between the electric wires in the blanket, and the bell begins to ring. This immediately produces reflexive cessation of urination and wakes up the patient, who then goes to the toilet. Gradually the conditioned response of waking up and going to the toilet is built up and, usually after a short time, the patient is cured of his enuresis. There is ample statistical and experimental evidence to show that this system is extremely successful in producing this particular conditioned response and that it also tends to eliminate all the fears and anxieties which have built up in the patient and his family because of his failure to keep dry at night.

Again, it is not suggested that this method can be applied directly to the kind of problems presented by the criminal. It is cited here merely to indicate that, with sufficient ingenuity, it is possible to make deductions from learning theory, which may lead to a solution of these problems. What may be the most appropriate method for the treatment of criminals remains to be discovered.

Before making suggestions in this connection, I would like to stress one point in particular which has usually been overlooked in many discussions of the treatment of criminals, and which is equally applicable to the upbringing of children. Throughout the centuries, there has been a swinging of the pendulum in opinions about the upbringing of children, between those who swear by the old saying, 'Spare the rod and spoil the child,' and those who accept the principles of *laissez-faire*, of letting children grow up more or less as they will. The arguments presented by the 'Spare the rod and spoil the child' school are that the child has to be trained in the social mores of his society, and that this cannot be done without some infliction of pain. The argument of the *laissez-faire* school, on the other hand, tends to be that the infliction of pain on children is unjustified and is likely to lead to neurotic disorders later in life. At the moment, the pendulum seems to have swung a long way towards the *laissez-faire* school, although there are indications that this may have gone too far and that the pendulum is about to swing back in the other direction. Can psychology say anything useful in relation to this particular conflict?

The main contribution which psychology can make in this connection is a very simple one. According to learning theory, we would say that both sides are right in what they positively assert, and that both sides are wrong, in leaving certain points unsaid. Certainly, sternness and discipline in some degree are required if the child is to grow up into a moral, law-abiding citizen. The failure on the part of so many parents to provide such a background is undoubtedly responsible, in part, for the present outbreak of juvenile delinquency and the growth of crime throughout the Western world. The *laissez-faire* school is quite right in postulating that too severe discipline may often lead to neurotic disorders of one kind or another. Clearly, the path to follow is through a middle ground, to treat children with a sufficient degree of severity to achieve the conditioning required by society, but not to treat them so severely that they fall prey to neurotic disorders.

Although this answer may seem quite obvious, unfortunately it is not at all easy to put into practice. The reason for the difficulty is that we tend to talk about an abstraction, that is, children in general, when what we have to deal with is a particular child at a particular moment. As we have seen, children are by no means all alike; some are introverted, some are extraverted, some condition poorly, some condition quickly. The severity of discipline required by an introverted child is very much less than the severity of discipline required by an extraverted child. Treat them both alike, and you might find that your extraverted child (because he conditions so poorly) ends up as a delinquent, whereas your introverted child (because he conditions so well) ends as a neurotic! What is required, of course, is to suit the type of upbringing to the type of child. Unfortunately, very few parents know whether their children will condition well or poorly; consequently they proceed largely by trial and error, supplemented by some knowledge of popular ideas of psychology and psychoanalysis. We cannot expect that the upbringing which the child gets in the usual case is the kind of upbringing that will be best suited to make him a normal, non-neurotic, law-abiding individual. A great deal of experimental work is needed before we will be able to give positive answers and guidance to parents who come with a request for help. Unfortunately, child guidance clinics are currently of little value in this connection. The evidence is fairly conclusive that even when children are referred to them with neurotic disorders of one kind or another, child guidance clinics do very little, if any, better than chance. In other words, here also spontaneous remission claims as many successes as does the most successful child guidance clinic with all its psychiatrists and clinical psychologists. The reason for this is the acceptance on the part of so many workers in this field of unproven theories and methods which have not been empirically validated. Until there is considerable change toward a more scientific approach to these issues, it is unlikely that parents will receive much help with their problems from those who are expected to be best able to aid them by virtue of their training and experience.

What has been said here of children applies equally to adult criminals. Those who are extraverted, who condition poorly, obviously require a good deal of firmness in their treatment; however, those who are introverted, who condition well, and who turn to crime largely as a result of conditioning in an unfavourable environment, might be permanently damaged by excessive severity. The attempts of society to treat both types alike probably means sitting between two stools and getting the worst of both worlds.

THE HUMANITARIAN THEORY OF PUNISHMENT*

C. S. Lewis

For some thirty years preceding his death in 1963, C. S. Lewis was a controversial and urbane gadfly within English literary circles. Though his own professional interest as Fellow of Magdalen College was literature, he often applied his incisive comments to political and social affairs as well. The following article, published originally in 1954, is representative not only of his refusal to accept the rehabilitative ideal but also of some widely held humanistic reservations which stem from one of the central issues in rehabilitative theory: What degree of free choice remains open to the individual who has been successfully "treated" and "cured"?

In England we have lately had a controversy about Capital Punishment. I do not know whether a murderer is more likely to repent and make a good end on the gallows a few weeks after his trial or in the prison infirmary thirty years later. I do not know whether the fear of death is an indispensable deterrent. I need not, for the purpose of this article, decide whether it is a morally permissible deterrent. Those are questions which I propose to leave untouched. My subject is not Capital Punishment in particular, but that theory of punishment in general which the controversy showed to be almost universal among my fellow-countrymen. It may be called the Humanitarian theory. Those who hold it think that it is mild and merciful. In this I believe that they are seriously mistaken. I believe that the "Humanity" which it claims is a dangerous illusion and disguises the possibility of cruelty and injustice without end. I urge a return to the traditional or Retributive theory not solely, not even primarily, in the interests of society, but in the interests of the criminal.

According to the Humanitarian theory, to punish a man because he deserves it, and as much as he deserves, is mere revenge, and, therefore, barbarous and immoral. It is maintained that the only legitimate motives for punishing are the desire to deter others by example or to mend the criminal. When this theory is combined, as frequently happens, with the belief that all crime is more or less pathological, the idea of mending tails off into that of healing or curing and punishment becomes therapeutic. Thus it appears at first sight that we have passed from the harsh and self-righteous notion of giving the wicked their deserts

* *The Humanitarian Theory of Punishment* by C. S. Lewis appears in GOD IN THE DOCK, published by Wm. B. Eerdmans Publishing Co. Reprinted by permission of Wm. B. Eerdmans and Goeffrey Bles Ltd.

to the charitable and enlightened one of tending the psychologically sick. What could be more amiable? One little point which is taken for granted in this theory needs, however, to be made explicit. The things done to the criminal, even if they are called cures, will be just as compulsory as they were in the old days when we called them punishments. If a tendency to steal can be cured by psychotherapy, the thief will no doubt be forced to undergo the treatment. Otherwise, society cannot continue.

My contention is that this doctrine, merciful though it appears, really means that each one of us, from the moment he breaks the law, is deprived of the rights of a human being.

The reason is this. The Humanitarian theory removes from Punishment the concept of Desert. But the concept of Desert is the only connecting link between punishment and justice. It is only as deserved or undeserved that a sentence can be just or unjust. I do not here contend that the question "Is it deserved?" is the only one we can reasonably ask about a punishment. We may very properly ask whether it is likely to deter others and to reform the criminal. But neither of these two last questions is a question about justice. There is no sense in talking about a "just deterrent" or a "just cure." We demand of a deterrent not whether it is just but whether it will deter. We demand of a cure not whether it is just but whether it succeeds. Thus when we cease to consider what the criminal deserves and consider only what will cure him or deter others, we have tacitly removed him from the sphere of justice altogether; instead of a person, a subject of rights, we now have a mere object, a patient, a "case."

The distinction will become clearer if we ask who will be qualified to determine sentences when sentences are no longer held to derive their propriety from the criminal's deservings. On the old view the problem of fixing the right sentence was a moral problem. Accordingly, the judge who did it was a person trained in jurisprudence; trained, that is, in a science which deals with rights and duties, and which, in origin at least, was consciously accepting guidance from the Law of Nature, and from Scripture. We must admit that in the actual penal code of most countries at most times these high originals were so much modified by local custom, class interests, and utilitarian concessions, as to be very imperfectly recognizable. But the code was never in principle, and not always in fact, beyond the control of the conscience of the society. And when (say, in Eighteenth Century England) actual punishments conflicted too violently with the moral sense of the community, juries refused to convict and reform was finally brought about. This was possible because, so long as we are thinking in terms of Desert, the propriety of the penal code, being a moral question, is a question on which every man has the right to an opinion, not because he follows this or that profession, but because he is simply a man, a rational animal enjoying the Natural Light. But all this is changed when we drop the concept of Desert. The only two questions we may now ask about a punishment are whether it deters and whether it cures. But these are not questions on which anyone is entitled to have an opinion simply because he is a man. He is not entitled to an opinion even if, in addition to being a man, he should happen also to be a jurist, a Christian, and a moral theologian. For they are not questions about principle but about matter of fact; and for such *cuiquam in sua arte credendum.* Only the expert "penologist" (let barbarous things have barbarous names), in the light of previous experiment, can tell us what is likely to deter: only the psychotherapist can tell us what is likely to cure. It will be in vain for the rest of us, speaking simply as men, to say, "but this punishment is hideously unjust, hideously disproportionate to the criminal's deserts." The experts with perfect logic will reply, "but nobody was talking about deserts. No one was talking about *punishment* in your archaic vindictive sense of the word. Here are the statistics proving that this treatment deters. Here are the statistics proving that this other treatment cures. What is your trouble?"

The Humanitarian theory, then, removes sentences from the hands of jurists whom the public conscience is entitled to criticize and places them in the hands of technical experts whose special sciences do not even employ such categories as Rights or Justice. It might be argued that since this transference results from an abandonment of the old idea of Punishment, and, therefore, of all vindictive motives, it will be safe to leave our criminals in such hands. I will not pause to comment on the simple minded view of fallen human nature which such a belief implies. Let us rather remember that the "cure" of criminals is to be compulsory; and let us then watch how the theory actually works in the mind of the Humanitarian. The immediate starting point of this article was a letter I read in one of our Leftist weeklies. The author was pleading that a certain sin, now treated by our Laws as a crime, should henceforward be treated as a disease. And he complained that under the present system the offender, after a term in gaol, was simply let out to return to his original environment where he would probably relapse. What he complained of was not the shutting up but the letting out. On his remedial view of punishment the offender should, of course, be detained until he was cured. And of course the official straighteners are the only people who can say when that is. The first result of the Humanitarian theory is, therefore, to substitute for a definite sentence (reflecting to some extent the community's moral judgment on the degree of ill-desert involved) an indefinite sentence terminable only by the word of those experts—and they are not experts in moral theology nor even in the Law of Nature—who inflict it. Which of us, if he stood in the dock, would not prefer to be tried by the old system?

It may be said that by the continued use of the word punishment and the use of the verb "inflict" I am misrepresenting Humanitarians. They are not punishing, not inflicting, only healing. But do not let us be deceived by a name. To be taken without consent from my home and friends; to lose my liberty; to undergo all those assaults on my personality which modern psychotherapy knows how to deliver; to be remade after some pattern of "normality" hatched in a Viennese laboratory to which I never professed allegiance; to know that this process will never end until either my captors have succeeded or I grown wise enough to cheat them with apparent success—who cares whether this is called Punishment or not? That it includes most of the elements for which any punishment is feared—shame, exile, bondage, and years eaten by the locust—is obvious. Only enormous ill-desert could justify it; but ill-desert is the very conception which the Humanitarian theory has thrown overboard.

If we turn from the curative to the

deterrent justification of punishment we shall find the new theory even more alarming. When you punish a man *in terrorem,* make of him an "example" to others, you are admittedly using him as a means to an end; someone else's end. This, in itself, would be a very wicked thing to do. On the classical theory of Punishment it was of course justified on the ground that the man deserved it. That was assumed to be established before any question of "making him an example" arose. You then, as the saying is, killed two birds with one stone; in the process of giving him what he deserved you set an example to others. But take away desert and the whole morality of the punishment disappears. Why, in Heaven's name, am I to be sacrificed to the good of society in this way?—unless, of course, I deserve it.

But that is not the worst. If the justification of exemplary punishment is not to be based on desert but solely on its efficacy as a deterrent, it is not absolutely necessary that the man we punish should even have committed the crime. The deterrent effect demands that the public should draw the moral, "If we do such an act we shall suffer like that man." The punishment of a man actually guilty whom the public think innocent will not have the desired effect; the punishment of a man actually innocent will, provided the public think him guilty. But every modern State has powers which make it easy to fake a trial. When a victim is urgently needed for exemplary purposes and a guilty victim cannot be found, all the purposes of deterrence will be equally served by the punishment (call it "cure" if you prefer) of an innocent victim, provided that the public can be cheated into thinking him guilty. It is no use to ask me why I assume that our rulers will be so wicked. The punishment of an innocent, that is, an undeserving, man is wicked only if we grant the traditional view that righteous punishment means deserved punishment. Once we have abandoned that criterion, all punishments have to be justified, if at all, on other grounds that have nothing to do with desert. Where the punishment of the innocent can be justified on those grounds (and it could in some cases be justified as a deterrent) it will be no less moral than any other punishment. Any distaste for it on the part of a Humanitarian will be merely a hang-over from the Retributive theory.

It is, indeed, important to notice that my argument so far supposes no evil intentions on the part of the Humanitarian and considers only what is involved in the logic of his position. My contention is that good men (not bad men) consistently acting upon that position would act as cruelly and unjustly as the greatest tyrants. They might in some respects act even worse. Of all tyrannies a tyranny sincerely exercised for the good of its victims may be the most oppressive. It may be better to live under robber barons than under omnipotent moral busybodies. The robber baron's cruelty may sometimes sleep, his cupidity may at some point be satiated; but those who torment us for our own good will torment us without end for they do so with the approval of their own conscience. They may be more likely to go to Heaven yet at the same time likelier to make a Hell of earth. Their very kindness stings with intolerable insult. To be "cured" against one's will and cured of states which we may not regard as disease is to be put on a level with those who have not yet reached the age of reason or those who never will; to be classed with infants, imbeciles, and domestic animals. But to be punished, however severely, because we have deserved it, because we "ought to have known better," is to be treated as a human person made in God's image.

In reality, however, we must face the possibility of bad rulers armed with a Humanitarian theory of punishment. A great many popular blue prints for a Christian society are merely what the Elizabethans called "eggs in moonshine" because they assume that the whole society is Christian or that the Christians are in control. This is not so in most contemporary States. Even if it were, our rulers would still be fallen men, and, therefore, neither very wise nor very good. As it is, they will usually be unbelievers. And since wisdom and virtue are not the only or the commonest qualifications for a place in the government, they will not often be even the best unbelievers. The practical problem of Christian politics is not that of drawing up schemes for a Christian society, but that of living as innocently as we can with unbelieving fellow-subjects under unbelieving rulers who will never be perfectly wise and good and who will sometimes be very wicked and very foolish. And when they are wicked the Humanitarian theory of punishment will put in their hands a finer instrument of tyranny than wickedness ever had before. For if crime and disease are to be regarded as the same thing, it follows that any state of mind which our masters choose to call "disease" can be treated as crime; and compulsorily cured. It will be vain to plead that states of mind which displease government need not always involve moral turpitude and do not therefore always deserve forfeiture of liberty. For our masters will not be using the concepts of Desert and Punishment but those of disease and cure. We know that one school of psychology already regards religion as a neurosis. When this particular neurosis becomes inconvenient to government, what is to hinder government from proceeding to "cure" it? Such "cure" will, of course, be compulsory; but under the Humanitarian theory it will not be called by the shocking name of Persecution. No one will blame us for being Christian, no one will hate us, no one will revile us. The new Nero will approach us with the silky manners of a doctor, and though all will be in fact as compulsory as the *tunica molesta* or Smithfield or Tyburn, all will go on within the unemotional therapeutic sphere where words like "right" and "wrong" or "freedom" and "slavery" are never heard. And thus when the command is given, every prominent Christian in the land may vanish overnight into Institutions for the Treatment of the Ideologically Unsound, and it will rest with the expert gaolers to say when (if ever) they are to re-emerge. But it will not be persecution. Even if the treatment is painful, even if it is life-long, even if it is fatal, that will be only a regrettable accident; the intention was purely therapeutic. Even in ordinary medicine there were painful operations and fatal operations; so in this. But because they are "treatment," not punishment, they can be criticized only by fellow-experts and on technical grounds, never by men as men and on grounds of justice.

This is why I think it essential to oppose the Humanitarian theory of punishment, root and branch, wherever we encounter it. It carries on its front a semblance of mercy which is wholly false. That is how it can deceive men of good will. The error began, perhaps, with Shelley's statement that the distinction between mercy and justice was invented in the courts of tyrants. It sounds noble, and was indeed the error of a noble mind. But the distinction is essential. The older view was that mercy "tempered" justice, or (on the highest level of all) that mercy and justice had met and kissed. The essential act of mercy was to pardon; and pardon in its very essence involves the recognition of guilt and ill-desert in the recipient. If crime is only a disease which needs cure, not sin which deserves punishment, it cannot be pardoned. How can you pardon a man for having a gumboil or a club foot? But the Humanitarian theory wants simply to abolish Justice and substitute Mercy for it. This means that you start being "kind" to people before you have considered their rights, and then force upon them supposed kindnesses which they in fact had a right to refuse, and finally kindnesses which no one but you will recognize as kindnesses and which the recipient will feel as abominable cruelties. You have overshot the mark. Mercy, detached from Justice, grows unmerciful. That is the important paradox. As there are plants which will flourish only in mountain soil, so it appears that Mercy will flower only when it grows in the crannies of the rock of Justice: transplanted to the marshlands of mere Humanitarianism, it becomes a man-eating weed, all the more dangerous because it is still called by the same name as the mountain variety. But we ought long ago to have learned our lesson. We should be too old now to be deceived by those humane pretensions which have served to usher in every cruelty of the revolutionary period in which we live. These are the "precious balms" which will "break our heads."

There is a fine sentence in Bunyan: "It came burning hot into my mind, whatever he said, and however he flattered, when he got me home to his house, he would sell me for a slave." There is a fine couplet, too, in John Ball:

> Be ware ere ye be woe
> Know your friend from your foe.

One last word. You may ask why I send this to an Australian periodical. The reason is simple and perhaps worth recording: I can get no hearing for it in England.

MORAL DILEMMAS IN REHABILITATION*

Shlomo Shoham

Shlomo Shoham, himself a concerned professional "treatment man," addresses his Crime and Social Deviation *in part to a discussion of the moral problems befalling the rehabilitative therapist. As a representative of legal society, the therapist assumes a position, vis-à-vis the patient, suggesting that the therapist has himself successfully internalized the norms of society to the extent of allegiance and personal conviction. Obviously, such a commitment does not always obtain. In any event, the interested reader will note herein a moral-educative theory of rehabilitation strongly contrasting with the conditioning mechanisms espoused by other treatment men.*

The moral dilemma of penal treatment confronts the probation officer, the prison warden, the police officer and others of the growing crowd of "treatment men" who are actively concerned with the Sisyphian task of prevention of crime and treatment of offenders.

The treatment man devotes himself to (and is paid for) making law-abiding citizens out of offenders. The ultimate aim is to "resocialize" the offender, to "re-adjust" him to society, to "rehabilitate" him, to "change him deep inside." The treatment man is generally equipped with a varying quantity and quality of knowledge about the causes of crime. He may be an adherent of the bio-physiological approach (fortunately quite rare since the Lombrosian and Neo-Lombrosian theories were proved to be largely myths); he may believe that mental defectiveness or psychopathy are causing crime; or he may subscribe to the currently popular sociological theory that a person turns into a criminal by association with criminal groups and identification with their values. He is only rarely told that most of these theories have been refuted by subsequent empirical testing, that the others are at the embryonic, hypothetical stage, and that overall knowledge of the pressures toward crime and social deviation is fragmentary and ambiguous. The ideal state of affairs for the treatment man would be if the knowledge of crime causation or the pressures toward crime had reached an advanced stage; then his task would be to prevent or "neutralize" these criminogenic factors. But, as we have already stated, this stage of knowledge is as far from us as ever and its attainment seems sadly remote.

Short of devising remedies based on the knowledge of causal processes, the treatment man may be equipped with pragmatic, trial and error, penological and correctional techniques: institutional

* Excerpted from Crime and Social Deviation by Shlomo Shoham, published by Henry Regnery Company, 1966. Reprinted by permission of the publishers.

routine, vocational training, guided recreation, individual psychological and psychiatric treatment, group therapy and group counseling. The overall achievements of modern penology and correction cannot be evaluated in a few sweeping statements, but treatment men usually make no secret of the fact that in spite of their correctional methods the rate of recidivism is steady or constantly rising,[1] and their search for the "philosopher's stone" to perform the alchemic trick of making law-abiding citizens out of offenders has not yet been successful. . . .

We propose to raise some problems that may, to a limited extent, account for our constant and frustrating failures in the field of correction and crime prevention. We may not have the solutions to these problems but we believe that by raising them we voice the views of many treatment men who have faced these problems every day for years, in actual work in the field of prevention of crime and treatment of offenders.

The first problem is the personal dilemma of the treatment man. To the offender he is the representative of "legitimate society." He personifies everything and everybody on the other side of the legal barricade. In this capacity the treatment man is in a peculiarly weak position. He is supposed to speak for an acquisitive, money-hungry, "cut-throat," competitive, morally confused and patently dishonest "affluent" society. The express or implied reaction of the offender to the treatment man's moralizing righteousness is, "Why do you want to make a saint out of me? What about the hordes of 'fixers,' politicians, businessmen and other white-collar criminals who get away with it because they have the right connections, who don't give two hoots today for the law, all they care about is not being caught. They are the same as me, only bigger thieves and a lot smarter, so they don't get caught; but they belong to the 'social elite' and I am a criminal." This attitude is not fiction, a logical and imaginary reconstruction, but is actually voiced by a large number of offenders who develop close and informal relations with their treatment men.

The personal dilemma of the treatment man becomes more apparent if we bear in mind that the rehabilitation process is basically an educational one, largely dependent on the link between the treatment man and his charge and the ability of the former to direct the thoughts and behavior of the latter. Educators and philosophers throughout the ages, especially those such as Plato, Rousseau, Pestalozzi and Dewey, who dealt intensively with pedagogical methodology, agree unanimously that a condition precedent to an effective educational process is not only that the educator knows and is able to transmit certain values and a set of norms but also that the educator himself is thoroughly convinced of the validity of these norms and regards them as binding in relation to his own behavior, i.e., has internalized these values and norms into his personality structure. . . .

Another problem, which is closely related to the first and may account for the low rate of "successful" treatment of offenders, is connected with the currently growing realization of many criminologists that the normative barrier against proscribed behavior (including crime) is strongly linked with the depth of the

[1] *See,* for instance, Professor P. A. H. Baan, "Causes of Recidivism," submitted to the Third International Congress on Criminology, London, 1955.

individual's internalization of norms and values. The extent to which the non- (or anti-) criminal norms have been incorporated into the personality of a particular person, i.e., his moral orientation,[2] may largely determine his chances for becoming an offender and his subsequent "reformation" or recidivism.[3]

This is a new trend, introduced into criminological theory mainly by social psychologists. Until recently the correctional field was thoroughly dominated (and is still largely dominated today) by the vehemently deterministic approach to human behavior, according to which morality is a dirty word, an atavism from the "unscientific" free-will approach to human behavior. Morality was therefore regarded by correctional theorists as an ambiguous, largely metaphysical concept by definition tainted with "value judgment"—the anathema of social sciences.[4] This attitude, which very likely stemmed from the Italian Scuola Positiva and its modern offspring, the Social Defense movement, resulted in a rather mechanistic approach to correction. The offender was regarded as a freak, the product of certain hereditary-biological traits *cum* very limited environmental pressures; American sociologists stressed the importance of social pressures to the exclusion of all others. The treatment man, therefore, was supposed to detect these crime-causing factors and pressures, and try to remove them (or remove the offender from their detrimental influence) or neutralize their harmful effects, so that the offender became "adjusted."

This mechanistic approach to the treatment of offenders may be necessary but it is certainly not sufficient. In order to achieve true reformation it is not enough to "neutralize" the criminogenic factors in a given offender's personality or socioeconomic background; it is necessary, in plain language, to provide the offender with a new set of norms and to strengthen his moral resistance against committing offenses. The crucial problem, however, is that we do not have a reasonably defined set of norms and values to offer the offender. We, the treatment men, come to the offender as representatives of a chaotic (and sometimes almost nonexistent) normative system. We represent a value vacuum where honesty in business, altruism, selfless devotion to a cause and even common decency are often regarded as archaic relics to which people may pay lip service but rarely adhere. The prevailing norms in business and everyday life are such ones as "everyone to himself," "never do any favor because you get into trouble," "push to the top, never mind the others" and "the crime is not doing something illegal but getting caught."

The frustration and helplessness of the treatment man is most apparent when, in moments of truth, he realizes that he stands before the offender as a

[2] N. Gross *et al.*, "Role Conflict and Its Resolution," in *Readings in Social Psychology*, ed. E. E. Maccoby *et al.* (New York: Holt, Rinehart & Winston, 1958), pp. 447 ff.

[3] *See* G. Trasler, *The Explanation of Criminality* (London: Routledge & Kegan Paul, 1962), pp. 40 ff.; W. C. Reckless, "A Non-Casual Explanation: Containment Theory," *Excerpta Criminologica,* II (1962), 131–34; W. C. Reckless, S. Dinitz and B. Kay, "The Self Component in Potential Delinquency and Potential Non-Delinquency," *American Sociological Review,* XXII (October, 1957), 566–70; and S. Shoham, "Conflict Situations and Delinquent Solutions," *Journal of Social Psychology,* LXIV (1964), 185–215.

[4] *See* A. W. Gouldner, "Anti-Minotaur: The Myth of Value-free Sociology," *Social Problems,* IX, No. 3 (Winter, 1962), 199. Gouldner doubts the ability of human beings (even sociologists) to be completely immune to value judgments.

deflated apostle lacking inner moral convictions and representing a morally bankrupt society. Offenders are not easily fooled; they realize very quickly that disillusioned treatment men become cynical and turn the vocation into a tool of personal ambition and the mission into a racket. Interservice rivalry occupies most of the working hours of some of the higher echelons of treatment personnel; high-ranking prison officers, directors of juvenile institutions and administrators of probation services may sometimes indulge in power skirmishes, personal feuds and petty intrigue, so that almost no time is left to devote any thought to correction programs. Penal services are not particularly worse in this respect than other services. These phenomena are only more accentuated and apparent in correctional institutions and services, where practical success and achievement in rehabilitating offenders are bound to be meager, so that disillusionment, cynicism and apathy may set in earlier; a cynical, power-thirsty or apathetic treatment man has little value as an educational or correctional figure. . . .

The treatment man is also vulnerable to a common occupational hazard: he may over-identify with the offender and be accused by his colleagues and superiors of neglecting the cause of law-abiding society, sympathizing with law-breakers and thus prejudicing public safety, taking things easy and "forgiving" the crimes of the offender. This, indeed, may occur with treatment men who realize that the behavior of some of their charges is more direct, that they are more consistent in their reactions and that they display more animal vigor and less calculated hypocrisy than supposedly law-abiding citizens. Without a positive set of values to offer, the treatment man may feel a subterranean affinity with the offender.

On the other hand, if the treatment man is unsympathetic, harsh in his reaction and pessimistic as to the chances for the offender's rehabilitation, he "does not understand" the case and forgets that "tout comprendre c'est tout pardonner." In the course of time the treatment man may get tired of fighting the Scylla of over-identification with the offender and the Charybdis of disciplinarian condemnation and peacefully degenerate into the atrophying apathy and hypocrisy of "Big Penology." Our purpose in the present context is to show that this attitude is mainly due to our inability to face (let alone solve) the moral issues of correction and penal treatment and to our tendency to escape from and evade moral decisions.

The low status of morality in the field of treatment (social welfare) and as a general regulating force of human behaviour stems from many sources. One we shall examine later is its close association with religion and the Judeo-Christian principle of the individual's moral responsibility. The other is closely linked with the constant attack of some modern schools of thought on "decadent bourgeois morality," "the tyranny of the weak against the strong," "the unconscious lust" and "sour-grapes" attitude underlying any moral and righteous indignation. Nietzsche, that great foe of Christian morality, led the attack by announcing:

> Weakness is to be falsified into desert. . . . And impotence, which requiteth not, is to be falsified into "goodness," timorous meanness into "humility"; submission to those whom one hates into "obedience" (namely, to one who they say commands this obedience; they call him God). The inoffensiveness of the "weak one," cow-

> ardice itself, in which he is rich, his standing at the door, his unavoidable necessity of waiting comes here by good names, such as "patience," they even call it the cardinal virtue. Not-to-be-able-to-take-revenge is called not-to-will-revenge, perhaps even forgiveness ("For they know not what they do; we alone know what they do"). They also talk of "love for their enemies" —and sweat in doing so.[5]

Those who have read the *Genealogy of Morals* (or have been directly or indirectly influenced by these ideas) may be reluctant to profess adherence to virtue, forgiveness and selfless idealism without feeling at least an aftertaste of hypocrisy. The psychoanalysts have carried on from here by declaring that morality feeds on our own inner struggles and the instability of our own emotional equilibrium; it is actually our own desire to commit immoral acts that disguises itself in righteous indignation. They say that righteousness is perverted sadism, that moral indignation helps us to overcome our own inner tendencies toward immorality and that it is never he who is without sin who casts the first stone.[6] The psychoanalysts make one positively uneasy and ashamed to have moral ideas, let alone impose them on others.

The patent (moral!) justification of the individual's sacrifice to the common good is the eventual attainment of Utopia; but Utopia seems to have vanished from humanity's fata morgana. A society dominated by the "American way of life" is, at best, seen as a racket of the "status seekers" operated by the "hidden persuaders" and by the "organization man" for the good and glory of the "power elite." At worst it displays its macabre leer through Huxley's *Brave New World*. The totalitarian Utopia is better known today, thanks to Orwell's portrayal of Big Brother, Doubletalk and Doublethink.

A mere glimpse at the main themes of contemporary literature and art reveals the overwhelming preoccupation with despair and helplessness: Sartre's nausea, Camus's absurd, Beckett's endless agony and aimlessness and the perverted monstrosities of Ionesco, Duerrenmatt and Max Frisch. These works don't deal with morality, because for them it does not exist. Morals belong to fairy tales and nurseries (where they are not taken seriously anymore). One might as well impute reality to the unicorn and the Pegasus.

This brief description of the status of morality in modern society may reveal the near futility and naïveté of our attempts to find answers to the moral dilemma of the treatment man. These answers, if any, must by their very nature be fragmentary and abstract, but if valid they could somewhat ease the confusion and present aimlessness in the field of correction.

THE RELIGIOUS ANSWER

This should not be mistaken for the dogmatic and somewhat tautological contention that crime is sin, therefore the struggle against crime is synonymous with the formal battle of the official religious bodies against sinful behavior.

The relevant religious answer to the dilemma of penal treatment is based on the conviction that the omnipotent, omniscient Divine Entity is by definition just and good. The treatment man might

[5] F. Nietzsche, *Genealogy of Morals,* trans. A. B. Samuel (New York: Modern Library, 1927), first essay, Section 14.

[6] *See* H. Weihofen, *The Urge to Punish* (Bloomington: Indiana University Press, 1956), p. 198. *See also* J. C. Flugel, *Man, Morals and Society* (London, 1955), pp. 205, 207-9.

convey to his charges the basic religious conviction that the power of God is not arbitrary and they need not fear Him if their behavior is right, for His basic nature and main characteristics are morality and justice.[7] This conception of a Divinity that willingly submits to morals and justice imputes order and meaning to life; according to the religious approach, good and bad (i.e., moral judgment) are meaningless if not backed by metaphysics and a Divine Entity.

Assuming that the religious belief is sincere and overlooking the religious hypocrites who feign piety for lucrative or other material ends, the difficulties with this approach to our dilemma are still obvious. Religious belief is closely connected with religious indoctrination and training from a very early age. The dogmas of Catholicism and the many daily rituals of Judaism are ingrained into the personality of the child by a conditioning process that cannot possibly be repeated at an advanced age. At the latter stage the chances of making a saint out of an adult (or even a juvenile) offender are sadly remote. Equally meager are the chances that he will suddenly see the light of his own accord. God's justice and moral integrity are more likely to be doubted (a mortal sin in itself) and Job's bitter accusation that "the earth is given into the hand of the wicked; He covereth the faces of the judges thereof; if not them, who is it?"[8] is likely to be hurled into the face of the priest, the minister or the rabbi.

THE RULES OF THE GAME

A common secular attempt at solving the dilemma of the treatment man is to persaude the offender that playing according to the rules of the (legitimate) game is simply more worthwhile, that the most important thing is to keep out of trouble. This is actually a completely amoral solution, a maxim of survival in a patently incomprehensible and absurd social system. This "rules of the game" approach is a direct corollary of the "adjustment" craze in the Western image (particularly in the U.S.) of a balanced personality.

The "rules of the game" answer advocates adjusting to harsh and cruel standards of competition and surmounting status and class barriers; or it points to the other alternative, i.e., social ostracism, economic hardship and "rotting half your life in prison." This obviously is a poor way out; it is more of an evasion than a solution, for it presupposes a utilitarian-hedonistic basis for behavior, which has long been discarded as an overall explanation for human motivation. The offender may also want to play his own game according to his own rules, which might be more risky—as if there were built-in securities in the "legitimate racket"—but sometimes very worthwhile. The choice offered the offender is based on convenience or on inconvenience, not on normative moral convictions. The "rules of the game" approach is, therefore, hardly relevant to our present issue and is probably not very effective as a treatment tool.

A PHILOSOPHIC ANSWER

On the abstract level the problem boils down to the interrelationship between criminal policy and the utilitarian conception of morality; the main clash is between the correctional task of the treatment man and the most common system of ethics, which states that moral behavior is not an end in itself but a

[7] According to the conceptions of Judaism.

[8] Job 9: 24

means to achieve material rewards and happiness.[9] This system of ethics has a built-in self-defeating mechanism; a man who anticipates any sort of gain, material or otherwise, as a direct corollary of his moral behavior is bound to be disappointed, feel deprived and cheated of a just reward and eventually become bitter and cynical. A more durable system of ethics is the one that sees righteousness as its own reward and the idea of justice as based on a categorical imperative to do right and punish the wrongdoer. Probably the most suitable conception of morality for our purposes is the one that regards the individual as a component of society, realizes that a system of ethics must start from the axiomatic existence of society and the necessity for its existence and proceeds to regulate the interrelation of individuals—not as individuals but as particles of a greater whole that is an entity by itself and not just a conglomeration of particles.

Durkheim, the chief exponent of this view, says:

> Law and morality are the totality of ties which bind each of us to society, which make a unitary coherent aggregate of the mass of individuals. Everything which is a source of solidarity is moral; everything which forces man to take account of other men is moral; everything which forces him to regulate his conduct through something other than the striving of his ego is moral, and morality is as solid as these ties are numerous and strong.[10]

This conception of morality does not need a metaphysical basis, because it stems from the fact of the existence of the individual and the existence of society. The philosophical counterpart of Durkheim's sociological conception of morality is modern existentialist thought —not Sartre's pessimistic brand, but Camus's more optimistic one. The latter's solution to the absurd, the meaninglessness of life and its value vacuum, is voiced by the two main heroes of *The Plague*:

> "Why do you show such devotion," asked Tarrou, "considering you don't believe in God?"
>
> "I have no idea what's awaiting me," answered Rieux. "For the moment I know this: there are sick people and they need curing. Later on perhaps they'll think things over and so shall I, but what's wanted now is to make them well. I defend them as best as I can, that's all. One thing I must tell you: there's no question of heroism in all this. It's a matter of common decency. That's an idea which may make some people smile but the only means of fighting a plague is common decency."[11]

Man's inevitable bonds with his fellowmen in society create mutual obligations and may serve as a basis for the war against the ills of society symbolized by the plague. This synthesis of Durkheim and Camus gives us a partial answer on the philosophical level and, as we shall see later, may serve as a pragmatic answer to the dilemma of the treatment man. It may also shed new light on Garofalo's wish to break the legalistic boundaries of the criminal law and include the "délit naturel" in the boundaries of criminology and crime prevention. Garofalo's idea was largely based on the premises of the "law of nature," which were very

[9] *See* E. Cahn, *The Moral Decision: Right and Wrong in the Light of American Law* (Bloomington: Indiana University Press, 1955), Part I, p. 9 ff.

[10] Cited by C. W. Mills, ed., in *Images of Man* (New York: Braziller, 1960), p. 477.

[11] A. Camus, *The Plague* (Baltimore: Penguin Books, 1960), p. 107.

popular at that time among legal philosophers. The point, however, which is rarely contested nowadays, is that nature is amoral. Morality can only have a meaning in relation to man in society. Nature does not know either pity or probity. The latter may, however, be included in our proposed synthesis of Durkheim's solidarity and Camus's obligation and duty of man toward his fellowman as the common basis of a practical ethical system that we can offer to our charges and that will supply us with a credo that may answer to a certain extent the dilemma of the treatment man. The white-collar criminals, the hordes of cynical officials, fixers and corrupt politicans may indeed worry us if our system of ethics is utilitarian, but not if we adopt social solidarity and obligation toward our fellowmen as a corollary of the fact of their existence, as the backbone of our professional and moral philosophy.

A PRAGMATIC APPLICATION

"All very nicely said," we hear Old Mike muttering through his pipe, "but how do you go on from here; is it a real 'new penology' or just some more of those ten-gallon hot-air words of 'Big Penology'?"

How do we convey our new moral convictions to our charges? It's the same old problem: you can lead a horse to water but you can't make him drink. How do we make an offender receptive to new values? We have already stated the difficulties involved in corrective reeducation. We start with a man with a twisted personality, very often without any education, with a tough, self-centered attitude toward everybody and everything, the result of a lifelong struggle for survival and continuous failure experiences. Many of them are almost incapable of love and pity for others. The treatment man's clue about an appropriate ethical system is clearly not enough. How does he convey it to his charge? There are, of course, no hard and fast rules; none of the following ideas have been tested but they may serve as a tentative basis for further hypotheses to be subsequently verified by empirical testing.

First of all, force, sheer force, is required to break the barrier of the charge's tough personality or to shock him out of his inner conflicts or to cast some doubts as to the infallibility of his image of the "legitimate racket." This initial battle of stamina and wit must end in victory for the treatment man, or the whole war is lost *ab initio*. At this stage dramatization of some principles is indeed necessary. We have already stressed the futility of moralizing as a treatment tool. Morals dished out verbally are very often flat and unpalatable. The Old Testament prophets fully realized this point when they used their lively and picturesque images; so did Goethe, when he saw that, from a whole line of blind beggars, one got most of the coins because instead of the usual poster saying "Help the blind" he held one saying "It is April, and I am blind." "Dramatisation," says Cahn, "has a magical capacity to arouse our moral constitutions; that is, if the drama is genuine and sincere in nature."[12]

Apart from the technical effect of dramatization, the treatment man must see his task as a continuous challenge where no "treatment sessions" and other correctional techniques by themselves are sufficient. The basic unit is the treatment man—offender dyad, and the link

[12] Cahn, *op. cit.*, p. 50.

must be intensive and close; at some stages "over-identification" is not only permissible but necessary. It should be understood that plucking an offender out of the criminal subculture and changing his values (without which the "rehabilitation" is temporary and illusory) is no mean trick. It is a minor Pygmalion-Galatea dyad, in which the treatment man's tenacious efforts are channeled through a close personal link with the offender.

This calls, of course, for special qualities in the treatment man; we realize that supermen might find better positions than as probation or parole officers or members of a prison correctional staff, but without the charisma in their personality structures that not only sustains moral convictions but also conveys them to others they will be of very limited use as treatment men. As Camus's Tarrou says:

> "On this earth there are pestilences and there are victims . . . and there are true healers. But it's a fact one does not come across many of them, and anyhow it must be a hard vocation."

THE REHABILITATIVE IDEAL*

Francis A. Allen

Francis A. Allen, dean of the Law School at the University of Michigan, formerly taught law at Northwestern, Harvard, and the University of Chicago. His interests, as reflected in his numerous publications, center about constitutional law and criminal law topics. The following selection, written in 1959, reflects his hesitancy to embrace wholeheartedly the rehabilitative ideal, at least until its scope has become better defined and less arbitrary. One of his critical questions is: To what extent, if any, has the rehabilitative ideal been detrimental to the science of criminology?

Although one is sometimes inclined to despair of any constructive changes in the administration of criminal justice, a glance at the history of the past half-century reveals a succession of the most significant developments. Thus, the last fifty years have seen the widespread acceptance of three legal inventions of great importance: the juvenile court, systems of probation and of parole. During the same period, under the inspiration of continental research and writing, scientific criminology became an established field of instruction and inquiry in American universities and in other research agencies. At the same time, psychiatry made its remarkable contributions to the theory of human behavior and, more specifically, of that form of human behavior described as criminal. These developments have been accompanied by nothing less than a revolution in public conceptions of the nature of crime and the criminal, and in public attitudes toward the proper treatment of the convicted offender.[1]

This history with its complex developments of thought, institutional behavior, and public attitudes must be approached gingerly; for in dealing with it we are in peril of committing the sin of oversimplification. Nevertheless, despite the presence of contradictions and paradox, it seems possible to detect one common element in much of this thought and activity which goes far to characterize the history we are considering. This common element or theme I shall describe, for want of a better phrase, as the rise of the rehabilitative ideal.

The rehabilitative ideal is itself a complex of ideas which, perhaps, defies com-

* From Allen, *Criminal Justice, Legal Values and the Rehabilitative Ideal*, 50 JOURNAL OF CRIMINAL LAW, CRIMINOLOGY AND POLICE SCIENCE 226 (1959). Reprinted with permission.

[1] These developments have been surveyed in Allen, *Law and the Future: Criminal Law and Administration*. 51 NW. L. REV. 207, 207–208 (1956). See also HARNO, *Some Significant Developments in Criminal Law and Procedure in the Last Century*, 42 J. CRIM. L., C. AND P.S. 427 (1951).

pletely precise statement. The essential points, however, can be articulated. It is assumed, first, that human behavior is the product of antecedent causes. These causes can be identified as part of the physical universe, and it is the obligation of the scientist to discover and to describe them with all possible exactitude. Knowledge of the antecedents of human behavior makes possible an approach to the scientific control of human behavior. Finally, and of primary significance for the purposes at hand, it is assumed that measures employed to treat the convicted offender should serve a therapeutic function, that such measures should be designed to effect changes in the behavior of the convicted person in the interests of his own happiness, health, and satisfactions and in the interest of social defense.

Although these ideas are capable of rather simple statement, they have provided the arena for some of the modern world's most acrimonious controversy. And the disagreements among those who adhere in general to these propositions have been hardly less intense than those prompted by the dissenters. This is true, in part, because these ideas possess a delusive simplicity. No idea is more pervaded with ambiguity than the notion of reform or rehabilitation. Assuming, for example, that we have the techniques to accomplish our ends of rehabilitation, are we striving to produce in the convicted offender something called "adjustment" to his social environment or is our objective something different from or more than this? By what scale of values do we determine the ends of therapy?[2]

These are intriguing questions, well worth extended consideration. But it is not my purpose to pursue them in this paper. Rather, I am concerned with describing some of the dilemmas and conflicts of values that have resulted from efforts to impose the rehabilitative ideal on the system of criminal justice. I know of no area in which a more effective demonstration can be made of the necessity for greater mutual understanding between the law and the behavioral disciplines.

There is, of course, nothing new in the notion of reform or rehabilitation of the offender as one objective of the penal process. This idea is given important emphasis, for example, in the thought of the medieval churchmen. The church's position, as described by Sir Francis Palgrave, was that punishment was not to be "thundered in vengeance for the satisfaction of the state, but imposed for the good of the offender: in order to afford the means of amendment and to lead the transgressor to repentance, and to mercy."[3] Even Jeremy Bentham, whose views modern criminology has often scorned and more often ignored, is found saying: "It is a great merit in a punishment to contribute to the *reformation of the offender,* not only through fear of being punished again, but by a change in his character and habits."[4] But this is

[2] "We see that it is not easy to determine what we consider to be the sickness and what we consider to be the cure." FROMM, PSYCHOANALYSIS AND RELIGION (1950) 73. See also the author's development of these points at 67–77.

[3] Quoted in DALZELL, BENEFIT OF CLERGY AND RELATED MATTERS (1955) 13.

[4] BENTHAM, THE THEORY OF LEGISLATION (Ogden, C. K., ed., 1931) 338–339. (Italics in the original.) But Bentham added: "But when [the writers] come to speak about the means of preventing offenses, of rendering men better, of perfecting morals, their imagination grows warm, their hopes excited; one would suppose they were about to produce the great secret, and that the human race was going to receive a new form.

far from saying that the modern expression of the rehabilitative ideal is not to be sharply distinguished from earlier expressions. The most important differences, I believe, are two. First, the modern statement of the rehabilitative ideal is accompanied by, and largely stems from, the development of scientific disciplines concerned with human behavior, a development not remotely approximated in earlier periods when notions of reform of the offender were advanced. Second, and of equal importance for the purposes at hand, in no other period has the rehabilitative ideal so completely dominated theoretical and scholarly inquiry, to such an extent that in some quarters it is almost assumed that matters of treatment and reform of the offender are the only questions worthy of serious attention in the whole field of criminal justice and corrections.

This narrowing of interests prompted by the rise of the rehabilitative ideal during the past half-century should put us on our guard. No social institutions as complex as those involved in the administration of criminal justice serve a single function or purpose. Social institutions are multi-valued and multi-purposed. Values and purposes are likely on occasion to prove inconsistent and to produce internal conflict and tension. A theoretical orientation that evinces concern for only one or a limited number of purposes served by the institution must inevitably prove partial and unsatisfactory. In certain situations it may prove positively dangerous. This stress on the unfortunate consequences of the rise of the rehabilitative ideal need not involve failure to recognize the substantial benefits that have also accompanied its emergence. Its emphasis on the fundamental problems of human behavior, its numerous contributions to the decency of the criminal-law processes are of vital importance. But the limitations and dangers of modern trends of thought need clearly to be identified in the interest, among others, of the rehabilitative ideal, itself.

My first proposition is that the rise of the rehabilitative ideal has dictated what questions are to be investigated, with the result that many matters of equal or even greater importance have been ignored or cursorily examined. This tendency can be abundantly illustrated. Thus, the concentration of interest on the nature and needs of the criminal has resulted in a remarkable absence of interest in the nature of crime. This is, indeed, surprising, for on reflection it must be apparent that the question of what is a crime is logically the prior issue: how crime is defined determines in large measure who the criminal is who becomes eligible for treatment and therapy.[5] A related observation was made some years ago by Professor Karl Llewellyn, who has done as much as any man to develop sensible interdisciplinary inquiry involving law and the behavioral disciplines:[6] "When I was younger I used to hear smuggish assertions among my sociological friends, such as: 'I take the sociological, *not* the legal, approach to crime'; and I suspect an inquiring reporter could still hear much the same (perhaps with 'psychiatric' often substituted for 'sociological')

It is because we have a more magnificent idea of objects in proportion as they are less familiar, and because the imagination has a loftier flight amid vague projects which have never been subjected to the limits of analysis." Id. at 359.

[5] Cf. HART, *The Aims of the Criminal Law,* 23 LAW AND CONT. PROB. 401 (1958).

[6] See LLEWELLYN AND HOEBEL, THE CHEYENNE WAY (1941). See also *Crime, Law and Social Science: A Symposium, 34* COLUM. L. REV. 277 (1934).

—though it is surely somewhat obvious that when you take 'the legal' out, you also take out 'crime.'"[7] This disinterest in the definition of criminal behavior has afflicted the lawyers quite as much as the behavioral scientists. Even the criminal law scholar has tended, until recently, to assume that problems of procedure and treatment are the things that "really matter."[8] Only the issue of criminal responsibility as affected by mental disorder has attracted the consistent attention of the non-lawyer, and the literature reflecting this interest is not remarkable for its cogency or its wisdom. In general, the behavioral sciences have left other issues relevant to crime definition largely in default. There are a few exceptions. Dr. Hermann Mannheim, of the London School of Economics, has manifested intelligent interest in these matters.[9] The late Professor Edwin Sutherland's studies of "white-collar crime"[10] may also be mentioned, although, in my judgment, Professor Sutherland's efforts in this field are among the least perceptive and satisfactory of his many valuable contributions.[11]

The absence of wide-spread interest in these areas is not to be explained by any lack of challenging questions. Thus, what may be said of the relationships between legislative efforts to subject certain sorts of human behavior to penal regulation and the persistence of police corruption and abuse of power?[12] Studies of public attitudes toward other sorts of criminal legislation might provide valuable clues as to whether given regulatory objectives are more likely to be attained by the provision of criminal penalties or by other kinds of legal sanctions. It ought to be re-emphasized that the question, what sorts of behavior should be declared criminal, is one to which the behavioral sciences might contribute vital insights. This they have largely failed to do, and we are the poorer for it.

Another example of the narrowing of interests that has accompanied the rise of the rehabilitative ideal is the lack of concern with the idea of deterrence—indeed the hostility evinced by many modern criminologists toward it. This, again, is a most surprising development.[13] It must surely be apparent that the criminal law has a general preventive function to perform in the interests of public order and of security of life, limb, and possessions. Indeed, there is reason to assert that the influence of criminal sanctions on the millions who never engage in serious criminality is of greater social importance than their impact on the hundreds of thousands who do. Certainly, the assumption of those who make our laws is that the denouncing of conduct as criminal and providing the means for the enforcement of the legislative prohibitions will generally have

[7] *Law and the Social Sciences—Especially Sociology*, 62 Harv. L. Rev. 1286, 1287 (1949).

[8] Allen, *op. cit. supra*, note 1, at 207–210.

[9] See, especially, his Criminal Justice and Social Reconstruction (1946).

[10] White-Collar Crime (1949) See also Clinard, The Black Market (1952).

[11] Cf. Caldwell, *A Re-Examination of the Concept of White-Collar Crime*, 22 Fed. Prob. 30 (March, 1958).

[12] An interesting question of this kind is now being debated in England centering on the proposals for enhanced penalties for prostitution offenses made in the recently-issued Wolfenden Report. See Fairfield, *Notes on Prostitution*, 9 Brit. J. Delin. 164, 173 (1959). See also Allen, *The Borderland of the Criminal Law: Problems of 'Socializing' Criminal Justice*, 32 Soc. Ser. Rev. 107, 110–111 (1958).

[13] But see Andenaes, *General Prevention—Illusion or Reality?* 43 J. Crim. L., C. and P.S. 176 (1952).

a tendency to prevent or minimize such behavior. Just what the precise mechanisms of deterrence are is not well understood. Perhaps it results, on occasion, from the naked threat of punishment. Perhaps, more frequently, it derives from a more subtle process wherein the mores and moral sense of the community are recruited to advance the attainment of the criminal law's objectives.[14] The point is that we know very little about these vital matters, and the resources of the behavioral sciences have rarely been employed to contribute knowledge and insight in their investigation. Not only have the criminologists displayed little interest in these matters, some have suggested that the whole idea of general prevention is invalid or worse. Thus, speaking of the deterrent theory of punishment, the authors of a leading textbook in criminology assert: "This is simply a derived rationalization of revenge. Though social revenge is the actual psychological basis of punishment today, the apologists for the punitive regime are likely to bring forward in their defense the more sophisticated, but equally futile, contention that punishment deters from [*sic*] crime."[15] We are thus confronted by a situation in which the dominance of the rehabilitative ideal not only diverts attention from many serious issues, but leads to a denial that these issues even exist.

Now permit me to turn to another sort of difficulty that has accompanied the rise of the rehabilitative ideal in the areas of corrections and criminal justice. It is a familiar observation that an idea once propagated and introduced into the active affairs of life undergoes change. The real significance of an idea as it evolves in actual practice may be quite different from that intended by those who conceived it and gave it initial support. An idea tends to lead a life of its own; and modern history is full of the unintended consequences of seminal ideas. The application of the rehabilitative ideal to the institutions of criminal justice presents a striking example of such a development. My second proposition, then, is that the rehabilitative ideal has been debased in practice and that the consequences resulting from this debasement are serious and, at times, dangerous.

This proposition may be supported, first, by the observation that, under the dominance of the rehabilitative ideal, the language of therapy is frequently employed, wittingly or unwittingly, to disguise the true state of affairs that prevails in our custodial institutions and at other points in the correctional process. Certain measures, like the sexual psychopath laws, have been advanced and supported as therapeutic in nature when, in fact, such a characterization seems highly dubious.[16] Too often the vocabulary of therapy has been exploited to serve a public-relations function. Recently, I visited an institution devoted to the diagnosis and treatment of disturbed children. The institution had been established with high hopes and, for once, with the enthusiastic support of the state legislature. Nevertheless, fifty minutes of an hour's lecture, delivered by a supervising psychiatrist before we toured the building, were devoted to custodial problems. This fixation on problems of custody was reflected in the insti-

[14] This seems to be the assertion of Garafalo. See his CRIMINOLOGY (Millar trans. 1914) 241–242.

[15] BARNES AND TEETERS, NEW HORIZONS IN CRIMINOLOGY (2nd ed. 1954) 337. The context in which these statements appear also deserves attention.

[16] See note 25, *infra*.

tutional arrangements which included, under a properly euphemistic label, a cell for solitary confinement.[17] Even more disturbing was the tendency of the staff to justify these custodial measures in therapeutic terms. Perhaps on occasion the requirements of institutional security and treatment coincide. But the inducements to self-deception in such situations are strong and all too apparent. In short, the language of therapy has frequently provided a formidable obstacle to a realistic analysis of the conditions that confront us. And realism in considering these problems is the one quality that we require above all others.[18]

There is a second sort of unintended consequence that has resulted from the application of the rehabilitative ideal to the practical administration of criminal justice. Surprisingly enough, the rehabilitative ideal has often led to increased severity of penal measures. This tendency may be seen in the operation of the juvenile court. Although frequently condemned by the popular press as a device of leniency, the juvenile court, is authorized to intervene punitively in many situations in which the conduct, were it committed by an adult, would be wholly ignored by the law or would subject the adult to the mildest of sanctions. The tendency of proposals for wholly indeterminate sentences, a clearly identifiable fruit of the rehabilitative ideal,[19] is unmistakably in the direction of lengthened periods of imprisonment. A large variety of statutes authorizing what is called "civil" commitment of persons, but which, except for the reduced protections afforded the parties proceeded against, are essentially criminal in nature, provide for absolutely indeterminate periods of confinement. Experience has demonstrated that, in practice, there is a strong tendency for the rehabilitative ideal to serve purposes that are essentially incapacitative rather than therapeutic in character.[20]

The reference to the tendency of the rehabilitative ideal to encourage increasingly long periods of incarceration brings me to my final proposition. It is that the rise of the rehabilitative ideal has often been accompanied by attitudes and measures that conflict, sometimes seriously, with the values of individual liberty and volition. As I have already observed, the role of the behavioral sciences in the administration of criminal justice and in the areas of public policy lying on the borderland of the criminal law is one of obvious importance. But I suggest that, if the function of criminal justice is considered in its proper dimensions, it will be discovered that the most fundamental problems in these areas are not those of psychiatry, sociology, social case work, or social psychology. On the contrary, the most fundamental problems are those of political philosophy and political science. The administra-

[17] As I recall, it was referred to as the "quiet room." In another institution the boy was required to stand before a wall while a seventy pound fire hose was played on his back. This procedure went under the name of "hydrotherapy."

[18] Cf. WECHSLER, *Law, Morals and Psychiatry*, *18* COLUM. L. SCHOOL NEWS 2, 4 (March 4, 1959): "The danger rather is that coercive regimes we would not sanction in the name of punishment or of correction will be sanctified in the name of therapy without providing the resources for a therapeutic operation."

[19] Cf. TAPPAN, *Sentencing under the Model Penal Code, 23* LAW AND CONT. PROB. 538, 530 (1958).

[20] Cf. HALL, JEROME, GENERAL PRINCIPLES OF CRIMINAL LAW (1947) 551. And see SELLIN: THE PROTECTIVE CODE: A SWEDISH PROPOSAL (1957) *9*.

tion of the criminal law presents to any community the most extreme issues of the proper relations of the individual citizen to state power. We are concerned here with the perennial issue of political authority: Under what circumstances is the state justified in bringing its force to bear on the individual human being? These issues, of course, are not confined to the criminal law, but it is in the area of penal regulation that they are most dramatically manifested. The criminal law, then, is located somewhere near the center of the political problem, as the history of the twentieth century abundantly reveals. It is no accident, after all, that the agencies of criminal justice and law enforcement are those first seized by an emerging totalitarian regime.[21] In short, a study of criminal justice is most fundamentally a study in the exercise of political power. No such study can properly avoid the problem of the abuse of power.

The obligation of containing power within the limits suggested by a community's political values has been considerably complicated by the rise of the rehabilitative ideal. For the problem today is one of regulating the exercise of power by men of good will, whose motivations are to help not to injure, and whose ambitions are quite different from those of the political adventurer so familiar to history. There is a tendency for such persons to claim immunity from the usual forms of restraint and to insist that professionalism and a devotion to science provide sufficient protections against unwarranted invasion of individual right. This attitude is subjected to mordant criticism by Aldous Huxley in his recent book, "Brave New World Revisited." Mr. Huxley observes: "There seems to be a touching belief among certain Ph.D's in sociology that Ph.D's in sociology will never be corrupted by power. Like Sir Galahad's, their strength is the strength of ten because their heart is pure—and their heart is pure because they are scientists and have taken six thousand hours of social studies."[22] I suspect that Mr. Huxley would be willing to extend his point to include professional groups other than the sociologists. There is one proposition which, if generally understood, would contribute more to clear thinking on these matters than any other. It is not a new insight. Seventy years ago the Italian criminologist, Garafalo, asserted: "The mere deprivation of liberty, however benign the administration of the place of confinement, is undeniably punishment."[23] This proposition may be rephrased as follows: Measures which subject individuals to the substantial and involuntary deprivation of their liberty are essentially punitive in character, and this reality is not altered by the facts that the motivations that prompt incarceration are to provide therapy or otherwise contribute to the person's well-being or reform. As such, these measures must be closely scrutinized to insure that power is being applied consistently with those values of the community that justify interferences with liberty for only the most clear and compelling reasons.

But the point I am making requires more specific and concrete application to be entirely meaningful. It should be pointed out, first, that the values of individual liberty may be imperiled by claims to knowledge and therapeutic technique that we, in fact, do not possess

[21] This development in the case of Germany may be gleaned from CRANKSHAW, GESTAPO (1956).

[22] HUXLEY, BRAVE NEW WORLD REVISITED (1958) 34–35.

[23] *Op. cit. supra,* note 14, at 256.

and by failure candidly to concede what we do not know. At times, practitioners of the behavioral sciences have been guilty of these faults. At other times, such errors have supplied the assumptions on which legislators, lawyers and lay people generally have proceeded. Ignorance, in itself, is not disgraceful so long as it is unavoidable. But when we rush to measures affecting human liberty and human dignity on the assumption that we know what we do not know or can do what we cannot do, then the problem of ignorance takes on a more sinister hue.[24] An illustration of these dangers is provided by the sexual psychopath laws, to which I return; for they epitomize admirably some of the worst tendencies of modern practice. These statutes authorize the indefinite incarceration of persons believed to be potentially dangerous in their sexual behavior. But can such persons be accurately identified without substantial danger of placing persons under restraint who, in fact, provide no serious danger to the community? Having once confined them, is there any body of knowledge that tells us how to treat and cure them? If so, as a practical matter, are facilities and therapy available for these purposes in the state institutions provided for the confinement of such persons?[25] Questions almost as serious can be raised as to a whole range of other measures. The laws providing for commitment of persons displaying the classic symptoms of psychosis and advanced mental disorder have proved a seductive analogy for other proposals. But does our knowledge of human behavior really justify the extension of these measures to provide for the indefinite commitment of persons otherwise afflicted? We who represent the disciplines that in some measure are concerned with the control of human behavior are required to act under weighty responsibilities. It is no paradox to assert that the real utility of scientific technique in the fields under discussion depends on an accurate realization of the limits of scientific knowledge.

There are other ways in which the modern tendencies of thought accompanying the rise of the rehabilitative ideal have imperiled the basic political values. The most important of these is the encouragement of procedural laxness and irregularity. It is my impression that there is greater awareness of these dangers today than at some other times in the past, for which, if true, we perhaps have Mr. Hitler to thank. Our increased knowledge of the functioning of totalitarian regimes makes it more difficult to assert that the insistence on decent and orderly procedure represents simply a lawyer's quibble or devotion to outworn ritual. Nevertheless, in our courts of so-called "socialized justice" one may still observe, on occasion, a tendency to assume that, since the purpose of the proceeding is to "help" rather than to "punish," some lack of concern in establishing the charges against the person before the court may be justified. This position is self-defeating and otherwise indefensible. A child brought before the court has a right to demand, not only the benevolent concern of the tribunal, but justice.

[24] I have developed these points in ALLEN, *op. cit. supra*, note 12, at 113–115.

[25] Many competent observers have asserted that none of these inquiries can properly be answered in the affirmative. See, e.g., SUTHERLAND, *The Sexual Psychopath Laws, 40* J. CRIM. L., C. AND P.S. 543 (1950) HACKER AND FRYM. *The Sexual Psychopath Act in Practice: A Critical Discussion, 43* CALIF. L. REV. 766 (1955). See also TAPPAN, THE HABITUAL SEX OFFENDER (Report of the New Jersey Commission) (1950).

And one may rightly wonder as to the value of therapy purchased at the expense of justice. The essential point is that the issues of treatment and therapy be kept clearly distinct from the question of whether the person committed the acts which authorize the intervention of state power in the first instance.[26] This is a principle often violated. Thus, in some courts the judge is supplied a report on the offender by the psychiatric clinic before the judgment of guilt or acquittal is announced. Such reports, while they may be relevant to the defendant's need for therapy or confinement, ordinarily are wholly irrelevant to the issue of his guilt of the particular offense charged. Yet it asks too much of human nature to assume that the judge is never influenced on the issue of guilt or innocence by a strongly adverse psychiatric report.

Let me give one final illustration of the problems that have accompanied the rise of the rehabilitative ideal. Some time ago we encountered a man in his eighties incarcerated in a state institution. He had been confined for some thirty years under a statute calling for the automatic commitment of defendants acquitted on grounds of insanity in criminal trials. It was generally agreed by the institution's personnel that he was not then psychotic and probably had never been psychotic. The fact seemed to be that he had killed his wife while drunk. An elderly sister of the old man was able and willing to provide him with a home, and he was understandably eager to leave the institution. When we asked the director of the institution why the old man was not released, he gave two significant answers. In the first place, he said, the statute requires me to find that this inmate is no longer a danger to the community; this I cannot do, for he may kill again. And of course the director was right. However unlikely commission of homicide by such a man in his eighties might appear, the director could not be certain. But, as far as that goes, he also could not be certain about himself or about you or me. The second answer was equally interesting. The old man, he said, is better off here. To understand the full significance of this reply it is necessary to know something about the place of confinement. Although called a hospital, it was in fact a prison, and not at all a progressive prison. Nothing worthy of the name of therapy was provided and very little by way of recreational facilities.

This case points several morals. It illustrates, first, a failure of the law to deal adequately with the new requirements being placed upon it. The statute, as a condition to the release of the inmate, required the director of the institution virtually to warrant the future good behavior of the inmate, and, in so doing, made unrealistic and impossible demands on expert judgment. This might be remedied by the formulation of release criteria more consonant with actuality. Provisions for conditional release to test the inmate's reaction to the free community would considerably reduce the strain on administrative decision-making. But there is more here. Per-

[26] A considerable literature has developed on these issues. See, e.g., Allen, *The Borderland of the Criminal Law: Problems of "Socializing" Criminal Justice, 32* Soc. Ser. Rev. 107 (1958), Diana, *The Rights of Juvenile Delinquents: An Appraisal of Juvenile Court Proceedings, 44* J. Crim. L., C. and P.S. 561 (1957), Paulsen, *Fairness to the Juvenile Offender, 41* Minn. L. Rev. 547 (1957); Waite, *How Far Can Court Procedures Be Socialized without Impairing Individual Rights? 12* J. Crim. L. and C. 430 (1921).

haps the case reflects that arrogance and insensitivity to human values to which men who have no reason to doubt their own motives appear peculiarly susceptible.[27]

In these remarks I have attempted to describe certain of the continuing problems and difficulties associated with, what I have called, the rise of the rehabilitative ideal. In so doing, I have not sought to cast doubt on the substantial benefits associated with that movement. It has exposed some of the most intractable problems of our time to the solvent properties of human intelligence. Moreover, the devotion to the ideal of empirical investigation provides the movement with a self-correcting mechanism of great importance, and justifies hopes for constructive future development.

Nevertheless, no intellectual movement produces only unmixed blessings. It has been suggested in these remarks that the ascendency of the rehabilitative ideal has, as one of its unfortunate consequences, diverted attention from other questions of great criminological importance. This has operated unfavorably to the full development of criminological science. Not only is this true, but the failure of many students and practitioners in the relevant areas to concern themselves with the full context of criminal justice has produced measures dangerous to basic political values and has, on occasion, encouraged the debasement of the rehabilitative ideal to produce results, unsupportable whether measured by the objectives of therapy or of corrections. The worst manifestations of these tendencies are undoubtedly deplored as sincerely by competent therapists as by other persons. But the occurrences are neither so infrequent nor so trivial that they can be safely ignored.

[27] One further recent and remarkable example is provided by the case, In re Maddox, 351 Mich. 358, 88 N.W. 2d 470 (1958). PROFESSOR WECHSLER, *op. cit. supra,* note 18, at 4, describes the facts and holding as follows: "Only the other day, the Supreme Court of Michigan ordered the release of a prisoner in their State prison at Jackson, who had been transferred from the Ionia State Hospital to which he was committed as a psycopath. The ground of transfer, which was defended seriously by a State psychiatrist, was that the prisoner was 'adamant' in refusing to admit sexual deviation that was the basis of his commitment; and thus, in the psychiatrist's view, resistant to therapy! The Court's answer was, of course, that he had not been tried for an offense."

IS PUNISHMENT NECESSARY?*

Jackson Toby

Jackson Toby is professor and chairman of the Department of Sociology in the College of Arts and Sciences at Rutgers University. From 1959 to 1963 he served as a regular consultant to the Youth Development Program of the Ford Foundation. In the following article, published originally in 1964, Dr. Toby considers the deterrent and rehabilitative goals of punishment and examines the current assumption that punishment will completely give way to treatment and rehabilitation measures. The reader may be surprised at Dr. Toby's suggestion that punishment may be an instrument devised by conformists to support and reward their own standards.

Of 11 contemporary textbooks in criminology written by sociologists, ten have one or more chapters devoted to the punishment of offenders.[1] All ten include a history of methods of punishment in Western society and, more specifically, a discussion of capital punishment. Seven discuss punishment in pre-literate societies. Seven include theoretical or philosophical discussions of the "justification" of punishment—usually in terms of "retribution," "deterrence," and "reformation." These theoretical analyses are at least as much indebted to law and philosophy as to sociology. Thus, in considering the basis for punishment, three textbooks refer both to Jeremy Bentham and to Emile Durkheim; three textbooks refer to Bentham but not to Durkheim; and one textbook refers to Durkheim but not to Bentham. Several textbook writers express their opposition to punishment, especially to cruel punishment. This opposition is alleged to be based on an incompatibility of punishment with scientific considerations. The following quotation is a case in point:

> "We still punish primarily for vengeance, or to deter, or in the interest of a 'just' balance of accounts between 'deliberate' evildoers on the one hand and an injured and enraged society on the other. We do not yet generally punish or treat as scientific criminology would imply, namely, in order to change antisocial attitudes into social attitudes."[2]

Most of the textbook writers note with satisfaction that "the trend in modern

* From Toby, *Is Punishment Necessary?* 55 Journal of Criminal Law, Criminology and Police Science 332 (1964). Reprinted with permission.

1 Barnes & Teeters, New Horizons in Criminology (3d ed. 1959); Caldwell, Criminology (1956); Cavan, Criminology (1955); Elliot, Crime in Modern Society (1952); Korn & McCorkle, Criminology and Penology (1959); Reckless, The Crime Problem (2d ed. 1955); Sutherland & Cressey, Principles of Criminology (5th ed. 1955); Taft, Criminology (3d ed. 1956); Tappan, Crime, Justice and Correction (1960); von Hentig, Crime: Causes and Conditions (1947); Wood & Waite, Crime and Its Treatment (1941).

2 Taft, *op. cit. supra* note 1, at 359.

countries has been toward humanizing punishment and toward the reduction of brutalities."[3] They point to the decreased use of capital punishment, the introduction of amenities into the modern prison by enlightened penology, and the increasing emphasis on nonpunitive and individualized methods of dealing with offenders, e.g., probation, parole, psychotherapy. In short, students reading these textbooks might infer that punishment is a vestigial carryover of a barbaric past and will disappear as humanitarianism and rationality spread. Let us examine this inference in terms of the motives underlying punishment and the necessities of social control.

Many crimes have identifiable victims. In the case of crimes against the person, physical or psychic injuries have been visited upon the victim. In the case of crimes against property, someone's property has been stolen or destroyed. In pressing charges against the offender, the victim may express hostility against the person who injured him in a socially acceptable way. Those who identify with the victim—not only his friends and family but those who can imagine the same injury being done to them—may join with him in clamoring for the punishment of the offender. If, as has been argued, the norm of reciprocity is fundamental to human interaction, this hostility of the victim constituency toward offenders is an obstacle to the elimination of punishment from social life.[4] Of course, the size of the group constituted by victims and those who identify with victims may be small. Empirical study would probably show that it varies by offense. Thus, it is possible that nearly everyone identifies with the victim of a murderer but relatively few people with the victim of a blackmailer. The greater the size of the victim constituency, the greater the opposition to a nonpunitive reaction to the offender.

It would be interesting indeed to measure the size and the composition of the victim constituencies for various crimes. Take rape as an illustration. Since the victims of rape are females, we might hypothesize that *women* would express greater punitiveness toward rapists than *men* and that degrees of hostility would correspond to real or imaginary exposure to rape. Thus, pretty young girls might express more punitiveness toward rapists than homely women. Among males, we might predict that greater punitiveness would be expressed by those with more reason to identify with the victims. Thus, males having sisters or daughters in the late teens or early twenties might express more punitiveness toward rapists than males lacking vulnerable "hostages to fortune."

Such a study might throw considerable light on the wellsprings of punitive motivation, particularly if victimization reactions were distinguished from other reasons for punitiveness. One way to explore such motivation would be to ask the same respondents to express their punitive predispositions toward offences which do not involve victims at all, e.g., gambling, or which involve victims of a quite different kind. Thus, rape might be balanced by an offense the victims of which are largely male. Survey research of this type is capable of ascertaining the opposition to milder penalties for various offenses. It would incidentally throw light on the comparatively gentle societal reaction to white-collar crime. Perhaps the explanation lies in the diffi-

[3] Reckless, *op. cit. supra* note 1, at 450.

[4] Gouldner, *The Norm of Reciprocity: A Preliminary Statement*, 25 Am. Soc. Rev. 161 (1960).

culty of identifying with the victims of patent infringement or watered hams.[5]

Conformists who identify with the *victim* are motivated to punish the offender out of some combination of rage and fear. Conformists who identify with the *offender,* albeit unconsciously, may wish to punish him for quite different reasons. Whatever the basis for the motivation to punish, the existence of punitive reactions to deviance is an obstacle to the abolition of punishment. However, it is by no means the sole obstacle. Even though a negligible segment of society felt punitive toward offenders, it might still not be feasible to eliminate punishment if the social control of deviance depended on it. Let us consider, therefore, the consequences of punishing offenders for (a) preventing crime, (b) sustaining the morale of conformists, and (c) rehabilitating offenders.

Durkheim defined punishment as an act of vengeance. "What we avenge, what the criminal expiates, is the outrage to morality."[6] But why is vengeance necessary? Not because of the need to deter the bulk of the population from doing likewise. The socialization process prevents most deviant behavior. Those who have introjected the moral norms of their society cannot commit crimes because their self-concepts will not permit them to do so. Only the unsocialized (and therefore amoral) individual fits the model of classical criminology and is deterred from expressing deviant impulses by a nice calculation of pleasures and punishments.[7] Other things being equal, the anticipation of punishment would seem to have more deterrent value for inadequately socialized members of the group. It is difficult to investigate this proposition empirically because other motivationally relevant factors are usually varying simultaneously, e.g., the situational temptations confronting various individuals, their optimism about the chances of escaping detection, and the differential impact of the same punishment on individuals of different status.[8] Clearly, though, the deterrent effect of anticipated punishments is a complex empirical problem, and Durkheim was not interested in it. Feeling as he did that *some* crime is normal in every society, he apparently decided that the crime prevention function of punishment is not crucial. He pointed out that minute gradation in punishment would not be necessary if punishment were simply a means of deterring the potential offender (crime prevention). "Robbers are as strongly inclined to rob as murderers are to murder; the resistance offered by the former is not less than that of the latter, and consequently, to control it, we would have recourse to the same means."[9] Durkheim was factually correct; the offenses punished most severely are not necessarily the ones which present the greatest problem of social defense. Thus, quantitatively speaking, murder is an unimportant cause of death; in the United States it claims only half as many lives annually as does suicide and only one-fifth the toll of automobile accidents. Furthermore, crimi-

[5] In this connection, it is well to recall that there is less reluctance to steal from corporations than from humans. See A. W. JONES, LIFE, LIBERTY, AND PROPERTY (1941).

[6] DURKHEIM, THE DIVISION OF LABOR IN SOCIETY 89 (1947).

[7] PARSONS, THE STRUCTURE OF SOCIAL ACTION 402–03 (1949).

[8] Toby, *Social Disorganization and Stake in Conformity: Complementary Factors in the Predatory Behavior of Young Hoodlums*, 48 J. CRIM. L., C. & P.S. 12 (1957).

[9] *Op. cit. supra* note 6, at 88.

nologists have been unable to demonstrate a relationship between the murder rate of a community and its use or lack of use of capital punishment.

Most contemporary sociologists would agree with Durkheim that the anticipation of punishment is not the first line of defense against crime. The socialization process keeps most people law abiding, not the police—if for no other reason than the police are not able to catch every offender. This does not mean, however, that the police could be disbanded. During World War II, the Nazis deported all of Denmark's police force, thus providing a natural experiment testing the deterrent efficacy of formal sanctions.[10] Crime increased greatly. Even though punishment is uncertain, especially under contemporary urban conditions, the possibility of punishment keeps some conformists law-abiding. The empirical question is: *How many* conformists would become deviants if they did not fear punishment?

Durkheim considered punishment indispensable as a means of containing the demoralizing consequences of the crimes that could not be prevented. Punishment was not for Durkheim mere vindictiveness. Without punishment Durkheim anticipated the demoralization of "upright people" in the face of defiance of the collective conscience. He believed that unpunished deviance tends to demoralize the conformist and therefore he talked about punishment as a means of repairing "the wounds made upon collective sentiments."[11] Durkheim was not entirely clear; he expressed his ideas in metaphorical language. Nonetheless, we can identify the hypothesis that the punishment of offenders promotes the solidarity of conformists.

Durkheim anticipated psychoanalytic thinking as the following reformulation of his argument shows: One who resists the temptation to do what the group prohibits, to drive his car at 80 miles per hour, to beat up an enemy, to take what he wants without paying for it, would like to feel that these self-imposed abnegations have some meaning. When he sees others defy rules without untoward consequences, he needs some reassurance that his sacrifices were made in a good cause. If "the good die young and the wicked flourish as the green bay tree," the moral scruples which enable conformists to restrain their own deviant inclinations lack social validation. The social significance of punishing offenders is that deviance is thereby defined as unsuccessful in the eyes of conformists, thus making the inhibition or repression of their own deviant impulses seem worthwhile. Righteous indignation is collectively sanctioned reaction formation. The law-abiding person who unconsciously resents restraining his desire to steal and murder has an opportunity, by identifying with the police and the courts, to affect the precarious balance within his own personality between internal controls and the temptation to deviate. A bizarre example of this psychological mechanism is the man who seeks out homosexuals and beats them up mercilessly. Such pathological hostility toward homosexuals is due to the sadist's anxiety over his own sex-role identification. By "punishing" the homosexual, he denies the latent homosexuality in his own psyche. No doubt, some of the persons involved in the administration

[10] TROLLE, SYV MÅNEDER UTEN POLITI (SEVEN MONTHS WITHOUT POLICE) (Copenhagen, 1945), quoted in Christie, *Scandinavian Criminology*, 31 SOCIOLOGICAL INQUIRY 101 (1961).

[11] DURKHEIM, *op. cit. supra* note 6, at 108.

of punishment are sadistically motivated. But Durkheim hypothesized that the psychic equilibrium of the *ordinary* member of the group may be threatened by violation of norms; Durkheim was not concerned about psychopathological punitiveness.

Whatever the practical difficulties, Durkheim's hypothesis is, in principle, testable. It should be possible to estimate the demoralizing impact of nonconformity on conformists. Clearly, though, this is no simple matter. The extent of demoralization resulting from the failure to punish may vary with type of crime. The unpunished traffic violator may cause more demoralization than the unpunished exhibitionist—depending on whether or not outwardly conforming members of society are more tempted to exceed the speed limit than to expose themselves. The extent of demoralization may also vary with position in the social structure occupied by the conformist. Thus, Ranulf suggested that the middle class was especially vulnerable:

> "[T]he disinterested tendency to inflict punishment is a distinctive characteristic of the lower middle class, that is, of a social class living under conditions which force its members to an extraordinarily high degree of self-restraint and subject them to much frustration of natural desires. If a psychological interpretation is to be put on this correlation of facts, it can hardly be to any other effect than that moral indignation is a kind of resentment caused by the repression of instincts."[12]

Once the facts on the rate and the incidence of moral indignation are known, it will become possible to determine whether something must be done to the offender in order to prevent the demoralization of conformists. Suppose that research revealed that a very large proportion of conformists react with moral indignation to *most* violations of the criminal laws. Does this imply that punishment is a functional necessity? Durkheim apparently thought so, but he might have been less dogmatic in his approach to punishment had he specified the functional problem more clearly: making the nonconformist unattractive as a role model. If the norm violation can be defined as unenviable through some other process than by inflicting suffering upon him, punishment is not required by the exigencies of social control.

Punishment can be discussed on three distinct levels: (a) in terms of the motivations of the societal agents administering it, (b) in terms of the definition of the situation on the part of the person being punished, and (c) in terms of its impact on conformists. At this point I am chiefly concerned with the third level, the impact on conformists. Note that punishment of offenders sustains the morale of conformists only under certain conditions. The first has already been discussed, namely that conformists unconsciously wish to violate the rules themselves. The second is that conformists implicitly assume that the nonconformity is a result of *deliberate defiance* of society's norms. For some conformists, this second condition is not met. Under the guidance of psychiatric thinking, some conformists assume that norm violation is the result of illness rather than wickedness.[13] For such conformists, pun-

[12] Ranulf, Moral Indignation and Middle-Class Psychology 198 (Copenhagen, 1938).

[13] Talcott Parsons has repeatedly suggested the analogy between illness and criminality. See also Aubert & Messinger, *The Criminal and the Sick*, 1 Inquiry 137 (1958), and Wootton, Social Science and Social Pathology 203–67 (1959).

ishment of the offender does not contribute to their morale. Since they assume that the nonconformity is an involuntary symptom of a disordered personality, the offender is automatically unenviable because illness is (by definition) undesirable. Of course, it is an empirical question as to the relative proportions of the conforming members of society who make the "wicked" or the "sick" assumption about the motivation of the offender, but this can be discovered by investigation.

In Western industrial societies, there is increasing tendency to call contemporary methods of dealing with offenders "treatment" rather than "punishment." Perhaps this means that increasing proportions of the population are willing to accept the "sick" theory of nonconformity. Note, however, that the emphasis on "treatment" may be more a matter of symbolism than of substance. Although the definition of the situation as treatment rather than punishment tends to be humanizing—both to the offender and to the persons who must deal with him—there are still kind guards and cruel nurses. Furthermore, it would be an error to suppose that punishment is invariably experienced as painful by the criminal whereas treatment is always experienced as pleasant by the psychopathological offender. Some gang delinquents consider a reformatory sentence an opportunity to renew old acquaintances and to learn new delinquent skills; they resist fiercely the degrading suggestion that they need the services of the "nut doctor." Some mental patients are terrified by shock treatment and embarrassed by group therapy.

What then is the significance of the increasing emphasis on "treatment"? Why call an institution for the criminally insane a "hospital" although it bears a closer resemblance to a prison than to a hospital for the physically ill? In my opinion, the increased emphasis on treatment in penological thinking and practice reflects the existence of a large group of conformists who are undecided as between the "wicked" and the "sick" theories of nonconformity. When they observe that the offender is placed in "treatment," their provisional diagnosis of illness is confirmed, and therefore they do not feel that he has "gotten away with it." Note that "treatment" has the capacity to make the offender unenviable to conformists whether or not it is effective in rehabilitating him and whether or not he experiences it as pleasant. Those old-fashioned conformists who are not persuaded by official diagnoses of illness will not be satisfied by "treatment"; they will prefer to see an attempt made to visit physical suffering or mental anguish on the offender. For them, punishment is necessary to prevent demoralization.

Rehabilitation of offenders swells the number of conformists and therefore is regarded both by humanitarians and by scientifically minded penologists as more constructive than punishment. Most of the arguments against imprisonment and other forms of punishment in the correctional literature boil down to the assertion that punishment is incompatible with rehabilitation. The high rate of recidivism for prisons and reformatories is cited as evidence of the irrationality of punishment.[14] What sense is there in subjecting offenders to the frustrations of incarceration? If rehabilitative programs are designed to help the offender cope with frustrations in his life situation, which presumably were responsible for

[14] Vold, *Does the Prison Reform?* 293 ANNALS 42 (1954).

his nonconformity, imprisoning him hardly seems a good way to begin. To generalize the argument, the status degradation inherent in punishment makes it more difficult to induce the offender to play a legitimate role instead of a nonconforming one. Whatever the offender's original motivations for nonconformity, punishment adds to them by neutralizing his fear of losing the respect of the community; he has already lost it.

Plausible though this argument is, empirical research has not yet verified it. The superior rehabilitative efficacy of "enlightened" prisons is a humanitarian assumption, but brutal correctional systems have, so far as is known, comparable recidivism rates to "enlightened" systems. True, the recidivism rate of offenders who are fined or placed on probation is less than the recidivism rate of offenders who are incarcerated, but this comparison is not merely one of varying degrees of punishment. Presumably, more severe punishment is meted out to criminals who are more deeply committed to a deviant way of life. Until it is demonstrated that the recidivism rates of strictly comparable populations of deviants differ depending on the degree of punitiveness with which they are treated, the empirical incompatibility of punishment and rehabilitation will remain an open question.

Even on theoretical grounds, however, the incompatibility of punishment and rehabilitation can be questioned once it is recognized that one may precede the other. Perhaps, as Lloyd McCorkle and Richard Korn think, some types of deviants become willing to change only if the bankruptcy of their way of life is conclusively demonstrated to them.[15] On this assumption, punishment may be a necessary preliminary to a rehabilitative program in much the same way that shock treatment makes certain types of psychotics accessible to psychotherapy.

It seems to me that the compatibility of punishment and rehabilitation could be clarified (although not settled) if it were considered from the point of view of the *meaning* of punishment to the offender. Those offenders who regard punishment as a deserved deprivation resulting from their own misbehavior are qualitatively different from offenders who regard punishment as a misfortune bearing no relationship to morality. Thus, a child who is spanked by his father and the member of a bopping gang who is jailed for carrying concealed weapons are both "punished." But one accepts the deprivation as legitimate, and the other bows before superior force. I would hypothesize that punishment has rehabilitative significance only for the former. If this is so, correctional officials must convince the prisoner that his punishment is just before they can motivate him to change. This is no simple task. It is difficult for several reasons:

1. It is obvious to convicted offenders, if not to correctional officials, that *some* so-called "criminals" are being punished disproportionately for trifling offenses whereas *some* predatory business men and politicians enjoy prosperity and freedom. To deny that injustices occur confirms the cynical in their belief that "legitimate" people are not only as predatory as criminals but hypocritical to boot. When correctional officials act as though there were no intermediate position between asserting that perfect justice characterizes our society and that it is a jungle, they make it more difficult

[15] McCorkle & Korn, *Resocialization Within Walls*, 293 ANNALS 88 (1954).

to persuade persons undergoing punishment that the best approximation of justice is available that imperfect human beings can manage.[16]

2. Of course, the more cases of injustice known to offenders, the harder it is to argue that the contemporary approximation of justice is the best that can be managed. It is difficult to persuade Negro inmates that their incarceration has moral significance if their life experience has demonstrated to them that the police and the courts are less scrupulous of *their* rights than of the rights of white persons. It is difficult to persuade an indigent inmate that his incarceration has moral significance if his poverty resulted in inadequate legal representation.[17]

3. Finally, the major form of punishment for serious offenders (imprisonment) tends to generate a contraculture which denies that justice has anything to do with legal penalties.[18] That is to say, it is too costly to confine large numbers of people in isolation from one another, yet congregate confinement results in the mutual reinforcement of self-justifications. Even those who enter prison feeling contrite are influenced by the self-righteous inmate climate; this may be part of the reason recidivism rates rise with each successive commitment.[19]

In view of the foregoing considerations, I hypothesize that punishment—as it is now practiced in Western societies—is usually an obstacle to rehabilitation. Some exceptions to this generalization should be noted. A few small treatment institutions have not only prevented the development of a self-righteous contraculture but have managed to establish an inmate climate supportive of changed values.[20] In such institutions punishment has rehabilitative significance for the same reason it has educational significance in the normal family: it is legitimate.

To sum up: The social control functions of punishment include crime prevention, sustaining the morale of conformists, and the rehabilitation of offenders. All of the empirical evidence is not in, but it is quite possible that punishment contributes to some of these and interferes with others. Suppose, for example, that punishment is necessary for crime prevention and to maintain the morale of conformists but is generally an obstacle to the rehabilitation of offenders. Since the proportion of deviants is small in any viable system as compared with the proportion of conformists, the failure to rehabilitate them will not jeopardize the social order. Therefore, under these assumptions, sociological counsel would favor the continued employment of punishment.

A member of a social system who violates its cherished rules threatens the stability of that system. Conformists who identify with the victim are motivated to punish the criminal in order to feel safe. Conformists who unconsciously identify with the criminal fear their own ambivalence. If norm violation is defined by conformists as willful, visiting upon the offender some injury or degradation will

[16] See the interesting discussions of human fallibility in the works of Reinhold Neibuhr—*e.g.*, THE CHILDREN OF LIGHT AND THE CHILDREN OF DARKNESS (1950).

[17] Trebach, *The Indigent Defendant*, 11 RUTGERS L. REV. 625 (1957).

[18] For a discussion of the concept of contraculture, see Yinger, *Contraculture and Subculture*, 25 AM. SOC. REV. 625 (1960).

[19] Sellin, *Recidivism and Maturation*, 4 NAT'L PROBATION AND PAROLE A.J. 241 (1958).

[20] MCCORKLE, ELIAS & BIXBY, THE HIGHFIELDS STORY (1958), and Empey & Rabow, *Experiment in Delinquency Rehabilitation*, 26 AM. SOC. REV. 679 (1961).

make him unenviable. If his behavior is defined by conformists as a symptom of pathology they are delighted not to share, putting him into treatment validates their diagnosis of undesirable illness. Whether he is "punished" or "treated," however, the disruptive consequence of his deviance is contained. Thus, from the viewpoint of social control, the alternative outcomes of the punishment or treatment processes, rehabilitation or recidivism, are less important than the deviant's neutralization as a possible role model. Whether punishment is or is not necessary rests ultimately on empirical questions: (1) the extent to which identification with the victim occurs, (2) the extent to which nonconformity is prevented by the anticipation of punishment, (3) what the consequences are for the morale of conformists of punishing the deviant or of treating his imputed pathology, and (4) the compatibility between punishment and rehabilitation.

PART III

Seeking a Unity for Punishment Theories

CHAPTER SIX

PLURALISM

In the main the preceding authors have emphasized their belief in the possibility of formulating a justification of punishment in terms of one or another overriding philosophical principle. Though these principles differ, their proponents agree at least in the contention that one and only one justification of punishment can be established.

While this ideal of a unitary explanation has motivated most of the past efforts at penal jurisprudence, there has lately arisen a strong minority feeling that no one theoretical label can be imposed on a phenomenon of such caprice or ambiguity. Pointing to the manifold meanings, applications, and forms of punishment, the five selections below propose, each in their own terms, a pluralism of rationales for justifying punishment.

Such pluralism might seem especially fitting for a type of patriotic pragmatism which would seek middle-of-the-road solutions by a merger of conflicting opinions. But for the authors in the following pages, no such indiscriminate pluralism will suffice. For one reason, the traditional aims of retribution, rehabilitation, deterrence, and social defense are mutually contradictory at several junctures in logic, criminal procedure, and prison technique—not to mention human psychology. Thus, in place of a random scattering of theories, the authorities in this section illustrate H. L. A. Hart's assertion that differing justifications correspond to differing aspects of the punishment process.

A moment's reflection reveals something of the rationale for this assertion. Punishment is as ambiguous as it is manifold. Despite Flew's lucid definition in the first section above, punishment remains a hundred-headed creature of many faces and few lasting names. It may be imposed by police, judges, courts, wardens, prison guards, juries, or psychiatrists. It may consist of a grab bag of penalties from fine to probation, restrictions, or imprisonment. Imprisonment itself may be short or long, absolute or interrupted, solitary or shared. Punishment may require deprivation of freedom, of companions, of material goods. It may involve cruel physical suffering, or a harsh blast of bad publicity, or confinement to a hospital bed. Thus the public image of punishment as corporeal suffering is an oversimplified stereotype. It admits of more gradations, varieties, and expressions than readers of Caryl Chessmann or the Bird Man of Alcatraz might imagine.

Thus it is not surprising that Professor Hart emphasizes the need to distinguish the issues of *why* we may punish (his "General Justifying Aim") from the question of *whom* we punish (his "Principle of Distribution") and to isolate these two issues from such other questions as *where* and *how much* we punish.

But even such a pluralistic interpretation of the justification of punishment as that given by Miss Silving seemingly involves giving priority to one theory or another. Almost in spite of themselves, some of the authorities below such as Hall and Radzinowicz seem to invoke in various ways the principle of retribution as justification for one human being imposing pain on another. Yet retribution alone is a dangerous penal explosive to handle without a protective buffer. It tends to be backward looking, viewing a past criminal act rather than the future well-being of the offender. It views the individual in isolation from society and often in isolation from the crime which his punishment supposedly fits. Further, retribution concentrates on the moral rather than the psychological state of the offender and, perhaps most crucially, it views the offender's guilt rather than the legitimate need of society to be protected.

Accordingly, retribution needs to be complemented by social-minded, forward-looking theories of punishment, as the report of the New York Governor's Committee on Criminal Offenders indicates. The relationship between retribution and these other rationales is both complex and intriguing, as seen in the following selections.

THE INCLUSIVE THEORY OF PUNISHMENT*

Jerome Hall

Professor Jerome Hall argues that the complexity of punishment demands a pluralistic rather than a univocal account of its justifying aims. In the following selection from his General Principles of Criminal Law, *he proposes an "inclusive theory of punishment" which makes room for an appraisal of the offender's moral guilt. A remaining important question concerns how non-retributive aims are related to retribution.*

Much of the voluminous writing on punishment reveals difficulties resulting from the apparently inevitable ambiguity of "punishment," the failure to articulate the postulates of a theory, and the fact that the problem involves ultimate "can't helps." Until quite recently this literature has also been characterized by the advocacy of particularistic justification of punishment—retribution, *or* deterrence, *or* correction. If correction is espoused, retribution is damned as a vestige of man's instinctual past, while deterrence is excluded as ineffective, rationalistic, and even as a cause of crime. This continues to be the main emphasis of certain psychiatrists, despite their avowals that there are many normal criminals and that punishment sustains the conforming individual's "sense of justice." In official circles, on the other hand, deterrence is vigorously supported as a necessary and potent defense of social values,[1] and there is the authority of the summary dismissal of correction by Holmes. Surviving also, but hardly noticed until recent years, are theories of retribution[2] which emphasize the justice of punishment.[3] Finally, there is the integrative view which is receiving increasingly wide support, in which all types of valid justification—justice, deterrence and reformation, with legality always presupposed—are combined in an inclusive

* Reprinted from Hall, General Principles of Criminal Law, second edition, copyright 1947 and 1960 by The Bobbs-Merrill Company, Inc.

[1] Elmer L. Irey, Former Chief, Enforcement Branch, United States Treasury, describes the trial and conviction of Ralph Capone for tax fraud and reports that the next day and every day after that for several weeks many underworld operators went to the collector's office "to pay Uncle Sam voluntarily $1,000,000 in taxes . . . [They] were afraid Uncle Sam would find out." Irey and Slocum, The Tax Dodgers 35 (1948). *Cf.* "On the other hand, to regard deterrence as the sole end of the criminal law is a confession either of defeatism or cynicism." Paton, A Textbook of Jurisprudence 352 (1946).

[2] For a brief discussion distinguishing the retributive theory of Plato and St. Thomas Aquinas from those of Kant and Hegel, see Hawkins, *Punishment and Moral Responsibility,* 7 Mod. L. Rev. 205 (1944). *Cf.* Bradley, Ethical Studies, Essay 1 (1876).

[3] After criticizing the defects of mechanical views of retribution, Morris Cohen wrote: "Despite the foregoing and other limitations of the retributive theory, it contains an element of truth which only sentimental foolishness can ig-

theory.[4] This theory implies, *e.g.* that it is fallacious (a) to ask *only,* "for what end is punishment imposed?" because this automatically excludes the intrinsic value of the relevant moral experience as well as the "vindication" of the law,[5] or (b) to assume that just punishment does not contribute to reformation and deterrence.[6]

In view of the persistent difficulties which envelop this important subject, it may help to delimit the areas of agreement and disagreement if we amplify the above observations in a very simple way. Let 1 = rehabilitation, 2 = deterrence, and 3 = justice. A affirms only 1; B affirms only 2; C affirms only 3; while D affirms 1 and 2 and 3. It should not be difficult to plot the issues involved in various discussions, and thus to articulate the different positions represented in the literature. For example, it will be clear that D, when he adversely criticizes deterrence or correction, cannot be understood to oppose those objectives. If he is consistent, he criticizes only exclusive or excessive claims in their behalf.

On the other hand, A, who espouses rehabilitation, may never inquire whether "corrective treatment" is wholly free of punitive elements or whether it is possible to eliminate retribution entirely; although he also assumes that involuntary incarceration is a necessary condition of correction.[7] Nor does A consider the application of his theory to persons like Professor Webster, the erudite homicide, Whitney, the former Wall Street embezzler, and many other criminals who are very well educated, extremely able and highly successful. Again, what does A say regarding the many thousands of apparently incorrigible minor offenders, such as pickpockets who are unwilling to surrender a skillful art of making an easy living? In the name of "science" or "humanitarianism," would he allow alleged experts to make the pertinent decisions, even to the extent of life imprisonment, uninhibited by "legalistic" control or "moralistic" proportionality? If A would articulate his

nore." Cohen, *Moral Aspects of the Criminal Law,* 49 Yale L. J. 1011 (1940). *Cf.* Cowan, *A Critique of the Moralistic Conception of Criminal Law,* 97 U. of Pa. L. Rev. 502 (1949) and Rooney, *Law Without Justice? The Kelsen and Hall Theories Compared,* 23 Notre Dame L. 140 (1948).

"Most intuitionists would perhaps take the view that there is a fundamental and underivative duty to reward the virtuous and to punish the vicious." Ross, The Right and the Good 57–58 (1930).

[4] Because the ethical validity of a sound body of criminal law is its most important attribute and since this had been greatly neglected, it has been emphasized by the writer. *Cf.* "A third theory, and it is the one which seems to me to come nearest the truth is that there must be an element of retribution or expiation in punishment: but that so long as that element is there, and enough of it is there, there is everything to be said for giving the punishment the shape that is most likely to deter and reform." Asquith, *The Problem of Punishment,* The Listener, May 11, 1950, at 821 (pub. by B. B. C.).

[5] Radin, *Natural Law and Natural Rights,* 59 Yale L. J. 214 (1950), and Coddington, *Problems of Punishment,* 46 Proc. Arist. Soc. (n. s.) 155 (1946).

[6] One of the most interesting changes in the history of ideas is represented in the shift from Plato's axiom that punishment, justly imposed, is always corrective, indeed, that it is a major educational institution, to the axiom of contemporary academic penologists, that punishment never has any beneficial effect. If corrective treatment unavoidably includes a punitive element, the two perspectives are not actually in such complete opposition as the polemics imply.

[7] The new Swedish Protective Code (Sellin ed. 1957) omits the word "punishment" and employs instead "consequence," "sanction" and "measure." Included among the "measures" are fines, imprisonment and imprisonment with hard labor.

theory with reference to such questions, he might make an important contribution to the existing knowledge of treatment and punishment.[8]

Some advocates of the theory of correction take a very critical view of "moralistic" theories of punishment.[9] But since this does not prevent them from speaking of "harmful consequences" or relieve them of the need to communicate the meaning of "imprisonment with hard labor" and the like, an already complex problem seems only to be aggravated by the gratuitous addition of verbal problems. In any case, it is difficult to apprehend what is "naive" about the formal public condemnation of normal adults who voluntarily inflict serious injuries on human beings. This "vulgar morality" seems to be at the foundation of the penal law of civilized countries and it is emphasized in the decisions of the courts. Indeed, while polemics against punishment are sometimes carried on without compromise, the courts in those countries are doing very much what the courts in all civilized countries are doing. Within the limits of their authority, they are attending to the gravity of the harm, the personality of the offender, the public interest, the available peno-correctional facilities, and so on. In other words, the courts are not functioning along doctrinaire lines but, instead, they are taking the important considerations into account.

B, the ardent advocate of deterrence, would be shocked by the suggestion that insane persons or petty thieves should be executed or that innocent persons should be punished or that wide publicity should be given to the "execution" of murderers who, in fact, were not punished at all, regardless of any amount of persuasive evidence that criminal conduct would thereby be deterred.[10] The execution of civilian hostages in the last war and the scientific treatment of "public enemies" by experts in dictatorial states seem to have been very effective deterrents. The relevant facts should not be ignored. But if B does not articulate his thinking in relation to these phases of deterrence, he is not apt to recognize that some degree of retribution is required in any legal order he can approve.

So, finally, C, the "pure retributionist," who sees only the intrinsic moral worth of the public condemnation of attacks on human beings, might reflect that from the very beginning of Western thought deterrence has been approved and the education of corrigible offenders has been urged by many great thinkers. The finest teachings of religion emphasize the forgiveness of transgressors by their victims[11] and that should also temper the administration of criminal law. At the same time, as the retributionist

[8] See Allen, *Criminal Justice, Legal Values and the Rehabilitative Ideal,* 50 J. Cr. L. Crim. and Pol. Sci. 226 (1959).

[9] *Cf.* Cowan, *op. cit. supra* note 3 and Lewis, *The Humanitarian Theory of Punishment,* 6 Res Judicatae 224, 519 (1953–54).

[10] "To achieve the maximum deterrent effect it would be necessary either to impose excessively long sentences or to inflict harsh treatment and impose rigid restrictions and deprivations on the prisoners." MacCormick, *The Prison's Role in Crime Prevention,* 41 J. Cr. L. Crim. and Pol. Sci. 42 (1950).

[11] "Criminals may well be called public enemies. But they are men and women. They are entitled to the benefit of the Biblical injunction that we must love our enemies. Perhaps we could come to love them if we made a sacrifice for them." Gausewitz, *Realistic Punishment,* pub. in The Administration of Criminal Justice, Virginia Law Weekly Dicta 47 (1948–49). *Cf.* St. Luke 23–41.

urges, the human cry for justice also makes its demands; and, in addition, the elementary needs of survival require the deterrence of potential harm-doers. We should not shut our eyes to these aspects of the problem and, regardless of social responsibilities, advocate the substitution of *agape* for criminal law no matter how generously we may treat those who have harmed us.[12]

If a theory of punishment took due account of the various problems indicated above, the outlook so far as scientific research is concerned, and consequently also with reference to the administration and reform of penal law, would be greatly altered. Attention could then be directed to carefully formulated, pertinent questions, *e.g.* within the limits set by the principle of legality in what particular offenses, regarding which types of offender, in relation to what prevalent crime rates, available facilities and so on, should the peno-correctional treatment be determined and adjusted thus and so in order to preserve the maximum intrinsic and instrumental values?[13]

Despite the unusual difficulties which beset the problem of punishment, important progress has been made in recent years in the above direction. For example, it is now recognized that the "prevention of crime" and the "protection of society" are ends accepted by everyone, and that the reiteration of such slogans does not solve problems. It seems also to be widely agreed that involuntary incarceration is punishment regardless of the kindness of the administrators or the unexceptionable quality of the treatment program.[14] And although there are unfortunate relapses,[15] only infrequently does one find the punitive sanctions of civilized laws equated with vengeance or other merely emotional reactions or the cruel imposition of suffering as an end in itself.[16] But the most important advance is that the inclusive theory of punishment has been gaining ground in

[12] "The effort to make life more decent therefore always involves a struggle against opposing forces. And in this struggle men find hatred as well as love, tonic emotions. Indeed, we must hate evil if we really love the good." Cohen, *supra* note 3, at 1018.

[13] See Coddington, *Problems of Punishment, op. cit. supra* note 5, reprinted in part in Hall, Cases and Readings on Criminal Law and Procedure 99 (1949). *Cf.* generally, Oppenheimer, The Rationale of Punishment (1913).

[14] See the Protective Code (Sellin ed. 1957). "Experienced penologists do not dismiss the idea of punishment. They recognize the fact that being sent to a prison, however humanely it is operated, is punishment in itself. They know that it is impossible to make a prison so pleasant that the prisoners will not consider their imprisonment punishment." MacCormick, *op. cit. supra* note 10, at 42–43.

[15] ". . . the tradition of legal revenge." Zilboorg, The Psychology of the Criminal Act and Punishment 114 (1954).

[16] The "right" to be punished is not quite the absurd thing that is sometimes assumed, *e.g.* by Quinton, *On Punishment,* pub. in Philosophy, Politics and Society 85 (Laslett ed. 1956). There is not only the psychiatric evidence of relief from a burdening sense of guilt, but also the statements of convicted persons, such as: "To punish a man is to treat him as an equal. To be punished *for an offence against rules* is a sane man's right." Macartney, Walls Have Mouths 165, quoted by Mabbott, *Punishment,* 48 Mind (n.s.) 158 (1939). Finally, ". . . prosecuted persons are often anxious to be sentenced to punishment instead of being interned in educative establishments, in mental hospitals or in establishments for the detention of certain abnormal criminals, although these forms of treatment are considered protective measures without a repressive character." Kinberg, *Punishment or Impunity?,* 21 Acta Psych. et Neur. 441–42 (1946).

recent years.[17] This has resulted largely from the recognition that retribution has an important part in any defensible theory, at least to the extent that punishment should be imposed only on the guilty[18] and that there should be a fair proportion of punishment to the gravity of the harm, even when acknowledgment of that is made in factual terms of "the traditional rating system."[19] Within the above general context of theories in justification of punishment, it is possible more precisely to delineate the distinctive attributes of the punitive sanction.

[17] ". . . no penal philosophy can today be based upon one single idea, be it retribution, prevention or whatever; rather will it be a somewhat dubious mixture of heterogeneous elements, perhaps with one element predominating in the mind of judge A, another in the mind of judge B. Moreover, this hybrid penal philosophy will often have to give way to the stark realities of life: orders to an approved school or probation orders cannot reasonably be made if no vacancies exist in such schools or if the probation officers concerned are already too overworked to look after another case." Mannheim, *Some Aspects of Judicial Sentencing Policy,* 67 Yale L. J. 961, 971–2 (1958).

See the current A. L. I. Model Penal Code, Tent Draft No. 2, sec. 1.02 (2). "Basic considerations of justice demand, moreover, that penal law safeguard offenders against excessive, disproportionate or arbitrary punishment, that it afford fair warning of the nature of the sentences that may be imposed upon conviction and that differences among offenders be reflected in the just individualization of their treatment." *Id.* at 4.

[18] Raphael, *Justice and Liberty,* 51 Proc. Artist. Soc. (n. s.) 167 (1951) and Shaw, Imprisonment 18 (1924). But *cf.* Bentham, Rationale of Punishment 3 (1830).

[19] It "is primarily a question of finding that penalty which corresponds to customary standards of punishment." Andenaes, *Choice of Punishment,* pub. in 2 Scandinavian Studies in Law 59–60 (1958). *Cf.* ". . . the courts can reasonably interfere only . . . where the punishment proposed is so severe and out of proportion to the offense as to shock public sentiment and violate the judgment of reasonable people." State v. Becker, 3 S. D. 29, 40, 51 N. W. 1018, 1022 (1892).

TOWARD A PRAGMATIC POSITION*

Leon Radzinowicz

Fellow of Trinity College, Professor Leon Radzinowicz is Wolfson Professor of Criminology and director of the Institute of Criminology at the University of Cambridge. His 1966 James S. Carpenter Lectures at Columbia University, published under the title Ideology and Crime, *argue for a diversity of purposes of punishment, with retribution seemingly retaining the role of a central regulating principle.*

What of the aims of punishment? . . . Any confidence in the possibility of establishing a single general principle has been abandoned. Even the liberal attitude, so highly pitched in its ideal of justice, could not escape the necessity of deterrence, could not wholly reconcile the illusory equivalence of offence and punishment with the practical need to prevent the offender and others from offending again.

A few quotations, like lights in a dark tunnel, may help us. In 1864 Sir Henry Maine could already say "All theories on the subject of punishment have more or less broken down . . . and we are again at sea as to first principles."[1] Some forty years later Professor Kenny, after examining current opinions of judges and legislators alike, reached the same conclusion: ideas on punishment had failed to assume "either a coherent or a stable form."[2] Twenty years later, discussing the position in the United States, Dean Roscoe Pound spoke of the "fundamental conflict with respect to aims and purposes" pervading both penal legislation and penal administration.[3] And now, after another lapse of twenty years, Professor Jerome Hall has shown that the divergence of views is as wide as it was a century ago.[4]

It is not that the past hundred years have provided no opportunity to arrive

* From RADZINOWICZ, IDEOLOGY AND CRIME (New York: Columbia University Press, 1966), pp. 113–127. Reprinted with permission.

[1] *Sir Henry Maine. A Brief Memoir of his Life,* by Sir M. E. GRANT DUFF with some of his Indian Speeches, etc. (ed. by Whitley Stokes, 1892), p. 125.

[2] See C. S. KENNY, *Outlines of Criminal Law* (1st ed., 1902), p. 36.

[3] See ROSCOE POUND, *Criminal Justice in Cleveland* (1922), p. 576.

[4] JEROME HALL, *General Principles of Criminal Law* (2nd ed., 1960), Chapter IX, pp. 296–324.

The literature on the subject is enormous and continues to grow. But it would be difficult to select three essays which show the many-sidedness and complexity of the subject in a more startling and sophisticated way than: M. R. COHEN, "Moral Aspects of the Criminal Law," *Yale Law Journal,* vol. 49 (April 1940), p. 987; C. S. LEWIS, "The Humanitarian Theory of Punishment," reproduced in *Res judicatae* (1953), vol. 6, p. 224 and the very basic article by HENRY M. HART, Jr., "The Aims of the Criminal Law," in *Law and Contemporary Problems* (Sentencing) (Summer 1958), vol. XXIII, No. 3, p. 401.

at a unifying theory, supposing that were possible. On the contrary, there have been the classical school, the positivist school and many shades of variation in between. There have been all the political changes, the criminological researches, the penological experiments of the present century. But still the question remains: is not the search for a single purpose in punishment like the search for a single cause of crime?

Indeed the dominant change in recent years has been an increasing acceptance of the diversity in the purposes of punishment. There are still those who yearn for the good old days when wrongdoers got their deserts. At the other extreme, there are those who claim that reformation of the offender is the only end compatible with a belief in the absolute value of the individual. But any realistic assessment must arrive at the conclusion that there is no single formula. The Streatfeild Committee in England, after careful scrutiny of the evolution of sentencing practices, concluded that four objectives of punishment must be recognized. The old element of retribution for a wrong committed in the past could not be ignored, but in addition there were three other objectives concerned with the attempt to control the future: to stop the offender from offending again, to deter other potential offenders and to protect society from the persistent offender.[5]

It is at once obvious that in particular cases those purposes must sometimes clash. The backward-looking element of retribution may clash with the forward-looking object of reform. To seek to rehabilitate the offender may clash with the deterrence of others or with the protection of society. There is no philosopher's stone—objectives and risks must be weighed against each other, whilst the authority of the criminal law must be upheld. It must be remembered, too, that any rational reformative measure will include some penal element; in some cases punishment may be the best means to reform. Above all, so wide is the range of offences and offenders, that no single penal approach can, in the nature of things, be effective for all.

A growing emphasis on the need to test the actual effects of different kinds of penal treatment is, indeed, another aspect of the pragmatic approach.

In this context the word "test" is crucial. I am particularly fond of quoting a comment by Sir Samuel Romilly when Bentham's famous treatise on punishment appeared in 1811: "Penal legislation hitherto has resembled what the science of physic must have been when physicians did not know the properties and effects of the medicine they administered."[6] In the period moulded by liberal ideology such questions were not even expected to be raised. To pursue the objectives of punishment beyond the just proportion of penalty to offence seemed an invasion of individual rights, an unjustifiable extension of state control.

It is only since social utility has edged "just retribution" out of its monopolistic position that this need to understand the effects of penal practice has been ac-

[5] See *Report of the Interdepartmental Committee on the Business of the Criminal Courts*, Cmnd 1289 (1961), §§ 257–287, pp. 76–83. It is instructive to compare the formula agreed upon by the Committee with the problem as seen by those in charge of drawing up the new penal code: see on this HERBERT WECHSLER's paper, "Sentencing, Correction, and the Model Penal Code," *University of Pennsylvania Law Review* (February 1961), vol. 109, No. 4, p. 465.

[6] See Sir SAMUEL ROMILLY, *Memoirs of the Life of . . .* (ed. by his Sons, 1840), vol. 2, pp. 385–386.

corded real recognition. The first step in evaluation was the collection of statistics of recidivism, which began towards the end of the nineteenth century and received a great impetus from the deterministic schools of criminology, both Marxist and positivist. They found in the sorry records of recidivism a ready weapon in their attacks on the classical school.

Even so, it was not until after the first world war that evaluation was undertaken on a wider basis. The consternation produced by Sheldon and Eleanor Glueck's findings in 1930 relating to results obtained by the Massachusetts State Reformatory showed how far from the facts were general public assumptions about the effectiveness of institutional training.[7] No less rudimentary was the information available in England before the war.[8]

It has only been in the last twenty-five years that we have really got to grips with the implications of this kind of research, involving as it does the attempt to assess the specific functions of punishment not in terms of theory but of practice, not in terms of what is intended but of what is achieved.[9] As Dr. Roger Hood has shown, we have still a long way to go.[10] But it is undeniable that our knowledge of these problems is much greater than in the past and so is our awareness of what we still need to know. I regard this as one of the most significant developments in contemporary criminology.

Some of the research findings have been unexpected. For example, in England, fines often prove more effective than either probation or deprivation of liberty, even for certain classes of sex offenders.[11] The success rate for borstal training (devised primarily as a reformative measure for young adults) has slumped since the second world war from seven out of ten not reconvicted within two years of release to less than four out of ten, a rate no better than that following the preventive detention devised for persistent offenders.[12] It may be true that those now being sent to borstal are tougher and more hardened offenders than those who went in the earlier period. But it also has to be considered whether the borstal system has lost its social relevance and reforming zeal, has settled into an unimaginative routine and failed to adapt to a changing world. Or whether, indeed, the social influences tending towards crime are becoming too strong for any of the existing penal measures to counteract.

The results of imprisonment as a reformative measure are particularly discouraging. The shorter sentences are, in

[7] See Sheldon and Eleanor T. Glueck, *Five Hundred Criminal Careers* (1930), pp. 167–169 and 182–192.

[8] On what was then available see L. Radzinowicz, "The After-Conduct of Discharged Offenders," in *Modern Approach to Criminal Law* (vol. IV of the Cambridge Series, 1945), p. 142.

[9] For excellent examples of analytical assessments of the value of a particular programme of training, see H. A. Weeks, *Youthful Offenders at Highfields* (1958); L. W. McCorkle *et al., The Highfields Story* (1958); H. Polksy, *Cottage Six* (1962).

[10] See R. Hood, "Research on the Effectiveness of Punishments and Treatments," Report presented to the Council of Europe (Criminological Division), Document DPC/CDJR (64)9 (Strasbourg, 15 November 1964).

[11] See *The Sentence of the Court. A Handbook for Courts on The Treatment of Offenders,* published by the Home Office (April 1964); see also *Sexual Offences* (Cambridge Series, vol. IX, 1957), pp. 234–235.

[12] See the *Annual Report of the Council of the Central After-Care Association* (1963), pp. 9 and 26.

general, followed by no more reconvictions than the longer ones, but fine or probation might well have been adequate in many of these cases.[13] Those who have been to prison only once are much the least likely to return, and this irrespective of the type of institution to which they are sent. Their rate of reconviction ranges, according to institution, from one in ten to one in four.[14] Professor Glaser believes he has refuted the myth that two-thirds of all offenders in American prisons return there again after release: he would put the proportion nearer one-third.[15] In England before the war it was shown that only about a quarter returned.[16] Unfortunately we lack the statistics to make a similar calculation for the present day, but what we do know is that around two-thirds of all those committed to prison have previous prison records. All evidence shows that the proportion of such recidivists who succeed is much lower than the general average, and after all it is the recidivist who presents the real problem. With him a longer sentence is no more likely to be successful than a shorter one. There has been little to choose, so far as subsequent conduct is concerned, between those sent to ordinary imprisonment for up to four years and those sentenced to preventive detention for eight to fourteen years, or between those in this last category released after serving two-thirds or five-sixths of their sentences.[17]

It is all very well for penal administrators, who can only use the resources society gives them, to adopt formulae such as "training for freedom," or "turn them out of prison better men and women . . . than they went in," or "an offender is sent to prison *as* a punishment not *for* punishment."[18] The hard figures combine with the studies of what actually goes on in the sub-cultures of existing prisons—studies so brilliantly pioneered in the United States and now taken up on our side of the Atlantic—to cast a heavy cloud over claims such as these.[19] They may provide a lofty charter, but they are far from expressing present penal realities.

It is evident that we cannot assume either that because a measure is intended to be reformative it will therefore prove to be so, or that a system that was effective at one period will necessarily remain so in changing social conditions. Indeed as Dr. Hood and others have pointed out, taking offenders as a whole, and allowing for such overwhelmingly

[13] See R. Hood, *Sentencing in Magistrates' Courts* (1962), pp. 121–122; see also R. G. Andry, *The Short Term Prisoner* (1963), pp. 115–116.

[14] See: Home Office, *Prisons and Borstals* 1963, Statistical Tables, Cmd. 2630 (1965), p. 47.

[15] D. Glaser, *The Effectiveness of a Prison and Parole System* (1964), pp. 13–16; and his paper, "Effectiveness of the Federal Correction System," in *Federal Probation,* vol. XXVIII (December 1964), p. I.

[16] See L. Radzinowicz, "After-Conduct of Convicted Offenders in England," in *The Modern Approach to Criminal Law* (1945), p. 142.

[17] W. H. Hammond and E. Chayen, *Persistent Criminals* (1963), p. 99.

[18] See *Prisons and Borstals, England and Wales.* Home Office (4th ed., 1963), p. 2.

[19] See, for example, G. Sykes, *The Society of Captives* (1958); D. Clemmer, *The Prison Community* (1958); R. A. Cloward *et al., Theoretical Studies in Social Organization of the Prison* (published in 1960 under the auspices of the Social Science Research Council) still serves as an excellent introduction to the subject and contains a good selection of the more recent literature; D. R. Cressey, ed., *The Prison: Studies in Institutional Organization and Change* (1961). In England the book by T. and P. Morris, *Pentonville* (1963) represents a considerable achievement in this field.

important variables as age and previous criminal record, there is considerable evidence that results vary little with different forms of treatment.[20] This does not, of course, rule out the probability that different treatments are more successful with some types of offender than with others.[21] Here, once more, there is the tendency to break down broad generalizations into more exact and significant groups. It is not enough to talk sweepingly of institutional or non-institutional treatment, or even of prison or borstal: it is a matter of analyzing the different kinds of institutional regime, the different kinds of probation supervision. It is not enough to discuss the response of offenders generally, or even of juvenile or adult offenders: it is necessary to try to divide them up, on the basis of their circumstances, personalities and attitudes, in ways relevant to their response to treatment. It is being realized more and more that there is no sovereign remedy.

This branch of research has still many difficulties to overcome and explorations, though promising, are still in their earliest stages.

The same is true of attempts to measure the effectiveness of general deterrence, the deterrence of potential offenders. In 1952 Professor Andenaes remarked that, so far as empirical studies of general prevention were concerned, we are "still in the pre-Lombrosian era."[22] Some advances have been made since then but the task of assessing the attitudes of the general population is one of great difficulty and what empirical data are available are still fragmentary.

Closely linked with general deterrence, however, is the question of the enforcement of the law. Neither fear of punishment nor respect for the law is likely to hold back potential offenders effectively if this is known to be inadequate. I have already referred to the size of the dark figure of crime. Let me drive the point home by quoting from a scale drawn up by the Cambridge Institute to show the degrees of impunity of robbers.[23] In no type of robbery does the proportion who escape fall below fifty per cent, in many it is seventy per cent, whilst in robbery of property in transit it rises as high as eighty per cent. Moreover, the gap is widening. Calculation of chances takes place in crime at least as much as in other activities. Except for the deeply abnormal, or the person subjected to extreme and sudden stress, offenders consider their chances of impu-

[20] See L. T. WILKINS, "A Small Comparative Study of the Results of Probation," *British Journal of Delinquency* (1957–1958), vol. VIII, p. 201; R. HOOD, "Research on the Effectiveness of Punishments and Treatments," paper presented to the Council of Europe, cited above, note 10, p. 117.

[21] See, for example, J. D. GRANT and M. Q. GRANT, "A Group Dynamic Approach to the Treatment of Nonconformists in the Navy," *Annals of the American Academy of Political and Social Science* (March 1959), vol. 322, p. 126; S. FOLKARD, "The Probation Research Project," *Probation* (1962), vol. 10, No. 4, p. 49.

[22] See J. ANDENAES, "General Prevention—Illusion or Reality," *Journal of Criminal Law, Criminology and Police Science* (1952), vol. 43, p. 176, at p. 197. Very wisely the International Society of Criminology has put on the agenda of its Congress in Montreal (27 August to 3 September 1965) the subject of "Punishment and the problem of general prevention" and it is very much hoped that Professor Andenaes, as general rapporteur, will be in a position to throw much more empirical light on this largely unexplored field.

[23] See F. H. MCCLINTOCK and E. GIBSON, *Robbery in London* (vol. XIV of the Cambridge Series, 1964), pp. 30–45 and my Preface, p. vii, at pp. xi–xiii.

nity and will seize on any grounds for considering it optimistically. The theorists who give priority to deterrence amongst the objects of punishment must learn to be as realistic as the criminals.

Yet even the criterion of effectiveness cannot stand alone. Account must still be taken of the need to strike a balance between the rights of the individual and the rights of society. It is the directness of this confrontation that lends much of its fascination to the study of the criminal law. Not even here, however, can there be any single and rigid formula. The line of demarcation must constantly be reassessed as society evolves. Each generation has to face the task afresh and none can claim its solution as final.

At the beginning of this century Enrico Ferri regarded preoccupation with the function of criminal justice in protecting the rights of the individual as a kind of anachronism. "The abuses of the judicial process," he wrote, "which at the end of the middle ages finally called forth the generous protest of Cesare Beccaria, followed by much glorious scientific thought in favour of making punitive justice more humane—also brought into the laws in force an affirmation of the rights of man, which affirmation, in the second half of the nineteenth century, was carried to an excess not now admissible, since it led to the sacrifice of the most obvious social necessities."[24] Certainly the rigidity of the classical school on the Continent of Europe made it almost impossible to develop constructive and imaginative penal measures. Had our system of dealing with crime been confined within the pattern laid down in *Dei delitti e delle pene* virtually all the reforms of which we are most proud would have been excluded, because they would have conflicted with the principle that punishment must be closely defined in advance and strictly proportionate to the offence. There would have been no discharge, no adjustment of fines to the means of offenders, no suspended sentences, no probation, no parole, no special measures for young offenders or the mentally abnormal.[25]

It was in America, mercifully exempt from the most rigid classical influences, that some of the most promising of such measures were first adopted: Elmira, probation, the juvenile court. Following the Gladstone Report and the work of the Police Court Missionaries similar measures were adopted in England. These were intended essentially as reformative devices, focused upon the needs of various classes of offender.

More sinister in its possibilities was another kind of special treatment, stemming equally from the positivist emphasis on the need to consider the offender rather than the offence. This was the use of the long semi-indeterminate sentence, less to reform the offender than to protect society against him. The introduc-

[24] See on this ENRICO FERRI, *Sociologia Criminale* (5th ed. by Arturo Santoro, 1930), vol. 2, pp. 107–110.

[25] It is impossible to visualize to-day the extraordinary amount of persuasion and argument which was needed to secure, for example, the adoption of a suspended sentence, conditional discharge, not to speak of probation. They were all regarded as violations of the sacred equation according to which crime must correspond to a determinate penalty. See, for instance, the article by A. GAUTIER, "A propos de la condamnation conditionelle," *Revue Penale Suisse* (1890), vol. 3, pp. 299–333 and that by FRANZ VON LISZT," "Bedingte Verurteilung und bedingte Begnadigung," in *Vergleichende Darstellung des Deutschen und Auslandischen Strafrechts* (1908), vol. III, pp. 1–94.

tion also first appeared in America, in relation to certain psychopaths, sexual offenders, and habitual criminals. This embodied the most conspicuous challenge of all to the basic principles of liberalism and classicism.

Its enforcement has been attempted in two ways. In America it was the kind of single indeterminate sentence proposed by the positivists. On the Continent, where the classical tradition was so much more powerful, the demand that there should be punishment proportionate to the offence resulted in a two-part sentence, the first related to the immediate crime, the second to the need for preventive custody.

The absurdity of this latter arrangement has been described as follows: "Imagine that an offender, having served his sentence of ten or fifteen years hard labour, is called before the Governor of the prison and told: 'To-day expires the term of your punishment. Justice requires that punishment shall now stop.' When the prisoner, however, is about to depart, the Governor adds: 'Oh no, now we must protect society: you will enter preventive detention.' Whereupon the offender asks: 'What change then is there to be in my life?' To which he will get the reply: 'Up to now you have been detained in the east wing of the prison; from now on you will be detained in the west wing.'" This was said over forty years ago and little has been done to change it.[26]

[26] See Professor Graf zu Dohna in the discussion on the subject of "protection of society against dangerous offenders," etc. at the 20th meeting of the German and Austrian societies of the International Association of Criminal Law (Innsbruck, 10–12 September 1925), reported in *Mitteilungen der Internationalen Kriminalistischen Vereinigung* (1926), N.F., 1 Band, p. 198, at pp. 201–202.

In England there has been experiment and attempts at compromises. In 1908 Parliament decided that the two-part sentence ought to be adopted so that the total length of detention could be related to the gravity of the crime for which the offender was before the court at the time. This was further emphasized by the restriction of preventive detention to cases where this crime was serious enough to warrant penal servitude. In practice, however, the courts felt it unjust to impose two sentences at once and the provision was little used. Such a feeling was even apparent when similar powers were introduced in Nazi Germany in 1933, but there the reluctance was soon overcome and within a year they were being applied to nearly five thousand alleged habitual offenders.

The so-called dual system was a fiction (it has been called an Etickettenschwindel, a fraudulent label) and in England it was abandoned. But the single sentence of "preventive detention" has been no more satisfactory, and has been equally regarded as unjust.

This whole history has been significant. Tales of disappointment, of uneasiness, if not of straight skepticism, have come in from many parts of the world where it has been tried, not least from its erstwhile proud parent, the United States. What has produced the revulsion has been specific experience rather than any set of ideas and beliefs. I had the depressing task, as a member of the Advisory Council on the Treatment of Offenders, of investigating the operation of preventive detention in England. It is the hopelessness and transparent unfairness that makes the strongest impression: a miserable assortment of petty offenders, too inadequate to be a danger to society, are detained under conditions that must make their reabsorption into the community still more difficult. The long preventive sentence has created more problems than it has solved.[27]

It is in this context that we had to reassess the old doctrine that the punishment must fit the crime. It is no use to say that this is just going backwards: the problem itself has changed. One of the greatest objections to the classical codes was that they resulted in a vast number of very short sentences of imprisonment which could only be corrupting. Now we have many alternatives. Such measures as discharge, probation and suspended sentence have weakened the nexus of crime and punishment. But when it comes to long-term detention following a comparatively trivial offence, we need to recall the older principle and allow it its due part in regulating the rights of individuals in relation to those of society.

Retribution remains in the background as a regulator of the proportion of punishment or treatment. In this it can contribute to both deterrence and reformation.

[27] See *Preventive Detention,* Report of the Advisory Council on the Treatment of Offenders (1963); see also D. J. West, *The Habitual Prisoner* (vol. XIX of the Cambridge Series, 1963).

The doubts and uneasiness felt by American criminal lawyers and penologists on this subject have been voiced on many occasions and with much force. A few examples selected at random may help to show the main direction of criticisms and indicate the wide range of sources for further study: "Court Treatment of General Recidivist Statutes" (Note), *Columbia Law Review* (1940), vol. 42, p. 238; G. K. Brown, "The Treatment of the Recidivist in the United States," Cambridge pamphlet series No. 12, published in *Canadian Bar Review* (October 1945), vol. 23, p. 640; "Statutory Structures for Sentencing Felons to Prison" (Note), *Columbia Law Review* (1960), vol. 60, p. 1134. See also the several significant papers by the late Paul Tappan quoted and expanded by him in his *Crime, Justice and Correction* (1960), pp. 411–420, 433–437 and 471–475. Many of the comments made by Helen Silving in her paper on " 'Rule of Law' In Criminal Justice," in *Essays in Criminal Science* (ed. by G. O. W. Mueller, 1961), p. 77, *passim,* are also relevant. So, in different ways, is the important report "Mental Illness and Due Process (1962), published under the auspices of a Special Committee of the Association of the Bar of the City of New York in co-operation with the Cornell Law School.

THE GENERAL AIM AND LIMITS FOR PUNISHMENT*

H. L. A. Hart

H. L. A. Hart is a distinguished British lawyer and philosopher who, until recently, held the chair of jurisprudence at Oxford. In his book Punishment and Responsibility *Professor Hart argues that there can be no indiscriminate merger of competing justifications of punishment, because some are mutually contradictory. Instead, differing penal principles respond to differing logical questions within the entire gamut of penal phenomena. Of central importance in this 1968 essay is the interrelationship between the general justifying aim and the principle of distribution of punishment.*

The main object of this paper is to provide a framework for the discussion of the mounting perplexities which now surround the institution of criminal punishment, and to show that any morally tolerable account of this institution must exhibit it as a compromise between distinct and partly conflicting principles.

General interest in the topic of punishment has never been greater than it is at present and I doubt if the public discussion of it has ever been more confused. The interest and the confusion are both in part due to relatively modern scepticism about two elements which have figured as essential parts of the traditionally opposed 'theories' of punishment. On the one hand, the old Benthamite confidence in fear of the penalties threatened by the law as a powerful deterrent, has waned with the growing realization that the part played by calculation of any sort in anti-social behaviour has been exaggerated. On the other hand a cloud of doubt has settled over the keystone of 'retributive' theory. Its advocates can no longer speak with the old confidence that statements of the form 'This man who has broken the law could have kept it' had a univocal or agreed meaning; or where scepticism does not attach to the *meaning* of this form of statement, it has shaken the confidence that we are generally able to distinguish the cases where a statement of this form is true from those where it is not.[1]

Yet quite apart from the uncertainty engendered by these fundamental doubts, which seem to call in question the accounts given of the efficacy, and the morality of punishment by all the old competing theories, the public utterances of those who conceive themselves to be expounding, as plain men for other plain men, orthodox or common-sense principles (untouched by modern psychological

* Excerpted from PUNISHMENT AND RESPONSIBILITY by H. L. A. Hart. Reprinted by permission of the Clarendon Press, Oxford.

[1] See Barbara Wootton *Social Science and Social Pathology* (1959) for a comprehensive modern statement of these doubts.

doubts) are uneasy. Their words often sound as if the authors had not fully grasped their meaning or did not intend the words to be taken quite literally. A glance at the parliamentary debates or the *Report of the Royal Commission on Capital Punishment*[2] shows that many are now troubled by the suspicion that the view that there is just one supreme value or objective (e.g. Deterrence, Retribution or Reform) in terms of which *all* questions about the justification of punishment are to be answered, is somehow wrong; yet, from what is said on such occasions no clear account of what the different values or objectives are, or how they fit together in the justification of punishment, can be extracted.[3]

No one expects judges or statesmen occupied in the business of sending people to the gallows or prison, or in making (or unmaking) laws which enable this to be done, to have much time for philosophical discussion of the principles which make it morally tolerable to do these things. A judicial bench is not and should not be a professorial chair. Yet what is said in public debates about punishment by those specially concerned with it as judges or legislators is important. Few are likely to be more circumspect, and if what they say seems, as it often does, unclear, one-sided and easily refutable by pointing to some aspect of things which they have overlooked, it is likely that in our inherited ways of talking or thinking about punishment there is some persistent drive towards an over-simplification of multiple issues which require separate consideration. To counter this drive what is most needed is *not* the simple admission that instead of a single value or aim (Deterrence, Retribution, Reform or any other) a plurality of different values and aims should be given as a conjunctive answer to some *single* question concerning the justification of punishment. What is needed is the realization that different principles (each of which may in a sense be called a 'justification') are relevant at different points in any morally acceptable account of punishment. What we should look for are answers to a number of different questions such as: What justifies the general practice of punishment? To whom may punishment be applied? How severely may we punish? In dealing with these and other questions concerning punishment we should bear in mind that in this, as in most other social institutions, the pursuit of one aim may be qualified by or provide an opportunity, not to be missed, for the pursuit of others. Till we have developed this sense of the complexity of punishment (and this prolegomenon aims only to do this) we shall be in no fit state to assess the extent to which the whole institution has been eroded by, or needs to be adapted to, new beliefs about the human mind. . . .

Before we reach any question of justification we must identify a preliminary question to which the answer is so simple that the question may not appear

[2] (1953) Cmd. 8932.

[3] In the Lords' debate in July 1956 the Lord Chancellor agreed with Lord Denning that 'the ultimate justification of any punishment is not that it is a deterrent but that it is the emphatic denunciation by the community of a crime' yet also said that 'the real crux' of the question at issue is whether capital punishment is a uniquely effective deterrent. See 198 *H. L. Deb* (5th July) 576, 577, 596 (1956). In his article, 'An Approach to the Problems of Punishment,' *Philosophy* (1958), Mr. S. I. Benn rightly observes of Lord Denning's view that denunciation does not imply the deliberate imposition of suffering which is the feature needing justification (p. 328, n. 1).

worth asking; yet it is clear that some curious 'theories' of punishment gain their only plausibility from ignoring it, and others from confusing it with other questions. This question is: Why are certain kinds of action forbidden by law and so made crimes or offences? The answer is: To announce to society that these actions are not to be done and to secure that fewer of them are done. These are the common immediate aims of making any conduct a criminal offence and until we have laws made with these primary aims we shall lack the notion of a 'crime' and so of a 'criminal.' Without recourse to the simple idea that the criminal law sets up, in its rules, standards of behaviour to encourage certain types of conduct and discourage others we cannot distinguish a punishment in the form of a fine from a tax on a course of conduct.[4] This indeed is one grave objection to those theories of law which in the interests of simplicity or uniformity obscure the distinction between primary laws setting standards for behaviour and secondary laws specifying what officials must or may do when they are broken. Such theories insist that all legal rules are 'really' directions to officials to exact 'sanctions' under certain conditions, e.g. if people kill.[5] Yet only if we keep alive the distinction (which such theories thus obscure) between the primary objective of the law in encouraging or discouraging certain kinds of behaviour, and its merely ancillary sanction or remedial steps, can we give sense to the notion of a crime or offence.

It is important however to stress the fact that in thus identifying the immediate aims of the criminal law we have not reached the stage of justification. There are indeed many forms of undesirable behaviour which it would be foolish (because ineffective or too costly) to attempt to inhibit by use of the law and some of these may be better left to educators, trades unions, churches, marriage guidance councils or other non-legal agencies. Conversely there are some forms of conduct which we believe cannot be effectively inhibited without use of the law. But it is only too plain that in fact the law may make activities criminal which it is morally important to promote and the suppression of these may be quite unjustifiable. Yet confusion between the simple immediate aim of any criminal legislation and the justification of punishment seems to be the most charitable explanation of the claim that punishment is *justified* as an 'emphatic denunciation by the community of a crime.' Lord Denning's dictum that this is the ultimate justification of punishment[6] can be saved from Mr. Benn's criticism, noted above, only if it is treated as a blurred statement of the truth that the aim not of punishment, but of criminal legislation is indeed to denounce certain types of conduct as something not to be practised. Conversely the immediate aim of criminal legislation cannot be any

[4] This generally clear distinction may be blurred. Taxes may be imposed to discourage the activities taxed though the law does not announce this as it does when it makes them criminal. Conversely fines payable for some criminal offences because of a depreciation of currency become so small that they are cheerfully paid and offences are frequent. They are then felt to be mere taxes because the sense is lost that the rule is meant to be taken seriously as a standard of behaviour.

[5] cf. Kelsen, *General Theory of Law and State* (1945), pp. 30–33, 33–34, 143–4. 'Law is the primary norm, which stipulates the sanction. . . . (ibid. 61).

[6] In evidence to the Royal Commission on Capital Punishment, Cmd. 8932. para. 53 (1953). *Supra*, n. 3.

of the things which are usually mentioned as justifying punishment: for until it is settled what conduct is to be legally denounced and discouraged we have not settled from what we are to *deter* people, or who are to be considered *criminals* from whom we are to exact *retribution,* or on whom we are to wreak *vengeance,* or whom we are to *reform.*

Even those who look upon human law as a mere instrument for enforcing 'morality as such' (itself conceived as the law of God or Nature) and who at the stage of justifying punishment wish to appeal not to socially beneficial consequences but simply to the intrinsic value of inflicting suffering on wrongdoers who have disturbed by their offence the moral order, would not deny that the aim of criminal legislation is to set up types of behaviour (in this case conformity with a pre-existing moral law) as legal standards of behaviour and to secure conformity with them. No doubt in all communities certain moral offences, e.g. killing, will always be selected for suppression as crimes and it is conceivable that this may be done not to protect human beings from being killed but to save the potential murderer from sin; but it would be paradoxical to look upon the law as designed not to discourage murder at all (even conceived as sin rather than harm) but simply to extract the penalty from the murderer.

I shall not here criticize the intelligibility or consistency or adequacy of those theories that are united in denying that the practice of a system of punishment is justified by its beneficial consequences and claim instead that the main justification of the practice lies in the fact that when breach of the law involves moral guilt the application to the offender of the pain of punishment is itself a thing of value. A great variety of claims of this character, designating 'Retribution' or 'Expiation' or 'Reprobation' as the justifying aim, fall in spite of differences under this rough general description. Though in fact I agree with Mr. Benn[7] in thinking that these all either avoid the question of justification altogether or are in spite of their protestations disguised forms of Utilitarianism, I shall assume that Retribution, defined simply as the application of the pains of punishment to an offender who is morally guilty, may figure among the conceivable justifying aims of a system of punishment. Here I shall merely insist that it is one thing to use the word Retribution *at this point* in an account of the principle of punishment in order to designate the General Justifying Aim of the system, and quite another to use it to secure that to the question 'To whom may punishment be applied?' (the question of Distribution), the answer given is 'Only to an offender for an offence.' Failure to distinguish Retribution as a General Justifying Aim from retribution as the simple insistence that only those who have broken the law—and voluntarily broken it—may be punished, may be traced in many writers: even perhaps in Mr. J. D. Mabbott's[8] otherwise most illuminating essay. We shall distinguish the latter from Retribution in General Aim as 'retribution in Distribution.' Much confusing shadow-fighting between utilitarians and their opponents may be avoided if it is recognized that it is perfectly consistent to assert *both* that the General Justifying Aim of the practice of punishment is its beneficial conse-

[7] Op. cit., pp. 326–35.

[8] 'Punishment' *Mind* (1939), p. 152. It is not always quite clear what he considers a 'retributive' theory to be.

quences *and* that the pursuit of this General Aim should be qualified or restricted out of deference to principles of Distribution which require that punishment should be only of an offender for an offence. Conversely it does not in the least follow from the admission of the latter principle of retribution in Distribution that the General Justifying Aim of punishment is Retribution though of course Retribution in General Aim entails retribution in Distribution.

We shall consider later the principles of justice lying at the root of retribution in Distribution. Meanwhile it is worth observing that both the old fashioned Retributionist (in General Aim) and the most modern sceptic often make the same (and, I think, wholly mistaken) assumption that sense can only be made of the restrictive principle that punishment be applied only to an offender for an offence if the General Justifying Aim of the practice of punishment is Retribution. The sceptic consequently imputes to all systems of punishment (when they are restricted by the principle of retribution in Distribution) all the irrationality he finds in the idea of Retribution as a General Justifying Aim; conversely the advocates of the latter think the admission of retribution in Distribution is a refutation of the utilitarian claim that the social consequences of punishment are its Justifying Aim.

The most general lesson to be learnt from this extends beyond the topic of punishment. It is, that in relation to any social institution, after stating what general aim or value its maintenance fosters we should enquire whether there are any and if so what principles limiting the unqualified pursuit of that aim or value. Just because the pursuit of any single social aim always has its restrictive qualifier, our main social institutions always possess a plurality of features which can only be understood as a compromise between partly discrepant principles. This is true even of relatively minor legal institutions like that of a contract. In general this is designed to enable individuals to give effect to their wishes to create structures of legal rights and duties, and so to change, in certain ways, their legal position. Yet at the same time there is need to protect those who, in good faith, understand a verbal offer made to them to mean what it would ordinarily mean, accept it, and then act on the footing that a valid contract has been concluded. As against them, it would be unfair to allow the other party to say that the words he used in his verbal offer or the interpretation put on them did not express his real wishes or intention. Hence principles of 'estoppel' or doctrines of the 'objective sense' of a contract are introduced to prevent this and to qualify the principle that the law enforces contracts in order to give effect to the joint wishes of the contracting parties.

This as in the case of property has two aspects (i) Liability (Who may be punished?) and (ii) Amount. In this section I shall chiefly be concerned with the first of these.[9]

From the foregoing discussions two things emerge. First, though we may be clear as to what value the practice of punishment is to promote, we have still to answer as a question of Distribution 'Who may be punished?' Secondly, if in answer to this question we say 'only an offender for an offence' this admission of retribution in Distribution is not a principle from which anything follows as to the severity or amount of punishment;

[9] Amount is considered below in connexion with Mitigation.

in particular it neither licenses nor requires, as Retribution in General Aim does, more severe punishments than deterrence or other utilitarian criteria would require.

The root question to be considered is, however, why we attach the moral importance which we do to retribution in Distribution. Here I shall consider the efforts made to show that restriction of punishment to offenders is a simple consequence of whatever principles (Retributive or Utilitarian) constitute the Justifying Aim of punishment.

The standard example used by philosophers to bring out the importance of retribution in Distribution is that of a wholly innocent person who has not even unintentionally done anything which the law punishes if done intentionally. It is supposed that in order to avert some social catastrophe officials of the system fabricate evidence on which he is charged, tried, convicted and sent to prison or death. Or it is supposed that without resort to any fraud more persons may be deterred from crime if wives and children of offenders were punished vicariously for their crimes. In some forms this kind of thing may be ruled out by a consistent sufficiently comprehensive utilitarianism.[10] Certainly expedients involving fraud or faked charges might be very difficult to justify on utilitarian grounds. We can of course imagine that a negro might be sent to prison or executed on a false charge of rape in order to avoid widespread lynching of many others; but a *system* which openly empowered authorities to do this kind of thing, even if it succeeded in averting specific evils like lynching, would awaken such apprehension and insecurity that any gain from the exercise of these powers would by any utilitarian calculation be offset by the misery caused by their existence. But official resort to this kind of fraud on a particular occasion in breach of the rules and the subsequent indemnification of the officials responsible might save many lives and so be thought to yield a clear surplus of value. Certainly vicarious punishment of an offender's family might do so and legal systems have occasionally though exceptionally resorted to this. An example of it is the Roman *Lex Quisquis* providing for the punishment of the children of those guilty of *majestas*.[11] In extreme cases many might still think it right to resort to these expedients but we should do so with the sense of sacrificing an important principle. We should be conscious of choosing the lesser of two evils, and this would be inexplicable if the principle sacrificed to utility were itself only a requirement of utility.

Similarly the moral importance of the restriction of punishment to the offender cannot be explained as merely a consequence of the principle that the General Justifying Aim is Retribution for immorality involved in breaking the law. Retribution in the Distribution of punishment has a value quite independent of Retribution as Justifying Aim. This is shown by the fact that we attach importance to the restrictive principle that only offenders may be punished, even where breach of this law might not be thought immoral. . . .

[10] See J. Rawls, 'Two Concepts of Rules,' *Philosophical Review* (1955), pp. 4–13.

[11] Constitution of emperors Arcadius and Honorius (A.D. 397).

A NEW PHILOSOPHY OF CRIMINAL JUSTICE*

Helen Silving

Helen Silving, professor of law at the University of Puerto Rico, was formerly an adviser to the Legislative Penal Reform Committee of the Commonwealth of Puerto Rico. In the important selection below, written in 1966, she argues for a theory of punishment responsive both to the well-being of the individual offender and that of society at large.

Once the belief prevailed that crime is a "natural phenomenon," not in the sense of being inherent in human nature but in the sense that one could determine by merely observing a conduct whether it is or is not a crime. For each such "natural" crime there was believed to be a corresponding punishment, a punishment "naturally" flowing from it. When it was realized that the crime concept is an artificial construct, a creature of men's minds, that it was possible to bring to an end a hitherto criminal conduct by terminating its qualification as a crime, it also became clear that there is no ontological relationship between crime and punishment. The coordination of crime and punishment then became rather a matter of justice and "legality." Thus there arose the demand of French Revolutionary Constitutions and of our Eighth Amendment—a demand of Biblical origin—that punishment must not be "excessive," meaning, harsh beyond proportion to the gravity of the crime. Soon, however, there arose alongside with a deterministic philosophy that made crime appear to be something the offender "could not help" committing—another type of "natural crime"—, a call for "scientific" handling of the offender. This demand became so urgent and was voiced so "self-righteously" that it obliterated two significant realities pertinent to this new "rehabilitative ideal:" (1) that no one apparently cares to ascertain what role the gravity of the precipitating crime [the crime in issue in the concrete case, the one on whose basis the criminal proceedings were conducted and for which the defendant was convicted] still plays or ought to play in the sanctioning process; (2) that we do not know how to rehabilitate offenders, if by "rehabilitation" we mean a cure that would prevent reincidence.

There developed an ideological conflict between a concept of criminal law oriented to the "act" which give rise to the criminal proceedings, visualizing a punishment adjusted to that act, and an ideal of criminal law concerned with the offender, the type of person he is, his rehabilitation potential, the length of time and the methods it takes to rehabilitate him, regardless of the type of

* Excerpted from Silving, *A Plea for a New Philosophy of Criminal Justice*, 35 Revista Juridica de la Universidad de Puerto Rico 401 (1966). Reprinted with permission.

"act" for which he was convicted or of the harm produced by that act. The so-called "criminal law of the actor" thus clashed with the "criminal law of the act" (*derecho penal del autor* versus *derecho penal del acto*). A would-be "scientific rehabilitation" declared a war against the "Rule of Law" which postulates the "law of the act."

To reconcile the demands of "Rule of Law" that a man not be punished unless he committed some anti-social, criminal act, and that he not be punished beyond the measure corresponding to the harm created by his "act," with the demand for so-called "scientific" treatment of offenders, a treatment that must be adjusted to rehabilitation needs rather than measured by the gravity of the act, there was invented in countries of common law tradition a peculiar set of separations of criminal law philosophies and functions, that by themselves violate principles of the "Rule of Law."

Sanctions are being separated from crimes, the latter following the philosophy of the "criminal law of the act" while the former are based on a philosophy of the "criminal law of the actor." In practical terms this means that a person is being convicted for what he "did," the appearance being preserved as if, indeed, it mattered what he did, whether he smoked a single marihuana cigarette in his own bedroom or committed mass murder, but is sentenced as if this difference did not matter for purposes of the consequences attached to such act, sentencing being adjusted, within certain broadly devised limits to what kind of person, he is, his personality—his personality as it will appear in the process of execution.

Our total criminal law is devised under the impact of a philosophy that deliberately ignores the implications of sanctions, as if it did not matter what happens to a criminal defendant after his sentence becomes final. This nonchalance is based on a more or less tacit belief that a person who has been found "guilty" is within the total, totalitarian power of the state, which can do almost anything with him or to him, since by his "guilt" he has forfeited all his civil rights. Our case books do not deal with what happens in a penitentiary. Nor do we hear much about court cases where a prisoner complains about, e.g., being unjustly placed in solitary confinement. Apparently, all the prisoners complain about in courts is something that happened twenty years ago at the time of their trial, something that may have vitiated the finding of their "guilt," like the absence of an attorney or a coerced confession. And so, it would seem that we should look more closely into the question of what precisely "guilt" means and why we have come to believe that by his "guilt" the prisoner has forfeited all his civil rights, regardless of the nature of that of which he has been found "guilty." We cannot today simply accept, as we do, a magical concept of "guilt.". . .

(1) I am postulating that *criminal law which operates by means of restrictions of constitutional rights of [the] individual adopt only strictly limited goals and do not admit interchangeability of goals.* No goal is pursuable as a primary one, that is, as determinative of the length and terms of freedom deprivation, by means of criminal law unless such goal cannot be reached in any other manner and unless it is functionally attainable by such means. This implies that if we do not know how a goal can be achieved or whether it can be achieved at all, we cannot adopt it as a primary goal, though we may try to pursue it within the limits set by a legitimate primary

goal. We are not permitted either to deprive an individual of his liberty or extend a liberty deprivation for the purpose of experimenting with methods of reaching a non-primary goal. Even "bad people" are not by the same token experimental rabbits. Thus, since we do not know how either deterrence or rehabilitation works, these cannot be assumed as primary goals, though they may be pursued within the limits set by the needs of primary goals. . . .

It is not permissible to adopt any criminal law method for interchangeable purposes, meaning, for example, to punish attempt on the theory that if such punishment should not deter, then perhaps it might rehabilitate, and if it does not do that, then it might serve a retributive purpose, etc. The legislators too must be prepared at any time to answer the basic *habeas corpus query*: Why, meaning, for what purpose, did you provide for the restriction of John Doe's liberty?

We have in our Penal Code a provision prohibiting "arresting" a person for a crime not provided for in the Code (33 L.P.R.A. § 5). There is no doubt that this also means that no one may be convicted for such crime. I believe that this should also be taken to mean that no one should be convicted for a conduct which the legislators had no business to make a crime and which is unconstitutional on this ground.

Proceeding from such philosophy of limited defined specific goals, I assumed that there are only two legitimate primary goals: so-called "retribution" and so-called "prevention." The former is not vengeance but rather a symbolic assertion of a legal prohibition, an assertion which at the same time indicates by the degree of the severity of the punishment imposed upon a crime what rank it occupies in the hierarchy of the negative value system in a "free society." Retribution is wholly "act-oriented." Punishment that is excessive, that is, disproportionate to the mischief of the crime, is barred. But whatever the gravity of the "act" charged, the latter ought not to be "punished" unless there obtains a conscious attitude of the accused toward the act and its consequences, that is, either intent or foresight.

Where the "act" charged can be shown to have been committed by the defendant, but he has not been shown to have possessed a conscious intent, knowledge or foresight as regards it or its consequences, or has not been shown not to have suffered from an exempting mental incapacity, retribution does not lie, but there may be an urgent need for prevention of recurrence or protection of the community against the danger emanating from the defendant whether he be insane or have acted in some uncommon type of error or in a state of inadvertent negligence. A man who kills another mistaking him for a tree stump, where most other people would have recognized that the object is a human being, may not be punishable; yet, he is extremely dangerous and we cannot stand by permitting him to kill another human being.

(2) In both the retributive and the preventive law, the "act" is a *sine qua non* and a limitative factor. Deprivation of a man's liberty by the methods of criminal law is barred (a) unless he committed some "act" described as criminal or (b) beyond the limits of the maximum period corresponding to such act.

(3) To the two goals or purposes of criminal law there correspond two types of sanctions: the retributive sanction, that is, punishment, and the preventive sanction, that is, a measure of security and cure. A system based on use of two

distinctive sanctions is referred to as a "dual system."

However, the "dual system" as known in countries of the civil law is characterized by the fact that only very few specific situations are earmarked as regions of protective treatment. Beyond these situations there obtains a confusion of criminal law goals. Such situations are those of persons acquitted by reason of insanity, alcoholics and drug addicts and habitual offenders. The system is "dual" because some distinctive "legality principles" are applied to the measures provided for such persons.

I assume a much broader view of a "dual system." Since only conscious conduct, meaning, conduct consciously directed to the specific proscribed act, may be punished, there remains a broad area of situations where because of some inadequacy of the mental element, either absence of conscious intent or knowledge, or mental incapacity, the defendant ought not to be "punished" but is nevertheless highly "dangerous." We must take account at this time of the phenomena of "unconscious intent" and "unconscious recklessness." We may find patterns of inarticulate recognition of such phenomena in laws of civil law countries. In all such situations, for example, negligence without foresight of consequences, preventive measures ought to be applied for the protection of society. My Draft* provides minimum detention periods for very grave situations of this type, just as there are minimum periods of imprisonment in cases within the area of retribution.

* The author had preposed a draft revision of the Penal Code of Puerto Rico for the Legislative Penal Reform Commission in 1966.—Editors

(4) By adopting a wider area of preventive law at the expense of punitive law it is possible to reach a less dogmatic view of certain categories of criminal law than obtains in our present law. The dogmatism of the ideology of the defense of "insanity" is considerably modified when error, drunkenness and inadvertent negligence are subject to similar categories of social reactions. Yet, there can be no relaxation of the insistence on defining all relevant concepts as strictly as at all possible. We cannot withdraw from the jury determination of the "insanity" issue. This is so because it has been so held in our law. All we can do, and must do to satisfy legality demands is to define the exemption of mental incapacity as intelligently as possible within our present scientific knowledge and within the requirement of certainty and precision of statutory defintions.

(5) The concept of "guilt" no longer appears as a fixed ontological reality of theological imprint. "Guilt" is but a shorthand expression for a set of postulates of democratic law as regards the mental ingredient of crime, its relationship to the outward occurrence, and rules regarding the proof of these items. Such purging of the notion of "guilt" permits realization of possibilities of diversity and change in its meaning. Together with relativisation of the concept of "insanity" it yields recognition that the traditional statement that "no one can be guilty if he is insane" is meaningless except in a historical context. We must endow these concepts with new meaning adopted to modern life conditions. The Constitution does not bar this, though it does bar a total elimination of the "guilt" or "insanity" concepts. . . .

THE PENAL SYSTEM: TREATMENT AS PREVENTION*

New York Governor's
Special Committee on Criminal Offenders

In 1968 the New York Special Committee on Criminal Offenders, authorized by Governor Rockefeller, issued a report which represents a practical compromise among the competing justifications considered previously. Deterrence and prevention of recidivism become guiding norms, with other traditional goals introduced only to the extent to which they contribute to these norms. The perceptive reader might well inquire into the latent foundations for these guiding norms.

The criminal treatment system,[1] although a distinct method of law enforcement, may be thought of as primarily a supporting operation for the other three levels of law enforcement and for the moral level. In a gross sense, the objective of the treatment system is the same as the objective of the other levels of law enforcement—prevention of crime—and the ideal of the treatment system is to bring offenders to the moral level. The role of the system in prevention of crime is twofold: (a) general deterrence, and (b) prevention of recidivism. General deterrence is the instrumentality of the threat level; and the various methods of preventing recidivism are aimed at either restraining the offender (a variation of the police intervention level) or at bringing him to the point where he will observe the self-executing level or, ideally, to the moral level.

Hence, the other three levels of law enforcement, and the moral level, furnish the key to all but one of the goals toward which treatment is directed and, therefore, form a large part of the framework of the functions of the treatment system.

The rest of the framework is formed by a concept that can be called prevention of anomie. The term "anomie" as used in this Report means a condition of society in which its members feel that normative standards of conduct and belief are weak or lacking. The aspect of anomie that the criminal treatment system is concerned with can be defined as a feeling on the part of the public that government is permitting certain community values and norms to deteriorate.

When government promulgates a prohibition against harmful conduct and

* Excerpted from PRELIMINARY REPORT OF THE GOVERNOR'S SPECIAL COMMITTEE ON CRIMINAL OFFENDERS (State of New York, 1968), pp. 72–88. Reprinted with permission.

[1] In this Report we use the term "treatment system," for want of a better term, as meaning the entire post adjudicatory system: from and including conviction or adjudication to final discharge from custody.

assumes the role of protecting the community from such conduct, it also assumes the role of guardian of the particular community norm that is to be protected from attenuation by that conduct. Because of this role, it must not only enforce the law but also demonstrate to the public that the law is being enforced. If the state, as the avowed guardian of a norm, does not demonstrate an interest in enforcing it, the public—should it feel strongly about the norm—will become anxious through fear that the norm is deteriorating. The public will then focus upon the avowed protector of the norm as the cause of its anxiety and unrest and the result will be lack of faith in government with all the ramifications that may follow.

Inasmuch as both prevention of anomie and threat of sanctions (general deterrence) are aimed at producing reactions in the general public, it is appropriate at this point to articulate the distinction between them. The distinction is that general deterrence is a method of enforcing the law, while prevention of anomie is aimed at maintaining the faith of the public in the law.[2]

Thus, the objectives of the criminal treatment system are to prevent crime and to prevent anomie. The system carries out these objectives as follows:

1. By administering sanctions that have a sufficient degree of unpleasantness to
   - (a) demonstrate to the public at large that the threats annexed to prohibitions cannot be ignored without consequences (*i.e.*, general deterrence), and to
   - (b) reinforce the confidence of the public in the fact that the state is determined to uphold norms, through a demonstration of action taken against wrongdoers (*i.e.*, prevention of anomie); and
2. By preventing recidivism through the use of sanctions as a vehicle for administering
   - (a) rehabilitative techniques to bring offenders to the point where they will voluntarily observe the prohibitions set forth in the criminal law, and
   - (b) preventive force through incarceration or close community supervision of the offender so as to limit his opportunity to offend again—a variation of the police intervention concept, and
   - (c) punishment to make the threats

[2] It is important to note the relationship of the concept of retaliation or retribution to the functions of the treatment system. The exaction of retaliation or retribution has no inherent value as a goal of the treatment system and is relevant only to the extent that it bears upon the function of preventing anomie.

The administration of justice in a civilized society does not include the principle of harming one individual for the purpose of placating another. Furthermore, vengeance taken for the sake of vengeance does not assist in law enforcement. Therefore, whatever its historical relationship to the system of criminal justice may be, it is clear that the concept of retribution is not one of the inherent goals of the modern treatment system.

The desire for retribution is, however, a factor in causing anomie, and prevention of anomie is a legitimate goal of the treatment system. When sanctions inflicted by the state are not severe enough to satisfy public desire for revenge, that unsatisfied desire translates into a belief that the state is not fulfilling its responsibility in upholding the norm. Therefore, the state must take the retributive feelings of the public into account to the extent that such feelings bear upon anomie. This involves appraisal of the extent of anomie, or loss of faith in government, that will be risked rather than direct assessment of the degree of retaliation that should be exacted for the criminal act.

a reality to the individual offender so that he will be more responsive to them in the future (*i.e.,* individual deterrence).

GENERAL PRINCIPLES UNDERLYING THE USE OF SANCTIONS

In the context of the criminal treatment system, the term "sanction" comprises formal community condemnation, deprivation of rights or privileges, and forfeiture of property for a purpose other than restitution or reparation, imposed and carried out by the state as a direct consequence of conduct that violates a prohibition promulgated by the state.

The sanctions presently acceptable for the criminal treatment system are: conviction, fine, field supervision, incarceration and death.[3] Conviction causes shame, blemishes reputation and, in many cases, deprives the offender of rights or privileges. A fine, of course, is forfeiture of property for a purpose other than restitution or reparation. Field supervision (*i.e.,* probation, parole or "aftercare") interferes with the right to self-determination. And incarceration can mean total deprivation of liberty. Thus, in varying degrees, all sanctions interfere with the ordinary liberties enjoyed by the public at large.

As previously indicated, the business of the criminal treatment system is to administer sanctions, and it is, therefore, important to consider the principles by which the extent and severity of sanctions are gauged.

Two basic factors are utilized in applying criminal sanctions to individuals: conduct and condition. Conduct means the specific act for which the offender has been convicted, and condition means the offender's personal characteristics (*e.g.,* mental, physical, developmental, and social). Conduct is the basis or trigger mechanism of the system. Conduct is also the basis for the maximum authorized sanction and for the appropriate sanction range in individual cases. Condition determines the sanction actually imposed within the appropriate sanction range.[4]

The fundamental precept of the criminal treatment system is that it can only be set in motion with respect to an individual if the individual has been found guilty of specific proscribed conduct. The condition of the individual, no matter how dangerous and no matter how closely related to criminal conduct (*e.g.,* addiction to a substance that is illegal to possess such as heroin), cannot trigger

[3] There is another disposition commonly used, and in New York State it is called "conditional discharge" (see Penal Law, §§65.05, 65.10). Under this form of disposition an offender is discharged, after conviction, subject to certain conditions. If he fulfills the conditions during a specified period of time, no sanction beyond conviction is imposed. If he violates the conditions during that period of time, the court may impose any sanction it originally could have imposed. Conditional discharge cannot be considered a sanction even though fulfillment of the conditions may require that the offender refrain from exercising rights or privileges (*i.e.,* options) he would ordinarily be free to exercise. When conditional discharge is used, fulfillment of the conditions does not involve submission to treatment imposed or administered by the criminal system. The offender has the option of avoiding criminal treatment beyond the conviction level by performing conditions outside of, and not officially supervised by, the system.

[4] Condition, of course, may be evidenced by behavior, and in this sense the terms conduct and condition as used herein might be confused. However, the distinction is that behavior is merely a factor that serves as an indication of something else: *i.e.,* condition. While "conduct," as used herein, means a specific criminal act, which is in itself a sufficient basis for action by the state.

the mechanism of the criminal system. The relevance of this precept is that it serves as the point of departure for distinguishing between the criminal treatment system and the civil treatment system. Such distinction is vital because there is and has been a tendency to confuse the rationale of the two systems by applying the civil model to the criminal system; and the danger in this is that such application may unjustifiably interfere with basic liberties of the individual.

As used herein the term "civil treatment" means mandatory treatment imposed by the state upon certain individuals who have not been found guilty of a criminal offense. The term is intended to apply to such measures as: quarantine of those with communicable diseases; institutionalization and aftercare and out-patient treatment (under threat of institutionalization) of the mentally ill, the mentally defective and the addicted; and institutionalization and aftercare and probation treatment (under threat of institutionalization) of children who are "habitually truant, incorrigible, ungovernable or habitually disobedient and beyond the lawful control of parent or other lawful authority" (see N.Y. Family Court Act, §712[b]). Whatever the historical origin of the right of the state to impose civil treatment may be (*e.g.,* the doctrine of *parens patriae,* the right to deal with obnoxious or dangerous persons, or some duty of society to care for those who cannot care for themselves), it is generally accepted today that the state has the right to impose such treatment. The right to do so, however, proceeds from the condition of the individual rather than—as under the criminal treatment system—from any specific conduct. In order to set the civil treatment system in motion it is necessary to prove that the individual is in a particular condition, and treatment must cease when the condition terminates.

The civil treatment system is similar to the criminal treatment system in that both systems utilize incarceration and both systems administer habilitative and rehabilitative services under coercive circumstances. Moreover, the training of persons for both civil system and criminal system habilitative and rehabilitative services is basically the same, and the same persons often work in both systems (*e.g.,* psychiatrists, psychologists, sociologists, social workers, educators), focusing, naturally, upon condition, rather than conduct, in both systems. These factors often lead practitioners and others to believe that the rationales of the two systems, so far as the right to impose treatment is concerned, are the same. What is overlooked is the fact that a person's condition is not a basis for imposing treatment under the civil system, unless the condition is one the law specifically recognizes as a basis for imposing treatment. The civil system can mandate treatment only if a particular, legally recognized, condition can be shown (*e.g.,* mental illness), while the criminal system can mandate treatment on the basis of conduct without the need to prove that a legally recognized condition exists. The danger lies in applying a principle of the civil system—*i.e.,* treatment based upon condition and lasting for duration of the condition—to a conduct-based system. In other words the danger lies in extending the period of treatment, under the criminal system, beyond the period warranted by conduct, for the purpose of treating a condition. Treatment can be mandated for duration of a condition only where the condition is one that is recognized by the civil system.

Examples may be found in the current problem of dealing with prostitutes and deteriorated alcoholics. In both of these cases—at least under present New York law—the civil system does not recognize the condition of the individual as a basis for mandatory treatment. The only justification for mandating treatment is conduct (*i.e.,* public intoxication or the offense of prostitution). However, the conduct is not considered grievous enough to warrant criminal system treatment for more than fifteen days, and it is unlikely that any effective rehabilitative impact can be made on the offender's condition in that period of time. Hence, there is substantial support for the position that the permissible criminal sanction for these offenses (*i.e.,* the maximum period of treatment) should be longer. The rationale for such support is that a longer period of time is required to treat the condition. This overlooks the fact that mandatory treatment must be justified on the basis of either conduct, or a condition recognized by the civil system. If it cannot be justified on the basis of either, it represents an unwarranted deprivation of the individual's basic right to self-determination.

In addition to serving as the trigger for the mechanism of the criminal treatment system, conduct is also the sole criterion for the permissible maximum sanction. The legislature evaluates the relative harmfulness of particular conduct and expresses its evaluation in terms of the authorized sanction (*i.e.,* the upper limits of the sentence). This process involves a weighing of the harmfulness of the conduct against the value of the individual's right to be free from the restraints of the treatment system (*i.e.,* sanctions). The greater the harm, the greater the right of the state to deprive the offender of his liberty.

The process of prescribing authorized sanctions does not involve assumptions or conclusions with respect to the condition of offenders. Such assumptions and conclusions are the business of the agencies that administer the treatment system. The legislature merely determines—and expresses in terms of the authorized sentence—the maximum power that the treatment system is permitted to exercise for all or any of its functions; and the sole basis for this determination is conduct.

The principle that conduct is the sole basis for the maximum permissible sanction is a useful tool in analyzing the nature of statutes that permit completely indefinite treatment as an alternative to a fixed term or that authorize extended terms (*e.g.*: so called "sexual psychopath" laws; the American Law Institute Model Penal Code, "MPC" [§§6.07, 7.03]; the NCCD Model Sentencing Act, "MSA" [§5]). Where the maximum legal term of imprisonment for specific conduct is a fixed number of years, but a person can receive an indefinite sentence that could amount to mandatory treatment for life (*e.g.,* former N.Y. Penal Law, §§2010, 2189-a) or a sentence of six times the ordinary maximum (*e.g.,* MSA §5) or twice the ordinary maximum (*e.g.,* MPC §6.07) because, in addition to having committed the crime, he has failed to measure up to some undefined standard of normality (former N.Y. law), or is found to have "a severe personality disorder indicating a propensity toward criminal activity" (MSA), the question arises as to whether the indefinite or extended treatment is based upon conduct or condition (*i.e.,* whether the civil model is being applied to the criminal system). The answer is furnished by the observation that, if the indefinite or extended treatment were based upon conduct, all persons who are convicted of such conduct would be subject to it; and, obviously, only those of the ones convicted who are found to have a certain condition are subject to it.

However, the harmfulness of conduct cannot be judged by the condition of the offender; and the fact that an offender is abnormal does not depreciate the value of his liberty. Such legislation permits the condition of the offender to trigger the operation of an added and distinct portion of treatment to be administered under the criminal system; and this violates the fundamental precept of the system. The danger in creating a part of the system which is not based upon conduct alone is the same as the danger in overlooking the precept that conduct is the sole basis of the entire criminal system: namely, that of unjustifiably interfering with the basic liberties of individuals. Whenever deprivation of liberty is legislated upon the basis of condition, such deprivation must proceed within the framework of the civil system and the individual is entitled to be treated, in every respect, in accordance with the concepts of the civil system; not the least of which is that the period of custody is governed by the duration of the condition, and that the various concomitants of a criminal sentence do not apply. If the condition is one that can be proved through a procedure that meets fundamental due process requirements, and the condition makes the individual dangerous to the community, the individual can and should be dealt with under provisions similar to those we have for dealing with the dangerous mentally ill. A law that utilizes condition as the basis for criminal treatment violates the principle of equal protection (see *Baxstrom* v. *Herold,* 383 U. S. 107 [1966]), and the prohibition against cruel and inhuman punishment (see *Robinson* v. *California,* 370 U. S. 660 [1962]).

The type of legislation discussed in the foregoing paragraphs can, perhaps, be distinguished, to some extent, from statutes that permit life imprisonment because of prior convictions (persistent felony offender legislation, *e.g.,* N.Y. Penal Law, § 70.10). Such multiple offender legislation seems to be based upon the theory that present conduct, taken together with past conduct, supplies legal justification for overcoming any right the offender otherwise would have had to further freedom. Stated otherwise, the cumulation of convictions seems to negate the obligation of society to take further risks with the offender (this obligation being the reciprocal of the value of his right to be free from the interference of the treatment system).

Once the authorized maximum has been prescribed for a category of conduct, the appropriate sanction range must be determined. This is done for the purpose of ascertaining the degree of sanction that would be appropriate for the offender's actual conduct. The determination is needed because the maximum authorized sanction is based upon the harmfulness of conduct as defined by statute in general terms, and this covers a range of ways in which the offense can be committed. In a conduct-based system the appropriate sanction must be based upon the actual facts and circumstances of the offense.

The object here is to determine where, within the range of the general statutory definition of the proscribed conduct, the offender's actual conduct falls, and to determine whether there are any aggravating or extenuating circumstances that would tend to make such conduct more or less shocking. In considering the actual facts and circumstances, there are three considerations: (1) that the statute defining the proscribed conduct, and fixing the maximum sanction, covers a range of ways in which the crime can be committed, some of which are more serious than others; (2) that the conviction may be for a crime which is less serious than the actual conduct (*e.g.*, a case where a lesser plea is taken); and (3) that there may be extenuating circumstances.

An example of the first consideration would be the crime of Robbery in the First Degree. Under New York law (Penal Law, §160.15), this crime may be committed by forcibly stealing property while armed with a deadly weapon; and the term deadly weapon includes both a machine gun and metal knuckles (§10.00). Therefore, when a number of men enter a bank armed with submachine guns and forcibly take money from the clerks, the crime is Robbery in the First Degree. The same crime is committed, however, if a person, with metal knuckles in his pocket, forcibly steals a bicycle from a ten year old in the park. The maximum sanction is twenty-five years of custody in both cases; but the degree to which each strikes at the peace and security of the community is quite different.

The facts in the bicycle case can also be used to illustrate the second consideration. If the bicycle robber is permitted to plead to the count of the indictment that charges him with possession of the knuckles (in satisfaction of all charges for his conduct), the appropriate sanction range would be higher—within the limits of the maximum sanction authorized for such possession—than would be the case if his actual conduct consisted merely of possession. In so determining the appropriate sanction range, we would be considering his actual conduct as an aggravating circumstance of the crime for which he was convicted. Here the theory is that the plea was accepted with the thought in mind that the authorized sanction for possession is adequate to cover the actual conduct.

The third consideration can be illustrated by the crime of Assault in the Second Degree (N. Y. Penal Law, §120.05). This crime is committed when one person intentionally—and without lawful justification—inflicts serious physical injury upon another. Provocation is not lawful justification. Therefore the crime is technically the same in an unprovoked assault as it is where the assault was provoked by the victim. Yet the community is much more disturbed in the former situation than it is in the latter.

The determination as to the appropriate sanction range, which gives us the maximum sanction justified for any or all of the purposes of the system, is based solely upon conduct. However, the key factor in determining the actual sanction to be applied, within the appropriate range, is the condition of the individual offender. The process of determining the actual sanction involves selection of the best method of fulfilling the purposes of the system (*i.e.*, general deterrence, prevention of anomie and prevention of recidivism), and the condition of the offender serves as the gauge of what is needed for these purposes.

The relationship between the condition of the offender and prevention of recidivism is obvious. The determination with respect to risk of recidivism is, in substance, a prediction as to future conduct based upon present condition (mental, emotional, physical, habits, attitudes, family life, employment, tendency to drug or alcohol abuse, etc.), including the effect that the present conviction has had as a deterrent to his future conduct. If it appears that the offender is likely to commit another offense, then a sanction beyond the conviction level must be selected from among those available in the appropriate range.

Of course, selection of the actual sanction to be used for prevention of recidivism depends upon a number of other decisions, which also utilize condition as a key determinant, such as (1) the needs of general deterrence and prevention of anomie, (2) whether prevention of recidivism in a particular case can best be accomplished by use of a non-custodial sanction (*i.e.,* a fine or intermittent jail) or whether custody is needed as a vehicle for rehabilitation or for preventive force, and (3) whether the term of custody justified for the conduct (*e.g.,* 15 day maximum) would be meaningful for rehabilitation or for preventive force, or would only serve the purpose of punishment. These and other matters are resolved on the basis of principles discussed in subsequent sections of this Part of the Report.

The relationship between the condition of the offender and general deterrence is that the sanction required for general deterrence is one which will have a value in deterring those who have the same degree of integration into the law-abiding community ("social integration") as the offender from committing similar crimes. Social integration is the aspect of the offender's condition that is represented by his contacts and ties with other parts of the law-abiding community (*i.e.,* reputation, employment, family relationships, group memberships, licenses and other privileges).

Social integration is utilized as a factor in determining the extent of the sanction appropriate for general deterrence because one of the hypotheses of general deterrence is that the less a person has to lose the less he will be deterred by threats. For example, if a person has already been convicted of one crime, and therefore has lost a certain degree of his reputation, the threat of conviction alone may not be a deterrent for him, while it might deter a person who has never been convicted. In applying this hypothesis, it is important to observe that general deterrence does not require the sanctioning of each offender at the level that would be used to fulfill the need of deterring the most hardened offender. The sanction applied for hardened offenders is used as a deterrent for other hardened offenders. Thus, for the purpose of general deterrence, it is appropriate to ascertain just what the offender has to lose at each level of sanction and the underlying assumption is that people in like circumstances will be impressed by the threat of that loss to the same extent as the loss is felt by the offender.

A person's degree of social integration is the best indicator of what he has to lose through a sanction. Social integration represents the offender's cohesion to other parts of the law-abiding community. These contacts can be affected by reputation and proximity. A conviction may affect reputation to the extent of causing loss of face in the community. This makes it more difficult for the offender to maintain social and business community acceptance and may even result in loss of employment. If the offender has close family ties, the pain to him is more severe because it is also felt by his family; and if he is removed from the community, by virtue of incarceration, loss of face is greater, loss of employment is usually automatic, and additional pain is inflicted because of separation from loved ones. The primary thing to bear in mind is that the social integration of each offender must be viewed in proportion to his own sphere of activity. The reason for this is that the essence of a sanction is the manner in which the recipient or potential recipient feels or would feel the infliction. Thus, the man whose contacts do not reach beyond his immediate neighborhood and a blue collar job should generally be viewed as having the same *relative degree* of social integration as the president of a large corporation who belongs to many exclusive clubs. The pain felt by the former in relation to conviction and imprisonment is as meaningful as the pain felt by the latter in relation to these factors.[5]

The considerations that apply in determining the level of sanction required for prevention of anomie are substantially the same as those that apply in the case of general deterrence. As indicated earlier, the distinction between general deterrence and prevention of anomie is that deterrence is a method of enforcing the law while prevention of anomie is aimed at maintaining the faith of the public in the law. In an area that cannot, in any event, be measured with mathematical precision, it would be cutting principles too fine to maintain that there is a practical distinction between what will make a man afraid to break the law and what will make a man believe that government is enforcing the law. There is, however, an important exception to this rule. In certain situations the shock of a crime to core values, or to core institutions, of society is such that it is necessary to reassure the entire community in each case that the state is determined to uphold the norm. This would require disregarding the social integration principle, and the use of sanction—for prevention of anomie—that is impressive to all members of the community. Such sanction might well be greater than the sanction needed for general deterrence.

All sanctions serve the purposes of general deterrence and prevention of anomie in varying degrees. Therefore, in utilizing sanctions for these purposes, we judge the appropriate sanction solely on the basis of the degree of unpleasantness needed. Moreover, there is a tendency to use the term sanction and the term punishment interchangeably. However, prevention of recidivism requires another dimension of thought. Here we recognize that treatment is applied to accomplish varying purposes with respect to the condition of the individual offender and that punishment is only one of three purposes. Prevention of recidivism also requires rehabilitation and preventive force; and, unless we separate the three concepts, we have no way—other than by degree of unpleasantness—to determine the sanction that should actually be applied. For example, it would be anomalous to state that we are placing a person who needs "rehabilitation" under probation supervision for "punishment." The thought must be that we are applying the sanction of field supervision for rehabilitation.

Therefore, in operationalizing the use of sanctions, it is essential to understand the differences between punishment, rehabilitation and preventive force, so that we can pinpoint our purpose or purposes and select the appropriate instrumentality for same.

Punishment can best be characterized

[5] The same principle applies where fines are concerned, but in such case we are not dealing with a factor that has the same value to persons in all social spheres: *i.e.*, human feelings. Therefore, in applying fines, the poor are more likely to be deterred by a small fine than the wealthy.

by two factors: (1) an intention to make the sanction unpleasant for the offender; and (2) recognition on the part of the offender that the sanction is unpleasant. The reason intent must be present, if a sanction is to be considered punishment, is that punishment is *aimed at* unpleasantness. Rehabilitation and preventive force may also have the effect of inflicting unpleasantness, but they are not aimed at that purpose. The reason that recognition of the unpleasantness is required is that unless the offender feels a substantial adverse impact, the sanction is not punishment. For example, a person who has two prior felony convictions would probably not view the conviction level of sanction as punishment; and the same would be true of all persons with a similar level of social integration.

It is important to recognize that the modern operational concept of punishment is focused upon interference with liberty and not upon corporal punishment. Therefore, when we speak of "levels of punishment" or of "an intention to make the sanction unpleasant for the offender," we are referring to steps taken to decrease normal liberties. Thus, punishment for individual deterrence varies from conviction, at one end of the scale, to "solitary confinement" at the other end of the scale.

Under our present system punishment is administered on three general levels: conviction, fine and incarceration.[6]

Punishment at the conviction level consists of formal community condemnation of the individual. Punishment at this level stems from two factors: (a) the feeling of shame felt by the individual; and (b) the assumptions that are made about his character (negative inferences) by the community from the time of conviction on. The first may be said to be the direct result of the conviction and the second the indirect result. It is important to recognize the distinction between direct and indirect results because the indirect results are usually more severe and more lasting and may, in fact, militate against the offender's chances of remaining or becoming a useful member of the community. The state recognizes this in its treatment system and there are many devices for preventing or ameliorating the effects of the indirect results. *E.g.:* youthful offender laws that require a formal adjudication but provide for the sealing of all records pertaining thereto and permit the offender to state that he has never been convicted of a crime; laws that permit the issuance of certificates that prevent mandatory forfeiture of licenses and remove mandatory bars to employment and licensing (see N. Y. Correction Law, Art. 23); and laws that permit the granting of amnesty or pardons.

The fine level involves the principle of using direct pecuniary deprivation. A

[6] The death penalty could be included as a form of punishment if such sanction were justifiable as a method of preventing recidivism. However, it seems more in accordance with modern thinking to view the death penalty as having value solely in the context of general deterrence and prevention of anomie. Therefore, the death penalty must be viewed as an extreme sanction rather than as punishment in the operational sense, because punishment in that sense is viewed as one of three methods of preventing recidivism.

It might also be noted that the death penalty, the last resort of the treatment system, is falling into increasing disuse in our society. The arguments pro and con with respect to this sanction have been the subject of lengthy and heated controversy, and the question of whether the death penalty should or should not be part of a modern treatment system has not as yet been definitively resolved.

fine is a necessary form of punishment in cases where the conviction itself is not of the type that would ordinarily result in a great deal of shame or community condemnation (*e.g.,* traffic offenses, conservation law violations). In these cases a fine is almost invariably used, except where mitigating or aggravating circumstances are found. A fine is also commonly used where the offender gained money or property through commission of the crime, or where the crime was committed while transacting some form of otherwise legitimate business (*e.g.,* anti-trust violations, housing violations). In some of these cases the theory is that the fine will take the profit out of the transaction, and in others that the crime was motivated by greed and that pocket book punishment strikes at the heart of the matter. Of course, fines also are used for other types of offenses on the theory that some form of punishment in addition to conviction is needed but that imprisonment is too severe.

The instrumentality of the incarceration level is institutional confinement. This may take the form of total incarceration or incarceration during certain hours of the day or night or on certain days of the week. When incarceration is inflicted, the punishment is deprivation of liberty and the infliction of additional shame along with the probability that the assumptions made by the community about the character of the offender will be even more damaging to him than those that would flow from the conviction itself.

When considering rehabilitation, it is first necessary to recognize that the term "rehabilitation," as used in the treatment field, covers more than a literal interpretation would denote. Literally, the term denotes restoration to a former condition. In the treatment system, the term means assisting an offender to raise himself to the point where he can function on an acceptable level in the community. Thus, in the treatment system, rehabilitation connotes restoration if the previous condition of the offender was satisfactory, and in all other cases the term connotes "habilitation."

The objectives of punishment for individual deterrence and of rehabilitation are somewhat similar (both seek to keep the offender from recidivating), and this can be a source of confusion. A firm understanding of the distinction between punishment and rehabilitation, is vital, however, in considering whether various treatment instrumentalities, such as probation and parole, are punishment or not and in coping with one of the fundamental problems of our correctional institutions, *i.e.,* administering punishment and rehabilitation simultaneously. Both involve treatment, but punishment is focused upon deprivation and is aimed at creating fear, while rehabilitation is focused upon accretion and is aimed at developing positive values, reactions and goals.

The theory of rehabilitation may be stated as follows:

1. There are certain personal characteristics that impede an individual's ability to function at a generally acceptable level in one or more basic social areas.

2. The difficulty in performing at a generally acceptable level in such areas significantly contributes to criminal conduct.

3. Treatment should be directed at overcoming the aforesaid personal characteristics.

Thus, the aim of rehabilitation is to treat those characteristics of the offender which are inconsistent with the basic characteristics needed to function acceptably. It is felt that, if the treatment has a positive impact, the offender will be more likely to satisfy his needs through socially acceptable conduct and the likelihood of his returning to crime will be reduced.

In the criminal treatment system preventive force means coercion applied to a specific offender for the purpose of limiting his opportunity to offend again. This may take the form of incarceration (full or part time); or a set of special rules to guide the offender's general activities in the community, enforced by threat of incarceration and by field supervision.

Preventive force may be characterized as a neutral concept. It is aimed at restraint of the offender and not at punishment or at rehabilitation. In some cases the objectives of punishment or the objectives of rehabilitation may coincide with the need for restraint and in some cases this may not be so. The distinction between situations where the needs of preventive force coincide with the needs of punishment or rehabilitation, and cases where they do not is crucial in developing and selecting appropriate instrumentalities for carrying out sanctions; for example, in determining whether a custodial instrumentality (*i.e.,* incarceration or field supervision) is necessary, and in making rational and efficient use of custodial instrumentalities.